National Citizenship and Its Evolution

National Citizenship and Its Evolution

Katie Miles

www.clanryeinternational.com

Clanrye International,
750 Third Avenue, 9th Floor,
New York, NY 10017, USA

Copyright © 2023 Clanrye International

This book contains information obtained from authentic and highly regarded sources. All chapters are published with permission under the Creative Commons Attribution Share Alike License or equivalent. A wide variety of references are listed. Permissions and sources are indicated; for detailed attributions, please refer to the permissions page. Reasonable efforts have been made to publish reliable data and information, but the authors, editors and publisher cannot assume any responsibility for the validity of all materials or the consequences of their use.

Trademark Notice: Registered trademark of products or corporate names are used only for explanation and identification without intent to infringe.

ISBN: 978-1-64726-622-6

Cataloging-in-Publication Data

National citizenship and its evolution / Katie Miles.
    p. cm.
Includes bibliographical references and index.
ISBN 978-1-64726-622-6
1. Citizenship. 2. Citizenship--History. I. Miles, Katie.
JF801 .N38 2023
323.6--dc23

For information on all Clanrye International publications visit our website at www.clanryeinternational.com

Contents

Preface XI

Part I **Putting a Price on Citizenship** 1

Chapter 1 **The Price of Citizenship: Global, National and European Perspectives** 3
Rainer Bauböck

Chapter 2 **Relationship between Money and Citizenship** 6
Ayelet Shachar

Chapter 3 **The Problematics Associated with Cash-for-Passports** 15
Peter J. Spiro

Chapter 4 **What is the Problem? The Price or the Sale** 18
Magni-Berton Raul

Chapter 5 **Selling Citizenship and its Cost** 21
Chris Armstrong

Chapter 6 **Investment Citizenship and Global Inequality** 25
Roxana Barbulescu

Chapter 7 **Citizenship for Sale in Malta** 29
Jelena Džankić

Chapter 8 **Sale of Citizenship and Democracy** 33
Rainer Bauböck

Chapter 9 **Citizenship and the Shortcomings of Monetary Power** 38
Paulina Ochoa Espejo

Chapter 10   Differentiating between Affording a Passport and
             Deserving a Passport..42
             Vesco Paskalev

Chapter 11   Citizenship and its Intrinsic Value...45
             Dimitry Kochenov

Chapter 12   European Union and the Trade of Citizenship for
             Human Capital..50
             David Owen

Chapter 13   Intervention of European Union and
             Citizenship for Sale..53
             Jo Shaw

Chapter 14   Connecting Income, Citizenship and
             European Values...57
             Hannes Swoboda

Chapter 15   Summary..60
             Ayelet Shachar

   Part II   Citizenship, Bloodlines and Belonging...62

Chapter 16   The Question of Abandoning Ius Sanguinis....................................64
             Costica Dumbrava

Chapter 17   Justifying Citizenship by Descent..73
             Rainer Bauböck

Chapter 18   Ius Sanguinis: A Historical Study..80
             Jannis Panagiotidis

Chapter 19   Ius Sanguinis and the Need for its Modernization........................85
             Scott Titshaw

Chapter 20   Issues with the Abolishment of Ius Sanguinis.................................90
             Kristin Collins

Chapter 21	**Problematizing Ius Sanguinis** 96
	Lois Harder

Chapter 22	**Ius Sanguinis and its Two Faces** 100
	Francesca Decimo

Chapter 23	**Rethinking the Requirement of State Citizenship** 104
	David Owen

Chapter 24	**Renouncing the Right of Blood** 107
	Kerry Abrams

Chapter 25	**Nationality Law, Ius Sanguinis and Children** 112
	David Armand Jacques Gérard de Groot

Chapter 26	**Ius Sanguinis Citizenship and Transmission of Privilege** 116
	Iseult Honohan

Chapter 27	**Taking Ius Sanguinis at Face Value and its Disadvantages** 121
	Eva Ersbøll

Chapter 28	**Limiting the Scope of Ius Sanguinis** 127
	Ana Tanasoca

Chapter 29	**The Right to a Suitable Citizenship at Birth: A Study of Naturalisation Debates** 133
	Katja Swider and Caia Vlieks

Chapter 30	**Concluding Remarks** 137
	Costica Dumbrava

Part III	**Revisiting the Concept of Banishment** 145

Chapter 31	**Impact of the New Denationalisation Policies on Citizenship** 147
	Audrey Macklin

Chapter 32 Expatriation of Terrorists and Counter Terrorism..........................157
             Peter J. Spiro

Chapter 33 Attacking the Nation and the Question of
             Citizenship..160
             Peter H. Schuck

Chapter 34 Repudiation of Citizenship by Terrorists......................................163
             Christian Joppke

Chapter 35 Citizenship: Us vs Them..167
             Vesco Paskalev

Chapter 36 Acquiring and Losing Citizenship..170
             Bronwen Manby

Chapter 37 The Politics of Revoking the Citizenship of
             Terrorists..178
             Kay Hailbronner

Chapter 38 Where do the Terrorists Belong..182
             Rainer Bauböck

Chapter 39 Citizenship Rights and Human Rights..187
             Daniel Kanstroom

Chapter 40 An American Perspective on
             Denationalization and Citizenship.......................................194
             Linda Bosniak

Chapter 41 Weakening of Citizenship by States...198
             Matthew J. Gibney

Chapter 42 Citizenship Revocation..203
             Reuven (Ruvi) Ziegler

Chapter 43 Micro-Banishments of our Times...206
             Saskia Sassen

Chapter 44	Citizenship Revocation and its Conflicts with EU Law ....209 Jo Shaw	
Chapter 45	A Glance at the Alien within ....215 Audrey Macklin	
Part IV	**Communities in the Digital Age** 225	
Chapter 46	Global Citizenship and the Rise of Cloud Communities ....227 Liav Orgad	
Chapter 47	Cloud Communities: Progressive Potential and Possible Problems ....237 Rainer Bauböck	
Chapter 48	**Blockchain Technology and Citizenship** ....243 Primavera De Filippi	
Chapter 49	**Global Citizenship and National Borders** ....254 Francesca Strumia	
Chapter 50	**Removing Law and Politics** ....260 Robert Post	
Chapter 51	Relationship between Violence, Cloud **Community and Human Rights** ....264 Michael Blake	
Chapter 52	**Citizenship and the Internet** ....269 Peter J. Spiro	
Chapter 53	**Algorithms, Cloud Communities and Citizenship** ....273 Costica Dumbrava	
Chapter 54	**Dividing Territory and State** ....278 Yussef Al Tamimi	

Chapter 55	Citizenship and Governance: A Futuristic Perspective	283
	Jelena Džankić	
Chapter 56	Global Citizenship and Access to Digital Devices	289
	Lea Ypi	
Chapter 57	Neo-Feudalism, Escapism and Technology	292
	Dimitry Kochenov	
Chapter 58	Digital Technologies, Materiality and Cloud Communities	298
	Stefania Milan	
Chapter 59	Virtual Public Spaces and Blockchain Technology	308
	Dora Kostakopoulou	
Chapter 60	Exploring the Possibility of a Global Cryptodemocracy	313
	Ehud Shapiro	
Chapter 61	Citizenship: Future Perspectives	322
	Liav Orgad	

Permissions

Index

Preface

This book has been an outcome of determined endeavour from a group of educationists in the field. The primary objective was to involve a broad spectrum of professionals from diverse cultural background involved in the field for developing new researches. The book not only targets students but also scholars pursuing higher research for further enhancement of the theoretical and practical applications of the subject.

Citizenship refers to the relationship between a nation and a person wherein the person owes their allegiance to the nation and in turn gets protection from the government of that nation. It indicates the status of freedom, which also involves accompanying responsibilities. A person can acquire citizenship mainly by three ways including citizenship by birth, citizenship by naturalization, and citizenship by descent. A recognized citizen of a country enjoys numerous legal benefits including the right to vote, social security, permanent residency, health services, hold public office, and public education. The evolution of citizenship can be traced from Greek city states where women, slaves and foreigners were denied citizenship, to the Renaissance, where it became an abstract idealized concept. This book provides significant information on the concept of national citizenship and its evolution. Its extensive content provides the readers with a thorough understanding of the subject.

It was an honour to edit such a profound book and also a challenging task to compile and examine all the relevant data for accuracy and originality. I wish to acknowledge the efforts of the contributors for submitting such brilliant and diverse chapters in the field and for endlessly working for the completion of the book. Last, but not the least; I thank my family for being a constant source of support in all my research endeavours.

Katie Miles

Part I: Putting a Price on Citizenship

Abstract

On 12 November 2013 the Maltese Parliament decided to offer Maltese and European citizenship at the price of € 650,000, but implementation of the law was postponed due to strong domestic and international critiques. On 23 December, the Maltese government announced significant amendments, including a higher total amount of € 1,150,000, part of which has to be invested in real estate and government bonds. Several other European states have adopted 'golden passport' programmes. Should citizenship be for sale? In November 2013 EUDO CITIZENSHIP invited Ayelet Shachar of the University of Toronto Law School to open a debate on these controversial policies. Twelve authors have contributed short commentaries, most of which refer to the initial law adopted by the Maltese Parliament. An executive summary by Rainer Bauböck provides an overview over the main questions raised in our Forum.

The contributions to this Forum on 'citizenship for sale' were published and disseminated to Members of the European Parliament shortly before a plenary debate on 15 January 2014 in the European Parliament. After hearing a statement by EU Commissioner Viviane Reding, the EP passed a resolution condemning the Maltese policy.

Keywords

Citizenship acquisition · Investor citizenship programmes · European citizenship · Commodification · Malta

1

The Price of Citizenship: Global, National and European Perspectives

Rainer Bauböck

The Forum Debate 'Should citizenship be for Sale?' collected comments representing a wide range of views and some highly original arguments. They can be summarised by distinguishing global, European and national perspectives.

(1) Global questions

From a global perspective, several authors argue that citizenship has become primarily a resource for mobility. Globalisation has already deeply undermined national citizenship as a bond between individuals and states and the sale of passports is just a symptom of an irreversible commodification of citizenship (Spiro). The primary value of citizenship lies in the mobility rights attached to passports. The high price put by the Maltese Parliament on Maltese passports reflects the instrumental value of free movement rights attached to EU citizenship for the wealthy and mobile global elites.

Some authors defend the sale of citizenship by pointing out that it is less arbitrary and more transparent than other ways of acquiring citizenship (e.g. Kochenov), while others suggest that giving the ultra-rich privileged access to 'global mobility corridors' (Barbulescu) raises concerns about fairness and justice (e.g. Owen). Instead of offering their citizenship for money, democratic states could bestow it on persons who are threatened by persecution or who fight for democratic values as a means of protection or exit option (Paskalev).

(2) European questions

Several comments emphasize that selling EU passports amounts to free-riding on the shared EU assets of free internal movement and external visa-waiver agreements created jointly by all Member States (e.g. Magni-Berton). Investor-citizenship programmes are, however, not the only instance. Many EU countries offer privileged access to EU citizenship to large populations outside the EU territory on grounds of distant ancestry or co-ethnic identity, obliging thereby all other Member States to admit immigrants from third countries to their territories and labour markets as EU citizens (Shaw).

Since EU citizenship is derived from Member State nationality and determining the latter remains an exclusive competence of Member States, EU law does not provide much leverage against either the sale of EU passports or other policies of creating new EU citizens without genuine links to any EU country. Several authors raise, however, the question whether the principle of proportionality established by the Court of Justice of the EU if withdrawal of Member State nationality leads to a loss of EU citizenship could also be applied to national rules regulating the acquisition of citizenship (Shaw, Shachar, Swoboda).

Independently of the issue of legality these authors suggest that the European Parliament is the institution that is best suited for addressing the issue. Instead of asking for intervention against particular Member States, they call for a broader debate on shared principles that ought to guide Member State policies in matters of citizenship.

(3) National questions

Most authors in our Forum defend a conception of citizenship as membership in a democratic community. From this perspective, selling membership seems odious in the same way that selling the franchise in elections is (Shachar, Bauböck). Citizenship is considered as the kind of good that money should not be able to buy (Ochoa).

Magni-Berton argues, however, that monetary investment can be a way of contributing to the common good of a political community and should therefore not be summarily dismissed as a legitimate reason for acquiring citizenship. In his view, the high price indicates the real problem, which is artificial scarcity created through exclusionary rules for access to national citizenship.

Authors disagree on whether citizenship acquisition based on purchase or investment is more arbitrary than the common rules of ius sanguinis, ius soli or residence-based naturalisation. Some consider all of these membership mechanisms as essentially arbitrary or discriminatory (e.g. Armstrong, Kochenov), whereas Bauböck defends them as supporting equal membership in intergenerational communities.

From a global justice perspective, 'golden residence programmes' that provide investors with privileged access to permanent residence status seem to be just as unfair towards the poor as 'golden passport programmes'. From a democratic citizenship perspective, however, the former are less problematic since they maintain a condition of residence and thus a 'genuine link test' for access to citizenship (e.g. Dzankic, Shachar, Owen).

Other authors acknowledge that states have legitimate interests in 'inviting the rich, the beautiful and the smart' (Kochenov) and that investor citizenship is not essentially different from the widespread practice of offering citizenship to prominent sportsmen and –women (Owen). Chris Armstrong observes that some states offer citizenship to foreigners who have served in their army or have otherwise provided exceptional service to the country. If investors really help to save a country from financial breakdown, offering them citizenship may be justified on grounds of emergency relief. Other authors are, however, sceptical that those who are only interested in additional mobility rights can be made to invest their wealth permanently and productively (Dzankic).

Apart from the lack of a 'genuine link' criterion, a global market for citizenship status is also seen as corrupting democracy by breaking down the wall that separates the spheres of money and power. Several contributions argue that there is a broader trend towards relinking citizenship acquisition to social class, which manifests itself, on the one hand, in offering citizenship to the rich and, on the other hand, in income and knowledge tests for ordinary naturalisations of foreign residents (Shachar, Barbulescu, Dzankic, Bauböck, Owen, Swoboda).

2

Relationship between Money and Citizenship

Ayelet Shachar

Vogue predictions that citizenship is diminishing in relevance or perhaps even vanishing outright, popular among jetsetters who already possess full membership status in affluent democracies, have failed to reach many applicants still knocking on the doors of well-off polities. One can excuse the world's destitute, those who are willing to risk their lives in search of the promised lands of migration in Europe or America, for not yet having heard the prophecies about citizenship's decline. But the same is not true for the well-heeled who are increasingly active in the market for citizenship: the ultra-rich from the rest of the world. They are willing to dish out hundreds of thousands of dollars to gain a freshly-minted passport in their new 'home country.' That this demand exists is not fully surprising given that this is a world of regulated mobility and unequal opportunity, and a world where not all passports are treated equally at border crossings. Rapid processes of market expansionism have now reached what for many is the most sacrosanct non-market good: membership in a political community. More puzzling is the willingness of governments – our public trustees and legal guardians of citizenship – to engage in processes that come very close to, and in some cases cannot be described as anything but, the sale and barter of membership goods in exchange for a hefty bank wire transfer or large stack of cash.

Everybody knows that immigration is among the most contentious policy issues of our times, and recent years have witnessed a 'restrictive turn'[1] with respect to ordinary immigration and naturalisation applicants, such as those who enter on the basis of a family reunification claim or for humanitarian reasons. The situation is different, however, for the world's moneyed elite, who can sidestep many of the standard requirements for settlement by 'buying' their way into the political community. The public act of naturalisation – of turning a non-member into a citizen – has always borne an air of legal magic, with the result that it is the 'most densely regulated and

---

[1] Joppke, C. (2007), 'Beyond National Models: Civic Integration Policies for Immigrants in Western Europe', *West European Politics* 30 (1): 1-22; Orgad, L. (2010), 'Illiberal Liberalism: Cultural Reflections on Migration and Access to Citizenship in Europe', *American Journal of Comparative Law* 58: 53-106.

most politicized aspect of citizenship laws'[2]. At stake is the regulation of the most important and sensitive decision that any political community faces: how to define who belongs, or ought to belong, within its circle of members. Not everyone knows, however, that governments are now proactively facilitating faster and smoother access to citizenship for those who can pay. Revealing insights about the current state of citizenship can be gained, I will argue in this short essay, by examining who is given this red-carpet treatment, and on what basis.

Consider the following examples. Affluent foreign investors were offered citizenship in Cyprus as 'compensation' for their Cypriot bank account deposit losses. In 2012, Portugal introduced a 'golden residence permit' to attract real estate and other investments by well-to-do individuals seeking a foothold in the EU. Spain recently adopted a similar plan. On 12 November 2013, Malta approved amendments to its Citizenship Act that put in place a new individual investor legal category that will allow high-net-worth applicants to gain a 'golden passport' in return for € 650,000; this sum was later increased to 1.15 million, opening a gilded backdoor to European citizenship. Under these cash-for-passport programmes, many of the requirements that ordinarily apply to those seeking naturalisation, such as language competency, extended residency periods or renunciation of another citizenship, are waived as part of an active competition, if not an outright bidding war, to attract the ultra-rich. Portugal, for example, offers a fast track for qualified applicants that entitles them to a 5 year permanent residence permit, visa-free travel in Schengen countries, the right to bring in their immediate family members, and ultimately the right to acquire Portuguese citizenship and with it the benefits of EU citizenship. This package comes with a hefty price tag: a capital transfer investment of € 1 million, a real estate property purchase at a value of € 500,000, or the creation of local jobs. The investment needs to remain active in Portugal for the programme's duration. Alas, the individual who gains the golden permit bears no similar obligation. Simply spending 7 days in Portugal during the first year and fourteen days in the subsequent years is enough to fulfil the programme's requirements. So much for the conclusion of the International Court of Justice in the 1955 *Nottebohm* decision that 'real and effective ties' between the individual and the state are expected to undergird the grant of citizenship.

---

[2] Bauböck, R. & S. Wallace Goodman (2010), 'Naturalisation', *EUDO Citizenship Policy Brief No. 2*, available at http://cadmus.eui.eu/handle/1814/51625, p. 1.

In Malta, recipients of the golden passport will be vetted in accordance with a discretionary ministerial act that puts in place little transparency and accountability. Government officials have made clear that applicants can expect an expedited treatment, meaning that they will not have to 'stand in the queue' like everyone else. In addition, the names of golden passport recipients would remain confidential, making it close to impossible ever to know to whom the polity has sold a precious part of its soul. This last provision has raised the ire of the opposition. Their concern is that concealing the identity of those who gain membership by literally purchasing citizenship makes it so that 'Maltese [a]re now being denied the right to know who is Maltese'[3]. The secrecy provision was eventually withdrawn in the eleventh hour, but the basic structure of the programme remains intact: privileged and fast-track naturalisation, allowing 'any Tom, Dick and Harry ... [to] buy a Maltese passport without ever setting foot on Maltese soil.' A recent survey[4] shows that the vast majority of the population opposes the sale of citizenship in principle, and rejects this scheme in particular, detached as it is from any residence or other requirements that would establish ties with the passport-granting country and society.

Beyond Europe, those seeking a new passport can look to St. Kitts and Nevis, where economic citizenship can be purchased for as low as $ 250,000 (for a lump sum) or $ 400,000 (if monies are directed to a real estate project), and issued within months. They might also consider Antigua and Barbuda, which is the latest in a growing list of countries to roll out a citizenship-by-investment programme or the Commonwealth of Dominica. Whereas ordinarily the law requires significant residence periods for those seeking naturalisation in these island nations (fourteen years in St Kitts and Nevis, seven years in the Commonwealth of Dominica and in Antigua and Barbuda, respectively), the residency requirement is reduced to merely seven days – a short vacation under the tropical sun – or even waived altogether for those who purchase their fast-tracked passport.

The citizenship-by-investment programmes that I have just described fall into the category of what we might call unfettered cash-for-passport exchanges. No '*nexi*' between the country and the passport recipient are

---

[3] 'Updated. Mario de Marco: "Opposition will not support prostitution of Malta's identity, citizenship"', *Malta Today*, 9 November 2013, available at https://www.maltatoday.com.mt/news/national/31325/opposition-proposes-change-of-name-to-individual-donor-programme-20131109#.Ws3jxHK-nZs

[4] 'Contentious citizenship scheme approved', *Malta Today*, 12 November 2013, available at https://www.maltatoday.com.mt/news/national/31402/contentious-citizenship-scheme-approved-20131112#.Ws3i9XK-nZs

required; only the investment monies must 'reside' in the country for a fixed term. This is to be distinguished from more traditional programmes, themselves the subject of perennial critique, under which migrant millionaires (to borrow David Ley's apt term) can receive an admission visa through a designated business-investment stream, but would then have to more or less comply with standard residency and naturalisation requirements[5]. Such programmes are found in, among other places, Australia, New Zealand, Hong Kong, the United Kingdom and the United States. Both kinds of programme raise serious ethical quandaries, but the unfettered cash-for-passport programmes are more extreme and blatant than the traditional investment programmes. They contribute to some of the most disturbing developments in 21st-century citizenship, including the emergence of new forms of inequality and stratification. Instead of retreating to the background as some theorists had forecasted, states are proactively creating and exacerbating inequalities through their selective and managed migration policies, setting up easy-pass citizenship for some while making membership more restrictive and difficult to achieve for others. This new world order reveals tectonic pressures and introduces urgent dilemmas about the proper scale, scope and relations of justice and mobility, citizenship and (selective) openness. These developments also bear a profound impact on immigration law and policy on the ground, since they entail processes through which the boundary between state and market is constantly being tested, eroded, and blurred.

It is these intricate and underexplored interactions between state and market that are at the heart of my inquiry into emerging selective migration regimes and transactional visions of citizenship[6]. Legally, the sovereign prerogative to issue a valid and internationally recognised passport is reserved in our international system to states alone. Governments and only governments – not markets – can secure and allocate the precious legal good of membership in the political community. But what happens when the logic of capital and markets infiltrates this classic statist expression of sovereignty? The proliferation of what I have called unfettered cash-for-passport programmes is a dramatic example of this pattern at work and it invites our

---

[5] Dzankic, J. (2012), 'The Pros and Cons of Ius Pecuniae: Investor Citizenship in Comparative Perspective', *Robert Schuman Centre for Advanced Studies, EUDO Citizenship Observatory Working Paper 2012/14*, Florence: European University Institute, available at http://cadmus.eui.eu/handle/1814/21476

[6] Shachar, A. (2006), 'The Global Race for Talent: Highly Skilled Migrants and Competitive Immigration Regimes', *NYU Law Review* 81 (2006): 148-206; Shachar, A. (forthcoming), *Olympic Citizenship: Migration and the Global Race for Talent*. Oxford: Oxford University Press.

critical scrutiny, especially since governments that use these programmes often do so in the name of advancing their country's national interest while paradoxically setting up dangerous connections between money and access to citizenship, possibly to the detriment of the basic egalitarian and participatory thrust of political membership as we currently know it. These developments raise core ethical and legal questions. Why are states putting citizenship up for sale? And what precisely is wrong with easy-pass naturalisation along the lines of the cash-for-passport programmes? Is it the queue jumping? The attaching of a price tag to citizenship? The erosion of something foundational about political membership itself? Or, perhaps, all of the above?

Surely, zealous free-marketeers will enthusiastically defend such programmes as freeing us from the shackles of culture, nation and tradition and moving citizenship forward to a new and more competitive global age of transactional contracting in which, as Nobel Prize laureate Gary Becker once put it, a price mechanism substitutes for the complicated criteria that now determine legal entry[7]. As much as Becker would like to deny it, though, these programmes have something of a 'whiff of scandal' not only due to frequent accusations of money laundering and fraud[8], but also because of something deeper and more profound. Citizenship as we know it (at least since Aristotle) is comprised of *political* relations; as such, it is expected to both reflect and generate a notion of participation, co-governance, and a degree of solidarity among those included within the body politic. It is difficult to imagine how these values could be preserved under circumstances in which insiders and outsiders are distinguished merely by the ability to pay a certain price. The objection here is to the notion that *everything*, including political membership, is 'commensurable' and reducible to a dollar value. This is what makes cash-for-passport exchanges, even if they account for only a limited stream or quota of entrants per year, deeply problematic and objectionable. The sale and barter of citizenship, even if initially reserved only for a small stream of recipients, nevertheless sends a loud and unmistakable message in both law and social ethics about whom the contemporary market-friendly state gives priority to in the immigration and naturalisation line and whom it covets most as a future citizen. This expressive conduct and the new grammar of market-infused valuation it entails tell us something

---

[7] Becker, G. (1992), 'An Open Door for Immigrants – the Auction', *Wall Street Journal*, October 14 1992, A1.

[8] 'Selling Citizenship: Papers Please', *The Economist*, September 28 2013, available at https://www.economist.com/news/international/21586843-hard-up-countries-flog-passports-papers-please.

important about the volatile state of citizenship today and the direction in which we may be heading.

Although economists will be quick to note that cash-for-passport programmes can create a hefty stream of revenue for governments, this is a hardly a strong enough justification to endorse them. The desire to enlarge their coffers may, as a matter of real-life experience, explain why some countries offer these programmes. From a normative perspective, however, such an exchange threatens to corrupt the good that is put on sale: what changes when we 'sell' citizenship is not just the price tag of membership, but its substantive content as well. As it plays a more and more important role in countries' immigration and naturalisation policies and priorities, citizenship-for-sale may also gradually reshape the greater class of those who are likely to enjoy political membership. Reliance on a price mechanism alone, to the exclusion of other important considerations, would not only prevent the vast majority of the world's population from ever gaining a chance to access citizenship in well-off polities. Taken to its logical conclusion (as *reductio*) it might also lead, corrosively and over time, to a world where *anyone* included in the pool of members must pay up, or risk 'falling helplessly to the wayside'[9].

Several scholars have taken up the task of imagining how our world might look were the market –rather than the state – to govern access to, and the acquisition of, political membership. As one study explains, '[i]f we take the basic incidents of citizenship to be protection of members and participation in modes of governance, the market for citizenship could form around offer of and demand for these services. Indeed, the offer of broader packages of citizenship services would be the basis for product differentiation'[10]. 'Product differentiation,' it should be noted, is a euphemism for providing lesser rights and services in exchange for lower fees[11]. Farewell, then, to the hard-earned ideal of inclusive citizenship as equal membership. In its absence, auction mechanisms and supply-and-demand rules may well replace our (however imperfect) procedures of exerting some degree of democratic governance and collective decision-making on what it means to belong to a political community, how to obtain a secure legal status of citizenship, and on what conditions.

---

[9] Spiro, P. J. (2008), *Beyond Citizenship: American Identity After Globalization*. Oxford: Oxford University Press, 134.
[10] Downes, D. M. & R. Janda (1998), 'Virtual Citizenship', *Canadian Journal of Law and Society* 13 (2): 27-61, at 55.
[11] Jordan, B. & F. Düvell (2003), *Migration: The Boundaries of Equality and Justice*. Cambridge: Polity Press.

Even staunch defenders of the market approach to citizenship understand that they are facing a hard sell. Becker, for one, admits that 'people object to the sale of permits because, as they say, "citizenship is not to be for sale"'[12], and this is a moral intuition that runs deep. As evidenced by recent debates over the instalment of cash-for-passport programmes, most people have strong reservations against attaching a price tag to citizenship[13]. The reasons are many. As already mentioned, such a move may cause irreparable harm to the vision of citizenship as grounded in long-term relations of trust and shared responsibility and may prefigure the conflation of the political and ethical with the economic and calculative. It may also undermine membership bonds grounded in co-authorship, cross-subsidisation of risk, and even sacrifice that might be expected in times of need. What is more, citizenship currently involves making collective decisions, and translating those decisions into binding commitments, in the context of a political project that is far larger than oneself, and that extends well beyond the lifespan of each generation of members – a time horizon that will be extremely hard to sustain under a regime of strategic transactions, according to which 'wealth buys membership.' Turning citizenship into a money-based prize also contradicts any notion of complex equality through blocked exchange according to which advantage in one sphere (here, wealth) cannot be legitimately transferred to another (in this case, membership)[14]. This makes the idea of selling membership unnerving for anyone who objects to the ultimate triumph of economics over politics, the reduction of our public life and ethics into mere pecuniary transactions, or the imperialistic idea that 'trades' occupy the full terrain of human value and meaning[15].

Another set of concerns arises in the context of supranational citizenship, as in the derivative structure of European citizenship. The actions of those member states that take the liberty to put their national citizenship 'on sale' indirectly affects the supranational political membership good that is shared by other countries, which may resist such commodification. There are also complex questions about *to whom* (beyond its own citizenry) the transacting

---

[12] Above n. 7.
[13] Borna, S. & J. M. Stearns (2002), 'The Ethics and Efficacy of Selling National Citizenship', *Journal of Business Ethics* 37 (2): 193-207, at 197.
[14] Walzer, M. (1983), *Spheres of Justice: A Defense of Pluralism and Equality*. New York: Basic Books.
[15] Radin, M. J. (1987), 'Market-Inalienability', *Harvard Law Review* 100: 1849-1937; Sunstein, C. R. (1997), 'Incommensurability and Kinds of Valuation: Some Applications in Law', in R. Chang (ed.), *Incommensurability, Incomparability, and Practical Reason*, 234-254. Cambridge, MA: Harvard University Press; Sandel, M. J. (2013), *What Money Can't Buy: The Moral Limits of Markets*. New York: Farrar, Straus and Giroux.

government is obliged to provide justificatory reasons concerning its selective admission and naturalisation policies. Need it justify itself to other member states? To the Commission of the European Union? To would-be entrants who might have had a shot at admission through standard migration streams (family, employment, and humanitarian) but who are priced out of the advantage given to those who can afford a 'golden passport'? From a global perspective, cash-for-passport programmes clearly exacerbate pre-existing inequalities rather than alleviate them. Should the sedentary populations of the migrant millionaires' countries of origin, which are typically less stable or poorer than the destination countries, get to weigh in as well? Or, if an expansive all-affected-interests principle is applied, perhaps anyone at all who may be unfairly and arbitrarily affected should have a voice in these decisions[16]. And what about migrants who are already settled in the country but ineligible to benefit from naturalisation schemes that require no knowledge or familiarity with the political structures, main civic institutions, history or language of the country, and who are subject instead to ever more demanding civic integration requirements? If civic integration is a required precondition to the bestowment of full membership by the state (as restrictive citizenship tests increasingly indicate), how can this demand only apply to some and not to others?

After all, there is no rational connection between delivering a stack of cash or sending in a bank wire transfer and establishing the kind of participation and equal standing among fellow citizens that the political bonds of membership are meant to represent and foster. From this vantage point, the transaction in citizenship, even if carefully regulated and implemented by monopolistic governments or their authorised delegates, should be prohibited. Taken to its dystopian extreme, this approach may lead to a situation whereby the size of their wallets, and nothing else, distinguishes suitable from unsuitable candidates for initial entry and eventual citizenship. This kind of transaction, as lawyers and philosophers like to put it, is value-degrading: the trading in citizenship 'taints,' 'degrades' or outrightly 'corrupts' (in the moral sense) its value as a good. We might in the same vein say that these cash-for-citizenship programmes detrimentally affect the 'character of the goods themselves and the norms that should govern them'[17]. As critics of commodification have been at pains to clarify in other contexts[18],

---

[16] Goodin, R. (2007), 'Enfranchising All Affected Interests, and Its Alternatives', *Philosophy and Public Affairs* 35 (1): 40-68.

[17] Sandel, M. J. (2013), *What Money Can't Buy: The Moral Limits of Markets*. New York: Farrar, Straus and Giroux, 113.

[18] Cohen, I. G. (2003), 'The Price of Everything, the Value of Nothing: Reframing the Commodification Debate', *Harvard Law Review* 117 (689): 689-710.

it is not that € 1 million is too high or too low a price, but that placing a 'for sale' tag on citizenship, no matter what amount is written on it, has a corrosive effect on non-market relations, eroding the ties that bind and altering our view of what it means to belong to a political community. Just as we should be critical of granting citizenship according to nothing but the fortuitous and arbitrary circumstances of station of birth[19], I believe we must resist, with even greater force, the notion that money can buy 'love of country' – or secure membership in it.

If governments and activists are listening, they should heed the warning signs. The ideal of equal citizenship has been inflicted with many wounds over the past decades, and has always been more of an aspiration than a reality. However, the dangerous and increasingly frequent links between money and access to political membership reflected in the more calculated, mercantilist-like perceptions of citizenship that have given rise to unfettered cash-for-passport programmes threaten not only the implementation of the ideal, but the ideal itself. Courting the world's moneyed elite by relaxing standard admission and naturalisation requirements may enrich the coffers of a country in the short run, but in the long haul it risks cheapening something far more important: citizenship itself.

---

[19] Shachar, A. (2009), *The Birthright Lottery: Citizenship and Global Inequality*. Cambridge, MA: Harvard University Press; Shachar, A. (2011), 'Earned Citizenship: Property Lessons for Immigration Reform', *Yale Journal of Law & the Humanities* 23: 110-158.

3

The Problematics Associated with Cash-for-Passports

Peter J. Spiro

Investor citizenship programmes are becoming increasingly commonplace in state practice. What was once the province of outlier Caribbean microstates is gaining traction among more substantial states. As an instrumental tool, states see citizenship-for-sale as a way to help get out of an economic hole on the cheap. There is no marginal material cost to minting new citizens, especially those with deep enough pockets to afford the price of admission. Hence the adoption of investor citizenship programmes by such countries as Cyprus, Malta, and Portugal.

I sympathise with Ayelet Shachar's powerful framing of these programmes. There is something unseemly, at least, about putting membership in the polity up for sale. Cash-for-passports, as Shachar derisively labels the phenomenon, clashes with our received understandings of citizenship as a marker of social solidarity in a Walzerian sense. The emerging market for citizenship literally commodifies the status, the tip of an iceberg that Shachar is describing in other work as states come to see immigration as a talent-pool competition.

But where Shachar sees investor citizenship programmes as a threat to robust citizenship ties, I see them more as a manifestation of citizenship that is already being hollowed out. If citizenship still meant what it used to mean, if it still represented special ties as a sociological matter, then investor citizenship schemes would not exist. In that context, citizenship-for-sale would have implicated serious symbolic societal costs by breaking the social contract, understood not as an arm's-length market transaction but rather as the locus of morally-inflected rights and responsibilities. In the old world, such programmes would have been inconceivable.

Today, far from inconceivable, they are becoming an accepted element of strategic immigration policy. Investor citizenship programmes remain controversial (perhaps especially in a small, distinctive society such as Malta, which may more represent the old norm rather the new). But they are obviously gaining traction. States have something to sell. There must be some sentiment in adopting states that the revenues will exceed costs, social or otherwise.

Investor programmes give the lie to notion that citizenship is sacred, in a civic sense. The programmes evidence the descent of citizenship from its former pedestal. Shachar extols a 'vision of citizenship as grounded in long-term relations of trust and shared responsibility, ... membership bonds grounded in co-authorship, cross-subsidisation of risk, and even sacrifice that might be expected in times of need.' That's the citizenship of the past, and passport-for-sale schemes supply another data point to prove it.

This is so notwithstanding externalities imposed on other states. In some contexts, these externalities will be miniscule (a citizen of Malta can travel to the United States visa free where the citizen of Russia cannot, but the numbers will be low, and the number who abuse visa-free entry will be even lower). In the European context they are potentially greater, as the EU member states become subject to lowest-common-denominator citizenship policies. Those who buy Maltese citizenship are less likely to settle in Valletta (one wonders how many could even name the capital city before – or perhaps even after – they have made the purchase) than in Berlin or Paris or Milan. When one buys Maltese citizenship one gets EU citizenship included in the price; it opens a backdoor to the rest of Europe. But the EU seems unlikely to complain. There is no legal basis for opposition, citizenship policy remaining exclusively within Member State discretion. Nor is there likely to be much pushback as a policy matter, so long as the price is high enough to depress numbers and maintain economic quality (as it were).

In material terms, the programmes are not much of a threat to provider states, either. The numbers will be low. (Portugal had only 330 takers in the first year of its program.) Because many buyers will remain non-resident, they will be invisible to the existing citizenry. They will not be politically engaged, to the extent they will feel no interest beyond protection of their bought-and-paid status. One possible cost would be with respect to diplomatic protection. It will be interesting to see whether that is a part of a bargain – whether in fact states will intercede with other states on behalf of their paying members (and whether international tribunals would recognise protection of cash-only nationals).

Shachar is correct that the investor programmes show that citizenship is still worth something. As the market thickens, we will see how much. With the reference point of states that sell permanent residency, we will be able approximately to isolate the value of citizenship itself – the premium states will be able to extract with the passport. Will investor programmes like Malta's, which offer citizenship, be priced much higher than Hungary's, which extends residency status only? (I will leave to the economists to deal with asymmetries among the various packages.) I suspect that premium will not be great, especially insofar as permanent residency includes the possibility of future eligibility for naturalisation. Finally, there is the possibility of price competition as more states enter the market and some seek to maximise revenues by attracting more buyers at a lower price point.

Investor citizenship programmes are a symptom, not a cause. Shachar sees citizenship as something that can be rescued through citizenship policy. As material forces of globalisation fragment citizens' solidarities, citizenship law cannot revive them.

4

What is the Problem? The Price or the Sale

Magni-Berton Raul

Roughly two thousand years ago, Roman citizenship began to be sold to rich foreigners. As a consequence, rather than a way to share equal duties and rights, citizenship by the third century C.E. had become an aristocratic title. It divided people instead of rallying them. It increased inequalities instead of reducing them.

The current situation is somewhat similar. Rich people have access to rich countries' membership, and poor people remain on the wrong side. Thus, I sympathise with Shachar's concerns and I think we should avoid to reproduce what we have already experimented in our ancient history.

However, I do not agree with the way in which both Shachar and Spiro have identified the problem. Consider, for example, a situation in which a foreigner asks for access to citizenship in those terms: 'I want to share the responsibility of my failures and achievements with you, and I'd like to invest in you and to be partly responsible of your achievements and your failures.' This is a touching statement of solidarity and identification with a group. I have called it the stockholder principle: individual citizens are like a joint-stock company in which fellow-citizens invest. The consequence of these collective investments is a shared responsibility for individuals' achievements. Moreover, the right to benefit from public support is associated with the duty to invest in other fellow-citizens' life projects. These duties are embodied in specific taxes for public investment. Thus, each citizen is also a stockholder with respect to other citizens.

Thus I would not say that the Maltese Parliament voted to 'sell' the Maltese passport when it granted citizenship for € 650,000. From a foreign investor's point of view, given that she makes the above statement and is ready to invest in the future of Maltese citizens, she acquires a moral claim to become citizen. She does not only give a sum of money in exchange for rights; she also becomes more largely committed to the duties of a Maltese citizen. In other words, she gains access to the Maltese nationality with an investment, which is a way to link her destiny to that of other Maltese.

So what is wrong with this beautiful story? Why are the Maltese people sceptical and why is international opinion critical? Of course, we could agree that the argument of externalities, mentioned by Shachar, is relevant: European citizens should also benefit from those new investments. Thus, the problem is identifying who decides the allocation of those investments: the government of Malta or the EU. Although these externalities are expected to be low, as Spiro points out, it can be argued that Maltese citizens free-ride because they alone benefit from the foreigners' will to become European, and this could be morally disputable.

Beyond that, the main argument I would like to develop here is that € 650,000 seems, at first sight, a lot. Not in absolute terms, of course. Suppose, for example, a society in which people spend € 200 on watching a film. Several others things are likely to be true in such a society. Firstly, there are some people that can afford to pay this price. Secondly, there are no other less expensive goods which are substitutable, such as for example theatre, sport or other entertainment. Perhaps this is because technological progress has improved cinema so that it delivers a specific pleasure one cannot find elsewhere. Alternatively, this may happen because theatres or circuses have simply gone bankrupt.

Analogically, in the case of naturalisation, several other things are likely to be true in virtue of the fact that people prefer to pay a considerable amount of money, rather than to proceed with alternatives. For example, in a society where people are ready to pay € 650,000 for a passport, many of these alternatives are likely to be extremely burdensome, impractical, or unfair.

Let me assume that, until now, the Maltese way to naturalise foreigners has been fair according to the stockholder principle. In other words, a 'poor foreigner' can be naturalised, if she is ready to share the responsibility for her failures and achievements with Maltese citizens, as well as to invest in them and become partly responsible for their achievements and failures. Under this assumption, investing money in Malta, whatever the amount, is one fair way, among others, to gain access to citizenship. There is no reason, after all, to distinguish between financial and human investments.

But, if the Maltese law was fair, people would not be likely to invest € 650,000 to be naturalised. Of course, they could love Malta. They also could be so wealthy that they prefer to pay this amount rather than spend time in human investments. More probably, however, the fact that people are ready to pay this amount reveals that the law is in fact too restrictive and does not provide other reasonable ways to become citizen.

Naturalisation in Malta is possible after five years of residence, but it includes discretionary conditions, the severity of which can vary across time. In other European countries specific conditions and varying periods of residence are required. The greater the severity, the greater the price for passports. Investor citizenship programmes should be used to create a fruitful community, not to maximise price.

To conclude, I do not believe that investor citizenship programmes in themselves are unfair. On the contrary, they can reveal, via a financial argument, how hard the naturalisation process is. All European countries are concerned with this issue: too restrictive laws prevent motivated people to give their contribution to the host country and they divide humanity into rich and poor, rather than into different united groups. Exactly as the Roman Empire did.

5

Selling Citizenship and its Cost

Chris Armstrong

Malta's decision to sell citizenship triggers strong reactions in many of us. It appears to wrongfully connect the awarding of citizenship to ability to pay. And as Ayelet Shachar's contribution points out, it disregards the other things that theorists often emphasise as key to citizenship acquisition: rootedness in a community, interaction with its institutions, long-standing residence, or participation in its political life.

On the other hand, we might ask, can these other things *always* be necessary criteria for awarding citizenship? Imagine that our country is waging a desperate war of self-defence. Just when defeat – and the collapse of our community – appears inevitable, a force of foreign volunteers enters the fray and swings the result in our favour. These volunteers have performed a tremendous service to our community – perhaps the greatest service we can imagine.

Imagine, next, that we decide to thank the volunteers by offering them citizenship in our country. Would this be morally repugnant? Far from it: the decision would, I think, be perfectly appropriate. What, then, of rootedness, interaction, residence, or participation? If giving citizenship to our imaginary volunteers is appropriate, then those things cannot be as important as we thought. Perhaps a massive, one-off contribution to the polity can be enough.

We might think the Maltese example is very different, of course. Perhaps what we object to here is the *selling* of citizenship, because this rides roughshod over the morally significant connection between citizen and community. Perhaps such 'deals' should never be made.

I'm not so sure. We can tweak the war example so that volunteers are not forthcoming, and our country still faces annihilation. We then *ask* for volunteers, promising to grant citizenship as a reward for their services. Obviously, this looks less palatable than the original example, because instead of a selfless sacrifice we now have a rather self-interested deal. Still, would it be wrong for our country to offer this deal? It seems to me that, though it might make some of us uncomfortable, the answer is no. Perhaps a country can be in such dire straits that such deals are, all-things-considered, an acceptable way of proceeding. But if *that* is true, what if the straits are financial ones, and the deal in question is, simply, the selling of citizenship?

I suspect that selling citizenship is perhaps not *always* wrong, even if it often will be. In the rest of this response I set out five reasons, though, for restricting the sale of citizenship. Some of these concerns can be avoided. Others remain genuine worries. But the *way* they ought to concern us is interesting, because they suggest that what is *wrong* with selling citizenship also applies to other instances of citizenship acquisition. Perhaps, then, selling citizenship is just the most visible case of a wider phenomenon. Perhaps, for all its blatancy, it is not even the most important case.

1. What if selling citizenship has not been democratically authorised (or, as Shachar suggests, it is veiled in secrecy), whereas if 'the people' had been properly consulted, they would not have endorsed such a policy? (A survey shortly before the Maltese decision showed 53 per cent disapproval.[1]) We know that citizens often feel their views are very poorly represented in policies on immigration. Then again, putting great weight on popular views about immigration may be unwise: those views are often hostile to immigration *in general*, and also, at the same time, often very badly informed. But regardless, this objection is a contingent one, and leaves open the deeper question: if the public *did* authorise selling citizenship, would there be anything wrong with doing so?

2. Perhaps admitting the kind of people who can afford to spend hundreds of thousands of Euros buying citizenship is unwise. Those (rich) people will probably turn out to wield disproportionate influence on domestic politics. I believe that we have every reason to fear their influence. But if this is so, it is not an objection to *selling* citizenship. It is an objection, surely, to *granting* citizenship to very rich individuals whether they pay for it or not. It would apply just as strongly to a policy which made it *easier* for rich individuals to access citizenship (free of charge). Less obviously, liberal democracies standardly grant automatic citizenship to the children of native citizens, some of whom also happen to inherit great wealth. Isn't *their* wealth a problem too? Isn't it just as large a danger to democracy? If so, what should we do?

---

[1] 'MaltaToday survey – Malta says yes to Budget, no to sale of citizenship', *Malta Today*, 11 November 2013, available at https://www.maltatoday.com.mt/news/data_and_surveys/31360/maltatoday-survey-budget-citizenship-20131111#.WtMg7HK-nZs

3. Perhaps it is unfair to allow people to buy citizenship, because other less fortunate outsiders are thereby disadvantaged. The playing-field is simply not even. If so, the same response follows: this is an objection not to *selling* citizenship, but to making it easier for *anyone* to obtain citizenship merely because they are wealthier or, indeed, because they possess 'desirable' skills. Selling citizenship is only a very visible instance of wider distributive unfairness in allocating citizenship. It may not be the most important example.

4. Perhaps selling citizenship cheapens that 'good', and, as Shachar rightly points out, sends a terrible signal to existing citizens about what makes a good citizen. This is, I agree, a profound concern, but we can respond in the same way as to the last objection. *Any* policy which makes it more likely that some, rather than others, will be admitted to citizenship sends such a signal. A policy which makes it easier for wealthier or more highly-skilled people to obtain citizenship sends just the same signal. If the objection is a good one, its implications ripple beyond the mere selling of citizenship.

5. Finally, we might object that what Malta is doing is unfair to other EU member states, since all of those states potentially bear the *costs* of granting citizenship to outsiders, but only Malta reaps the *benefits*. This, I suspect, is at the heart of much of the resistance to what Malta is doing. But several responses can be made. First, this objection obviously applies only to EU-member states, and not to states more generally. Second, for an EU member state to link citizenship to buying property or investing in their country should be equally objectionable. Third, and more importantly, we can point to ripple effects again. If it is wrong for one state to pursue a citizenship policy which delivers benefits to itself but imposes costs on others, what *else* might fall foul of that principle? What about countries that attract wealthy citizens of other states by offering them lower taxes and which thereby make it more difficult for progressively-minded states to pursue egalitarian policies? What if state competition for those wealthy individuals always imposes externalities, making progress towards a more equal world more difficult? Selling citizenship might then be, as Peter Spiro observes, merely the tip of a very large iceberg. And not necessarily the worst part.

I am not sure, in the end, that I agree with Shachar that selling citizenship is always wrong. Perhaps it is safer to say that it *usually* is, though we can imagine situations where the reverse is true. But either way, selling citizenship, even if it (often) appears repugnant, pales in comparison to many of the other inequities attendant on the ordinary transmission of citizenship, as Shachar's own work has forcefully hammered home. I am tempted to conclude precisely this: for all that selling citizenship troubles us, it might do us the considerable service of forcing us to think (more) about the way in which many people already obtain citizenship, and the way in which citizenship practices more broadly both feed off, and make it harder to tackle, underlying global inequalities. As Spiro observes, writing better citizenship laws can only be part of the solution to that problem. There are many other important ways of tackling global inequalities that deserve at least equal attention.

6

Investment Citizenship and Global Inequality

Roxana Barbulescu

The problem with investment citizenship ain't that it is for sale, the problem is global inequality. Citizenship-by-investment schemes do not themselves produce injustice but they are unjust because they build on pre-existing large disparities in the world: If all countries were equal in living conditions would the scheme be objectionable? If the answer is no, as I think it is, then the source of injustice is global inequality rather than policies that do not themselves produce injustice.

In the real world, however, citizenship-by-investment together with similar schemes for residence opens global mobility corridors for the ultra-rich. In what follows I discuss how investor citizenship impacts on international migration and how it alters the institution of citizenship. I end by calling for more systematic analysis of the political conditions under which this transformation of citizenship has come about.

From an international migration perspective citizenship-by-investment is a means for opening borders, even if only for very few affluent individuals (and their families). In abstract terms, the logic is the same as with the different competitive schemes for high-skilled migrants. The latter use talent, reputation, skill, work experience, previous salary and even age as proxies for admitting only those who can make an important contribution[1]. So do investors through their investments. The two schemes are also similar in their consequences: they both immobilise the less well-off individuals. The twin phenomena of global competition for the worlds' best and brightest and for the richest correspond to the nationalisation of poverty and the confinement of less well-off citizens within their national borders. For me, this indicates that the questions the scheme raises are indeed about global social justice and it is this problem on which states need to focus their efforts.

---

[1] Shachar, A. (2006), 'The Race for Talent: Highly Skilled Migrants and Competitive Immigration Regimes', *New York University Law Review* 81 (1): 148–206.

Here is one qualifier: many citizens of the rich countries benefit from similar privileged access to citizenship or residence in less developed countries around the world. They call themselves expats instead of migrants and often need not go through the normal immigration route. A basic state pension from the UK, for instance, can make one a particularly well-off person in the Global South. The citizenship-by-investment scheme just mirrors a worldwide state of affairs, but it is more visible because of the high threshold of capital needed for access. The fact that this matter has only now entered the citizenship debate indicates how heavily theoretical and ethical debates build on Western cases.

My second remark has to do with the profound transformation of the institution of citizenship. My point here is that citizenship-by-investment largely contradicts the very recent efforts of states to re-substantiate citizenship through tests and integration requirements (see the earlier debate hosted by this Forum[2]). Waiving these requirements for the ultra-rich raises serious doubts over the credentials of the previous citizenship reforms and states will need to justify why civic knowledge and other integration requirements are needed or useful and provide proof that they are something more than a filter to make immigration more selective.

The third point has to do with the fact that using capital as the sole condition for citizenship for investors (waiving requirements such as residence, language skills or ancestry) departs from traditional foundations of (national) citizenship which tended to privilege cultural and social ties. It also marks a break with the historically younger project of social citizenship which went in the opposite direction and sought to incorporate the economically disenfranchised into the citizenry[3]. As Peter Spiro argues in

---

[2] Bauböck, R. & C. Joppke (eds.) (2010), 'How Liberal are Citizenship Tests?', *Robert Schuman Centre for Advanced Studies, EUDO Citizenship Observatory Working Paper 2010/41*, Florence: European University Institute, available at http://cadmus.eui.eu/bitstream/handle/1814/13956/RSCAS_2010_41corr.pdf?sequence=3.

[3] See Marshall, T. H. (1973 [1950]), 'Citizenship and Social Class', in *Class, Citizenship, and Social Development*, Westport, CT: Greenwood Press; Soysal, Y. (2012), 'Citizenship, Immigration and the European Social Project: Rights and Obligations of the Individuality', *British Journal of Sociology* 36 (1): 1-21.

his contribution, with this revision citizenship aligns itself with other neo-liberal and free market-inspired developments. However, such withdrawal of the state and the advancement of the free market in the traditional sphere of state sovereignty still need to be better explained rather than just diagnosed.

In the case of citizenship-by-investment, we need to understand better whether this was a supply or demand driven policy change, what stakeholder alliances lobbied for this policy, what channels they used, who set the price tag (for an overview of varieties of citizenship- and residence-by-investment programmes across the world see Barbulescu 2016), and what arguments persuaded political elites to implement it. Neoliberalism does not spread like the flavour of a bag of tea in a cup of water: it needs promoters and legitimisation that will align support against other competing paradigms, especially in citizenship policies where there are strong path-dependency dynamics. These are important questions because citizenship-by-investment departs from citizenship traditions everywhere, because such policy revisions are largely unpopular and may have a high political cost and, not least, because they de-legitimise the very existence of state bureaucracies administrating citizenship for the ultra-rich. With naturalisation becoming a transaction over-the-counter, the organisation that implemented it partly loses its purpose.

So why is it important to understand how citizenship-by-investment has come about? Because of its large impact on an essential political institution and its success in carving out global mobility corridors through entangled states.

One final note: As several states have already implemented citizenship-by-investment schemes, states should quickly lose their naivety about investors as do-gooders. Those schemes that – unlike Malta's – rely on investment rather than direct payment should check that the capital is indeed invested. The UK, one of the first states to introduce Investor Visa (with a price tag of £ 1 million or a bank loan from an UK financial institution and personal assets worth 2 million) recently revised this policy as it came to its attention that investors used the capital for investment as security to back up loans and that investments were placed in offshore custody[4,5].

---

[4] UK Border Agency (2013), *Guidelines Tier 1 (Investor)*. Available at http://www.ukba.homeoffice.gov.uk/sitecontent/applicationforms/pbs/tier1investor-guidance1.pdf, p. 1; revision HC 760 came into force in December 2012; see also Nathan, M., H. Rolfe & C. Vargas-Silva (2013), 'The Economic and Labour Market Impacts of Tier 1 Entrepreneur and Investor Migrants', *Report to the Migration Advisory Committee*, available at www.ukba.homeoffice.gov.uk/sitecontent/documents/aboutus/workingwithus/mac/economic-research.pdf

[5] Barbulescu, R. (2016) Investment Migration in the World. IMC Geneva https://investmentmigration.org/investment-migration-in-the-world/

7

Citizenship for Sale in Malta

Jelena Džankić

'We didn't exactly believe your story, Miss O'Shaughnessy. We believed your 200 dollars. I mean, you paid us more than if you had been telling us the truth, and enough more to make it all right.' These were the words of Sam Spade played by Humphrey Bogart in the 1941 film 'The Maltese Falcon'. Malta's recent amendments to the Citizenship Act suggest that for the country's policymakers the amount of € 650,000 is just enough 'to make it all right' for investors to purchase the Maltese and by extension the European Union (EU) citizenship. But is cash-for-passport really 'all right', and does it affect the value of citizenship?

Magni Berton suggests in his contribution to this Forum that what is wrong with the Maltese law is that ordinary naturalisation is too difficult and discretionary. Indeed, for most applicants, meeting the criteria for ordinary naturalisation takes a long time and a lot of effort. During the years of residence that the applicants spend in their country of destination they make that country the focal point of their lives: they learn its language, its customs and establish social links with other citizens living there. Their claim to citizenship of that country is based – following Shachar – on *ius nexi*. Hence the integration of such individuals is of high value for citizenship as a public good, as a network of communal contributions and responsibilities, as shared love for the country.

Yet, Magni Berton claims that the rich may as well love the destination country and that money may merely be an instrument for facilitating their access to citizenship. Instead of a 'human investment', which would entail time, establishment of social links, and acquisition of language skills, the wealthy can make a monetary contribution. However, as highlighted in other contributions to this debate, the rich usually do not spend much time in their destination countries. Rather, as Spiro noted, they mostly use the opportunities provided to them by virtue of possessing its passport. Now, what is love in this context? The one who truly loves is willing to wait and invest time and effort. Otherwise, we would not speak about love. Offering money in exchange for practical benefits together with a claim of love sounds rather like something else. And that 'something else' is simply wrong.

In justifying investor citizenship programmes, Magni Berton further compares citizenship with stockholding: 'individual citizens are like a joint-stock company in which fellow-citizens invest'. This reduces the scope of citizenship, because the interests of stockholders are determined by the share of stocks that they have in the company. In addition to this, stocks are tradable – not only from the government to an individual, but also among individuals themselves.

It makes more sense if, instead of regarding citizenship as stockholding, we compare it to stakeholding, as Bauböck has suggested[1]. A citizen-stakeholder is a person who has a fundamental interest in membership in a particular polity (rather than in economic or other benefits for which membership may be instrumental). We can identify such stakeholder citizens by looking at how a person's interest in autonomy and well-being are structurally linked to the collective autonomy (self-government) and well-being (flourishing) of a country. This means that those who have obtained citizenship merely on grounds of investment cannot be stakeholders, because they only have an accidental and instrumental interest in citizenship in a state that offers them a favourable investment environment.

It is worth mentioning that there are different ways in which countries offer citizenship to the rich, which is often overlooked both in the media and in academic circles.[2] The way in which an investor programme is regulated could potentially turn this instrumental interest of the rich in possessing a passport of a country into stakeholder citizenship. In her initial contribution to this debate, Shachar highlighted the difference between 'golden residence' and 'investor citizenship' programmes. While the former require the investors to reside in their country of destination for a number of years and to undergo a standard naturalisation procedure (including the knowledge of language, customs, etc.) before becoming citizens, the latter is an exchange of a fixed amount of money and citizenship (most governments do run criminal record and due diligence checks of applicants). There is also a third mechanism for turning investors into citizens, which is discretionary

---

[1] Bauböck, R. (2009), 'The Rights and Duties of External Citizenship', *Citizenship Studies* 13 (5): 475-499.
[2] Dzankic, J. (2012), 'The Pros and Cons of Ius Pecuniae: Investor Citizenship in Comparative Perspective', *Robert Schuman Centre for Advanced Studies, EUDO Citizenship Observatory Working Paper 2012/14*, Florence: European University Institute, available at http://cadmus.eui.eu/handle/1814/21476

naturalisation on grounds of national interest. These provisions exist in 22 out of the 28 EU Member States. Such discretionary naturalisation is the prerogative of the state and it is used only in a few cases annually. In several countries, including Austria, discretionary naturalisation has resulted in corruption and secret deals, which tells us that too much discretion can have adverse effects on citizenship.

Even with this in mind, we can find some support for Armstrong's argument that investor citizenship programmes are not always wrong. That is, well-conceptualised 'golden residence' schemes may bring economic benefits to the state while also turning investors into genuine stakeholders. However, such 'golden residence' programmes should not be based merely on real estate purchase, as recently approved by Spain, and they should require more than a compulsory residence of only a few weeks per year as a mechanism of eventually qualifying for citizenship, as they do in Portugal. The argument here is that neither the possession of real estate nor the lack of residence can help the wealthy to establish a true connection with the destination country. Only 'golden residence' programmes that are based on multi-annual investment, jobs for citizens of the destination country, and compulsory residence for the investor before qualifying for citizenship, as is the case in Canada, help the investor to become integrated and interested in the well-being of the citizens of her or his adopted country.

By contrast, the program recently passed by the Maltese government is a 'pure investor citizenship' scheme, which differs from programmes in other EU countries that have recently adopted various 'golden residence' schemes (Bulgaria, Hungary, Portugal, Spain). Besides the crisis-struck Cyprus, which in May 2013 opened several routes to naturalisation on grounds of economic contribution to the state, Malta is the only other European state with such a scheme. The programmes in Malta and Cyprus are thus more similar to the ones in the Caribbean islands – Saint Kitts and Nevis, the Commonwealth of Dominica, and Antigua and Barbuda, all of which operate 'investor citizenship' schemes.

Two things make the Cypriot and Maltese programmes more attractive for investors than those of the Caribbean islands. First, in the former cases the naturalised investor will be granted visa-free travel to 151 (Cyprus) or 163 (Malta) states. This is considerably more than they would have by virtue of possessing the best-ranked Caribbean passport, that of Saint Kitts and Nevis which allows visa-free entry to 131 countries. Second, and more importantly, since in the EU the regulation of citizenship is decided by each Member State for herself, an individual may now obtain EU citizenship for roughly the price of a Porsche 918 Spyder. Hence the investor gains access to all the rights stemming from EU citizenship, including free movement and residence within the EU, the right to vote for and stand as a candidate in European Parliament and municipal elections, diplomatic protection, etc. This raises the question of whether it is proportionate and just that access to this array of rights is exchanged for the price of a sports car. Doesn't this dilute the value of citizenship to a tradable commodity, voiding it of the sense of rights and duties and undermining citizens' solidarity? If states sell citizenship, what the buyer gets will no longer look like citizenship at all.

8

Sale of Citizenship and Democracy

Rainer Bauböck

Like the Roman god Janus, whose head was displayed above city gates, citizenship has two faces: one looks outwards, the other one inwards. The external face turns to other states and demands that they recognise the country's passport as well as to citizens living abroad whom it promises the right to return and diplomatic protection. The internal face speaks to citizens as members of a democratic community. It tells them that, in spite of their different interests and identities, they are equal as individuals and collectively govern themselves through their right to vote. The two faces belong to the same head, but sometimes the stories that they tell become dangerously disconnected.

The European Union has strongly increased the external value of its member states' citizenships. It has expanded the right to return into freedom of movement throughout the Union. The EU passport is, moreover, a key that opens the doors of a large number of third countries for visa-free entry. Finally, EU citizenship offers now also diplomatic protection by other member states to EU nationals residing in third countries. When selling its passport for € 650,000 to non-resident foreigners, Malta intends to cash in on this European added value of its external citizenship. It is not hard to understand why this irritates EU institutions and other member states. Malta behaves like a member of a cooperative that sells membership to outsiders at a price that in no way reflects her own contributions.

Beyond the obvious unfairness in the division of monetary gains from the value of EU citizenship, member states also have reasons to be concerned about any one of them naturalising persons born and residing abroad without genuine links to the country. As Shachar and Dzankic point out, these people are likely to use their passports for other purposes than a 'return' to the state whose citizenship they have obtained. In this respect, Italy, Hungary and Romania, whose ethnic citizenship policies have created hundreds of thousands of new EU citizens abroad, are worse sinners than Malta. What the Maltese and similar programmes do is to transform an inherited privilege of co-ethnic populations residing abroad into a global commodity.

This makes it quite natural to consider the external value of citizenship from a global perspective, as Spiro, Armstrong and Barbulescu do in different ways. Spiro regards the sale of citizenship as yet another symptom of its inevitable decline due to globalisation, alongside the increasing toleration of dual citizenship, as he has argued previously. While the instrumental value of citizenship of an EU member state for transnationally mobile populations has increased, citizenship as a 'sacred bond' between an individual and a state has unravelled. Armstrong and Barbulescu look instead at citizenship through a lens of global (in)justice and conclude that the sale of EU passports is merely one instance – and not the most significant one – of how citizenship policies 'both feed off, and make it harder to tackle, underlying global inequalities.' This echoes Shachar's initial comment that we should be equally critical of the comparatively rare practice of putting up citizenship for sale and of 'granting citizenship according to nothing but the fortuitous and arbitrary circumstances of station of birth'.

I suggest that it is useful to consider the external and internal perspectives separately. From a global perspective, birthright citizenship may indeed look suspiciously arbitrary, although I would not regard it as a cause of global injustice. To see why, consider the EU as a regional model for a potentially more just global regime. In the EU, free movement and access to opportunities elsewhere is linked to citizenship in a member state, which is again based on birthright in each of these states. So it seems misconceived to point to birthright citizenship as the culprit that causes global social inequalities instead of blaming unequal resources, global economic governance and immigration control.

Once we walk through the city gates and listen to the voice of Janus from the other side, our critique of citizenship for sale will change quite radically. Barbulescu asks rhetorically: 'If all countries were equal in living conditions would the scheme be objectionable?' From inside a democratic community, the answer to this question must be an emphatic yes! To understand why, let us focus for a moment on the core political right of citizenship, the franchise in democratic elections. Isn't it objectionable to sell the right to vote to outsiders? Suppose that, in reaction to critiques by the other EU states, Malta decides to sell the franchise in its national elections rather than its passports. The price it could achieve would be of course much lower, but would it be all right to do so? Let me hasten to say that Malta and Cyprus are among the very few European states that currently do not allow their citizens residing abroad to cast their vote in national elections. So while investors can get citizenship without taking up residence, they will need to move to these island states in order to vote. Yet this seems a fortuitous coincidence rather than a policy design.

The corruptive political influence of linking citizenship to investment can be nicely illustrated by the story of Frank Stronach, a billionaire of Austrian origins who made his fortune in Canada. Under Austrian law, Stronach lost his Austrian citizenship upon becoming a Canadian citizen. When he established European headquarters of his company in Austria, he was granted citizenship under a special provision that requires neither residence nor renunciation of another nationality and that has also been used to naturalise Russian oligarchs alongside famous artists and sportsmen on grounds of "extra-ordinary achievements in the interest of the republic". Once he had retrieved his Austrian citizenship, Stronach started buying political influence by recruiting former politicians for his company. In 2012, Stronach bought himself also a political party that he called 'Team Stronach' and ran an expensive election campaign. He made a bit of a fool of himself in TV debates and got fewer votes than expected, but there is now a party in the Austrian Parliament established by and named after an investor-citizen. Maybe Stronach should not have lost Austrian citizenship in the first place. But the way in which he was able to reacquire it through his investment opened the doors widely to his subsequent corruptive influence on Austrian politics.

Of course, citizenship-from-the-inside is not only about voting and being elected. I am not so sure that it requires loving your country, as Dzankic suggests. But it certainly means being treated as an equal member and treating others as equal members of a political community. Magni Berton also looks at citizenship from the inside but does not emphasize sufficiently equality among citizens. He is right that the state invests into citizens and citizens invest into each other. But citizenship status and rights must not be proportional to the investments citizens make, or even conditional on such investments.

Voting rights provide again the test. Throughout much of the 19th century, the franchise was still a class privilege. 'No taxation without representation' also meant 'no representation without taxation.' Only those who contributed to the state coffers had a right to be represented in the making of laws. This is no longer our vision of democracy. True, democratic societies have hardly become more egalitarian since then and, as Stronach's example demonstrates, wealth can rather shamelessly buy influence in politics. Turning the status of citizenship itself into a marketable commodity would mean more than this. It would tear down a wall of protection that keeps social class from becoming, once again, a formal marker of inequality of citizenship rights and status. One could object that, once they are citizens, the votes of foreign investors will not formally count for more than everyone else's. But it seems quite naïve to think that a club that starts to sell its membership at a price that only the ultra-rich can afford will keep treating its poorer members as equals.

Barbulescu makes an interesting point that 'citizenship-by-investment largely contradicts the very recent efforts of states to re-substantiate citizenship through tests and integration requirements.' It seems indeed inconsistent to waive integration conditions for investors while at the same time insisting that citizenship can only be granted to foreign immigrants as a reward for their individual integration efforts. Yet from a democratic perspective both of these policies represent the same worrying trend: they link access to citizenship once again to social class. While income tests for naturalisation have an explicit class bias, knowledge tests have an implicit one, since education and the capacity to learn for tests is strongly related to social class.

But isn't the way citizenship is obtained anyhow morally arbitrary? Why should those who have citizen parents or who have been born in the state's territory have a stronger moral claim to citizenship than foreigners who are ready to pay or invest? Why should even long-term residence count, if those who can naturalise on that basis have been pre-selected by immigration controls that do not offer the same chances to the rest of the world's population? These may be relevant questions from a global justice perspective. From an internal democratic perspective, they are wrongly asked. Long-term residence is what makes immigrants' relation to the political community equal to that of native citizens in the relevant sense and is therefore not at all an arbitrary criterion for access to citizenship as membership in a particular polity. The same can be said for ius soli and ius sanguinis. Instead of giving citizens specific privileges based on a claim to land or to parental inheritance, these birthright rules make them equal amongst each other by referring to the circumstances of birth that they share in common, be it birth in a territory or to citizen parents. Moreover, by providing individuals with citizenship at birth and for life, states protect them in a much stronger way than clubs who select their members based on present members' interests in their contributions or in choosing new ones who are like themselves. Selecting future citizens on grounds of either investment or income and knowledge tests departs fundamentally from the egalitarian thrust that underlies rules of birthright citizenship as well as residence-based naturalisation.

So how should the EU and its member states react to citizenship-for-investors laws? They should protest that these policies undermine solidarity between member states, but they should also protest against the internal hollowing out of democratic standards. As a union of democracies, the EU must be concerned when democracy is corrupted by the rule of money in any of its member states. Bribing officials is not the only way in which this happens. Selling citizenship is, too.

9

Citizenship and the Shortcomings of Monetary Power

Paulina Ochoa Espejo

Brief visit to Valletta: € 2,500. Maltese Passport (and visa-free travel to the United States and 163 other countries): € 650,000. Partaking in a democratic community built on principles of equality and solidarity: Priceless.

In her article, Ayelet Shachar argues a point similar to the tagline of Master Card's famous advertisement: 'there are certain things money can't buy, for everything else...' Yet, as Peter Spiro remarks, pointing it out in our current circumstances may appear as banal as a TV ad. The hoax in the Master Card ad is that the numbers appearing on screen are not presented as the price tag of the 'priceless' item. Yet the ad also tacitly reminds us that we live in a society where the most 'meaningful' experiences are, in fact, bought and sold all the time; a society where what *really* matters to the beautiful woman may well be the expensive ring's promise of future riches, not the engagement with her fiancé. The campaign exploits our fear that priceless moments would simply not happen if they were not preceded by hefty purchases. Indeed, we daily discover things that, in a democratic society, are not supposed to be for sale, and yet go to the highest bidder. For example, the work of such public servants as soldiers, prison wardens, and government social workers is today frequently given by governments to private contractors. And today, more and more countries are selling citizenship.

But does 'everyone's doing it' make it *right*? I agree with Shachar that it ought not to happen: citizenship should not be for sale. However, I think that she has not chosen the best grounds to argue *why* it shouldn't. In her view, selling passports is wrong for many reasons, but what I take to be the most important are: first, because it undermines community; second, because it lets the economic sphere control the political sphere, and in doing so corrupts the value of citizenship. As to the first, Shachar argues, a person who has enough ready cash to buy citizenship in Malta has no incentives to establish relations of mutual trust and responsibility with other Maltese, so giving them a golden passport weakens a community built on solidarity and collective decision-making. As to the second, says Shachar, selling the privileges of citizenship brings economic inequality into the political sphere, thus undoing democracy's historic commitment to shield each citizen's political power from the effects of economic inequality. At first sight, these arguments seem overwhelming. Yet further reflection shows that they in fact prove too much. For if they were right, then we ought to forbid what I deem an unobjectionable practice: economic immigration by the poor.

Let's see how this could be so. On Shachar's argument, we object to selling passports, even when it is profitable, because the buyer's character and attitude undermines democratic institutions. A buyer of a golden passport is motivated to be a member for the wrong reasons: she is not seeking citizenship so as to establish relations of mutual trust and responsibility with Maltese. Notice, however, that this is also true of the economic immigrant who jumped the fence and worked illegally in the receiving country in order to pull herself out of poverty. In both cases the immigrant acts primarily according to her own interests, rather than any desire to build relationships of trust and mutual responsibility with her fellows. Both types of immigrants move money according to their transnational personal connections and concerns, both invest according to their personal needs. Both immigrants often bought their way in: either legally or illegally. Both value their new dual-citizenship status highly, and are not willing to forgo the advantages of either one, and both may spend huge amounts of money on immigration attorneys and fees to regularise their immigration status and get citizenship. So Shachar's own criterion, at least as presented, seems to rule out most economic immigration by the poor.

Something seems amiss. A better argument against a golden passport, I think, would use a criterion that would unambiguously imply both that it is wrong to admit rich immigrants simply because they will pay big money, and that it is wrong to deny admission to the poor simply because of their economic hopes. Let's examine some candidates for such a criterion.

Could it be time? In Shachar's essay, there is a muted factor that does seem to explain why we should not make ability to pay sufficient for citizenship: Time. Both the rich and the poor immigrants pay for their new membership in one way or another, but the rich can get citizenship *fast*. The world's rich have a degree of mobility that mirrors the speed of capital. They can follow the money, and they profit from their well-heeled hyper-mobility. This, of course, gives them few incentives to build 'long-term relations' and commitments 'expanding beyond their life-span'. So time might seem a good candidate for explaining why purchase shouldn't itself get you citizenship. Yet, as Chris Armstrong argues in his response, one can in a flash make deep commitments that do indeed seem to expand beyond one's life-span.

He reminds us of foreign volunteer soldiers like the Lincoln Brigade, who enter a foreign war to defend a country that is not theirs. It takes them no time to make a deep and seemingly long-lasting commitment. So if we think our criterion needs ultimately to track long-term commitments, then this criterion seems not to work for all cases.

Could it be the depth of the roots, then? Here is another way to explain why it is wrong to admit the rich passport-buyer simply because of ability to pay. Let's say that the criterion should be how much and how deeply the would-be immigrant's life and concerns are and will be rooted in the new country. For poor immigrants invest their work and efforts in becoming a part of the new society they join, while it might seem that a rich jetsetter buying a passport need make no such effort. Yet economic investment can be a very deep tie, as Raul Magni Berton argues in his reply. Committing a big sum to a new country can be done in a flash, and indeed, it can be done without even visiting the country in question; but if the investment is serious, it shows commitment and concern for others, and it lays down deep roots. So depth-of-roots cannot adequately distinguish the golden-passport holder from the poor immigrant.

Could it then be physical presence? This is the candidate criterion I favour. One of Shachar's concerns is that the rich passport-buyers need hardly ever be present in the new country. Territorial presence is particularly important because it forces individuals to partake in a particular way of doing things. Standing in queues, letting others go through, gather in certain occasions, stay indoors at other times. This type of action is face-to-face, and requires commitment to local institutions and local life. *By being there*, a person must become part of a civic organisation requiring solidarity and trust. And by being present in a democratic action, one can show a commitment to a civic community without having to share ethnic or cultural ties. This way of coming into a civic organisation can be immediate (as in the case of the person who volunteers to defend a country), but it does distinguish between an immigrant who is truly invested in the new country's institutions, from one who has just engaged in a one-time uncommitted monetary transaction. And most importantly, physical presence and face-to-face interactions can explain why citizenship is valuable in itself: it allows us to have relations as political equals, regardless of economic status. If we award passports to those without any likelihood of ever being there, we undermine the relevant connections built on regular interactions and participation in the institutions that organise local life, which is, after all, where equality takes place.

At bottom, what makes the golden passport wrong is that it undermines political equality, not that it puts closed communities in question, or shatters the separations between the spheres of justice. What remains priceless is the active face-to-face partaking and building of democratic institutions on the basis of principles of equality and solidarity: that is what money can't buy.

10

Differentiating between Affording a Passport and Deserving a Passport

Vesco Paskalev

The Maltese idea to 'sell' citizenships was met with almost universal criticism, not only within our Forum discussion but throughout Europe. While it is difficult to disagree with most of the arguments against monetization of citizenship, in my view they all aim at the wrong target. It is not the sale of citizenship *per se* which violates principles of justice and democracy; it is the existing international system of inclusion and exclusion of third country nationals which is deeply skewed and denigrates the value of citizenship. For all that I know, even the ultra-rich do not easily throw € 650,000 to the wind, so a condition under which anyone would give huge amounts of money for a travel document is deeply troubling. It is not membership but mobility which is at issue. Moreover, as Paulina Ochoa aptly notes, not only the rich but also the poor seek naturalisation for economic rather than civic reasons.

Bauböck distinguishes two sides of citizenship – an internal and an external one. Focusing on the former, he persuasively argues that selling citizenship undermines democracy. In a similar vein, Dzankic notes that in some cases the very fact of putting a price to a good corrupts the good. As a decent republican I fully agree with both of them. But as Spiro notes, the corruption of *this* good may have started long ago for reasons which have nothing to do with the recent fashion of investor citizenship schemes. While the policy makers and academics were predominantly concerned with the internal aspect of citizenship, various forces – from the Schengen Agreement via Ryanair to Moneygram – have brought the external aspect to the fore.

Is citizenship all about travel indeed, or about identity and democracy? A natural experiment occurred between Bulgaria and Macedonia. Most Bulgarians believe that Macedonians are actually ethnic Bulgarians, who happen to live in an artificial country because of some historic contingencies. Naturally, most Macedonians are annoyed (to put it mildly) by that suggestion and vehemently assert their Macedonian identity against Bulgarian imperialism. Yet, when Bulgaria joined the EU, Macedonians flocked to the Bulgarian consulates to apply for a passport. Suddenly, thousands were claiming that they are 'of Bulgarian origin'. Very few of these people had any actual bonds with Bulgaria and it is difficult to believe that anyone had suddenly woken up to her or his true Bulgarian identity. Apparently their Macedonian self-consciousness was in harmony with a Bulgarian passport and the opportunities it gives to 'Bulgarians abroad'.

I hasten to add that Macedonia tolerates dual citizenship; if people had to renounce their Macedonian citizenship in order to obtain a Bulgarian passport, the numbers could be very different. Yet, the story is telling. It shows how easy it is for people to claim certain origins when this is convenient despite of firmly holding on to a different identity, which in the Macedonian case has been explicitly constructed as excluding the Bulgarian one. For all the value we attach to citizenship, the relative weight of its internal aspect is by far superseded by that of its external dimension. When asserting that a passport is more about travel than about anything else I am not being cynical – most citizens do care about membership, too. But when your passport matters so much outside of your country, you are under pressure to adjust your priorities. Thus, in the extreme case, your passport may be completely unrelated to your emotional belonging. Virtually all countries in the world discriminate among those wishing to enter on the basis of the completely arbitrary facts of their birthplace and descent. It is this arbitrariness which corrupts the value of citizenship (and by implication of domestic democracy), not the availability of a bypass or two for a tiny minority, be it rich or poor.

So what should an EU Member State do in the face of the Maltese scheme if it is concerned with rescuing the value of citizenship as Shachar pleads? For sure, trying to prevent the Maltese from making some cash from a system which is already so unjust and distortive would not help much. Yes, selling citizenship does not do anything to help either, but if a wealthy European democracy is truly appalled by the idea of selling passports to the rich, why not start giving its passports for free to a more deserving crowd? The only decent response to the opening of a mobility corridor for the rich would be to open mobility corridors for the righteous – those who have shown exemplary civic virtue, have made sacrifices for democracy or human rights or are subject to outrageous persecution. A tentative list of candidates would include convicted Russian punks, jailed Egyptian protesters and Chinese dissidents, American whistle-blowers, Iranian adulterers facing stoning, etc. Certainly, one can immediately think about a number of problems that such a policy could create, yet if Raoul Wallenberg took the risk of handing out Swedish passports to save hundreds of Hungarian Jews from the Nazis, why shouldn't a proud member of the EU do something similar?

In practical terms granting citizenship to prominent civil rights activists can spare them from persecution at home and provide them with a mobility corridor to the Western world. Symbolically, it can become a way of recognition of their civic virtues and exploits (certainly, despotic regimes may frame it as evidence for treason). Critics are right to claim that the very fact that an immaterial value has a price tag undermines it, but the opposite can also be true – giving passports to highly esteemed figures can make these passports highly esteemed, too. If you are rich, go get a passport from Malta! If you are righteous, maybe you should be able to get a passport from say, Sweden. Comparing the existing investor citizenship schemes, the Financial Times feared that selling citizenship may start a race to the bottom.[1] Why not try launching a race to the top instead?

---

[1] '"Passport for sale" plan raises concern among EU members', *Financial Times*, 9 December 2013, available at https://www.ft.com/content/b8a2adfa-6106-11e3-b7f1-00144feabdc0

11

Citizenship and its Intrinsic Value

Dimitry Kochenov

Peter Spiro's tactful diagnosis of the flaws in Ayelet Shachar's kickoff text to this Forum is correct: Shachar fails to convince when arguing for saving citizenship against itself. (1) She understates the hypocrisy and randomness underlying any determination of citizenship. (2) She ignores the problem of *de facto* statelessness, which reveals a questionable understanding of discrimination. (3) She exaggerates the importance of the political dimension of citizenship and presents the link between citizenship and political participation as unproblematic. (4) Shachar claims that the sale of EU citizenship affects other member states, but this is perfectly legitimate since there is no breach of EU law involved. (5) There are multiple ways how to acquire EU citizenship which shows why Shachar's acceptance of naturalisation as a state-mandated purification ritual fails to capture reality. Overall, Shachar's argument against the Maltese policy does not stand. If we take democracy seriously, then it should be for the Maltese alone to set the price. I thus disagree also with Magni Berton when he claims that the high price at which Malta sells EU passports is problematic.

I.

There are many stories about how selling things is bad: land is not for sale; love is not for sale; salvation is not for sale. Such proclamations make one wonder whether the purpose of ethical high points is to totally contradict reality. Hypocrisy itself is difficult to sell as an argument: land can be bought, prostitution is often legal and some of the greatest art was sponsored by those who wanted to buy salvation for themselves. To insist that citizenship is not for sale is to ensure the perpetuation of the outright randomness of its conferral as well as hypocritical and self-righteous excuses lurking behind fundamental mechanisms of exclusions. Those boasting Italian great grandparents in Paraguay, members of Polish diasporas in Australia and elsewhere, large benefactors and talented sportsmen – all these people can become Europeans, however random the rules. But the critique focuses on those countries that offer citizenship for sale in a perfectly transparent way.

It is wrong to pretend that any other principle than outright randomness is at the core of the assignment of citizenship statuses in today's world. Once the inevitable randomness of exclusion is admitted – as Shachar did in her book on the birthright lottery[1] – we need to ask what citizenship is *actually* about.

II.

Shachar is worried about any discrimination at the point of acquisition of citizenship. However, a strict non-discrimination approach would deprive citizenship of its main function, i.e. random exclusion of large parts of society. Crucially, both *de facto* and *de jure* aspects of exclusion must be taken into account, a point that Shachar ignores in her statement. The fact that many *de jure* citizens are *de facto* stateless, in the sense of not receiving protection by their state of origin or enjoying substantive rights to return there, is of crucial importance. Idealistic images of a citizenship of the past are based on misrepresentation of social facts, perpetuating an often repugnant *status quo* where plenty of people are failed by their states day after day. Thus real citizenship starts with the actual extension of rights and giving the voice to those who are already formally included: women, minorities, the poor and the weak: plentiful problems remain in this regard.

Naturalisation is but a second step which serves three functions: providing citizenship status to long-term resident immigrants, respecting and recognising citizens' family ties through special naturalisation rules for family members, and reinforcing the society with talent, money, inspiration and diversity – which translates into inviting the rich, the beautiful and the smart (sometimes these three categories overlap of course).

No confusion between different groups of applicants should arise: to ask that all follow the same path is rarely helpful. Arguing for making the rules as strict as possible for all misses the different purposes of conferring nationality in the first place. Be it sports, science, money or family, it is up to the national democratic process to determine the criteria. Crucially, there is no ethical point to be made in arguing against money when loving a citizen, expensive education, or muscular power can also do the trick. Money is no less random a criterion and this is exactly what citizenship is about. Real discrimination would be to sell a partial rather than fully fledged citizenship, as Tonga does when selling its 'Tongan Protected Person Passport', which is not recognised by many other states and does not entail a right to enter and settle in Tonga. The attractiveness of such a second class citizenship is clearly limited.

---

[1] Shachar, A. (2009), *The Birthright Lottery. Citizenship and Global Inequality.* Cambridge, MA, Harvard University Press.

III.

Shachar overstates the actual importance of the political dimension of citizenship. In the age of post-heroic geopolitics plenty of people naturalise or cherish the nationality they already have for entirely different reasons. Indeed, the political aspect, rather than being at the core of citizenship, regrettably becomes the scapegoat for justifying refusals to extend the status to those who already belong to the society. The idea that only the right people participate in political life is so important that you will be discriminated, threatened with deportation, exploited and humiliated in order to protect the sacred body politic. The troubling truth is that more and more people do not care about politics, as opinion polls amply testify. And those who do can be politically engaged despite not having the formal status of membership – as the German citizen Daniel Cohn-Bendit was in Paris 1968. The basic presumption of the necessary connection between citizenship and political participation should be approached critically and is hardly defensible, especially in the EU (see the earlier EUDO CITIZENSHIP Forum on national voting right for EU citizens in other member states[2]). Insisting on the political dimension misrepresents thus what citizenship is about and ruins many lives by blowing a luxury right to politics totally out of proportion for the sake of justifying random exclusion.

IV.

It is clear that, just as the passports of other micro-states, Maltese citizenship as such is of very little practical value apart from visa-free travel. All the rights it brings – to work and live in the EU, non-discrimination in the EU and diplomatic protection outside the EU (when was the last time you saw a Maltese embassy?) – are related to the EU and the EU only. Clearly, what the Maltese are selling is EU citizenship and they are quite right to do so, since Member States are fully competent in this field, as international and also European law teaches us. Rich newly-minted Maltese will satisfy all the formal requirements of the EU Citizenship Directive 2004/38, thus becoming ideal EU citizens in London and Paris.

Following the *Micheletti* and *Rottmann* decisions of the Court of Justice of the European Union, the principles of EU law should be respected – and

---

[2] Bauböck, R., P. Cayla & C. Seth (eds.) (2012), 'Should EU citizens living in other Member States vote there in national elections?', *Robert Schuman Centre for Advanced Studies EUDO Citizenship Obervatory Working Paper 2012/32*, Florence: European University Institute, available at http://cadmus.eui.eu/handle/1814/22754.

they are, since it is unlikely that the number of Maltese investor-citizens will represent a problem in the EU context: the scale of sales will remain small – even compared with the extension of EU citizenship by other states where a connection with the state itself is unnecessary, such as turning Argentinians into Italians based on the romantic ideas of inter-generational continuity or distributing Hungarian passports in the Serbian province Voivodina. Importantly, there is nothing wrong at all with these practices which are democratic and legal and supply thus a strong argument in support of the Maltese law. Indeed, investing into your nationality is at least as random (read 'sound') as investing in a lawyer to discover your Italian heritage for the sake of claiming an Italian passport.

V.

EU citizenship provides the most vivid reminder of the radical shift in the meaning of citizenship that made it a more ethically acceptable institution. Non-discrimination on the basis of nationality – the very core of EU law – provides the litmus test for what national citizenship is really about in the EU today. France is prohibited from 'loving' its own nationals more than, say, resident Estonians or Maltese. The stigmatising function of citizenship is thus deactivated: humiliation of a randomly proclaimed other is not any more an option, at least legally speaking, among EU Member States. Full belonging to a society is thus not subjected any more to an arbitrary approval, putting all the bizarre language, culture and other tests that states subject newcomers to in a very interesting perspective: the very existence of the EU disproves their validity and relevance. They consist in nothing else but purification through humiliation: the 'others" language and culture is presumed as not good enough and social learning is dismissed, forcing people to waste their time by subjecting them to profoundly disturbing rituals[3]. The very success of EU citizenship is the strongest argument against these practices, which Shachar wants to see applied to all without questioning their effectiveness and common sense. Indeed, if a Romanian is good enough to be embraced by British society as equal, subjecting a Moldovan to any kind of tests is utterly illogical: the arguments of the protection of culture, language, etc. are simply devoid of relevance when more than half a billion EU citizens a exempted from them.

---

[3] Kochenov, D. (2011), 'Mevrouw de Jong Gaat Eten: EU Citizenship and the Culture of Prejudice', *Robert Schuman Centre for Advanced Studies EUDO Citizenship Observatory Working Paper 2011/06*, Florence: European University Institute, available at http://cadmus.eui.eu/bitstream/handle/1814/15774/RSCAS_2011_06.corr.pdf?sequence=3.

For the reasons above, I do not find Shachar's arguments convincing. Maltese democracy should be respected. Distorted dreams of the past, just as contemporary hypocrisy, are not worth defending. From a purely legal perspective, Malta's case is solid: EU law is unquestionably on its side. From a human perspective, if I could have done it, I would definitely have bought EU citizenship instead of naturalising, which I experienced as a deeply humiliating process.

12

European Union and the Trade of Citizenship for Human Capital

David Owen

In 2003 the brilliant Kenyan steeplechaser Stephen Cherono switched his allegiance to Qatar and took the name Saif Saaeed Shaheen. Under this name he has set a world record and won a number of global medals for Qatar which, alongside Bahrain, pioneered the explicit policy of recruiting athletes who have no prior connection to the state but whose human capital would contribute to its self-determined goals. Such practices are not entirely new – for example, the Australian and New Zealand national rugby teams (union and league) have maintained their standing in world rugby in part by actively recruiting young talent from the Pacific nations - Fiji, Papua New Guinea, Cook Islands, Tonga and especially Samoa – to the detriment of the national teams of those states. But, as with the case of Malta selling its citizenship for € 650,000, the policies adopted by Qatar and Bahrain are blatant in making explicit what was merely implicit in the rather widespread policies of other states, namely, the trading of access to citizenship for forms of capital (economic, cultural, political, etc.) held by individuals which the state deems valuable to acquire. Whether it is inducements to foreign millionaires (where other EU countries are playing catch up with long-standing UK policies) or to skilled workers in medical, finance or IT sectors, the immigration policies of states are perennially engaged in the practice of identifying valued forms of capital and facilitating the inward flow of such capital. The emigration policies of states exhibit similar patterns whether in terms of the deliberate creation of human capital for export markets (e.g., Indian medics and Filipino nurses) and/or the maintenance of thick links to diasporic communities to support trade, knowledge transfers, remittance flows and the recruitment of sporting talent. The state as a self-determining agent has a clear and well-established interest in structuring 'access to citizenship' in ways that support its goals, whether these goals concern economic development, health and social welfare, cultural standing or sporting glory. The legitimacy of the ways in which it pursues these goals is however another question.

For the states that compose the EU, we can distinguish three dimensions of democratic legitimacy that address, respectively, the composition of the demos of the state, associative obligations between member states and democratic obligations to non-members. Let's take them in turn.

If we focus on the composition of the demos, then it is important to acknowledge the difference of selling citizenship in a global market with schemes that, as Ayelet Shachar rightly notes, simply facilitate residence for selected types of highly valued persons and hence the acquisition of citizenship via residence-based naturalisation procedures. As Bauböck, Dzankic and Ochoa all stress, the 'golden residence permit' schemes (whatever other faults they may have) require a multi-year period of residence within, and hence subjection to, the authority of the state in question prior to, and as a condition of, the acquisition of citizenship. Such required residence grounds the claim to political equality that is given expression in access to membership of the demos.

Turning to the second dimension of democratic legitimacy of EU states, the associative obligations of member states, we can note that the explicit Treaty-based commitment to solidarity among these states has a specific implication for their democratic composition in that, normatively, it constrains states to treat their own citizenship (over which the EU has no – or via the Court of Justice of the European Union, very limited – competence) as integral to the democratic character of the EU. In this respect, Bauböck is surely right to highlight the point that selling national citizenship (and hence also EU citizenship) is incompatible with the associative obligations of member states as it admits persons to EU citizenship in all member states who do not have any genuine connection to any of these states. However, the scope of such obligations is not merely tied to such blatant examples of the commodification of citizenship but extends to the wider range of practices that are brought into focus by such extreme examples insofar as these undermine political equality with the EU by, for example, importing class and status differentials into access to citizenship.

The third dimension of democratic legitimacy for EU member states concerns those non-members whose morally significant interests are affected by the citizenship policies of these states. The requirement here is that these interests are impartially considered within the policy-making process. In contrast to Bauböck's distinction between democracy and global justice, I want to stress that this third dimension links the two and ties the concerns acutely raised by Barbulescu and, in more fatalistic mode, by Spiro directly to democratic legitimacy. As Barbulescu notes, the neo-liberalisation of citizenship that is expressed in practices of trading citizenship entails that the policy-making process does not give impartial consideration to all those whose morally significant interests are affected by these citizenship policies. Rather, the duty of justification owed to those affected is abrogated through a deliberate practice of partiality in which the rich and those who possess talents that are highly valued by the states in question are provided with unequal access to residence and hence to citizenship. Practices that support the emergence of transnational class and status stratification in which mobility rights become radically unequally distributed are not compatible with the democratic legitimacy of states or of the EU.

Oddly then we have reason to be grateful to states such as Qatar and Malta whose policies, in pushing to the neoliberal extreme, help bring into focus a wider range of policies that are hollowing out democratic citizenship from within.

13

Intervention of European Union and Citizenship for Sale

Jo Shaw

On 15 January 2014, the European Parliament will debate[1] the issue of 'EU citizenship for sale' as a 'topical subject' in its plenary. The Council and the Commission will both make statements on the issue, and the debate will be the culmination of a process whereby numerous parliamentarians from various political groups (ALDE, Verts/ALE, PPE – although not the S&D group of which the Maltese Labour Party currently in government is a member) have addressed questions to the Commission and the Council and expressed their concerns about the trend towards selling citizenship.

Can such critiques rely on European law or should the case be argued politically? And if the latter, is the Commission or the European Parliament the right institution to take the lead?

Dimitry Kochenov has made the point that there does not appear to be a case to argue that the decision by Malta to 'sell' its citizenship – whatever the price – raises an issue of EU law. It is well established that the conditions under which the Member States provide for the acquisition or loss of their citizenship are a matter to be decided by these states, provided that the rules put in place observe the requirements of EU law. The 1992 *Micheletti* judgment of the Court of Justice of the EU established that Member States must recognise the 'EU part' of a person's dual citizenship, as to do otherwise would deprive that person of the benefit of the free movement rights. In its 2010 *Rottmann* decision, the Court acknowledged that decisions on the *loss* of citizenship, where these would entail the loss of EU citizenship and thus deprive the person concerned of their rights and duties under that status, should be subject to a test of proportionality. In *Rottmann*, Advocate General Maduro did suggest a broader basis in the norms of EU law for constraining the actions of the Member States. He referred specifically to the case of mass naturalisations of third country nationals by a Member State undertaken

---

[1] European Parliament Resolution on the sale of EU citizenship, 2013/2995(RSP), available at http://www.europarl.europa.eu/oeil/popups/ficheprocedure.do?lang=en&reference=2013/2995%28RSP%29

without consulting the other Member States. Maduro argued that such practices might entail a breach of the duty of loyal or sincere cooperation contained in Article 4(3) of the Treaty on European Union.[2] According to that provision 'The Member States shall facilitate the achievement of the Union's tasks and refrain from any measure which could jeopardise the attainment of the Union's objectives.' But, as Kochenov notes, compared to the large numbers of Italian citizenships given out in Latin America to those demonstrating Italian ancestry, or indeed the effects of the external citizenship provisions of some of the newer Member States (e.g. Hungary in Serbia or Croatia in Bosnia and in many non-European countries where there are large Croatian diasporas such as in Australia), the effects of the Maltese provisions will be marginal in terms of numbers and thus have little impact on other Member States. The case for a legal obligation under the Treaties to moderate this type of national citizenship policy seems rather weak. It may be a mercantilist practice, but it is not arbitrary according to the norms of EU law.

So is that the end of it? Will the debate on 15 January be limited to the Commission rehearsing these legal points and pointing out its lack of competence in the matter, and MEPs wringing their hands about the 'abuse of rights' and the 'lack of respect'[3] for other Member States which is said to be involved in the creation of new citizens by such means? And will objections to the actions of Malta (and potentially other Member States which have introduced variants of these schemes) have no more traction than objections to a Member State exploiting its own natural resources, or exporting things for profit that it is particularly good at making, even if these might have environmental costs (such as cheaply produced French nuclear power or large German cars)?

As the contributions to this Forum have shown, the proposal by Malta to sell citizenship is just one example of why and how (national) citizenships can be most effectively monetized precisely because those citizenships are more attractive to those who 'invest' (it does not matter whether by means of work, long residence and civic integration or by direct financial contribution to the national exchequer), because they confer the benefits of EU citizenship. EU citizenship thus connects the external and internal dimensions of citizenship and offers incentives to states to exploit citizenship (and associated rights such as residence or the right to work) as a tradable good in a market system.

---

[2] Consolidated version of the Treaty on European Union, available at https://eur-lex.europa.eu/legal-content/EN/TXT/?uri=celex%3A12012M%2FTXT

[3] Parliamentary questions, 4 December 2013, Subject: EU citizenship for sale, available at http://www.europarl.europa.eu/sides/getDoc.do?type=OQ&reference=O-2013-000138&format=XML&language=EN

If Malta's policy exploits EU citizenship in a way that does not conflict with EU law, should the European Parliament – as an institution rooted in the principle of representative democracy – not use the opportunity to reflect instead more deeply upon the meaning of (national and EU) citizenship in a compact between states such as the European Union?

In that context, a comparison of the position of the Commission and the Parliament can be instructive. The Commission – unlike the Parliament – can speak with one voice, and has been assigned executive and enforcement powers under the Treaties. So a standard argument based on the duty of Member States to comply with EU law involves trying to get the Commission to say something about a situation in a given Member State, perhaps as a precursor to doing something such as bringing an enforcement action. But time and again, the argument fails, precisely because the issue falls outside the scope of EU law.

The powers of the Commission to take such actions are often overestimated because observers have watched how it has dealt with accession states. However, the context of enlargement deceives us, because it is during that phase of pre-accession negotiations – and whilst states live in fear of being told they do not comply with the Copenhagen criteria in relation to democracy and fundamental rights – that the Commission can make pointed interventions in areas of national sovereignty, including citizenship. Changes to the citizenship regimes of many of the Western Balkan states can be attributed directly or indirectly to pressure from 'Europe'. Perhaps the most obvious example is that of Macedonia[4], which changed its rules on acquisition of citizenship as one step towards a more consociational settlement involving the majority of ethnic Macedonians and the minority Albanian group. Similar effects via the implementation of national visa liberalisation roadmaps can be seen in Montenegro and Serbia. On the other hand, as the case of the controversial constitutional amendments in Hungary has shown, there is little the Commission can do to intervene in Member States, given the limitations of its current enforcement instruments[5], however egregious would appear to be the effects of the amendments introduced upon the 'entitlement' of that particular state to be a full member of Europe's democratic community of states.

---

[4] Spaskovska, L. (2011), *Macedonian Citizen: 'Former Yugoslav', Future European?*, CITSEE Study, available online at http://www.citsee.eu/citsee-study/macedonian-citizen-%E2%80%98former-yugoslav%E2%80%99-future-european

[5] *Ungarn – was tun? Folge 2: ein besonderes Vertragsverletzungsverfahren*, Verfassungsblog, available at https://verfassungsblog.de/category/debates/ungarn-was-tun-folge-2-ein-besonderes-vertragsverletzungsverfahren/

It is therefore not for the Commission to make the point that the creation of EU citizenship has indeed contributed to the hollowing out of national citizenship, not by taking away the prerogatives of national citizens (voting in national elections remains overwhelmingly reserved to national citizens only), but by incentivising its instrumentalisation for reasons of domestic gain (in Malta's case, a wish to improve the financial situation of a micro state buffeted by the effects of the Eurozone crisis).

But what about the European Parliament? As the democratically elected representative of the people(s) of the European Union and its Member States, and as a body elected on a franchise that deliberately goes beyond borders, the European Parliament can and indeed should take a careful look at the issues that the Maltese case raises. Yet it should do so not through a narrow focus on Malta, but rather through taking a sober look at the wider injustices and negative effects on democratic principles that may be highlighted by this newly identified dimension of the Fortress Europe construction (and how ironic it is, that Malta is also at the frontline of the *physical* Fortress Europe, as an island state located close to the southern shoreline of the Mediterranean sea).

'Intervention' is much too strong a word for whatever it is that the European Parliament could and should do on 15 January, when it debates the issue of EU citizenship for sale. But a first and wide-ranging reflection on some of the emerging consequences of EU citizenship for national democracies would at least be a start. 2013 was the year of the EU citizen. It did not do much to raise public awareness about EU citizenship and it ended with moves towards its commodification. Wouldn't it be appropriate for the European Parliament to start the new year with a real debate on the relation between national and EU citizenship?

14

Connecting Income, Citizenship and European Values

Hannes Swoboda

The decision by the Maltese Parliament to offer Maltese citizenship – and consequently – EU citizenship to third country nationals who can afford to pay € 650.000 comes as a closure of the EU year of citizens and reflects a worrying trend in the conception of all those rights related to EU citizenship, including above all freedom of movement.

Malta is not an isolated case, though. As highlighted by other contributions to this Forum, other EU Member States have in time come to link access to residence and hence – albeit indirectly – to citizenship to income or to economic investment, although the Maltese proposal goes a step further by introducing a direct and free gateway to citizenship purely based on a monetary payment.

Some may say that access to nationality is an exclusive competence of Member States and that the European Union has no right to interfere in these choices. From a purely legal perspective I would agree, but I believe we would miss the point if we did not see that, behind monetization of citizenship and residence, there is a vital political issue for the European Union to face, if we believe that Europe is more than just a wide single market.

The political debate about the so-called 'poverty migration' in the EU and on limitations to free movement for Romanian and Bulgarian citizens is just another side of the same coin. The supporters of the idea that 'free movement has to be less free' base their belief on the assumption that free movement should be free for those citizens who have a suitable income and less free for those who have not.

This questions the idea of citizenship as the core of a society, as the set of rights and duties defining active participation in the political, social and economic life of a community on an equal basis. And it questions the very idea of a European citizenship as a set of special rights connected to being a member of the European Union as a political Union, where individuals, notwithstanding their income and social position, can on an equal footing organise, participate in decisions in a wider European public space and feel part of a common project because that project is a collective benefit for all.

I would say that the very idea of the European Union as a community of values is put in question by these trends, particularly the idea that it is the duty of the EU to reinforce social cohesion, to eliminate discriminations and to provide a level playing field for the material exercise of the fundamental rights defined in the EU Charter.

I have often expressed the idea, including in the framework of EUDO debates, that access to EU citizenship needs to be expanded and not limited further, if we believe in making progress in the conception of a political and social Union.

I have often mentioned, for example, that many 'new Europeans' already live, study, work in our societies and contribute to them – some have been born and raised in Europe – but still are limited in their access to citizenship. These fellow Europeans have to go through detailed and lengthy citizenship tests before they can hope to achieve naturalisation in a Member State and therefore be fully EU citizens. I am convinced that – should Member States go in the direction of a privileged gateway to national citizenship solely based on income – this would create an unacceptable discriminatory situation that is probably also incompatible with EU law as it currently stands.

This is why I believe that a serious reflection at EU level is necessary ahead of European elections this year – also taking stock of the debates that characterised 2013 as the Year of EU citizens – on which common and shared criteria and guidelines should guide access to national citizenship and hence to EU citizenship at national level.

I think this is a necessary and urgent discussion we need to face. The background for the trend in citizenship policies that we are currently witnessing is of course more complex and it has to do with the on-going erosion of trust in institutions and with the fact that more and more among those who possess citizenship of the Union feel that they are not yet (or not fully) citizens, both at national and European level.

The real challenge is how European citizenship can be relaunched in a bottom-up process where EU citizens can enter the stage of the EU political arena, campaign for policy options, actively debate in a truly European public space and select legislators representing their views and working for their objectives.

If we don't want to leave a golden opportunity to Eurosceptics, nationalists and populists, we must seize the chance for a leap forward in the European process involving a much wider concept of citizenship than that defined in the letter of the EU Treaties.

15

Summary

Ayelet Shachar

That the European Parliament will debate the sale of 'golden visas' and 'golden passports' on 15 January 2014 is a victory for democracy and a testament to the vital importance of the issues raised by this Forum Debate, with its rich and illuminating contributions.

The 'selling of citizenship,' as many of my commentators have rightly noted, is indicative of larger and deeper transformations of our conception of political membership in a more globalized and competitive world. It is hoped that these tectonic changes will, on the whole, ultimately prove emancipatory and inclusionary. Placing a price tag on citizenship is not, however, a step in that direction. Globally, it secures privileged access to membership for multimillionaires who can afford it, while excluding all others. Domestically, it strains the ties that bind us together, which may in turn lead to erosion of the civic bonds and practices that allow a democratic society not only to survive, but to thrive.

The grant of citizenship is, as a pure legal matter, a last bastion of sovereignty. This is precisely what makes cash-for-passport programmes so controversial. They may be formally permissible, but they are nevertheless open to ethical and political contestation. Laws do not only guide action. They also carry meaning and have an expressive function. The grant of citizenship in exchange for nothing but a large pile of cash sends a loud message in both law and social ethics about whom the contemporary market-friendly state gives priority to in the immigration and naturalisation line and whom it covets most as future citizens.

These pressures are felt everywhere, but Europe is unique. It has developed the world's most advanced system of supranational-citizenship-in-action. In this system, when one member state 'sells' national citizenship as a gateway to gaining Union citizenship, tension inevitably arises, since the state's action in doing so also affects other EU member states as well as the very membership good at issue: European citizenship. For policymakers, there is an unfavourable track record to consider. Citizenship-by-investment schemes have in the past been closed down after concerns about their integrity led to the revocation of visa waiver policies in third countries. The programme set up by Grenada, for instance, was suspended after Canada imposed visa requirements on the island's passport holders. It is unclear whether similar responses by third countries are to be expected here, but this is a risk factor that must be acknowledged if European member states proceed with their plans to grant immediate citizenship based on payment alone and without requiring grantees to ever live in, or even visit, the passport-issuing country.

The discomfort we may feel toward the mercenary-like quality of cash-for-passport programmes brings additional, hard questions to the forefront: is citizenship merely about rights, or also responsibilities? Could (and should) proportionality apply not only to the loss of citizenship but also to its acquisition? And what justification, if any, is owed (and to whom) if a member state's action 'cheapens' the fundamental status of Union citizenship, in this case by commodifying it?

We are dealing here with some of the most foundational aspects of our collective and public life. The decision to place 'citizenship for sale' on the agenda for debate in the European Parliament and possibly the Commission as well is meaningful, both expressively and practically. It will offer a unique opportunity for all involved stakeholders to think critically about the law as we know it, while imagining the law as it could be.

Part II: Citizenship, Bloodlines and Belonging

Abstract

Can the widespread legal rule of ius sanguinis, through which citizenship is transmitted at birth from parent to child, still be justified in the contemporary world? Together with addressing more traditional objections to ius sanguinis, such as its alleged ethno-nationalist character or its negative effects on the global distribution of wealth and opportunities, the debate also looks into more recent challenges to ius sanguinis, such as those posed by dramatic changes in family norms and practices and the rapid development and spread of reproductive technologies. One major worry is that current forms of ius sanguinis are unable to deal adequately with uncertainties related to the establishment of legal parentage, especially in cross-border surrogacy arrangements. Whereas most contributors agree that ius sanguinis should be reformed in order to adapt to contemporary circumstances, plenty of disagreement remains as to how this reform should be done. The debate also tackles the questions of whether and in what way ius sanguinis could be justified as a normative principle for admission to citizenship. Authors discuss important normative considerations, such as the need to prevent statelessness of children, to ensure the preservation of family life and to provide opportunities for intergenerational membership.

Keywords

Ius sanguinis · Citizenship · Ethno-nationalism · Reproductive technologies · Statelessness · Family law

16

The Question of Abandoning Ius Sanguinis

Costica Dumbrava

The transmission of citizenship status from parents to children is a widespread modern practice that offers certain practical and normative advantages. It is relatively easy to distribute legal status to children according to parents' citizenship, especially in the context of high mobility where the links between persons and their birthplace are becoming increasingly strained. Granting citizenship status to children of citizens may also be desirable as a way of avoiding statelessness, acknowledging special family links and fostering political links between children and the political community of their parents. These apparent advantages of ius sanguinis citizenship are, however, outweighed by a series of problems. In what follows I argue that ius sanguinis citizenship is (1) historically tainted, (2) increasingly inadequate and (3) normatively unnecessary. Ius sanguinis citizenship is historically tainted because it is rooted in practices and conceptions that rely on ethno-nationalist ideas about political membership. It is inadequate because it becomes increasingly unfit to deal with contemporary issues such as advances in assisted reproduction technologies and changes in family practices and norms. Lastly, ius sanguinis citizenship is normatively unnecessary because its alleged advantages are illusory and can be delivered by other means.

Tainted

As a key instrument of the modern state, the institution of citizenship has been closely linked to nationalism. Ius sanguinis citizenship was reintroduced in Europe by post-revolutionary France, which sought to modernise French citizenship by discarding feudal practices such as ius soli.[1] Whereas in modern France the adoption of ius sanguinis was premised on the idea of a homogenous French nation, in countries with contested borders, such as Germany, ius sanguinis played a key role in maintaining ties with co-ethnics

---

[1] Weil, P. (2002), *Qu'est-ce qu'un Français?* Paris: Grasset.

living outside borders and thus in nurturing claims to territorial changes. Although ius sanguinis citizenship is not conceptually 'ethnic' (in the same sense in which ius soli citizenship is not necessarily 'civic'), there are a number of ways in which the application of the ius sanguinis principle has been used in order to promote ethno-nationalist conceptions of membership.

Firstly, the application of unconditional ius sanguinis in the context of a long history of emigration means that emigrants can pass citizenship automatically to their descendants regardless of the strength of their links with the political community. No less than twenty countries in Europe maintain such provisions.[2] Whereas one can find several non-nationalist arguments for justifying emigrants' citizenship, these weaken considerably when applied to successive generations of non-residents.

Secondly, there are cases in which countries rely on the principle of descent in order to confirm or restore citizenship to certain categories of people whom they consider to be linked with through ethno-cultural ties. Apart from cases where ethnic descent is an explicit criterion of admission (e.g. in Bulgaria, Greece), there are countries where ethnicity is camouflaged in the language of legal restitution or special duties of justice (e.g. in Latvia, Romania). In this way, persons can have their citizenship status 'restored' on the basis of descent from ancestors who had been citizens or residents in a territory that once belonged, even if briefly, to a predecessor state with different borders.

Thirdly, the combination of unconditional ius sanguinis citizenship with the reluctance to accept alternative ways of incorporating children of residents (such as ius soli) is also a strong indicator of an ethnic conception of citizenship, especially in the context of a long history of immigration. Convoluted attempts to adopt and expand ius soli provisions in Germany and Greece illustrate this point. In 2000 Germany adopted ius soli provisions[3] but maintained that, unlike persons who acquire German citizenship through ius sanguinis, those who acquire citizenship via ius soli could retain

---

[2] Dumbrava, C. (2015), 'Super-Foreigners and Sub-Citizens. Mapping Ethno-National Hierarchies of Foreignness and Citizenship in Europe', *Ethnopolitics* 14 (3): 296–310.

[3] Hailbronner, K. & A. Farahat (2015), *Country Report On Citizenship Law: Germany*. Florence: EUDO Citizenship Observatory, Robert Schuman Centre of Advanced Studies, European University Institute, available at http://cadmus.eui.eu/bitstream/handle/1814/34478/EUDO_CIT_2015_02-Germany.pdf?sequence=1

it only if they relinquish any other citizenship before their 23rd birthday. In 2011 the Greek Council of State halted an attempt to introduce ius soli citizenship in Greece[4] by claiming that ius sanguinis is a superior constitutional principle whose transgression would lead to the 'decay of the nation'.[5]

Inadequate

Consider the following two real cases.

Samuel was born in November 2008 in Kiev by a Ukrainian surrogate mother hired by Laurent and Peter, a married gay couple of Belgian and French citizenship respectively.[6] Samuel was conceived through in vitro fertilisation of an egg from an anonymous donor with Laurent's sperm. Upon his birth and according to practice, the surrogate mother refused to assume parental responsibility and thus transferred full parentage rights to Samuel's biological father. When Laurent requested a Belgian passport for Samuel, the Belgian consular authorities refused on grounds that Samuel was born through a commercial surrogacy arrangement, which was unlawful according to Belgian law. After more than two years of battles in court, during which Laurent and Peter also attempted and failed to smuggle Samuel out of Ukraine through the help of a friend pretending to be Samuel's mother, a Brussels court recognised Laurent's parentage rights and ordered authorities to deliver Samuel a Belgian passport. With it, Samuel was able to leave Ukraine and settle with Laurent and Peter in France.

---

[4] Christopoulos, D. (2011), 'Greek State Council strikes down ius soli and local voting rights for third country nationals. An Alarming Postscript to the Greek Citizenship Reform', *Citizenship News, EUDO Citizenship Observatory*, available at http://globalcit.eu/greek-state-council-strikes-down-ius-soli-and-local-voting-rights-for-third-country-nationals-an-alarming-postscript-to-the-greek-citizenship-reform/

[5] The Greek parliament has recently pushed forward another proposal regarding ius soli in an attempt to overcome the deadlock. See Christopoulos, D. (2015), *The 2015 reform of the Greek Nationality Code in brief*, Florence: EUDO Citizenship Observatory, Robert Schuman Centre of Advanced Studies, European University Institute, available at http://globalcit.eu/wp-content/plugins/rscas-database-eudo-gcit/?p=file&appl=countryProfiles&f=The%20 2015%20reform%20of%20the%20Greek%20Nationality%20Code%20in%20 brief.pdf

[6] European Parliament (2013), *A comparative study on the regime of surrogacy in EU Member States*. Directorate-General of Internal Affairs, Policy Department: Citizen's Rights and Constitutional Affairs, available at http://www.europarl.europa.eu/thinktank/en/document.html?reference=IPOL-JURI_ET(2013)474403.

In 2007 Ikufumi and Yuki, a married Japanese couple, travelled to India and hired Mehta as surrogate mother for their planned child.[7] Using Ikufumi's sperm and an egg from an anonymous donor, the Indian doctors obtained an embryo, which they then implanted in Mehta's womb. Only one month before the birth of Manji, the resulting child, Ikufumi and Yuki divorced. When Ikufumi attempted to procure a Japanese passport for Manji, the Japanese authorities refused on grounds that Manji was not Japanese. According to the Japanese Civil Code, the mother is always the woman who gives birth to the child. Despite having three 'mothers' – a genetic mother, who contributed with the egg, an intended mother who later declined involvement, and a surrogate mother, who did not plan to take up parental responsibilities – Manji had no obvious legal mother. Indeed, Manji's Indian birth certificate mentioned Ikufumi as the father but left the rubric concerning 'the mother' blank. After much legal wrangling Manji was issued a certificate of identity stating that she was stateless, with which Ikufumi managed to take her to Japan.

These are just two of a growing number of cases that test the legal and normative linkage between human reproduction, legal parentage and citizenship. Not only do they question conventional assumptions about the biological and cultural basis of citizenship, but they also show the limits of the principle of ius sanguinis in ensuring the adequate determination of citizenship status.

The incongruity between reproduction, legal parentage and citizenship is not an issue triggered solely by advances in reproductive technologies. Traditionally, children born out of wedlock could not acquire the father's citizenship through descent. Many countries still maintain special procedures for the acquisition of citizenship by children born out of wedlock to a foreign mother and a citizen father. In most cases this implies submitting a request for citizenship after parentage is legally established, although in Denmark these children can acquire citizenship only if the parents marry. In the Czech Republic and the Netherlands (for children older than 7), the determination of parentage for the purpose of citizenship attribution requires showing evidence of a genetic relationship between the father and the child. As argued by the European Court of Human Rights in its 2010 judgment on

---

[7] Points, K. (undated), *Commercial surrogacy and fertility tourism in India: The case of Baby Manji*. Durham: The Kenan Institute for Ethics at Duke University, available at https://web.duke.edu/kenanethics/CaseStudies/BabyManji.pdf

Genovese v Malta,[8] the differential treatment of children born within and out of wedlock with respect to access to citizenship amounts to discrimination on arbitrary grounds. This practice is also at odds with contemporary trends that indicate an impressive surge in births out of wedlock; the share of such births in the EU27 rose from 17 per cent of total births in 1990 to 40 per cent in 2013.[9]

One of the biggest challenges to ius sanguinis citizenship comes from the spread of assisted reproduction technologies (ART). About 7 million babies worldwide have been born through ART since the birth of Louise Brown, the first 'test-tube baby', in 1978.[10] ART have developed rapidly generating a multi-billion dollar market in assisted reproduction. A significant share of this market involves the international movement of doctors, donors, parents, children and gametes. In order to avoid legal restrictions or to cut costs, a growing number of infertile men and women, usually from high-income countries, travel to destinations such as India, Thailand or Ukraine in order to have 'their' babies conceived through in vitro fertilisation procedures using sperm or eggs (or both) donated by people from places such as Spain or Romania.

Many problems arise because the international market for assisted reproduction is not properly regulated, which means that national regulations often conflict with one another. Countries that oppose surrogacy consider the surrogate mother as the legal mother even if they are not genetically related to the child. According to this reasoning, the husband of the surrogate mother is the presumed father of the child. However, countries that encourage surrogacy usually recognise the intended mother and father as the legal parents, regardless of whether they are genetically related to the child. As the stories on Samuel and Manji show, when these two approaches collide the children risk becoming, as Justice Hedley put it, 'marooned, stateless and parentless'.[11]

---

[8] Genovese v. Malta, Application no. 53124/09, *European Court of Human Rights*, 11 October 2011, available at http://hudoc.echr.coe.int/sites/eng/pages/search.aspx?i=001-106785#

[9] 'Two in five EU babies born out of wedlock', BBC News, 26 March 2013, available at http://www.bbc.com/news/world-europe-21940895

[10] This number has been updated to the most recent figure. See: The European Society of Human Reproduction and Embryology (2017), *ESHRE fact sheets 1, available at* https://www.eshre.eu/~/media/sitecore-files/Press-room/Resources/1-CBRC.pdf?la=en

[11] Re: X & Y (Foreign Surrogacy), [2008] *EWHC (Fam) 3030 (U.K.)*, available at http://www.familylawweek.co.uk/site.aspx?i=ed28706

In some cases intended parents have the possibility to establish parentage and citizenship for their children born through surrogacy. However, such special arrangements often discriminate between (intended) mothers and fathers. For example, in the US children born to surrogate mothers outside the country are treated as children born out of wedlock, so fathers can be recognised as legal parents and therefore extend citizenship to children if they provide proof of a genetic relationship with the child (through a DNA test). Intended mothers, however, cannot be recognised as mothers even if the child was conceived using their eggs and even if they are married to the intended father.[12] It follows that, in cases where another woman's womb is involved, paternity and citizenship can still follow the sperm but not the eggs.

The practice of gamete donation has become increasingly accepted and regulated, so donors are in principle discharged of parental responsibilities with regard to children they help to conceive. However, it is not always clear what counts as donation. In a recent US case, a man successfully claimed parentage with regard to a child who was born after an informal agreement in which he agreed to 'donate' sperm to a friend. The Court decided in the man's favour arguing that his act did not count as donation because the procedure used in the insemination did not involve 'medical technology' (they used a turkey baster). The ultimate test of paternity in this case relied on a mere technicality, which can hardly be seen as a morally relevant fact for establishing fundamental ties of filiation and citizenship.[13]

The development of ART is likely to further complicate questions about parentage and citizenship. The new techniques of embryo manipulation, for example, make now possible the transfer of a cell nucleus from one woman's egg to the egg of another, which means that the resulting child will have three genetic parents. Advances in technologies for freezing gametes and embryos raise questions about the rights and responsibilities over future births and about the status of future children. There have already been a number of cases of posthumous conception in which the sperm or eggs of a deceased person were used by the spouse or another relative in order to conceive children. For example, it was recently reported that a 59 years old

---

[12] Deomampo, D. (2014), 'Defining Parents, Making Citizens: Nationality and Citizenship in Transnational Surrogacy', *Review of Medical anthropology* 34 (3): 210–225.

[13] Brandt, R. (2015), 'Medical intervention should not define legal parenthood', *Bionews*, 11 May 2015, available at http://www.bionews.org.uk/page.asp?obj_id=523229&PPID=523190&sid=282.

woman from the UK gave birth to 'her' daughter's child.[14] These practices raise obvious questions as to whom these children belong to and they may as well trigger issues of citizenship. Lastly, progress has been made on the creation or 'artificial' gametes through the modification of other types of human cells. Apart from opening possibilities for bypassing the heterosexual model of procreation,[15] these techniques raise concerns about abuse or reproductive 'crime'. Imagine a world in which it would be possible to create a child from a tissue sample collected from somebody's cup of coffee. Those famous actors and footballers would probably think twice before shaking their fans' hands.

Unnecessary

One could argue that the main problems do not lie with ius sanguinis citizenship but with the determination of legal parentage. Once we solve issues related to legal parentage, then the ius sanguinis principle will effectively address citizenship matters. However, this view ignores that dilemmas regarding the attribution of parentage are often triggered or complicated by citizenship (and migration) issues. It can also be argued that relying solely on legal parentage to settle citizenship issues disregards fundamental normative questions about who should be a citizen in a political community.

Despite much liberal-democratic talk about social contract, democratic inclusion and active citizenship, the overwhelming majority of people in the world acquire citizenship by virtue of contingent facts about birth (descent or place of birth). While ius soli citizenship has received considerable political and academic attention recently due to pressing concerns about the inclusion of children of immigrants, ius sanguinis continues to be taken for granted. In the remainder of this essay, I briefly challenge two main theoretical defences of ius sanguinis: (a) that ius sanguinis citizenship recognises and cements the special relationship between the parent and child; (b) that ius sanguinis citizenship ensures the intergenerational stability of the political community.

The main problem of ius sanguinis citizenship is that it is parasitic on external factors concerning the legal determination of parentage. As one of the examples presented above shows, it may only take a choice between a

---

[14] Smajdor, A. (2015), 'Can I be my grandchild's mother?', *BioNews*, 9 March 2015, available at http://www.bionews.org.uk/page_504476.asp.

[15] Shanks, P. (2015), 'Babies from Two Bio-Dads.' *Biopolitical Times*, 3 April 2015, *Center for Genetics and Society*, available at http://www.biopoliticaltimes.org/article.php?id=8418.

petri dish and a turkey baster to make somebody a parent and hence a supplier of citizenship status. The relevance of horizontal family ties between spouses in citizenship matters has largely diminished, as a flipside of the spread of gender equality norms, since in liberal states wives no longer automatically acquire their husbands' citizenship. By contrast, parental ties continue to remain paramount for the regulation of citizenship. Even if there are good reasons for seeking to ensure the swift transfer of citizenship from parents to children (e.g. to prevent statelessness), this approach is questionable because it renders children vulnerable. Ius sanguinis citizenship makes access to citizenship for children dependent on parents' legal status, actions or reproductive choices.

As in the case of spouses, joint citizenship adds little to the legal and normative character of the parent-child relationship. There is little doubt that the law should treat children and the parent-child relationship with special attention. However, this could and should be achieved regardless of the citizenship status of children and parents. One could, for example, extend the legal rights associated with parentage and filiation (e.g. conferring full migration rights to children of citizens) or seek to establish a universal status of (legal) childhood that confers fundamental right and protection to children regardless of their or their parents' citizenship or migration status.

The second argument for ius sanguinis citizenship is that the automatic transition of membership status from parents to children ensures the smooth reproduction of the political community. As children of citizens grow, they become socialised in the political community of their parents and develop political skills necessary for furthering their parents' project of democratic self-government, skills that they will eventually pass on to their own children. An easy objection to this view is that it is empirically naïve, especially in the context of increased migration and diversification of family practices. Citizenship is thus based on a contested expectation. Instead of granting citizenship ex-ante to persons who are likely to develop desirable citizenship attitudes and skills, we could delay the attribution of citizenship until such attitudes and skills are confirmed. Alternatively, there may be other normative considerations for turning children into citizens. For example, being born in the country and/or living there at a young age makes children not only subject to the law of the country but also highly dependent on the state, which, for example, is required to provide regular and reliable access to medical care such as vaccinations. These considerations could justify granting children at least provisional citizenship.

The intergenerational dimension of democratic membership can hardly be achieved by relying on legal fictions or on biological contingencies. Our efforts should rather be channelled towards consolidating democratic institutions and promoting citizenship attitudes and skills among all those who find themselves, by whatever ways and for whatever reasons, in our political community. As for the children who happen to be born here, we should treat them as political foundlings and give them all the care and support they need to become full political members.

17

Justifying Citizenship by Descent

Rainer Bauböck

Aristoteles famously defined a citizen as someone 'giving judgment and holding office' in the polity.[1] Yet, this does not settle the issue since we first need to know who qualifies for holding office. And so he continues: 'For practical purposes a citizen is defined as one of citizen birth on *both* his father's *and* his mother's side'.[2] Times have changed. From the French Revolution, which revived ius sanguinis, until the second half of the 20th century, citizenship was mostly transmitted only from the father to the child. Today, largely as a result of international conventions against the discrimination of women, all democratic states define a citizen as one of citizen birth on either the father's or the mother's side. Yet ius sanguinis remains the dominant rule for acquisition of citizenship worldwide. True, in the Americas the stronger principle is ius soli, the acquisition of citizenship through birth in the territory. But even there those born abroad to citizen parents who were themselves born in the country are recognised as nationals by birth.

Given this overwhelming presence of ius sanguinis in nationality law, Costica Dumbrava's call for abandoning it is bold. Some might even say, it is quixotic, but I disagree. It is indeed time to reflect on the future of ius sanguinis and to abandon it as a doctrine linking citizenship to biological descent. Yet there are good practical and normative reasons why the principle of citizenship transmission from parents to children will remain alive and ought to be retained.

Dumbrava runs three main attacks against ius sanguinis: It is tainted by its association with ethno-nationalism; it is inadequate because, in an age of artificial reproduction technologies, same sex marriage and patchwork families, biological descent no longer traces social parenthood; and it is unnecessary since its protective effects can be achieved by other means. I will accept the first and second argument with some modifications but reject the third.

---

[1] Aristotle (1962), *The Politics*. Transl: T.A. Sinclair, revised and commentary: T. J. Saunders (ed.). London: Penguin, III. i: 169.
[2] Ibid, III.ii: 171-2, original emphasis.

Not the only one tainted

As Dumbrava points out, modern ius sanguinis was seen as a democratic and revolutionary principle in contrast with ius soli that had its origins in the feudal idea that any person (or animal) born on the territory was subject to the ruler of the land. Deriving citizenship from citizen descent rather than territorial birth made it possible to imagine a self-governing people reproducing itself. Dumbrava is of course right that seeing the nation as a community of shared descent across generations made it also easier to justify the exclusion of foreigners as well as the inclusion of co-nationals across the border. Yet this is not a sufficient reason for abandoning ius sanguinis.

First, an ethnonationalist disposition can be overcome while maintaining ius sanguinis if this principle is supplemented with ius soli and residence-based naturalisation. The latter has created an ethnically highly diverse citizenry in continental European immigration countries even in the absence of the additional inclusionary effects of ius soli. The reason for this ethnically inclusive effect of ius sanguinis is simple: If first generation immigrants have access to citizenship and take it up, then ius soli and ius sanguinis does not make much difference: the children of immigrants will be citizens under either rule.

Secondly, a pure ius soli regime is also tainted and not only because of the feudal origins of the principle. Territorial nationalism can be just as nasty as ethnonationalism and may be fanned by thinking of ius soli as the right of the 'sons of the soil'. Even the case of Romania that Dumbrava lists among the problematic ones is ambiguous in this regard. If Romania awards citizenship to the descendants of those born in its lost territories, is this an instance of ius soli or ius sanguinis and an illustration of ethnic or of territorial nationalism? The answer is probably: both. Ius soli and ius sanguinis are therefore not alternatives, but can be combined in benign ways that neutralise the potentially illiberal effects of either principle, as well as malign ways that enhance their nationalist potential for ethnic exclusion and territorial expansion.

Thirdly, pure ius soli also has vicious exclusionary effects for migrants. In most American states, the immigrant generation 1.5 – those who have entered the country as minor children – cannot acquire citizenship before the age of majority. President Obama's Dream Act is an attempt to mitigate some of the worst consequences for the children of irregular immigrants. Even more problematic is the common distinction between nationals and citizens in many Latin

American states.[3] Only those born in the territory are considered nationals (they are sometimes also called 'naturals'). They turn into citizens with full voting rights at the age of majority. Immigrants who naturalise become citizens, but not nationals. They remain excluded from many public offices (also the US president still has to be a 'natural born citizen') and they can be deprived of their citizenship status, whereas nationality can often never be lost. In Uruguay even the concept of 'naturalisation' does not exist because those who are not born in the territory can never become 'naturals'. Similar exclusionary effects of ius soli traditions apply to those born abroad to citizen parents. They often do not acquire citizenship unless they are registered in time by their parents and they may lose it unless they 'return' before the age of majority.

If both ius sanguinis and ius soli are tainted in these ways, should we consider an even more radical alternative of abandoning citizenship by birth altogether? Why not replace it with *ius domicilii* so that citizenship is acquired automatically with taking up residence and lost with outmigration? Or should we maybe replace it with *ius pecuniae*,[4] i.e. a global market for citizenships in which individuals can bid for membership status anywhere and states can set the admission price? Neither of these alternatives is morally attractive and something important is lost when we give up birthright citizenship.

Why not *ius filiationis*?

Dumbrava's second argument is that developments in reproduction technologies and in the social and legal recognition of new family patterns make ius sanguinis increasingly unworkable and obsolete.

This problem is not entirely new and a solution is already available. International law has long abandoned the idea that children should acquire only one citizenship at birth. Since they can inherit two different citizenships from the mother's and the father's side (maybe in addition to a third one acquired iure soli), why should they not receive the citizenship of both an

---

[3] Acosta D, (2016), 'Regional Report on Citizenship: The South American and Mexican Cases', *EUDO Citizenship Observatory Comparative Reports 2016/01*, Florence: European University Institute, available at http://cadmus.eui.eu//handle/1814/43325

[4] Stern, J. (2011), 'Ius Pecuniae – Staatsbürgerschaft zwischen ausreichendem Lebensunterhalt, Mindestsicherung und Menschenwürde', *Migration und Integration – wissenschaftliche Perspektiven aus Österreich, Jahrbuch 1/2011*, Dahlvik/Fassmann/Sievers (eds.). See also Part I of this volume; Dzankic, J. (2015), 'Investment-based citizenship and residence programmes in the EU', *Robert Schuman Centre for Advanced Studies Working Papers 2015/08*, Florence: European University Insitute.

intended and a surrogate mother or an intended father and a sperm donor? Asking the question makes it already clear that the problem is not the multiplicity of citizenships per se, but the mismatch between biologically determined citizenship and parental care arrangements that would also open the door to abusive claims. The traditional solution that is already available in most nationality laws for cases where the biological parent is not the social parent is transmission of citizenship through adoption.[5] Why should it not be possible to generalise this model from the marginal case of adoption so that a modified ius sanguinis refers to social rather than biological parenthood (as it already does in several jurisdictions)?

The main issue with such a new *ius filiationis* might be that determination of citizenship is less automatic than it used to be for children born in wedlock to their biological mother and father. Yet states that are committed to the welfare of children have to figure out anyhow how to determine legal parenthood in the more complex family arrangements of contemporary societies. In order to avoid statelessness it is important that every child obtains at least one citizenship immediately at birth. And in order to make sure that children are not caught between conflicting legal norms and can develop stable relations to their countries of citizenship it is important that their citizenship status does not change automatically when they become part of a new family. If these concerns are taken into account through a combination of ius soli with legally determined initial parenthood, what objections can be raised against recognizing primary caregivers as well as persons with additional custodial rights as legal parents who can transmit their citizenship to the child?

Don't abandon the children!

Dumbrava's third argument is that ius sanguinis is not necessary because children's rights can be protected through other means. He claims that ius sanguinis renders children vulnerable by making their 'access to citizenship ... dependent on parents' legal status, actions or reproductive choices This is indeed a reason why the children of immigrants need ius soli as an independent right to citizenship in their country of birth. Unfortunately, in the US, their birthright citizenship does not prevent them from being deported together with their undocumented parents, whereas immigrant minors who are EU citizens have a right to stay that protects also their primary caregivers from deportation.[6]

---

[5] See the EUDO CITIZENSHIP Database on Modes of Acquisition of Citizenship in Europe, available at http://eudo-citizenship.eu/admin/?p=dataEUCIT&application=modesAcquisition.

[6] Case C-200/02 Zhu and Chen v Secretary of State for the Home Department, 2004; Case C-34/09 Ruiz Zambrano v Office National de L'emploi, 2011.

Yet small children are in any case dependent on their parents' migration decisions. This is a an equally strong reason why they also have a claim to share their parents' citizenship, since they risk otherwise to remain stranded in their country of birth or be treated as foreigners in their parents' country of nationality. Dumbrava suggests preventing this by 'conferring full migration rights to children of citizens'. But would migration rights become more secure if they are disconnected from the legal status of citizenship that is the only one obliging states to unconditionally admit them? Alternatively, he suggests to 'establish a universal status of (legal) childhood that confers fundamental rights regardless of their or their parents' citizenship or migration status'. This is what the Children's Rights Convention, which is one of the mostly widely signed and ratified human rights documents, aims to do. The question is not only whether states are willing to respect these rights, but whether they can be held responsible for protecting them. For this, children need not only human rights, they also need their parents' citizenship.

Delayed citizenship for all?

Dumbrava has, however, a much more fundamental objection that targets both ius sanguinis and ius soli: Citizenship as membership in a political community should not depend on 'contingent facts of birth (descent or place of birth)'. This is a common critique that always leaves me puzzled.[7] My very existence depends on these contingent facts. Humans cannot will themselves into being but are thrown into the world without choosing where to be born and to which parents. What is morally arbitrary is not that states use these fundamental features of personal identity to determine membership in political communities, but that in our world citizenship provides individuals with hugely unequal sets of opportunities. This is not an inherent feature of birthright citizenship but of the global economic and political (dis)order. If we want to overcome it, we have to address the causes of global inequality directly instead of attributing them to those rules that make individuals equal in status and rights as citizens of a particular state.

Dumbrava's critique focuses, however, on another birthright puzzle that has bothered republican theorists. Shouldn't membership in a self-governing political community be based on consent? And does it not presuppose cer-

---

[7] For nuanced critiques of birthright citizenship based on this idea see Carens, J. H. (2013), *The Ethics of Immigration*. Oxford: Oxford University Press; Shachar, A. (2009), *The Birthright Lottery. Citizenship and Global Inequality*. Cambridge, MA: Harvard University Press.

tain attitudes and skills that first need to be developed?[8] We may expect that children who are born and grow up in the state territory or who are raised by citizen parents will eventually want to join the political community and will also acquire the skills required for political participation. Yet these are expectations rather than certainties. Dumbrava suggests therefore that 'we could delay the attribution of citizenship until such attitudes and skills are confirmed'. However, since children also depend on the state for their health and education, he adds that they could at least be granted provisional citizenship. The Latin American distinction between nationality acquired at birth and citizenship acquired at majority seems to approximate this idea.

One reading of Dumbrava's proposal is that this is just a terminological distinction harking back to Aristotle's two definitions of citizenship. If we consider as citizens those who 'give judgments and can hold office', i.e. the members of the demos, then children are indeed only provisional citizens but will automatically become full citizens at the age of majority. The other interpretation draws, however, a line between the two statuses that can only be crossed by demonstrating the right attitude and skills. Instead of naturalising immigrants into a birthright community, this community itself would be denaturalised and reconstituted through a citizenship test imposed on all provisional native citizens. It may seem a form of poetic justice to treat natives like immigrants. Yet there is a big difference between expecting and promoting citizenship attitudes and skills and making them a requirement for access to citizenship rights. The only reason why immigrants can be expected to spend a few years as residents before becoming citizens, which gives them time to develop citizenship skills, and to apply for naturalisation, which demonstrates a civic attitude, is that they are birthright citizens of another state who have grown up there.

Citizenship across generations

Dumbrava concludes by suggesting that the intergenerational continuity of democratic membership should be achieved through consolidating institutions and educating citizens rather than the legal fictions and biological contingencies of birthright citizenship. One might ask why democracies need intergenerational continuity. The answer leads us back to the original justification for ius sanguinis after the French Revolution. It should not be the rulers who determine who the citizens are, nor the citizens themselves through

---

[8] See Dumbrava, C. (2014), *Nationality, Citizenship and Ethno-Cultural Belonging, Preferential Membership Policies in Europe*. Houndmills Basingstoke: Palgrave Macmillan, chapter 8, 9.

some democratic procedure in which they decide whom to admit or reject, nor the mere fact of subjection to the laws due to temporary presence in the territory. All of these rules lead to too much contingency and discontinuity with regard to the composition of the citizenry. Promoting civic attitudes and skills among those who are citizens is important, but it cannot resolve the puzzle who has a claim to be a citizen in the first place. Automatic acquisition of membership at birth and for life sets this question aside. It makes citizenship a part of citizens' personal identities that they are likely to accept. And it allows democracies to tap into resources of solidarity and to promote a sense of responsibility towards the common good and future generations.

In a nutshell, these are my two arguments why a modified version of ius sanguinis should be accepted as necessary for democratic states:

In a world of territorial states that control immigration, ius sanguinis (or *ius filiationis*) is as indispensible as ius soli for protecting the children of migrants. It provides them with the right to stay and to be admitted in their country of birth as well as their parents' country of origin. No other legal status can secure these rights as well as a birthright to dual nationality.

Deriving citizenship from unchosen and permanent features of personal identity – where and to whom one is born – sets aside the politically divisive membership question for the vast majority of citizens, creates a quasi-natural equality of status among them and signals that membership is linked to responsibilities for the common good and for future generations. No citizenship education programme can fully substitute for these signalling effects of birthright citizenship.

18

Ius Sanguinis: A Historical Study

Jannis Panagiotidis

In his thought provoking piece, Costica Dumbrava rejects ius sanguinis as 1) historically tainted, 2) increasingly inadequate and 3) normatively unnecessary. In my response, I will mainly focus on the first, historical dimension. Drawing on examples from the case of Germany, often used as the prime example to show what is wrong with ius sanguinis, I will contest the idea that ius sanguinis as such has been discredited by history.

Regarding the second and third points, I will restrict myself to the following brief observations, which are broadly in line with Rainer Bauböck's comments: while the issue of ART and citizenship raised by Dumbrava is indeed intriguing, I would go along with his own observation that this is more about the determination of legal parentage than about ius sanguinis, and with Bauböck's emphasis on social rather than biological parenthood. Discarding the ius sanguinis principle due to certain specific cases it might not adequately cover would mean throwing the baby out with the bathwater.

I am also simultaneously intrigued and sceptical regarding the suggestion to introduce a sort of 'a-national', universal status for children. Against the backdrop of recent historical research into children as the object of nationalist contestation and agitation during the first half of the twentieth century, a scenario in which 'children belonged more rightfully to national communities than to their own parents', this idea appears intuitively attractive.[1] Having said that, one can turn the argument around and see the suggested disconnection of parent and child citizenship as another attempt to claim children from their parents, this time on behalf on an imaginary inter- or supranational community. Yet in a world still (and for the foreseeable future) structured by nation states, where most so-called human rights are in fact citizens' rights,

---

[1] Zahra, T. (2008), *Kidnapped Souls: National Indifference and the Battle for Children in the Bohemian Lands, 1900–1948*. Ithaca: Cornell UP, 3; See also: Zahra, T. (2011), *The Lost Children: Reconstructing Europe's Families after World War II*. Cambridge, MA: Harvard UP, 20.

one may indeed wonder about the benefits of such a status 'above' or perhaps 'beyond' the nation if the parents cannot enjoy similar rights.

Tainted by history?

As to the argument of ius sanguinis being historically tainted, Dumbrava first of all needs to be commended for recognising that 'ius sanguinis citizenship is not conceptually "ethnic"'. Nevertheless, he argues that 'there are a number of ways in which the application of the ius sanguinis principle has been used in order to promote ethno-nationalist conceptions of membership'. These include 1) the maintaining of emigrant citizenship beyond the first generation of emigrants; 2) the use of 'the principle of descent in order to confirm or restore citizenship to certain categories of people whom [states] consider to be linked with through ethnocultural ties'; and 3) the exclusion of immigrant children from citizenship by an exclusive use of ius sanguinis with no ius soli elements.

Regarding the third point, I fully agree with Bauböck that it can be remedied quite easily by combining these two principles of citizenship allocation and simultaneously allow for residence-based naturalisation. The first issue is similarly unproblematic: extra-territorial transmission can simply be interrupted at a certain generational stopping point, much like the rule Germany introduced in section 4, paragraph 4 of its reformed 1999 citizenship law regarding the non-acquisition of German citizenship by the offspring of German citizens who themselves were born abroad after 31 December 1999.[2] There is no rule that says that the transmission of citizenship to descendants has to be possible ad infinitum.

Not all types of 'descent' are the same

I would like to discuss the second point in more detail, which touches upon the topics of preferential membership policies and co-ethnic citizenship and migration.[3] Here we are dealing with a terminological confusion quite typical for much of the literature in this field. The 'ethnic descent' that Dumbrava

---

[2] Joppke, C. (2003), 'Citizenship Between De- and Re-Ethnicization', *Russell Sage Foundation Working Paper No. 204*, 12–13. The full text of the law can be found at: http://www.gesetze-im-internet.de/rustag/BJNR005830913.html

[3] Dumbrava, C. (2014), *Nationality, Citizenship and Ethno-National Belonging: Preferential Membership Policies in Europe*. Basingstoke: Palgrave MacMillan; Panagiotidis, J. (2012), *Laws of Return? Co-Ethnic Immigration to West Germany and Israel (1948–1992)*. PhD Diss., European University Institute.

mentions as a criterion of admission to citizenship in some cases and the descent implied in the ius sanguinis principle are not the same and should not be conflated. In fact, they are mutually exclusive: 'descent' in ius sanguinis is about descent from a citizen, whatever his or her 'ethnicity'. The 'ethnic descent' used as a criterion in some cases of co-ethnic inclusion is precisely about people who are not citizens.

The supposed historical taintedness of the ius sanguinis principle results from the conflation of these different types of 'descent', and of the related unhappy connotations of the term 'blood', which invokes associations of 'race'. A lot of this confusion was created in the Brubaker-inspired debates of the 1990s about German citizenship. In a telling example, political scientist Patricia Hogwood claimed that 'the concept and law of citizenship in Germany were originally formulated in the context of nation-state development based on cultural or '*völkisch*' nationalism. ... The fact that the German legal framework for citizenship and naturalisation remains firmly rooted in the jus sanguinis principle has meant that citizenship policy in Germany is inextricably entangled in concepts of ethnicity and race. ... The principle of legal privilege [for ethnic Germans] on the basis of *racial* origins smacks of the racial policies of the Nazi period ...' (my emphasis, J.P.).[4]

Yet ius sanguinis per se has nothing to do with 'ethnicity' and 'race'. As Dieter Gosewinkel pointed out in his important book on German citizenship, the 'blood' here is a 'formal and instrumental' notion, not to be confused with 'substantial' blood conceptions of racial biology.[5] Those only entered German citizenship law through the Nazi Nuremberg laws. Before, a German Jew, whom the Nazis would later construe to be of a different 'race' for having the wrong 'blood', would transmit his German citizenship to his children iure sanguinis, just like other Germans whom the Nazis would construe as 'Aryans'. Ius sanguinis is ethnicity-blind. In fact, when young Israelis nowadays claim German citizenship with reference to an ancestor who fled from Germany, they also do so iure sanguinis. I would find it hard to interpret this as an objectionable *völkisch* practice. This example shows that the problem is not with ius sanguinis itself, but with the respective contexts in which it is embedded.

---

[4] Hogwood, P. (2000), 'Citizenship Controversies in Germany: the twin legacy of Völkisch nationalism and the Alleinvertretungsanspruch', *German Politics* 9 (3): 125–144, here 127, 132–133.

[5] Gosewinkel, D. (2001), *Einbürgern und Ausschließen: Die Nationalisierung der Staatsangehörigkeit vom Deutschen Bund bis zur Bundesrepublik Deutschland* [Naturalising and Excluding: Nationalisation of Citizenship from the German Confederation to the Federal Republic of Germany]. Göttingen: Vandenhoeck & Rupprecht, 327.

Co-ethnic citizenship is a different story

Nor is ius sanguinis particularly useful (or even necessary) for the conveying of citizenship upon 'co-ethnics' in other countries. This is a whole different discussion in my opinion which cannot be used to make a case against the ius sanguinis principle. Taking again the example of Germany, the main European supplier of co-ethnic citizenship in past decades, it needs to be stressed that 'ethnic Germans' from Eastern Europe did not receive German citizenship by means of the ius sanguinis of the 1913 citizenship law. This was not possible, as in most cases they had no ancestor with German citizenship to refer to. Their claim to citizenship rested on special provisions in the constitution and expellee law, which equalised the status of German *Volkszugehörige* with that of German citizens.

At this point we leave the solid ground of formal citizenship and enter into the murky territory of 'ethnicity'. But even here, it is not all about 'descent'. While the peculiar notion of *Volkszugehörigkeit* is often identified with 'ethnic descent', it was much more complex than that: it was actually very much a political-plebiscitary notion predicated on self-avowal (*Bekenntnis*) as German to be confirmed by an 'objective' criterion, which could be language, descent, upbringing, or culture (section 6 of the 1953 Federal Expellee Law).[6] 'Descent' (*Abstammung*) – notoriously hard to define in administrative practice – was thus neither a necessary nor a sufficient condition for recognition as a German.[7]

Conclusion

In sum, I would argue that the supposed 'taintedness' of ius sanguinis has to do with issues not intrinsic to this principle of transmitting citizenship, namely restrictive admission practices and racially based exclusion. The issue of co-ethnic citizenship should be kept apart from this discussion altogether. History cannot provide the justification for abandoning ius sanguinis, as its use in certain problematic ways and contexts in the past does

---

[6] See: http://www.bgbl.de/xaver/bgbl/start.xav?startbk=Bundesanzeiger_BGBl&jumpTo=bgbl153022.pdf

[7] I elaborate on the plebiscitary, quasi-'Renanian' nature of the German conception of Volkszugehörigkeit in: Panagiotidis, J. (2012), 'The Oberkreisdirektor Decides Who Is a German': Jewish Immigration, German Bureaucracy, and the Negotiation of National Belonging, 1953–1990. *Geschichte und Gesellschaft 38*, 503–533, esp. 511.

not mean it necessarily has to be used like that in the future. If complemented by other, inclusionary mechanisms of allocating citizenship in conjunction with increased tolerance for multiple citizenship it certainly remains a useful – and necessary – method of transmitting citizenship in the day and age of multiple transnational migrations.

19

Ius Sanguinis and the Need for its Modernization

Scott Titshaw

I appreciate the ideas that Costica Dumbrava and others have introduced into this debate. States' concerns about the quality and political consequences of their citizenship are important. But citizenship is a two-way street. Our discussion of ius sanguinis laws should extend beyond the concerns of states to also consider the serious practical consequences of citizenship laws on citizens, including the long-term unity and security of their families. Families facing instability or separation because children are denied their parents' citizenship are unlikely to be satisfied with the explanation that ius sanguinis is inadequate or historically tainted; the resulting individual sense of injustice might even discourage the loyalty and identification states seek in citizens.

This debate about citizenship transmission is necessary because of two modern changes in the facts of life: (1) increased international mobility based on cheap and easy transportation and communication; and (2) the advent and diffusion of assisted reproductive technology (ART) and new legal family forms (e.g., same-sex marriage and different-sex registered partnership). I will address each in turn. First, I'll explain why Dumbrava's proposal to abandon the ius sanguinis principle is an undesirable response to increased international mobility. Second, I'll build on Dumbrava's and Bauböck's recognition of the inadequacy of unlimited and exclusive ius sanguinis rules for today's families by suggesting that ius sanguinis be modernised rather than abandoned altogether. I'll also illustrate how citizenship in federal states can add an additional layer of complexity to any universal proposal regarding citizenship.

In a mobile world children need their parents' citizenship

Dumbrava's proposal to eliminate the ius sanguinis principle would increase, rather than decrease, problems based on greater international mobility. It would eliminate one tool parents currently use for transmitting citizenship to children conceived through ART. While current versions of ius sanguinis are inadequate to deal with other ART issues, that problem can be corrected. And, as Jannis Panagiotidis points out, abandoning ius sanguinis because of this inadequacy would be like 'throwing the baby out with the bathwater'. Most children are still conceived through sexual reproduction rather than ART, and many of their families would be worse off without ius sanguinis.

An example is easy to imagine. Let's say an Indian couple moves every seven years for employment reasons. They obtain residence permits, but not citizenship, in South Africa, the United Kingdom, and the United States, in turn. They also have a child in each country. Under ius soli regimes with no ius sanguinis rules, the children of these Indian parents would each have different passports (from South Africa, the UK, and the US). This might pose no problem in the short term. But what happens if a parent dies or loses his job?

Under a ius sanguinis regime, the surviving family members would be able to enter India and remain there together permanently as citizens.[1]

Dumbrava argues that such common citizenship is unnecessary to recognise and cement parent-child relationships if children of citizens have 'full migration rights. But 'migration rights' or benefits are substantially less stable than citizenship rights. What if a non-citizen family member becomes deportable because he or she commits a crime?[2] What if both Indian parents die while the children are minors? Without ius sanguinis, the children with their different nationalities might not be allowed to remain together anywhere, let alone in India where their extended family members (grandparents, aunts and uncles) most likely live.

Dumbrava's proposal of a universal legal status for all children would ameliorate some of these problems, but only until each child reaches the age of majority. At that time they might be separated from their parents and siblings.

---

[1] India would have automatically recognised these children as Indian citizens through 2004; it still recognises a greatly eased path to apply for citizenship in this context. http://www.loc.gov/law/help/citizenship-pathways/india.php

[2] While hardship of citizen relatives is sometimes considered, US immigration law generally requires removal of non-citizens who commit any of a long list of criminal infractions. 8 USC §1227(a)(2). https://www.law.cornell.edu/uscode/text/8/1227

ART requires fixing family and citizenship law

I agree with Dumbrava's and Bauböck's rejection of exclusive, unconditional ius sanguinis rules as inadequate in dealing with the consequences of ART and modern family law.

I disagree, however, with the conclusion Dumbrava draws from his argument that 'joint citizenship adds little to the legal and normative character of the parent-child relationship'. In fact, the permanence and stability stemming from common citizenship among close family members can have profound consequences for the unity required to develop and maintain family relationships.

I also disagree with Dumbrava's argument that 'the main problem' is that ius sanguinis 'is parasitic on external factors concerning the legal determination of parentage'. In fact, some federal States already delink federal citizenship determination and state or provincial family law,[3] creating greater problems than do citizenship laws that reflect legal parentage. In the United States, for example, legal parentage is generally a matter of state law. Yet, the US Constitution defines citizenship as an exclusively federal matter,[4] and Congress has established and revised a complex, autonomous algorithm for determining when a citizen parent transmits US citizenship to a child born abroad.[5] The problematic example Dumbrava points out regarding parents' inability to transmit US citizenship to children conceived through ART was created by a misguided autonomous federal policy, not parentage determinations under family law.[6] It could, and should, be

---

[3] HCCH (2014), *A Study of Legal Parentage and the Issues Arising from International Surrogacy Arrangements*, Prel. Doc. No 3C. Hague Conference on Private International Law,66–68 (listing Australia, Canada and the United States as examples). Available at http://www.hcch.net/upload/wop/gap2015pd03c_en.pdf

[4] The Fourteenth Amendment guarantees that '[a]ll persons born or naturalized in the United States and subject to the jurisdiction thereof are citizens of the United States and the state in which they reside'. Not only does this Amendment adopt a nearly absolute ius soli rule, but it clarifies that citizenship is a purely federal matter, with no meaningful state role beyond establishment of its own standards for recognising state residence.

[5] 8 USC §§1401–1409. Available at http://www.uscis.gov/sites/default/files/ilink/docView/SLB/HTML/SLB/0-0-0-1/0-0-0-29/0-0-0-9696.html

[6] Under current US law, a genetic and legal father and/or one or more legal and 'biological' mothers (i.e., genetic and gestational mother(s)) transmit birthright citizenship to children conceived through ART, but non-biological parents do not. Titshaw, S. (2014), 'A Transatlantic Rainbow Comparison: "Federalism" and Family-Based Immigration for Rainbow Families in the U.S. and the

corrected by federal reinterpretation of its rules to rely on family law parentage determinations.[7]

Rather than misplaced reliance on family law, the problems Dumbrava and Bauböck describe regarding the application of ius sanguinis following ART are consequences of outdated family law or of international conflict-of-law issues where relevant jurisdictions define parentage differently.

To the extent that the problems stem from conflict-of-law issues, it is worth noting that the Hague Conference on Private International Law is currently exploring whether to draft a multilateral instrument on international parentage and surrogacy, which might resolve some issues.[8]

To the extent that the problems stem from outdated family law, the best solution is to fix the family law. Family law generally reflects a more individualized, in-depth understanding of parent-child relationships than do citizenship or migration laws. Based on long experience and empirical data, family law tends to favour the stability of permanent family relationships with commensurate duties and benefits in the best interests of children. By tending to ensure the same citizenship for children and their parent(s), ius sanguinis rules also generally promote stable solutions in the best interests of children in a way that less permanent migration rules do not.

I agree with Bauböck that multiplicity of citizenships for children is generally not a problem, and I support his call for a more generous understanding of parenthood for purposes of citizenship transmission. But I would not opt for a *ius filiationis* proposal if it requires an entirely independent determination of social parenthood for citizenship transmission purposes. Officials dealing with citizenship issues are not as well suited to determine these issues as those administering family law. Also, too much generosity in this area might instigate cross-border mischief in familial disputes by 'social parents'.

E.U.', in C. Casonato & A. Schuster (Eds.), *Rights on the Move: Rainbow Families in Europe*: Proceedings of the conference: Trento, 16–17 October 2014, Trento: 189–200 (194-9). Trento: Università degli Studi di Trento, Facoltà di Giurisprudenza, available at http://eprints.biblio.unitn.it/4448/

[7] Titshaw, S. (2013), 'Revisiting the Meaning of Marriage: Immigration for Same-Sex Spouses in a Post-*Windsor* World', *Vand. L. Rev.* (66): 167–177 (174–75), available at http://www.vanderbiltlawreview.org/2013/10/revisiting-the-meaning-of-marriage-immigration-for-same-sex-spouses-in-a-post-windsor-world.

[8] At: http://www.hcch.net/upload/wop/gap2015pd03a_en.pdf

Instead, I would suggest replacing all outmoded rules that fail to consider parental intent and the best interests of the child in the context of children conceived through ART, whether these are family laws determining parentage or autonomous federal citizenship laws reading ius sanguinis as a literal 'right of blood'.

20

Issues with the Abolishment of Ius Sanguinis

Kristin Collins

Costica Dumbrava maintains that ius sanguinis citizenship is a historically tainted, outmoded, and unnecessary means of designating political membership. He argues that it is time to abandon it. His proposal is bold, and it has significant implications for an array of policies and practices. The parent-child relationship not only serves as a basis for citizenship transmission; it also entitles individuals to immigration preferences, and – in some countries – it facilitates automatic or 'derivative' naturalisation of the children of naturalised parents. In many countries that recognise ius soli citizenship, the parent-child relationship serves as an added requirement: one must be born in the sovereign territory and be the child of a citizen or a long-term legal resident. Dumbrava limits his challenge to ius sanguinis citizenship per se, and even suggests that family-based migration rights could be used to minimise the disruptive effect of abolishing citizenship-by-descent. But his core complaints about ius sanguinis citizenship – the mismatch of biological parentage and political affinity, the difficulties of determining legal parentage – can be, and have been, levied against these various family-based preferences and statuses, which are likely found in every nation's nationality laws. It is therefore important to consider his proposal in light of the role that the parent-child relationship plays in the regulation of migration, naturalisation, and citizenship more generally. With this broader context in mind, I concur with Rainer Bauböck and Jannis Panagiotidis that Dumbrava's proposal rests on an under-informed assessment of the historical record. I also argue that that, as a remedy for the problems that he has identified, Dumbrava's proposal is at once too restrained and too radical.

The complex history of ius sanguinis citizenship

Dumbrava first argues that ius sanguinis citizenship should be abolished because, historically, it has been associated with ethno-nationalist conceptions of citizenship. I appreciate Panagiotidis' insistence that 'the problem is not with ius sanguinis itself, but with the respective contexts in which it is embedded'. Panagiotidis also reminds us that ius sanguinis citizenship has sometimes functioned to create political communities that draw from different ethnic and religious groups, as in the case of German Jews whose membership in the German polity was secured by the country's ius sanguinis laws prior to the Nazi era. I want to elaborate and underscore the importance of this point with an additional example from United States history: During seventy years of Chinese exclusionary laws, ius sanguinis citizenship provided one of the very few routes to entry, and to American citizenship, for ethnic Chinese individuals born outside the U.S. For precisely that reason, exclusionists sought to limit or repeal the ius sanguinis statute, which recognised the foreign-born children of American fathers as citizens.[1] If one expands the historical frame to include parent-child immigration preferences and derivative naturalisation, the story becomes even more complex. By 1965, the race-based exclusions and national-origins quotas had been abolished, and previously excluded Asian families began immigrating to the U.S. in unprecedented numbers.[2] They were able to do so by relying on the generous family-based preferences in American immigration and nationality laws, which facilitated entry, settlement, and – especially significant to this discussion – derivative naturalisation for children.[3]

Even a cursory review of the historical record thus counsels a cautionary assessment of the contention that ius sanguinis citizenship's tainted past justifies its abolition. First, calls to end ius sanguinis citizenship have their own ugly history. Second, although one cannot gainsay that, in certain circumstances, ius sanguinis citizenship has been used to maintain ethnic homogeneity, the notion that parents and children do and should share the same political affiliation has also facilitated racial, ethnic, and religious diversification of some political communities. Rather than abolish ius sanguinis citizenship wholesale, we should be alert to the ways that it can operate as a tool

---

[1] For a discussion of these laws and efforts to restrict the recognition of ethnic Chinese individuals under the ius sanguinis citizenship statute, see Collins, K.A. (2014), 'Illegitimate Borders: *Jus Sanguinis* Citizenship and the Legal Construction of Family, Race, and Nation', *Yale Law Journal* 123 (7) 2134–2235 (at 2170–2182). Starting in 1934, the ius sanguinis statute also allowed American mothers to transmit citizenship to their foreign-born children. See id. at 2157.

[2] See Reimers, D. (1983), 'An Unintended Reform: The 1965 Immigration Act and Third World Immigration to the United States', *Journal of American Ethnic History* 9 (3): 23–24; Ong Hing, B. (1999), *Making and Remaking Asian America Through Immigration Policy, 1850–1900*. Stanford: SUP, 81–120.

[3] See, for example, *Immigration and Nationality Act of 1952*, 66 Stat. 163, 245, § 323.

of ethnic exclusion and degradation in particular socio-legal contexts, and work to minimise those effects.[4]

A proposal too restrained and too radical

To be fair, Dumbrava does not extend his proposal to migration and naturalisation policies that enlist the parent-child relationship; indeed, he would preserve such migration policies. He speaks only of traditional ius sanguinis citizenship, and argues that it often fails to map on to the reality of modern family formation, making it inadequate to 'deal with contemporary issues such as advances in assisted reproduction technologies' (ART), same-sex coupling and marriage, and the steady rise of nonmarital procreation. The problems Dumbrava identifies in this regard are important and difficult. But as a remedy for these problems, abolishing parent-child citizenship transmission is simultaneously too restrained and too radical. It is too restrained because, after abandoning ius sanguinis citizenship we would still be confronted with the difficulty of determining which parent-child relationships should count for purposes of regulating migration, derivative naturalisation, and (in many countries) ius soli birthright citizenship. Moreover, in all of these contexts, the 'fundamental normative questions about who should be a citizen in a political community' – and about the role that the parent-child relationship should play in that determination – would persist.

At the same time, Dumbrava's proposal is too radical. He argues that ius sanguinis citizenship is not necessary to protect children from statelessness and 'adds little to the legal and normative character of the parent-child relationship'. On this point I agree entirely with Bauböck and Scott Titshaw that Dumbrava underestimates the disruptive potential of his proposal. If all countries recognised unrestricted ius soli citizenship, Dumbrava's assertion that ius sanguinis citizenship is unnecessary to prevent statelessness would be basically correct. But, in fact, very few ius soli countries go that far. Instead, as noted, they use ius sanguinis concepts to restrict the operation of ius soli birthright citizenship, thus leaving some children at a risk of statelessness if traditional ius sanguinis citizenship were abolished. And it is not just formal statelessness that would increase in a world without ius sanguinis citizenship. Children whose citizenship does not align with that of their

---

[4] A particularly notable example of how ius sanguinis principles can operate as tools of ethno-racial exclusion is the 2013 ruling of the Constitutional Tribunal of the Dominican Republic, TC/0168/13, which effectively expatriated ethnic-Haitian individuals born and residing in the D.R., leaving hundreds of thousands of people stateless.

parents can find themselves divided by nationality from the individuals who are charged, ethically and legally, with their care. As Bauböck and Titshaw observe, in an era of voluntary and compelled migration, ius sanguinis is the most effective method of protecting against such destabilising and precarious circumstances.

How to modernise?

I agree with Titshaw and Bauböck that the modernisation of ius sanguinis citizenship, rather than its complete repudiation, offers a better way to address the problems Dumbrava identifies. The difficult question is how? I am hesitant to embrace Titshaw's proposed method of modernisation, and I offer a friendly but important amendment to Bauböck's proposal.

Titshaw argues that the officials who administer citizenship law should adhere to the parentage determinations made by officials who generally administer family law. In the U.S., these are state-level family law judges applying state law. But domestic family law, in the U.S. and elsewhere, does not necessarily generate ideal or even tolerable outcomes on questions of citizenship. Titshaw holds up a particularly poorly drawn U.S. federal policy that regulates ius sanguinis citizenship as it applies to foreign-born children conceived using ART, but there are many examples of how the use of state family law to regulate citizenship transmission has generated equally objectionable outcomes.[5]

Alternatively, Bauböck would have us adopt a '*ius filiationis*' standard that recognises the 'social parent' or the 'primary caregiver' as the parent for purposes of ius sanguinis citizenship. He urges that this would help remedy the 'mismatch between biologically determined citizenship and parental care arrangements that would also open the door to abusive claims'. He is correct. My concern, however, is that his emphasis on 'social parenting' and 'primary caregiving' is insufficient and has its own perils. First, it could

---

[5] For example, in 1940 the federal ius sanguinis citizenship statute was amended to include the nonmarital children of U.S. citizen fathers under certain circumstances, such as when the father had 'legitimated' the child. Federal officials turned to the law of the father's domiciliary state to determine whether legitimation had, in fact, occurred. In the 1940s and 50s, marriage to the child's mother was a very common mode of legitimation, but federal officials making citizenship determinations would not recognise an interracial marriage as the basis of a child's citizenship claim if the father's home state banned such marriages – and many did. See Collins, 'Illegitimate Borders', above n. 2, at 2210.

increase the likelihood of abusive denials of citizenship by officials who, at least in the U.S., are often all too eager to find reasons to reject claims to citizenship.[6] In the case of nonmarital children – who make up a far greater portion of the global population than children conceived through ART – the restriction of parent-child citizenship transmission to 'primary caregivers' could lead to circumspect treatment, or outright rejection, of the father-child relationship as a basis for citizenship transmission. Indeed, the primary caregiver standard could stymie the caregiving efforts of unmarried fathers who are divided by nationality from their children, and hence may never be able to establish themselves as the 'primary caregiver'. The emphasis on caregiving as a prerequisite could also aid unmarried fathers who prefer to avoid parental responsibility by distancing themselves geographically from their children. The result: a ius sanguinis citizenship regime that would buttress gender inequality by undermining men's parental rights and helping them to avoid their parental responsibilities.[7] Moreover, and regardless of one's view of the equities as between parents, it is ultimately the nonmarital child's citizenship and migration rights that could be destabilised, depending on how officials understood the concept of 'social parent'. Dumbrava recognises the inequities associated with 'the differential treatment of children born within and out of wedlock with respect to access to citizenship', but his solution – to abolish parent-child citizenship transmission altogether – would give cold comfort to nonmarital children and marital children alike.

This is not an endorsement for a purely genetic model of citizenship transmission. Despite the references to 'blood', ius sanguinis citizenship has never rested on purely biological conceptions of citizenship. Traditionally, marriage was fundamental to the ability of fathers to secure citizenship for their children, and – at least in the development of U.S. law – the presumption that the mother is the sole caregiver of the nonmarital child led to the recognition of the mother-child relationship as a source of citizenship for foreign-born nonmarital children.[8] Rather, I suggest that – unless and until we move beyond citizenship as the enforcement mechanism for basic human rights, and beyond the family as a foundational source of material and psychological support for children, we cannot overstate the importance of

---

[6] See, for example, Saldana Iracheta v. Holder, 730 F.3d 419 (5th Cir. 2013).
[7] I develop this argument in: Collins, K.A. (2000), 'When Fathers' Rights Were Mothers' Duties: The Failure of Equal Protection in Miller v. Albright', *Yale Law Journal* (109) 1669–1708 (1699–1705), and in 'Illegitimate Borders', above n. 2, at 2230–34.
[8] See Collins, 'Illegitimate Borders', above n. 2, at 2199–2205.

the generous recognition of the parent-child relationship for citizenship transmission. The modernisation of ius sanguinis citizenship should thus include the recognition of 'social parents' and parents with 'custodial rights'– as Bauböck rightly asserts – and also recognition of all who can be held legally responsible for a child's care or support. Dumbrava may be unhappy that the whims of parents, people's reproductive choices, and factors beyond the control of the individual would continue to determine membership in a political community. But it is precisely because citizenship designations rest on factors such as these that I wholly agree with his admonition that we channel our efforts 'towards consolidating democratic institution and promoting citizenship attitudes and skills among all those who find themselves, by whatever ways and for whatever reason, in our political community'.

21

Problematizing Ius Sanguinis

Lois Harder

I share Costica Dumbrava's critique of ius sanguinis citizenship, and ultimately what is, I think, his rejection of birth as the basis for political membership generally. Of course, there are issues of practicality – of the world as we find it – that might limit whether and how one would advance the abolishment of birthright citizenship in light of specific political dynamics. But it is precisely those practicalities, and the near unthinkability of alternatives to birth-based citizenship that demand our interrogation of birthright in the first instance. As Joseph Carens has argued with respect to his advocacy of open borders, 'even if we must take deeply rooted social arrangements as givens for purposes of immediate action in a particular context, we should never forget about our assessment of their fundamental character. Otherwise we wind up legitimating what should only be endured'.[1]

In his contribution to this Forum, Rainer Bauböck defends birthright citizenship and argues that in both of its iterations (ius sanguinis and ius soli) it avoids political division and 'creates a quasi-natural equality of status' among citizens who are entitled to claim it. But what about the inequality that divides the entitled from the unentitled? Political communities may be unavoidably bounded, but if a normative commitment to human rights is our guiding frame, it seems incumbent upon us to advance methods or prospects for membership that reduce the barriers to belonging as much as possible. Moreover, as Jacqueline Stevens trenchantly observes, in defining the bounds of equal citizenship, borders also form the boundaries of our non-emergency expressions of compassion.[2] To the extent that birthright entitlement advances a seemingly unassailable claim to exclusionary membership, its advocacy runs counter to a broader commitment to humanitarianism.

---

[1] Carens, J. (2013), *The Ethics of Immigration*. New York: Oxford University Press, 229.
[2] Stevens, J. (2010), *States without Nations: Citizenship for Mortals*. New York: Columbia University Press, 9.

Bauböck's description of birthright citizenship evades the fact that establishing citizenship through birth, as with any other basis for membership, is an inherently political decision. One of the central appeals of birthright is that it involves innocent, vulnerable babies, infants who are not (yet) marked by misdeeds, criminality, inadequate knowledge or commitment, or the wrong ideological proclivities. It is this innocence that helps to obscure the profoundly political basis of birthright; that makes it possible to describe birthright citizenship as avoiding political division and establishing a quasi-natural equality. However, the use of criteria of birth to determine political membership – whether it is birth to a citizen parent (variously defined) or birth in the territory (variously defined) – is not innocent. Prevailing views about

- wedlock and patriarchal forms of social organisation (e.g. unwed mothers having responsibility for their children and conferring citizenship, but unwed fathers having no such responsibility or capacity);
- the relative significance of biological and social parenting as well as gender and sexuality (can a lesbian co-mother confer citizenship on her genetic progeny to whom she did not give birth – just as fathers do?);
- national attachment (is this child born abroad as second or subsequent generation?); and
- how generous territorial definitions should be (is a child born to a Ugandan mother on an American airline flying in Canadian airspace from Amsterdam to Boston a Canadian? Answer = yes) [3]

all play out in the rules that determine birthright entitlement. The magical power of birthright citizenship is that it makes it possible for us to know and rehearse these rules while simultaneously making birthright seem straightforward, static and apolitical. In contrast to citizenship debates that engage migration, legal and illegal status and naturalisation, birthright citizenship makes these political choices disappear with a wave of a wand.

I am currently researching a book on the lost Canadians. These are people who thought they had a birthright claim to Canadian citizenship, but subsequently learned that they were mistaken. Their difficulties arose

---

[3] 'Birth and joy midflight' *Boston Globe*, 1 January 2009, available at http://www.boston.com/news/local/massachusetts/articles/2009/01/01/birth_and_joy_midflight/?page=full

for various reasons, and have now largely been resolved through statutory amendment (a rule change). In making their case to Parliament, the courts and the media, their primary, and highly successful, strategy, was to denigrate the rule-boundedness of 'mean-minded bureaucrats' and advance the merits of their claims through appeals to lineage and blood-based belonging.[4] Despite being born in the UK, residing in Canada for five years as a small child, and having subsequently lived in the UK for six decades, one such lost Canadian insisted, 'I, sir, am a Canadian. To the roots of me, to the spirit of me, to the soul of me, I'm Canadian'.[5] This impassioned claim to Canada – not exactly your 'go to' example of an ethnic nation – nonetheless succeeds as a rhetorical strategy because it re-enchants the nation,[6] underscoring the country's desirability to the Canadian public, and insisting that this connection is an essential feature of her identity. This is a logic that only works in a world of birthright citizenship. And it is a strategy that eventually succeeded in securing legislative amendments, because the birth-based claims of the lost Canadians (and not necessarily residency or connection) carried an overwhelming political potency.

To the extent that birthright citizenship enables progressive people to cordon off a substantial portion of membership determination from a potentially nasty political debate, one can certainly understand its attractions. But the occlusion of politics with an unsupportable appeal to nature is ethically dubious. If we are committed to democratic equality, we need principles to manage how we live together that refuse the privilege of birth over naturalisation, and that require us to come to terms with our mortality.[7] Political membership should be a lively, on-going process of negotiation in which everyone has a stake. Some critics might argue that abandoning birthright citizenship and its intergenerational character will create the conditions for decision making in which we are no longer future-oriented, or indeed, that we will neglect the lessons and obligations of our past. If our children do not

---

[4] Canada, 26 February 2007, House of Commons Standing Committee on Citizenship and Immigration 39th Parliament 1st Session no. 38. (at 11:50).
[5] Canada, 26 February 2007, House of Commons Standing Committee on Citizenship and Immigration 39th Parliament 1st Session no. 38. (at 11:45).
[6] Honig, B. (2001), *Democracy and the Foreigner*. Princeton: Princeton University Press, 74.
[7] For a full elaboration on the dangers of intergenerational citizenship, see Stevens (2010), at n.2 above.

have a stake in the polity to come, why should we commit ourselves to making it better? This kind of argument is morally bereft. We can continue to care about the future and attend to the damages we, and our ancestors, have wrought, even if, or precisely because, our political membership is limited by our mortality. It was, of course, ever thus.

22

Ius Sanguinis and its Two Faces

Francesca Decimo

Costica Dumbrava's proposal for abandoning ius sanguinis is timely and bold. My intuition is to reject his suggestion that children's citizenship might be disconnected from that of their parents, but to join his advocacy for a radical rethinking of the ius sanguinis principle with a view towards eliminating it once and for all. These are rather contrasting stances in relation to the same principle. Let us see if the apparent contradiction can be resolved.

To begin, let us consider the element of Costica Dumbrava's proposal that has elicited most attention and controversy among the respondents, but was picked up and expanded by Lois Harder, namely the assertion that granting citizenship at birth is unnecessary and, above all, that making children dependent on the legal status of their parents exposes them to a form of vulnerability. The idea of postponing the acquisition of citizenship until adulthood, taking into account birthplace and residence or possession of the appropriate attitudes and skills, derives from the classic opposition between ius sanguinis and ius soli according to which the former is considered ethnic and exclusive while the latter is considered civic and inclusive. Yet Rainer Bauböck's comments on this point explain how, in the absence of parental transmission of citizenship to children, ius soli and *ius domicilii* can generate individual and familial conditions that are both legally paradoxical and morally unfair.

I share the doubts and critiques raised by Rainer Bauböck, Scott Titshaw and Kristin Collins regarding the alleged emancipatory value of a citizenship system that disconnects children from their parents. Particularly, I consider any legal system that fails to specifically protect the relationship between parents and children to be highly risky. Indeed, who should children depend on if not their parents? Dumbrava's proposal that children might instead be subject to, and protected by, a kind of international law faces the problem of subordinating the individual and familial reproductive spheres to institutional logics.

As Luc Boltanski has noted,[1] the event of birth is inextricably linked to the definition of belonging and social descent – and therefore legal, political, cultural, national, etc. descent as well. Historically, devices for legitimating the procreative event were provided by religion, ancestry, the nation-state and, in more recent times, a long-term relationship among a couple. In a scenario in which parentage and citizenship are not tightly connected from the beginning, the risk is not only that of generating stateless children but also an excess of state power. Even after World War Two, the Catholic Church in Ireland took children considered illegitimate away from their unmarried mothers. It was nationalist demographic policies, both in Europe and overseas, that shaped the reproductive choices of individuals and families during the 20th century with a view to producing children for the fatherland. We might recall these policies when interpreting some recent nationally-oriented arguments encouraging the children of immigrants to rid themselves of the burden of their cultures of origin in which their inadequately assimilated mothers and fathers remain stuck.[2] With this in mind, do we really want to define children's citizenship irrespective of their parents'? Do we really want to shift the task of determining the legitimate membership of our offspring from relationships to institutions?

The considerations made thus far therefore lead me to agree with those who have argued that, as long as the system of nation-states regulates our rule of law, children's citizenship must be linked from birth to that of their parents.

At the same time, it seems to me that ius sanguinis is a legal instrument which, especially in a global context of increased geographical mobility, opens the way to policies of attributing nationality that go far beyond protecting the parent-child relationship. This point relates to Dumbrava's observation that ius sanguinis is historically tainted that was critically addressed by Jannis Panagiotidis but has not yet been decisively refuted.

As scholars have noted, ius sanguinis makes it possible to recognise a community of descendants as legitimate members of the nation regardless of its territorial limits, but that is not all. This principle has been used to grant the status of co-national to individuals dispersed not only across space but also across time, leading to the construction of virtually inexhaustible intergenerational chains.[3] This principle is based on blood, identified as the

---

[1] See Boltanski, L. (2004), *La condition foetale*. Paris: Gallimard.
[2] See Hungtinton, S. (2004), *Who are we?* New York: Simon and Schuster.
[3] See: Brubaker, R. (1992), *Citizenship and Nationhood in France and Germany*. Cambridge: Harvard University Press.

essential and primordial element of descent, belonging and identification. It is true that this potential for unlimited intergenerational transmissibility is effectively defused by the fact that many countries interpret ius sanguinis narrowly, applying it generally only up to the second generation born abroad. And yet, is this limit enough to bind and delimit the potential of ius sanguinis? In national rhetoric the image of a community of descendants continues to exert a powerful appeal that goes beyond the attribution of birthright citizenship. In historical emigration countries – but also others –,[4] ius sanguinis as a legal practice is used to grant preferential conditions and benefits to descendants as part of the direct transmission or 'recovery' of ancestral citizenship well beyond the second generation.[5] Generational limits in the granting of citizenship to descendants can thus be bypassed because, in principle, ius sanguinis itself poses no particular restrictions in this regard.

The most controversial aspects of ius sanguinis emerge when this principle ends up competing with ius soli or *ius domicilii*, that is, when individuals born and raised elsewhere enjoy a right to citizenship in the name of lineage and an assertion of national affiliation while immigrants who participate fully in the economic, social and cultural development of the country are denied this same right or face serious obstacles in accessing it. In such context – Germany in the past and Italy today – the right to citizenship effectively becomes a resource which, like economic, human and social capital, is distributed in a highly unequal way, benefitting certain categories of people – 'descendants' – at the expense of others – 'foreigners'.

In view of its unlimited intergenerational potential, I conclude that, if its purpose is merely to bind children's citizenship to that of their parents, ius sanguinis as a legal instrument suffers from ambiguity and disproportionality. All of these critical points seem to be implicitly overcome in Bauböck's proposal of a *ius filiationis* principle, which would focus entirely on linking children's citizenship to that of their parents, especially for migrants and non-biological offspring. Under a different name and with distinct content,

---

[4] Joppke's comparison of three highly divergent countries, France, Italy and Hungary, is quite effective in shedding light on this issue in Joppke, C. (2005), *Selecting by Origin*. Cambridge: Harvard University Press, 240–250.

[5] For an in-depth analysis of the Italian case, see Decimo, F. (2015). Nation and reproduction: Immigrants and their children in the population discourse in Italy. *Nations and Nationalism, 21*(1), 139–161; Tintori, G. (2013), *Naturalisation Procedures for Immigrants*. Florence: European University Institute Robert Schuman Centre for Advanced Studies, EUDO Citizenship Observatory, available at http://cadmus.eui.eu/bitstream/handle/1814/29787/NPR_2013_13-Italy.pdf?sequence=1

does this move not suggest that, rather than modifying or modernising ius sanguinis as advocated by Rainer Bauböck and Scott Titshaw, it is time to abandon it once and for all, adopting in its place a principle that explicitly protects parentage and citizenship in contexts of geographical mobility instead of linking it to genealogical lineage and nationhood?

23

Rethinking the Requirement of State Citizenship

David Owen

In his kick-off contribution, Costica Dumbrava offers a threefold critique of ius sanguinis as a norm of citizenship acquisition. In reflecting on this critique, I share the scepticism expressed by Rainer Bauböck, Jannis Panagioditis, Scott Titshaw and Kristin Collins. In particular I would note, along the lines of Titshaw's Indian family example, that the abolition of ius sanguinis would have led in my own family context to four siblings, of whom I am one, being split among three different nationalities: Nigerian, British and Malaysian). However rather than address Dumbrava's critique head on, I want to suggest that the kind of critique of ius sanguinis that he offers – and the same point would apply to the critique or defence of any of the classic membership rules taken singly as free-standing norms – gets things moving askew from the start. To see this, one needs to take a step back and situate this debate within a slightly different context. When asking what citizenship rules we ought to endorse or reject, we ought to begin with a prior question: 'what do we need state citizenship rules for?'

In a world of plural autonomous states, there are two basic functions that such rules are to play:

1. to ensure that each and every human being is a citizen of a state and hence that everyone has, at least formally, equal standing in a global society organised as a system of states;
2. to allocate persons to states in ways that best serve the common interest, that is, where this allocation supports protection of the fundamental interests of individuals, the realization of the common good within states and the conditions of cooperation between states.

A plausible response to these requirements is a general principle that Ayelet Shachar calls '*ius nexi*' which highlights the importance of a genuine connection between persons and the state of which they are citizens.[1] The notion

---

[1] Shachar, A. (2009), *The Birthright Lottery: Citizenship and Global Inequality*. Cambridge: Harvard University Press.

of 'genuine connection' can be glossed in terms of Bauböck's 'stakeholder' view which proposes that those and only those individuals have a claim to membership of a polity whose individual autonomy and wellbeing is linked to the collective self-government and flourishing of that polity.[2] It seems to me that we should see ius soli, ius sanguinis and *ius domicilii* under the general principle of *ius nexi* as denoting different routes through which a genuine connection is presumptively established: through parental citizenship, through place of birth and through residence.

Seeing each of these rules under this more general principle, rather than seeing each as a single free-standing norm, makes clear two points that are salient to this discussion. First, that in adopting any of these rules we are not reifying 'blood' or 'territory' or 'residence'. We regard them instead simply as acknowledgments of the diverse ways in which *ius nexi* may be given expression – and we need each of them if we are to do justice to the relations of persons to states. Second, that each of the ius soli, ius sanguinis and *ius domicilii* rules should be qualified by the general principle of *ius nexi* that they serve. So, for example, an unlimited ius sanguinis rule or a ius soli rule that included a child born to visiting tourists or a *ius domicilii* rule that granted citizenship after three months residence would be incompatible with the overarching *ius nexi* principle.

Still it would be in line with Dumbrava's argument for him to object that the 'birthright' rules of ius soli and ius sanguinis can only operate on the basis of the general presumption that parental citizenship and place of birth establish a genuine connection, so why not wait until the children reach their majority? Here I concur with the view advanced by Bauböck that the adequate protection of children's rights implies that 'children need not only human rights, they also need their parent's citizenship'. Titshaw's example of the serially mobile Indian family and my own peripatetic family history suffice to make this point. Contra Harder, I don't think that 'birthright' rules disguise the political character of membership norms, rather they acknowledge important interests of children, parents and states. Harder's stress on the relationship of those entitled to citizenship of a given state and those not so entitled doesn't provide reasons to drop either ius soli or ius sanguinis, what it does is provide reasons for relatively generous *ius domicilii* rules, of

---

[2] Bauböck, R. (2015), 'Morphing the Demos into the Right Shape. Normative Principles for Enfranchising Resident Aliens and Expatriate Citizens', *Democratization* 22 (5): 820–839 988146.

rights to dual/plural nationality and of a more equitable distribution of transnational mobility rights.

And perhaps there may be a clue here to an unstated background commitment of Dumbrava's critique. If we ask under what, if any, circumstances in a world of plural states, it could make sense to abolish ius sanguinis rules, then I think that the only answer that has any plausibility is a world of open borders characterised by rapid access to citizenship through *ius domicilii* rules. It may even be plausible that the abolition of ius sanguinis rules would generate political support for more open borders given the problems liable to be posed for sustaining the human right to a family life after the removal of such rules. Whether this is a prudent way of seeking to realise such a world and whether such a world is desirable are, of course, further questions.

24

Renouncing the Right of Blood

Kerry Abrams

Problems have plagued the ius sanguinis principle – the transmission of citizenship from parent to child – for as long as it has existed. Costica Dumbrava is surely correct that the time has come to ask whether ius sanguinis is still necessary. But the core problem with ius sanguinis, I would argue, is not that it uses the parent-child relationship to determine membership but that it overemphasizes the importance of the genetic tie to this relationship.

The very term ius sanguinis – 'right of blood' – makes the genetic tie the sine qua non of belonging. It is this obsession with genetic purity that has linked ius sanguinis to tribalism, xenophobia, and even genocide. This problem, I believe, is distinct from the very real need to ensure children's access to the same geographic territory and legal system as that of their parents. Rainer Bauböck's proposal for a '*ius filiationis*' based on family association rather than genetic ties would excise many of the problems caused by a focus on blood while protecting the parent-child relationship and the stability for children that flows from it.

Let me explain in more detail why I think that retaining recognition of parent-child relationships while abandoning the other features of ius sanguinis is sensible. At first glance, protecting the tying of children's citizenship to that of their parents may appear problematic because of that relationship's historical ties to property ownership. But a closer look shows that children really do deserve different legal treatment than adults, and *ius filiationis* is one critical way the law can recognise that difference.

Ius sanguinis feels retrograde today because it developed during a time in which relationships between parents and children, as well as relationships between husbands and wives and masters and servants, were much more akin to property-chattel relationships than we understand them to be today. Today's family law was yesterday's law of the household, which set forth entitlements and obligations based on reciprocal legal statuses – parent and child, husband and wife, master and servant, master and apprentice (and sometimes master and slave). Each of these relationships was hierarchical, involving responsibilities on the part of the superior party in the hierarchy (father, husband, or master) and obligations of service on the part of the inferior party (child, wife, servant, apprentice, or slave).[1] The inferior party derived identity from the superior: a wife or a child's nominal citizenship often followed that of the husband or father, but this identity did not confer the same rights enjoyed by the superior party. In early America, for example, male citizens were often entitled to the right to vote, right to contract, and right to own property (in fact, ownership of property was often a prerequisite for voting) but their wives – also technically citizens – were not entitled to any of these rights. Their political participation took the form of providing moral guidance to their husbands and raising virtuous sons who could themselves exercise political power. [2]

Today, we no longer think of citizenship in this way. The rights conferred by citizenship are understood in Western democracies as universal. If, for example, I become a naturalised U.S. citizen, the same neutral voting laws apply to me that apply to any other citizen, regardless of my gender, marital status, race, or national origin. Likewise, laws that imposed derivative citizenship on wives, and even laws that expatriated women upon marriage – both of which used to be widespread – are no longer the norm. In many parts of the world, women are no longer understood as intellectually and financially dependent on their husbands but instead as autonomous adults, capable of making their own economic, moral, and legal decisions, including the decision to consent to citizenship or renounce it. And even more dramatically, we no longer think of servants as deriving legal identity from their masters; instead, workers are free to participate in free, if regulated, labour markets and their citizenship status is independent of their employee status. [3]

The one legal distinction, however, that all countries still maintain in determining the capacity to exercise the rights associated with citizenship is age. Children are generally considered to be incapable of giving legal

---

[1] Halley, J. (2011), 'What is Family Law?: A Genealogy, Part I', *Yale Journal of Law & Humanities* 23 (1): 1–109, at 2.
[2] Kerber, L. (1980), *Women of the Republic: Intellect & Ideology in Revolutionary America*. Chapel Hill: UNC Press.
[3] In contrast to the independent citizenship status of workers, employer-sponsored immigration provisions may represent the vestiges of the ancient master-servant status relationship. See Raghunath, R. (2014), 'A Founding Failure of Enforcement: Freedmen, Day Laborers, and the Perils of an Ineffectual State,' *C.U.N.Y. L. Rev.* 18 (1): 47–91.

consent and in need of legal protection. The particular age at which they become capable of reasoning is contested, but it is incontestable that a newborn cannot care for himself nor meaningfully choose a nationality. In many circumstances, the law provides the protection children need by requiring children's parents to provide for them, care of them, and make decisions for them; in some instances, the state takes on this responsibility (foster care and universal public education are both examples). Children occupy a very different legal space than women or workers, one that makes them vulnerable when their ties to their parents are weakened. Providing children with a citizenship that they can exercise simultaneously with that of at least one of their parents is a critical protection for their wellbeing. We can believe this to be so while simultaneously rejecting the traditional hierarchies of parent-child, husband-wife, and master-slave. The United Kingdom's move away from conceptualizing parent-child relationships as 'custodial', property-like relationships and instead describing them as involving 'parental responsibility' is a good example of this shift. The emphasis has changed from ownership and control to care and protection.

If, then, we still need a form of parent-to-child citizenship transmission, is ius sanguinis as traditionally understood what we need? Scholars, courts, and government agencies often take ius sanguinis literally, as the 'rule of blood'. But I think that rigidity is misplaced. Even centuries ago the notion of ius sanguinis meant something distinct from a pure genetic tie. For men, who could never be certain of their child's paternity, transmission 'through blood' often really meant transmission through choice. A man chose to acknowledge his children by marrying, or already being married to, their mother. Children born to unmarried mothers generally took on the citizenship of their mothers, not their fathers, regardless of whether the father was known. The notion of 'blood', then, was complicated by the requirement of marriage for citizenship transmission through the father and the man's unique ability to embrace or repudiate his offspring based on his marital relationship to their mother. Presumably, many children, prior to blood and DNA testing, acquired citizenship iure sanguinis when there was actually no blood tie, sometimes in circumstances where the father was ignorant of this fact and sometimes where he knew full well no blood relationship existed.[4] Ius sanguinis has always been about more and less than simply blood.

---

[4] Abrams, K. & K. Piacenti (2014), 'Immigration's Family Values', *Va. L. Rev.* 100 (4): 629–709, at 660, 663, 692.

Thus, Bauböck's notion of *ius filiationis* seems to me both the most appropriate form today for citizenship transmission from parent to child to take, and a more accurate description of what really occurred historically. As I see it, the most challenging obstacle to implementing a *ius filiationis* system is that birthright citizenship is fixed in time. Courts are not in a position to predict on the date of a child's birth the adult who will ultimately assume parental responsibility for a child, but they can determine who the genetic or marital parent is. Shifting to a *ius filiationis* system, then, requires a multifaceted response. First, statutes outlining the requirements for citizenship transmission at birth should be amended to identify the intended parents. In most circumstances, the intended parents will be the genetic parents, but in some instances they might be someone else – for example, a non-genetic parent who contracts with a gestational surrogate or the spouse or partner of a genetic parent. Various pieces of evidence, from birth certificates to contracts to court judgments, would be necessary to determine parentage. In cases involving ART, this solution would solve many of the current problems. A genetic tie would be but one piece of evidence in determining citizenship at birth.

In addition to reforming ius sanguinis statutes, however, I believe we must also broaden the other available pathways to citizenship outside of birthright citizenship and traditional forms of naturalisation. There could be a deadline – perhaps by a specified birthday – by when a functional parent could request a declaration of citizenship for the child he or she has parented since birth. This alternative means of citizenship transmission should not substitute for birthright citizenship; as Kristin Collins points out, making citizenship determinations using only functional tests would put children at the mercy of officials seeking to deny citizenship and could disadvantage genetic or intentional fathers who may be unable to demonstrate that their care has been substantial enough to be 'functional.' But combined with a robust recognition of genetic and intentional parentage at birth, recognition of functional parentage later on could serve a supplemental purpose, ensuring that children will ultimately have access to citizenship rights in the country in which their functional parents reside. Full recognition of parent-child relationships requires going beyond the moment of birth so that we can recognise the individuals who actually take on parental responsibility.

It is premature to forsake the recognition of parent-child relationships in citizenship law, not when citizenship is still the mechanism for ensuring that every human being has membership in at least one state and providing access to basic human rights. But it is time that we abandoned the idea that 'blood' is the sole basis of these relationships.

25

Nationality Law, Ius Sanguinis and Children

David Armand Jacques Gérard de Groot

I agree to certain extent with Costica Dumbrava that ius sanguinis encompasses certain problematic issues, especially where it concerns newer forms of procreation, like IVF for lesbian couples and surrogacy. However, the origin of the problem cannot be attributed to ius sanguinis, but to non-solidarity of states that overuse the *ordre public* exemption for the denial of the recognition of parentage. But before delving into family relations and private international law conflicts, I would like to first argue that ius sanguinis is still the most suitable option for the main purposes of nationality law where it concerns children.

The main purposes of nationality

The commonly accepted main purposes of nationality are, first of all, that there is a territory to which an individual can always return and from which he cannot be deported, as was already pointed out by Bauböck and Titshaw; secondly, diplomatic and consular protection while being abroad; thirdly, national political participation in the state of nationality; and lastly, for EU citizens, free movement rights within the EU.

An abandonment of ius sanguinis in favour of ius soli might lead to the situation described by Titshaw, where within the same family the children might have different nationalities, which could, for example, lead to the situation that they would have to move to different countries in case of their parents' death while they are minor or that they might need to seek diplomatic protection from different foreign representations. Such a break-up of the family unit due to differing nationalities would certainly conflict with the right to family life. Therefore, for the purpose of preserving the unity and protection of the family, ius sanguinis is the most suitable option. If, when having attained majority the children feel that they have a closer bond with another nationality, they could still apply for naturalisation in that state.

This bond of attachment brings me to the national political participation purpose of nationality which is connected to Dumbrava's argument concerning the reproduction of the political community. Having the nationality of a certain state does not automatically mean integration into its society. This problem, depending on the mobility of the persons involved, does, however, not only occur with ius sanguinis and ius soli, but also with every other form of nationality transmission that one could think of. It should therefore be decided whom national political participation concerns most. If the definition of a 'state' refers primarily to a permanent population within its borders, long-term (non-national) residents should have national political participation rights and long-term absent nationals should not (except if they are working abroad in service of the state). National political participation rights should then be detached from nationality and therefore actually not be seen as a purpose of nationality (but that is a different discussion).

It should however be noted that for purpose of inclusion of long-term resident families, who for some reason have not acquired the nationality by naturalisation, into the national population, a third generation ius soli or even a second generation ius soli, in cases where the first generation migrant has entered the country at a young age, would be appropriate. However, this should not come with an option requirement for dual nationals at reaching majority, as in Germany, in order to avoid a conflict of identity if one is forced to make a choice between the nationality acquired iure soli and another nationality acquired iure sanguinis.

Non-solidarity of states

The problems that arise when a state does not grant its nationality to a child due to non-recognition of parentage can only occur in cases where parentage has been established by another state in accordance with its national family law. In surrogacy cases this means a non-recognition of a foreign judgement or birth certificate and in cases of dual motherhood of married or registered lesbian couples a non-recognition of the extended *pater est quem nuptiae demonstrant* principle. The *pater est* principle means that the husband of the woman that gives birth to the child is automatically considered to be the father and therefore directly at birth has a parentage link to the child. Increasingly, states have extended this principle to stable non-marital relationships and to same-sex marriages.

If the child is born in the state of the discussed nationality the national family law (mostly) applies to the establishment of parentage. It would therefore not make any sense that parentage ties to a national could be established at birth by the state in question, without also granting the nationality (if ius sanguinis is applied). The problems that arise are thus nearly always recognition issues between states.

There is a general principle of recognition of a civil status which was legally established abroad. Recognition can only be refused in cases of overriding reasons of *ordre public*. This *ordre public* principle should be limited by the best interest of the child and the right to family life. It can never be considered to be in the best interest of the child to have no parents at all instead of having parents with whom (s)he has no blood ties who want to care for her or him. This has also been stated by the European Court of Human Rights in the *Paradiso and Campanelli v. Italy case*. In that case an Italian couple had gotten a child through a surrogacy arrangement in Russia. When they brought the child to Italy the state refused to recognise the parentage ties, took the child away and placed him under guardianship. The Court stated in the Chamber judgment that Italy had failed to take the best interest of the child sufficiently into consideration when weighting it against *ordre public*. It had especially failed to recognise the de facto family ties and imposed a measure reserved only for circumstances where the child is in danger. In 2017 in its Grand Chamber judgment the Court overruled this considering that in cases where there are no biological ties there must have been a longer period of cohabitation in order to establish family life with the child compared to cases where there is a biological tie. However, one should consider that if the parents had not moved to Italy, but to another Member State where the Russian birth certificate is recognised, the child might have been stateless, but family life would have been assured. After some years of family life, Italy would have no choice but to recognise this parentage and consequently grant the nationality. Therefore, slightly paradoxically, it would be in the best interest of the child if Italy would grant the nationality immediately if the parents reside in another Member State, while it is under no such obligation if they reside in Italy. Another example where the best interest of the child should prevail is when the child from a second (polygamist) marriage is put in a worse position than a child born out of wedlock.

The problem is thus a lack of solidarity between states that do not recognise family ties legally established in another state. The parentage for the purpose of acquisition of nationality should thus be based on family law, including a more lenient approach in the private international law rules to recognition of a civil status acquired abroad.

I therefore like Bauböck's proposal of a *ius filiationis*. I see it, however, more as a change from 'law by blood', meaning parentage ties based on blood relationship, to a 'blood by law' relationship, meaning that parentage ties are seen to be established by the law. This thus means only an extension of the 'blood' definition. Bauböck's fear that this could create a situation where the child could not acquire a nationality at birth, due to the complex determination of parenthood, could technically be avoided by a pre-birth determination of parentage.

26

Ius Sanguinis Citizenship and Transmission of Privilege

Iseult Honohan

Costica Dumbrava has done a great service in stimulating us to reconsider the justification of ius sanguinis and to disaggregate its different forms.

I am sympathetic to critiques of ius sanguinis as a dominant mode of citizenship acquisition. Yet I acknowledge that the significance of family life for parents and children seems to offer some grounds for ius sanguinis citizenship – at least in a world of migration controls where citizenship is the only firm guarantee of right of entry to a country. I will argue here that to limit the extension of inherited privilege in this domain, however, this form of citizenship should be awarded provisionally.

Others here have shown convincingly that there is nothing inherently ethnically exclusive about ius sanguinis. Furthermore, it does not have to be understood in terms of bare genetic descent; so sorting out the deficiencies of current ius sanguinis provision does not depend on resolving all the issues of biological parenthood raised by the new reproductive technologies. If ius sanguinis can be detached from the strict genetic interpretation, it no longer provides a warrant for indefinite transmission across successive generations on the basis of biological descent. Thus two of the sharpest criticisms of ius sanguinis seem to have been defused.

It remains to consider in what way ius sanguinis might be necessary. On the one hand, various forms of ius soli can be seen as giving continuity of membership for the state and security for children born in the country. For those born in the country of their parents' citizenship there is little material difference between ius soli and ius sanguinis. But ius sanguinis citizenship may be seen as necessary when a child is born to parents living outside the state of their citizenship. Even if the child gains ius soli citizenship in the country in which she is born, this does not guarantee the security of the family. Focusing on what have been termed 'social parenthood', or functional parenting relationships of care, rather than simply biological descent, others here (Bauböck, Owen and Collins) have pointed to the way in which common citizenship best secures family life in allowing parents and children to stay together or move back to the country of their parent's citizenship.

What I want to address here is the further question: what forms or extent of ius sanguinis citizenship are warranted on the basis of this account?

Protecting families but not privilege

We may start from the consideration that those in the position of parents have an interest in and a particular responsibility to care for their children when young, implying a clear and fundamental interest in living together and being able to move together. These can be seen as necessary conditions for realising many of the intrinsic and non-substitutable goods of family life, or what have been called 'familial relationship goods', which include child-rearing and asymmetric intimacy.[1] These involve agent-specific obligations that can be realised only within family relationships of care and throughout childhood.[2] Thus this fundamental interest should be protected. Brighouse and Swift emphasise however, that we should not, in protecting these intrinsic goods, fail to distinguish them from other advantages external to familial relationship goods that parents can confer on their children, such as private education or concentrated wealth, which do not warrant protection. [3]

Can ius sanguinis citizenship, even if not based solely on genetic descent, support such unwarranted transmission of privilege? Citizenship grants more than the opportunity to live with and be cared for by your parents when you are a child. It provides membership of a political community and the benefits at least of entry and residence in that state, the right to participate in national elections and sometimes access to other rights. Under a regime of ius sanguinis, even understood as grounded in the rights of parents and children to share citizenship, the transmission of citizenship to children born to citizens abroad can mean that people with no connection to the country retain the benefits of citizenship, and, at the very least, can lead to a mismatch between the citizen body and the community of those who live in, and are particularly subject to, the state. Thus, life-long citizenship in the absence of real connec-

---

[1] Brighouse, H. & A. Swift (2014), *Family Values: The Ethics of Parent-Child Relationships*. Princeton: Princeton University Press.
[2] Honohan, I. (2009), 'Rethinking the claim to family re-unification', *Political Studies* 57 (4): 765–87.
[3] Brighouse, H. & A. Swift (2014), *Family Values: The Ethics of Parent-Child Relationships*. Princeton: Princeton University Press.

tions could well be seen as falling into the category of advantages that parents should not necessarily be able to convey to their children.

This is not to suggest that ius sanguinis citizenship is just a form of property or unearned privilege.[4] But there are still concerns about how to secure the legitimate interests of parents to care for their children, and of children to be protected, without justifying the transmission of privilege. My focus here is on considering how to guarantee the security of children to live and move with their parents through shared citizenship without supporting the unwarranted extension of privilege in the domain of citizenship.

This suggests the following limited justification for birthright ius sanguinis citizenship - rather than the universal child status and deferred, or provisional, ius soli citizenship that Dumbrava recommends.

Provisional ius sanguinis

First, birthright citizenship per se is justified because people need the protection of citizenship from birth.[5] Note that this is not mainly because they are children and thus innocent or particularly vulnerable (pace Harder), nor despite the fact that they are children and thus (arguably) not capable of consenting or participating politically, but while they are children, and like others, are both subject to the power of a state and in need of protection by a state. Dumbrava's proposal that children might gain a universal status of childhood and that citizenship should depend on their being able to choose, have established a connection, and developed capacities and virtues of citizenship overlooks the centrality of the legal status of citizenship to security, and the fact that this security should not be conditional on the qualities or practices of citizens.

The specific justification of ius sanguinis citizenship then derives from the way in which common citizenship between parents and children is the most secure way of guaranteeing their ability to live and move together. This can be in addition to the citizenship the child may acquire by ius soli; dual citizenship of the state of birth and that of parents' is not in itself problematic if a person has connections in both countries.

---

[4] Shachar, A. (2010), *The Birthright Lottery: Citizenship and Global Inequality*. Cambridge MA: Harvard University Press.
[5] Of course, not all birthright provisions apply from birth, rather than on the basis of birth, but they generally apply from the establishment of the fact of birth, whether in the country or to a citizen.

Because children need citizenship from birth, there is an argument for birthright citizenship; because young children need to be able to live with (and be cared for by) their parents, there is an argument for ius sanguinis citizenship at the time where this is most needed. Both of these concerns support an award of citizenship that is not deferred, but that is also not always retained indefinitely.

It may be objected that the withdrawal of citizenship should not be lightly recommended. Indeed this is true. But the strongest ground for withdrawal is the absence of any genuine link between a person and the state of citizenship. Thus, writing on birthright citizenship, Vink and De Groot offer a similar suggestion[6]: 'an alternative to limiting the transmission of citizenship at birth is the provision for the loss of citizenship if a citizen habitually resides abroad and no longer has a sufficient genuine link with the state involved'.[7] Indeed they go on to say that '[f]rom our perspective, a provision on the loss of citizenship due to the lack of a sufficient link is to be preferred to limiting the transmission of citizenship in case of birth abroad', on the grounds that this gives the child herself the opportunity to decide whether to establish that link, which thus should remain available until after majority, at the point when the child is better placed to make an independent decision.[8]

Thus, the parsimonious account of ius sanguinis defended here suggests that it should be awarded only provisionally – held through childhood, but requiring the establishment of connections of certain kinds, most clearly by a period of residence in the country of that citizenship by, or soon after, majority.[9] Confirmation would not depend on abjuring any other citizenship, as the aim would not be to avoid or reduce dual citizenship, but rather to reduce the numbers of citizens whose connections to a country are minimal or non-existent.

---

[6] Vink, M. P. & G. R. De Groot (2010), 'Birthright citizenship: trends and regulations in Europe', *EUDO Citizenship Observatory Comparative Report No. RSCAS/EUDO-CIT-Comp. 2010/8*. Florence: Robert Schuman Centre for Advanced Studies.

[7] Such provisions already exist in Belgium, Denmark, Finland, France, Iceland, the Netherlands, Norway, Sweden and Switzerland (see above n. 6). In many of these cases, however, loss of citizenship can be pre-empted by submitting a request to retain it.

[8] Above n. 6, at 12.

[9] This would not necessarily be the only basis for retaining citizenship. If, for example, the parent(s) had returned to the country of their citizenship, this also could create a connection of their potential care in old age by adult children, which might justify their retaining citizenship.

Such a conditional citizenship could take seriously the justifiable claims of families without leading to the unwarranted extension of family advantage.

27

Taking Ius Sanguinis at Face Value and its Disadvantages

Eva Ersbøll

There is no doubt that Costica Dumbrava has raised an important question about whether to abandon ius sanguinis citizenship. His arguments are that ius sanguinis is historically tainted and unfit to deal with contemporary issues such as developments in reproductive technologies and changes in family practices and norms; he also claims that ius sanguinis is normatively unnecessary, as it is possible to deliver its advantages by other means.

In my opinion, it is not time to abandon ius sanguinis, mainly because it is impossible to secure its advantages by other means. Admittedly, ius sanguinis, if taken literally, is unfit to deal with contemporary issues such as complex family arrangements involving, among other things, assisted reproduction technologies (ART). However, it seems possible to solve many problems by applying a modified principle of ius sanguinis translated into *ius filiationis*, as suggested by Rainer Bauböck and supported by most of the participants in this debate.

What matters is, as also expressed by many authors, that children from a human rights perspective need their parents' citizenship - or rather, the citizenship of their primary caretakers, be they biological parents or not.

A solution to many of the problems related to reproductive technologies has been advanced by the Council of Europe, the Committee of Ministers, in Recommendation CM/Rec(2009)13 on the nationality of children:

> Member states should apply to children their provisions on acquisition of nationality by right of blood if, as a result of a birth conceived through medically assisted reproductive techniques, a child-parent family relationship is established or recognised by law.[1]

Still, it is of course necessary to examine more closely the arguments against ius sanguinis and the practical solutions to its shortcomings.

---

[1] See the recommendation at https://wcd.coe.int/ViewDoc.jsp?id=1563529

History is not an argument

As Jannis Panagiotidis writes, history cannot justify abandoning ius sanguinis. The use of the principle may have been problematic in the past, and still, it may be all right today. Besides, as argued by Rainer Bauböck and others, it is possible to overcome ethno-nationalist dispositions by modifying a ius sanguinis principle, supplemented with ius soli and residence-based modes of acquisition.

As things stand, ius sanguinis citizenship is in my opinion irreplaceable. It provides, in accordance with the Convention on the Rights of the Child (article 7) for automatic acquisition of citizenship by birth. In addition, it seems to be one of the most simple and secure acquisition modes when it comes to protection against statelessness, as it has the ability to protect (most) children against statelessness from the very beginning of their life.

What is more, it is a central international law principle. For instance, state parties to the European Convention on Nationality are obliged to grant citizenship automatically at birth to children of (one of) their citizens (if born on their territory, cf. article 6(1)).

To me, it seems risky to jettison such an effective principle anchored in binding human rights standards.

Unity of the family

Ius sanguinis is not the only relevant principle. Others, like the unity of the family, safeguard the same interests and may be applied in a broader perspective. To mention a few situations, take acquisition by adoption and acquisition by filial transfer based on the fact that the target person is a natural, adopted or foster child of a citizen.

In addition, new automatic modes of acquisition by birth are developing. Denmark, for instance, has amended its law in 2014 to provide for automatic acquisition of citizenship by birth by children with 'a Danish father, mother or co-mother'. [2] This is an example of citizenship acquisition based on *ius filiationis* as advanced by Rainer Bauböck.

---

[2] Costica Dumbrava gives an inadequate Danish example regarding the acquisition possibilities for children born out of wedlock. For long, such children have been entitled to naturalise regardless of residence in Denmark, although until 2013, it was a requirement that the father had (shared) custody over the child. This requirement is now repealed.

As Costica Dumbrava rightly anticipatesd, a reasonable reservation in this debate has been that the main problems connected with the development of ART do not lie with ius sanguinis citizenship but with the determination of legal parentage. Such determination may take long time and involve a number of legal uncertainties and ethical dilemmas. Still, as argued by among others Rainer Bauböck and Scott Titshaw, states have in any case to fix their family law and figure out how to determine legal parenthood. Subsequently, children's right to their legal parents' citizenship may not raise major problems.

Ius filiationis benefits

Developing a *ius filiationis* principle may entail even more advantages. Among others, it may solve some of the problems originating from loss or so-called quasi-loss of citizenship following the disappearance of a family relationship.[3] Disappearance or annulment of a family relationship may have consequences for a person's citizenship based on that family relationship. Many states assume that if a person has acquired his or her citizenship through a child-parent family relationship that citizenship will be lost or even nullified if the family relationship disappears.[4] If, however, states recognise citizenship based on social rather than biological parenthood, the threat of loss or quasi-loss may not arise in the case of disappearance of a biological family relationship.

Human rights protection at this stage

According to the Council of Europe recommendations on the nationality of the child, quoted in the introduction, member states should apply the ius sanguinis principle in ART-cases where the child-parent family relationship is established or recognised by law. The crucial question is of course under which conditions the intended parents' country must recognise such a family relationship if it has been legally established abroad.

David de Groot points out that states can only refuse recognition in case of overriding reasons of *ordre public*, and he criticises states' overuse of the *ordre public* exemption for the denial of parentage. As he rightly argues, it cannot be in the best interest of the child to have no parents at all, instead of

---

[3] See more about quasi-loss of citizenship at http://www.ceps.eu/publications/ reflections-quasi-loss-nationality-comparative-international-and-european-perspective

[4] See more about quasi-loss etc. at http://www.ceps.eu/publications/ how-deal-quasi-loss-nationality-situations-learning-promising-practices

caring parents without blood ties. David de Groot refers to the 2015 judgment of European Court of Human Rights (ECtHR) in *Paradiso and Campanelli v. Italy*.[5] Here, the Court ruled that the removal of a child born to a surrogate mother and his placement in care amounted to a violation of the European Convention on Human Rights article 8 on respect for private and family life.

In 2014, the ECtHR dealt with another case concerning the effects of non-recognition of a legal parent-child relationship between children conceived through assisted reproduction, *Mennesson v. France*.[6] A French married couple had decided to undergo in vitro fertilisation using the gametes of the husband and an egg from a donor with the intention to enter into a gestational surrogacy agreement with a Californian woman. The surrogacy mother gave birth to twins, and the Californian Supreme Court ruled that the French father was their genetic father and the French mother their legal mother. France, however, refused on grounds of *ordre public* to recognise the legal parent-child relationship that was lawfully established in California as a result of the surrogacy agreement.

The ECtHR ruled that the children's right to respect for their private life – which implies that they must be able to establish the substance of their identity – was substantially affected by the non-recognition of the legal parent-child relationship between the children and the intended parents. Having regard to the consequence of the serious restriction on their identity and right to respect for their family life, the Court found that France had overstepped the permissible limits of its margin of appreciation by preventing both recognition and establishment under domestic law of the children's relationship with their biological father. Considering the importance of having regard to the child's best interest, the Court concluded that the children's right to respect for their private life had been infringed.

The Court also dealt with the children's access to citizenship as an element of their identity (see also *Genovese v Malta*).[7] Although the children's biological father was French, they faced a worrying uncertainty as to their possibilities to be recognised as French citizens. According to the Court, that uncertainty was liable to have negative repercussions on their definition of their personal identity.

---

[5] Case of *Paradiso and Campanelli v. Italy*, judgment of 27 January 2015.
[6] Case of *Mennesson v. France*, judgment of 26 September 2014 (Final).
[7] Case of *Genovese v. Malta*, judgment of 11 October 2011.

In *Mennesson*, the ECtHR's analysis took on the special dimension where one of the parents was the children's biological parent; it is, however, in my opinion difficult to imagine that the Court should reach a different conclusion in a similar case where both gametes and egg were from a donor. *Paradiso and Campanelli* may underpin this position that also appears to be supported by the fact that the Court has explicitly recognised that respect for the child's best interest must guide any decision in cases involving children's right to respect for their private life. In this context the Court has made it clear that respect for children's private life implies that they must be able to establish the substance of their identity, including the legal parent-child relationship.

Other ways to protect parent-child relationship

Costica Dumbrava argues that there are other and better ways to protect the parent-child relationship than through the same citizenship status, for instance by conferring full migration rights to children of citizens or establishing a universal status of legal childhood that protects children regardless of their or their parents' status.

I find it hard to believe that any of these means can afford children a similarly effective protection of their right to a family life with their parents in their country.

Children need their parents' citizenship, as pointed out by Rainer Bauböck and many others, because citizenship is a part of a person's identity. Where and to whom one is born are facts that feed into developing a sense of belonging. Moreover, the unity of the family in relation to citizenship secures that children can stay with their parents in their country.

The course of events that followed the independence of women in citizenship matters seems illustrative. In Denmark for instance, when married women gained independence in citizenship matters in 1950, it was a major concern that in mixed marriages, where the spouses had different citizenship, the woman might lose her unconditional right to stay in her husband's country. The legislator assumed that the aliens' law would be administered in such a way that a wife would not be separated from her husband unless a pressing social need necessitated the separation.[8] Things have, however, developed differently. Nowadays, foreigners married to Danish citizens are subject to the same requirements for family reunification as foreign couples.

---

[8] See the Danish citizenship report at http://cadmus.eui.eu/bitstream/handle/1814/36504/EUDO_CIT_CR_2015_14_Denmark.pdf?sequence=1

Thus, a foreign spouse may be expelled if for instance her Danish husband has received cash benefits within the last three years before a residence permit could be granted; notably, this may apply regardless of whether the couple has a child with Danish citizenship.

A need for international guidelines on legal recognition of parenthood

As already mentioned, there is no doubt that Costica Dumbrava has raised an important discussion about continuous application of ius sanguinis citizenship. While there seems to be little support for abandoning the ius sanguinis principle, there seems to be almost unanimous support for modifying and modernising it. As recommended by the Council of Europe, states should apply to children conceived through medically assisted reproductive techniques their provisions on ius sanguinis acquisition of citizenship.

The problem remains that states must establish or recognise the child-parent family relationship by law, and often, two states with different approaches are involved in the recognition procedure. Therefore, *ordre public* considerations may arise as demonstrated in many of the concrete cases mentioned in this Citizenship Forum. In order to achieve consensus about the recognition of a parent-child family relationship in the best interest of the child, states should engage in international cooperation with a view to adopting common guidelines – as they have done in adoption matters.

28

Limiting the Scope of Ius Sanguinis

Ana Tanasoca

In an article published in 1987 Joseph Carens famously remarked that '[c]itizenship in Western liberal democracies is the modern equivalent of feudal privilege – an inherited status that greatly enhances one's life chances. Like feudal birthright privileges, restrictive citizenship is hard to justify when one thinks about it closely'.[1] Some 30 years after, he himself offers a justification of birthright citizenship, a change of heart and mind that he partly explains by the following: 'I thought that my open borders argument was getting at an important truth. At the same time, I recognised that it was not a practical proposal and that it did not provide much guidance for actual policy issues…'; 'In thinking about what to do in a particular situation, we have to consider questions of priority and questions of political feasibility, among other factors. One cannot move always from principles to a plan of action'.[2] Yet succumbing too much to such feasibility constraints, to use a popular term in the field, is dangerous. Moral (political) theorising should not be too tightly hemmed in by empirical facts. Rather it should be the other way around, insofar as our moral and political theory aims to tell us what existing empirical facts we should strive to change or overcome.

That is why Costica Dumbrava's critique of the ius sanguinis principle of citizenship ascription is, in a way, a much-needed intervention.[3] While I overall agree with Dumbrava's argument that ius sanguinis is unable to cope with the diversification of family structures and is not that morally appealing to begin with, I disagree with him on the details. I disagree especially with his background assumption that family ties (although not exclusively genetic, as it is presently the case) must play a salient role in the distribution of citizenship – although in the second part of this contribution I do offer a

---

[1] Carens, J. (1987), 'Aliens and citizens: the case for open borders', *Review of Politics* 49 (2): 251–73.
[2] Carens, J. (2013), *The Ethics of Immigration*. Oxford: Oxford University Press, x, 3.
[3] I say 'in a way' because he also relies heavily on empirical facts when arguing against ius sanguinis.

potential defence of his view against what is probably the strongest objection to his argument, which is that the abolishment of ius sanguinis would split families apart.

The main question is: Why should we insist on ius sanguinis except because it would ensure that nobody is stateless, that is, that everyone's human right to citizenship is satisfied? And insofar as statelessness can be equally avoided via ius soli, why should blood ties create an entitlement to citizenship?

The problem of making citizenship dependent on family ties

Dumbrava notices that ius sanguinis is unable to cope with the increased diversification of family structures made possible by the assisted reproduction technologies (ART). Yet there are solutions to that problem.

One would be, as Scott Titshaw notices, to reform family laws as to recognise diverse forms of parentage. Another one would be to replace ius sanguinis with *ius filiationis*, as Rainer Bauböck proposes. If the purpose of upholding ius sanguinis citizenship is to recognise and protect the family, we should replace it with more reliable indicator(s) of parenthood in the case where parenthood is no longer uniquely a matter of biology. As Kerry Abrams argues, the recognition of parenthood now requires 'going beyond the moment of birth'.

Notice, however, were multiple indicators of parenthood to be accepted, those individuals born via ART might be entitled to multiple citizenships. They might, for example, be entitled to the citizenship of the egg donor or the sperm donor or the surrogate mother, as well as to the citizenship of those who intend to raise the child. Such a situation may be deemed problematic in various respects: first because it would create great inequalities; second, because it would end up trivializing citizenship if all types of parenthood (e.g., the relationships the surrogate mother, the egg donor or the sperm donor, and the intended parents have with the child) were to be treated as equally morally relevant and therefore worthy of state recognition.

Dumbrava also bemoans ius sanguinis as failing to capture the political function of citizenship. If we grant citizenship to the children of citizens because we expect such children to develop the attitudes and skills required for political participation in their parents' state, why not wait to confer citizenship until these attitudes and skills are actually confirmed? And what if they never developed these skills and attitudes? Should people be deprived of their birthright citizenship altogether, or perhaps only of their political rights? Besides, while we might have a clear idea of what skills (e.g., reading and writing to enable voting) citizenship requires, what can we say of the attitudes citizens should display? Should apathetic voters be stripped of their political rights for failing to display the right attitude towards their right to vote? According to Dumbrava's reasoning, perhaps they should.

But the main problem both with Dumbrava's critique and the other contributors' accounts is that they conceive of citizenship as primarily reflecting a bond (genetic or affective or intentional) between two individuals – the parent and the child – and not as a bond between an individual and a state, or an individual and a political community. Such accounts overlook the political nature and function of citizenship and are also likely to leave us with a very limited, rigid, and exclusionary conception of the demos, one that is at the same time unjust and inefficient. As Rainer Bauböck put it elsewhere, '[n]ormative principles for membership must instead lead to boundaries that avoid both under- und over- inclusiveness',[4] particularly in the context of increased global mobility.

In his contribution to this Forum, however, Bauböck argues that birthright citizenship creates a 'quasi-natural equality of status' among those entitled to it. He represents it as avoiding divisions, by making citizenship part of people's unchosen and permanent personal features, namely, where and to whom one is born.[5] Yet as such birthright creates exclusion and inequality between those entitled and those unentitled that can be hard to justify or overcome, as Lois Harder rightly notices. Why should the son of a citizen of state *A* be entitled to citizenship in that state, but not a regular immigrant residing for years in state *A*, paying taxes there and having virtually all of his interests deeply affected by the institutions of state *A*? While the first has unconditional and automatic access to citizenship – a right to citizenship in virtue of his blood ties to another citizen – the second has to apply for naturalisation, which is subject to the state's discretionary powers. That is, his residence in that state, contributions to the community, or his interests being affected by that state's institutions do not automatically ground any right to citizenship for him in the same way blood ties do for the citizens' progeny.

---

[4] Bauböck, R. (2015), 'Morphing the demos into its right shape. Normative principles for enfranchising resident aliens and expatriate citizens', *Democratization* 22 (5): 820–39.

[5] This last bit is problematic in itself. Tying citizenship – that has an immense influence on individuals' life opportunities and welfare – to underserved and permanent personal features like ancestry is after all morally problematic even if practically convenient for states.

Why should the boundaries of the demos be defined by family ties, rather than by social or political kinship? By ascribing citizenship on the basis of blood ties we conceive of political communities as big extended families rather than communities gathered around common interests, values, and goals. Such a conception of the demos is disrespectful of individual consent (no one consents to being born, to having these parents rather than others, or to the colour of their passport). It attaches too much value to contingencies and too little value to individual choices. A political community based on ancestry is, after all, just an overinflated dynasty.

Limiting the scope of ius sanguinis

While abolishing ius sanguinis might be a good idea, we could nonetheless be worried that the transition costs would outweigh potential benefits. After all, most families today are still founded on blood ties. Abolishing ius sanguinis altogether could create situations where parents and children are not citizens of the same state. Such policy, it is argued by several contributors, would have the disruptive effect of potentially separating families, preventing parents from discharging their parental duties, and leaving children deprived of the care they are entitled to. (Of course, nothing prevents parents from applying for a visa or for citizenship if they wish to reside or share a citizenship with their progeny; but let us assume that the parents do not have the means to do that, or that even doing that would not guarantee that they can be reunited with their child immediately as we would wish.) This is, I think, the strongest argument against Dumbrava's proposal.

One solution would be, of course, to replace ius sanguinis with another principle for citizenship allocation, perhaps affected interests or perhaps *ius domicilii*. As children's and parents' interests are interdependent, the affected interests principle would ensure that children and parents are members of the same state. So would *ius domicilii*, at least in cases where parents and children are currently domiciled in the same state (although it would provide no citizenship-based grounds for family reunion, in cases where they are not).

My proposal, however, takes a different tack. Notice that in a world with genuinely open borders we need not be worried that parents and children would be separated if they are citizens of different states. The solution I propose would therefore be to limit the scope of ius sanguinis – that is distribute some, but not all rights traditionally associated with citizenship, on the basis of ius sanguinis. This would be an appealing compromise, insofar as some of us may think citizenship should not be distributed on the basis of blood ties, while nonetheless accepting that blood ties are one (albeit not the only) relevant ground for the distribution of some categories of rights.

As Bauböck notices in his contribution, immigrant minors who are EU citizens have a 'right to stay' that protects their primary caregivers from deportation. Yet, most likely, this policy is a recognition of an entitlement to care that the child has – not a recognition of a right the parents have to stay strictly in virtue of their blood ties to the child. Blood ties may simply serve as the operational indicator of the primary caregivers.

My preferred solution, however, would entitle a person to the limited enjoyment of some rights in a state, on the basis of having blood ties to someone who is already a citizen of that state. I primarily have in view, among that limited subset of rights, the right to enter and leave the state and the right of residence. By 'limited' I also mean that the enjoyment of these rights, purely on the basis of ius sanguinis, should be time-constrained. [6]

Take the case of minors having a different citizenship from their parents. My proposal would be: either the parents should be granted extensive residence rights, until the minor reaches adulthood as in the case above; or else the minor should be granted these rights, provided the parents wish to remain in their country of citizenship. Consider the case of a couple, both citizens of state *A*, who move to state *B* and give birth there to a child, who becomes via ius soli citizen of *B*. Under my proposal, the parents would be automatically entitled to residence in state *B* until the child is 18, provided the family decides to reside in state *B*; equally, the child would be automatically entitled to reside in state *A* until 18 if the family decides to reside there.

Things would be different in the case of adults. Say my mother and I are citizens of different countries, she of state *A* and I of state *B*. Under my proposal, I as an adult would not be entitled to all the current rights of citizenship in state *A* on the basis of ius sanguinis. Still, I may nonetheless be automatically entitled on the same ground to a right to freely enter state *A* and reside there for a limited period of time (for example, 1 month). That would allow me to visit and spend time with my mother, preserving my family ties intact and allowing me to discharge whatever ordinary duties I have towards family members. But what if my mother becomes frail or ill,

---

[6] In the same vein, Iseult Honohan proposes in her contribution to this debate that minors born in another states other than that of their parents should also be entitled to their parents' citizenship but only until they reach adulthood; from then on, they can lose this citizenship if they do not continue residing in the country of parental citizenship. This would be another way of limiting ius sanguinis entitlements.

and I become her main caregiver and thus need to spend more than one month in state *A*? If the circumstances require it, I should be able to petition for my right to remain to be extended, and that petition should be automatically granted so long as authorities are satisfied that the requisite circumstances really do prevail. The period for which one can enjoy such rights, and the categories of rights one enjoys, might be extendable in this way. Alternatively, of course, I could bring my mother to reside with me in state *B* on a (elderly) dependent visa.

Under my proposal, there would thus be a limit to what one is entitled to under ius sanguinis alone. We should not think of the distribution of citizenship rights as an all-or-nothing affair. Among the many component rights currently associated with citizenship, different rights can and should be distributed separately according to different criteria. By the same token, many different criteria can serve as a legitimate ground for the distribution of any one of those constituent rights.

29

The Right to a Suitable Citizenship at Birth: A Study of Naturalisation Debates

Katja Swider and Caia Vlieks

Citizenship has a political and a legal dimension. In his opening contribution, Costica Dumbrava only marginally addresses the legal dimension of citizenship, acknowledging its importance, but suggesting that it is replaceable with alternative arrangements, such as a universal status for children. Maybe he is right in his priorities; maybe citizenship status should primarily be reserved for the purpose of fostering a political community. But in reality much legal baggage is attached to citizenship, and one cannot simply shake it off, even if this appears normatively attractive. In a way, the whole human rights movement can be seen as an effort to separate access to legal rights from possessing a status of political membership, and this attempt has not reached its goal (yet). As Jannis Panagiotidis points out, 'most so-called human rights are in fact citizens' rights'. Citizenship is still the 'right to have rights'. Avoidance of statelessness is therefore not just a legal whim; it is a human rights failsafe mechanism.

In our contribution we start from the assumption that leaving anyone, including (and especially) children, without a citizenship for any significant period of time is not an option due to the essential legal rights that are attached to the status of national citizenship. The question therefore is not whether children should acquire a citizenship at birth, but which citizenship they should acquire at birth. Should it be the citizenship of their parents? And if not, what alternatives to birthright citizenship arrangements are adequate?

While we consider attribution of citizenship at birth to be necessary, we also maintain that it is inherently unfair, regardless of what mechanisms of attribution are relied upon. There is nothing fair about attaching the fate of a child to one state, when states differ so tremendously in their ability (and willingness) to provide access to basic rights, such as education, healthcare, physical safety and pursuit of happiness for their minor citizens. Rainer Bauböck shifts attention from this unfairness by suggesting that 'we have to address the causes of global inequality directly' instead of criticising the contingencies of birthright citizenship. However, we should not forget that this discussion takes place largely among the privileged 'winners' of the 'birthright lottery'.[1] There is no doubt that global inequalities need to be addressed, but is it morally justifiable to suggest to the 'losers' of the birthright lottery to wait for global equality?

If fairness in birthright citizenship cannot be achieved and leaving children without any citizenship is unacceptable, what is the normative ideal that we could strive towards in attributing citizenship at birth? As Lois Harder correctly argues here, rules about birthright attribution of citizenship are as politically charged as rules about acquiring and losing a nationality during adulthood, even though the former are not as much part of the public debate. According to Harder, '[t]he magical power of birthright citizenship is that it makes it possible for us to know and rehearse [politically charged] rules while simultaneously making birthright seem straightforward, static and apolitical'. Can we reverse this logic, and perhaps also learn from the extensively politicised discourse on migrants' rights to naturalisation in order to improve birthright citizenship rules?

In particular, we suggest applying the concept of appropriate citizenship to strengthen the normative foundation of birthright citizenship attribution. This notion is based on the ideas of Ernst Hirsch Ballin, who advocates 'a citizenship that is appropriate to everyone's life situation, where he or she is at home – which can change during the course of a person's life: a natural right to be recognized as a citizen, born free'.[2] He believes that this type of citizenship and citizens' rights can overcome the existing gap between 'the universality of human rights' and 'the changing political and social settings of people's lives'.[3] Drawing on that, we feel that appropriate citizenship, even when acquired at birth, could do the same. Appropriate citizenship is of course a highly subjective concept, the interpretation of which would be dependent on numerous cultural and specific national legal factors. Ensuring that birthright citizenship is appropriate would imply a case-by-case evaluation of the individual situation of each new-born, a process which in most cases would be as simple as the registration of birth, but in some cases would require a complex investigation to be conducted in a very brief period of time.

---

[1] Shachar, A. (2009), *The Birthright Lottery: Citizenship and Global Inequality.* Cambridge, MA: Harvard University Press.
[2] Hirsch Ballin, E. (2014), *Citizens' Rights and the Right to Be a Citizen.* Nijhoff: Brill, 145.
[3] Ibid. 144.

While perhaps logistically counter-intuitive, introducing the normative standard of appropriateness into the attribution of citizenship at birth is not more complex than trying to solve ad hoc 'hard cases' of citizenship within the traditional logic of ius sanguinis versus ius soli. This complexity of some birthright citizenship cases has been extensively discussed in the contributions by Dumbrava and Scott Titshaw. Requiring that birthright citizenship is appropriate emphasises the importance of (meaningful) ties[4] of a person (including a child) to a country, and thus incorporates the idea of *ius nexi* discussed by David Owen. With the criterion of appropriateness we accept that birthright citizenship is a political issue, not a contingent biological fact of life, and therefore should be based in a reasoned decision-making process and subjected to normative criticism.

The requirement that citizenship acquired at birth needs to be appropriate is far from being precise. However, we believe that a certain amount of flexibility is necessary in order to ensure that attribution of citizenship at birth has a normative foundation in each individual case. The exact modes of implementation of the criterion of appropriateness would need to be developed within the individual legal systems, but important factors to be considered include the ones that have been discussed elaborately in this Forum discussion:

- the nationalities of the persons that are expected to care for the child (biological, social or functional parents or otherwise, thus including and reinforcing the *ius filiationis* proposal put forward by Bauböck);
- the country where the child is born;
- the country where the child is expected to build his or her future, receive education and effectuate his or her rights as a citizen;
- the necessity of ensuring that at least one nationality is acquired and that the best interests of the child are safeguarded (in line with the almost universally ratified Convention on the Rights of the Child).[5]

It is not always easy to determine all the relevant criteria for establishing appropriateness of citizenship with a high degree of certainty. Kerry Abrams, for example, identifies some possible obstacles when discussing Bauböck's *ius filiationis* proposal, namely that courts sometimes cannot determine who will ultimately be the parent that is truly (legally) responsible for the child. However, since the proposal of appropriate nationality is based on multiple relevant factors rather than a single one, the risks associated with the inability

---

[4] Or 'genuine connection(s)', see also *Nottebohm (Liechtenstein v Guatemala) ICJ Reports* 1955, p. 4; General List, No 18.
[5] See Articles 3(1) and 7 of the Convention on the Rights of the Child.

to assess some of the factors are ameliorated by the availability of other factors that can compensate for uncertainties.

Finally, we would like to emphasize that Hirsch Ballin's ideas and the concept of appropriate nationality that we have introduced are compatible with having multiple nationalities, as well as changing one's nationality over the course of one's life. It is appropriate to enable children, as well as adults, to acquire a new nationality to reflect the changes in their personal circumstances. When attributing an appropriate nationality at birth to a child, states therefore do not need to embark on the impossible task of predicting the future.

30

Concluding Remarks

Costica Dumbrava

This has been a fascinating debate that succeeded in unravelling some of the major issues about the past, present and future of ius sanguinis citizenship. I was delighted to see that many of the contributors shared my concerns about the failings of the current system of transmission of citizenship from parent to child. I learned a great deal from reading the various reactions to my deliberately provocative propositions. With these concluding remarks, I use the privilege of the last word to engage with several key points emerging from the debate and to clarify and, as much as possible, elaborate my position. However, I am hopeful that this debate does not finish here and I look forward to continuing through other ventures.

How ethnic is ius sanguinis and why does it matter?

I think we are in agreement that ius sanguinis is not inherently ethnic and that it can take on ethnic connotations depending on particular historical and policy contexts. The apple of discord is whether the gravity of such occurrences recommends the abolishment of ius sanguinis. I concede that empirical evidence is not conclusive for dismissing the principle of ius sanguinis. However, I caution that we should not underestimate the dangers of ethnonationalist instrumental uses of ius sanguinis.

Panagiotidis explains clearly the difference between legal descent (descent from a citizen) and ethnic descent (descent from a non-citizen of a particular ethnicity) and shows that the objection about the ethnic character of ius sanguinis is founded on a big conceptual confusion. While I agree that ius sanguinis is conceptually distinct from ethnic or racial descent, I would hesitate to say that the two have 'nothing to do' with one another. Unfortunately, it is not only distracted scholars that make this confusion. The ambiguity between legal and ethnic descent is often present in legal practices and political discourses about birthright citizenship. In my initial contribution I mentioned co-ethnic citizenship because these policies frequently rely on the ambivalence between legal and ethnic descent. For example, legal criteria of descent from citizens (or from former citizens or from former citizens of a former part of a country, etc.) are often used as a smoke screen for selecting future citizens according to (perceived) ethnic descent. It matters less that these policies rarely achieve the goal of ethnic selectivity as long as the very statement of the commitment to include co-ethnics is likely to bring significant political and ideological gains. As Decimo and Harder argue, despite being a technical and legalistic principle, ius sanguinis carries significant ideological connotations, among which the myth of commonality of blood or ethnic descent is often prevalent.

I also doubt that the ethnonationalist uses of ius sanguinis are only a matter of the past and I am not convinced that they are unlikely to be 'used like that in the future' (Panagiotidis). What else if not the fear of ethno-national extinction drove Latvia and Estonia in 1990 to reinstate their pre-war citizenship laws and to apply ius sanguinis retrospectively back to pre-1940 citizens? It is besides the point that not all newly recognised citizens were ethnic Latvians or Estonians (as not all of the pre-war citizens were). The political-nationalist gains obtained from the perception that the overwhelming majority of them were co-ethnics and from the symbolic reinstatement of the original national citizenry were significant. The same can be said about the Romanian policy to restore citizenship to all those who lost Romanian citizenship independently of their will. In this case, ius sanguinis has been used to trace descendants of citizens several generations back in view of recovering the 'national stock' lost with the territorial changes during WWII.

It is true, as Bauböck and Collins rightly point out, that both ius sanguinis and ius soli (and combinations thereof) can have either emancipatory or exclusionary implications, depending on the context. Since empirical facts do not translate well into normative arguments (Tanasoca), I think that wrestling over empirical evidence about the positive or negative effects of ius sanguinis is not going to help us settle the normative questions about the justification of the principle of ius sanguinis. If we have strong moral reasons for maintaining ius sanguinis, we should endorse it regardless of how wrong it is applied in practice and how often this happens. Of course, we should adjust the ways in which to implement a morally justified principle to match changing empirical circumstances. Yet, the prior question is whether ius sanguinis can be morally justified as a principle of admission to citizenship.

Why bother fixing ius sanguinis?

Many contributors to this debate grant that ius sanguinis is a morally justified principle and propose ways to reform the ways in which we implement it. Bauböck, Ersbøll and Abrams argue that the ethno-nationalist disposition of ius sanguinis can be counterbalanced through adopting supplementary ius soli and residence-based naturalisation. Bauböck, Titshaw, Abrams and De Groot discuss possibilities of rethinking legal parentage in order to accommodate complex cases of citizenship determination in the context of ART birth.

There is a broad consensus that ius sanguinis should be reformed, albeit disagreements prevail as to how and by whom. Bauböck's proposals of *ius filiationis*, which reinterprets legal parenthood as a combination of genetic and social parenthood, is cheered by some but welcomed with scepticism by others. Titshaw and Collins, for example, worry that *ius filiationis* will not eliminate the uncertainty related to the determination of legal parentage and that it may also encourage abuse. Another contention is about the administrative level at which decisions about ius sanguinis should be taken. Writing in the context of the US federal system, Titshaw argues that fixing the family law will solve many problems related to legal parentage and therefore to ius sanguinis citizenship. Yet, Collins fears that leaving citizenship determination to those applying the family law will unwarrantedly expose citizenship to parochial concerns (e.g. immigration control). I think this is an important point, which we should consider beyond the level of administrative decision-making. I argue that the recognition of legal parentage and the determination of citizenship should not only be implemented through two separate procedures, but also regarded as two normative processes driven by distinct principles. While I appreciate the practical importance of the proposals for reforming ius sanguinis, I am not convinced that the strategy of fixing legal parentage addresses the prior and more fundamental question about the moral justification of ius sanguinis as a principle of admission to citizenship.

It is surprising to me that in a debate about ius sanguinis citizenship so little is being said about citizenship. Most contributors seem to take for granted the normative link between parentage and citizenship and to give priority to instrumental arguments over normative ones. Let me explain this point by discussing three key arguments in support of ius sanguinis: (1) ius sanguinis protects children against statelessness; (2) ius sanguinis enables and protects family life; and (3) ius sanguinis expresses the social identity of the child.

Preventing statelessness

There is a wide consensus in the debate that children need (at least one) citizenship from birth and that ius sanguinis provides the 'most simple and secure' means (Ersbøll) to prevent statelessness. This view is accepted even by those who argue that birthright citizenship is ultimately an unfair arrangement (Swider and Vlieks). It is true that in today' world the possession of the legal status of citizenship (aka nationality) predetermines access to a set of important rights and privileges, in the absence of which a person's life is significantly constrained. It is also true that, despite a number of complications caused by changing family patterns and the spread of assisted reproductive technologies, ius sanguinis still provides a relatively simple solution to tackle statelessness at birth. However, one can think of other ways to prevent statelessness that are equally convenient, as well as better justified normatively.

The problem of statelessness could be arguably solved by a system of generalised unconditional ius soli or by a citizenship lottery in which newborns are assigned randomly the citizenship of a state. These alternatives remove the uncertainties associated with the determination of legal parenthood for the purpose of ius sanguinis. However, convenience alone does not count for normative justification. Against the citizenship lottery suggestion, defenders of ius sanguinis would probably insist that new-borns should receive the citizenship of 'their' parents. Notice that this is not an argument about convenience anymore but one about the importance of a shared citizenship between parents and children. But nothing in the argument about avoiding statelessness requires shared citizenship between parents and their children. To avoid statelessness at birth (in the absence of ius soli), it is sufficient that a child receives one citizenship from either of the parents. This means that in international families only one parent needs to transmit citizenship to the child and, if a parent has multiple citizenships, he or she needs to transfer only one these citizenships to the child. The argument about avoiding statelessness does not offer any guidance as to which citizenship should be shared between parents and children and why.

Alternative solutions based on ius soli elements may offer better normative justifications. I argued elsewhere that states have a collective duty to grant access to a fundamental status of legal protection (nationality) to those born and living in their jurisdiction due to states' joint participation in an international system that leaves individuals no real possibility of opting out, i.e. to establish a new citizenship or to remain stateless. My point here is not that the parent-child relationship has no normative implications for citizenship; it is merely that the argument about avoiding statelessness is unable to bring such normative concerns to the surface.

Protecting family life

The second major argument in defence of ius sanguinis is that the (automatic and immediate) transmission of citizenship from parent to child enables and protects family life. In the absence of a shared citizenship between parents and children, it is feared, family life would be severely disrupted as family members risk being separated from one another by borders and immigration restrictions. I do not contest that family life deserves special protection and that the legal recognition of parent-child relationship provides 'critical protection for their [children's] wellbeing' (Abrams). However, I am not convinced that the automatic and immediate transfer of citizenship from parent to child is a major normative prerequisite of family life.

It appears to me that the overwhelming majority of contributors subscribe to an indirect and instrumental defence of ius sanguinis. The biggest concern is about securing joint migration rights for family members, which are instrumental for family life. De Groot mentions two other important citizenship privileges, i.e. diplomatic and consular protection and political participation, but surrenders quickly to the concern about migration rights. The prevailing argument in these interventions is not so much a defence of ius sanguinis citizenship but a defence of *ius migrationis sanguine* – the right to migrate in virtue of a blood relationship. The downside of linking too tightly ius sanguinis to family migration rights is that the argument only holds as long as migration rights are strictly determined by citizenship status and as long as there are no other ways to secure migration rights for family members apart from ius sanguinis. Hence in a world of (more) open borders, where children would not be separated from their parents or siblings by migration restrictions, ius sanguinis citizenship loses its importance. However, a system of generalised family migration policies, such as the one suggested by Tanasoca, could provide the 'permanence and stability' (Titshaw) required for achieving meaningful family life in the absence of ius sanguinis citizenship.

Expressing social identity

Another intriguing argument in defence of ius sanguinis rests on the idea that (birthright) citizenship is an important part of a child's social identity. According to the judgement of the European Court of Human Right in the case *Genovese v Malta*, the failure to acquire a particular citizenship at birth is likely to affect negatively the identity of the child. I distinguish two versions of this argument: a softer/instrumental version, according to which the ius sanguinis principle 'makes citizenship a part of citizens' personal identities that they are like to accept' (Bauböck); and a harder/essentialist version, for which the ius sanguinis principle recognises and confirms the (inherited) identity of the child.

The essentialist version of the argument about a child's social identity can be easily dismissed by pointing at the fact that citizenship is a contingent social and legal convention rather than a mechanism that confirms prior genetic, ethnic or cultural identities. Recall that in the *Genovese* case the Court used this argument in connection with the principle of non-discrimination. The failure to acquire citizenship via ius sanguinis by a child born out of wedlock will affect negatively his or her social identity because children born in wedlock do not face similar restrictions of ius sanguinis as children born out of wedlock. The situation can be remedied not only by removing the discriminatory treatment in the application of ius sanguinis but also by abolishing ius sanguinis altogether. The instrumental version of the identity argument is more interesting, not least because it supports our intuition that (birthright) citizens are likely to feel attached to their country of birth. However, this is valid for both ius sanguinis and ius soli, so the instrumental argument cannot show why we should preserve ius sanguinis or why we should chose one form of birthright citizenship over another.

Long-lasting institutions usually shape people's attitudes and generate attachments and identities. They acquire the kind of 'quasi-naturalness' that Bauböck ascribes to birthright citizenship. However, the test of time and familiarity is not a valid moral test because bad institutions can also acquire that kind of 'magical power' (Harder). We ought to question the moral foundations of deeply rooted institutions such as birthright citizenship especially because they are so popular and because they shape our identity.

Opportunities for intergenerational membership

There are several arguments in the debate that deal more seriously with normative aspects of ius sanguinis citizenship. I agree with Owen that the principle of *ius nexi* or genuine connection is the best we have for determining access to citizenship and that this general principle can be served by different policy arrangements, including some form of qualified ius sanguinis. I assume that the principle of 'appropriate citizenship' defended by Swider and Vlieks goes along the same path. My concern with their proposal is that allowing for 'a case-by-case evaluation of the individual situation of each newborn' (Swider and Vlieks) might not serve well the commitment to avoid statelessness, which seems essential to the principle of appropriate citizenship.

Honohan endorses the principle of genuine connection and defends a limited version of ius sanguinis by arguing for imposing restrictions to the intergenerational transmission of citizenship. She endorses ius sanguinis but proposes that citizenship be withdrawn from (adult) citizens who fail to develop a genuine link with the country. I am sympathetic to this proposal but I am not fully convinced about its underpinning justification. Honohan's main objection to ius sanguinis, which is shared by Decimo and Harder, is that the unconditional acquisition of citizenship by children from their parents can amount to an unfair privilege. Although I acknowledge the implications of citizenship policies in today's world characterised by sharp economic inequalities, I think that the concern with economic privilege should be disconnected from the concern about admission to citizenship. I agree with Bauböck that there are more appropriate means to fight global inequality and injustice than redistributing citizenship (e.g. economic redistribution, fairer migration policies).

Honohan rightly argues that citizenship 'provides membership of a political community' but she does not explain why children should be admitted in the political community of their parents rather than in another (e.g. the best political community). My answer is that both parents and children have an interest in the continued participation to a particular intergenerational political project. This interest can be served through providing opportunities for intergenerational membership in the form of provisional ius sanguinis. The citizenship acquired provisionally at birth should be withdrawn upon majority from those (provisional) citizens who do not have a genuine link with the country. However, if a person fails to prove a genuine link with at least one country, his or her provisional citizenship should still be extended but only in the form of formal legal membership, i.e. without political rights.

Notice that the argument for intergenerational provisional citizenship stands even after we solve the problems related to the recognition of parenthood and to migration restriction for family members. Bauböck points at this when talking about the 'signalling effects of birthright citizenship' but his argument slides into an instrumental and collectivist defence of birthright citizenship. My argument for intergenerational citizenship puts emphasis on the individual interests in continued political membership. Incidentally, this solution is also likely to have positive implications for the political community as a whole, e.g. by fostering 'a sense of responsibility towards the common good and future generations' (Bauböck). I am sympathetic to

Harder's idea of political membership as a 'lively on-going process of negotiation in which everyone has a stake'. However, I disagree that admission to political membership should be entirely up to negotiation, as I maintain that there are certain concerns that demand inclusion regardless of people's preferences and abilities. I also no not think that political membership should be 'limited by our mortality' (Harder). While I reject continuation based on genetic, ethnic and racial traits or simply convenience, I argue that there should be opportunities for intergenerational political continuity, which can be provided through provisional ius sanguinis.

It is beyond dispute that any attempt to dislodge a deeply rooted and widespread institution such as ius sanguinis is bound to pose serious practical challenges. However, if one has compelling moral reasons for dismantling such an institution, one ought to work towards this end. Babies are born into a physical world and from actual bodies but they are not naturally born into families and citizenship. The latter are social conventions that demand our acceptance when they are justified and our courage to change and replace them when they are not. To my critics who worried that abolishing ius sanguinis amounts to throwing out the baby with the dirty bathwater I reply that we should not put the baby in the dirty bathwater in the first place.

Part III: Revisiting the Concept of Banishment

Abstract

There is a growing trend in Europe and North America of using denationalisation of citizens as a counter-terrorism strategy. The deprivation of citizenship status, alongside passport revocation, and denial of re-admission to citizens returning from abroad, manifest the securitisation of citizenship. Britain leads in citizenship deprivation, but in 2014 Canada passed new citizenship-stripping legislation and France's Conseil Constitutionnel recently upheld denaturalisation of dual citizens convicted of terrorism-related offences. In the wake of the on-going crisis in Iraq and Syria, assorted legislators in Austria, Australia, the Netherlands, and the United States have expressed interest in enacting (or reviving) similar legislation. The contributors to the Forum Debate consider the normative justification for citizenship deprivation from a variety of disciplinary perspectives. There is relatively little disagreement among commentators about the limited instrumental value of citizenship revocation in enhancing national security, and more diversity in viewpoint about its significance for citizenship itself. The contributors discuss the characterisation of citizenship as right versus privilege, the relevance of statelessness and dual nationality, the relative merits of citizenship versus human rights as normative framework, and the expansiveness of banishment itself as a concept.

Keywords

Denationalisation · Deprivation · Citizenship · Terrorism · Banishment · Exile

31

Impact of the New Denationalisation Policies on Citizenship

Audrey Macklin

After decades in exile, banishment is back. Britain resuscitated the practice as part of its counter-terrorism strategy in the wake of the 9/11 and 7/11 terrorist attacks in New York, Washington and London. Canada followed suit with the 2014 Strengthening Canadian Citizenship Act.[1] As we enter the third decade of the 21st century, assorted legislators in Austria, Australia, Netherlands, and the United States expressed interest in enacting, reviving, or extending citizenship stripping laws.[2]

From antiquity to the late 20th century, denationalisation was a tool used by states to rid themselves of political dissidents, convicted criminals and ethnic, religious or racial minorities. The latest target of denationalisation is the convicted terrorist, or the suspected terrorist, or the potential terrorist, or maybe the associate of a terrorist. He is virtually always Muslim and male.

Citizenship-stripping is sometimes defended in the name of strengthening citizenship, but it does precisely the opposite. The defining feature of contemporary legal citizenship is that it is secure. Making legal citizenship contingent on performance demotes citizenship to another category of permanent residence. Citizenship revocation thus weakens citizenship itself. It is an illegitimate form of punishment and it serves no practical purpose.

---

[1] The Canadian legislation was subject to constitutional challenge following completion of this article. It was repealed by a new government in 2017 before the legality of hte legislation was determined and beforeany revocations went into effect.
[2] For a more elaborate comparative analysis of recent legislative developments in the United Kingdom, Canada and the US, see Macklin, A. (2014), 'Citizenship Revocation, the Privilege to Have Rights and the Production of the Alien', *Queens Law Journal* 40 (1): 1–54.

Denationalisation refers to involuntary loss of citizenship.[3] Denaturalisation is a subset of denationalisation, and applies selectively to those not born into citizenship via ius soli or ius sanguinis. The most common basis for denaturalisation is fraud or misrepresentation in the acquisition of citizenship. The operative premise is that had the material facts been known at the relevant time, the state would not have conferred citizenship in the first place. Denaturalisation for fraud simply annuls the erroneously conferred citizenship and restores the *status quo ante*.[4]

My remarks focus exclusively on denationalisation for allegedly disloyal conduct by a citizen, while a citizen. In its present incarnation, citizenship revocation is best understood as a technique for extending the functionality of immigration law in counter-terrorism. Since 2001, states have turned to deportation to resolve threats to national security by displacing the embodied threat to the country of nationality. But deporting one's own citizens is exile, and exile extinguishes a singular right of citizenship, namely the right to enter and to remain. Citizenship revocation circumvents that problem by introducing the two-step exile: first, strip citizenship; second, deport the newly minted alien.

The British Nationality Act authorises the Secretary of State for Home Affairs (Home Secretary) to deprive a person of British citizenship where she 'is satisfied that deprivation is conducive to the public good.' That happens to be the same low and vague standard for depriving a person of permanent resident status (indefinite leave to remain), which provides one illustration of the downgrading of citizenship. In Canada, the executive power to revoke citizenship depends on a criminal conviction for a listed

---

[3] Before the widespread acceptance of dual citizenship, acquisition of a second citizenship or marriage to a foreign man commonly triggered denaturalisation. In a world where states tolerated only one legal bond between individual and state at a time, acquisition of a second nationality denoted a transfer of membership from one state to another.

[4] The United States law combines renunciation of citizenship and denaturalisation for birthright citizens into a category labelled expatriation. The US Constitution guarantees the citizenship of ius soli citizens as a constitutional right. The doctrine of expatriation operated on the legal fiction that certain acts by a citizen denoted an intention to renounce citizenship. In a series of judgments culminating in 1967 in Afroyim v. Rusk, the US Supreme Court progressively restricted the government's ability to deem conduct short of explicit renunciation as conclusive proof of an intention to expatriate, and the executive effectively abandoned attempts to pursue constructive expatriation in the 1980s.

offence and a minimum sentence of either five years or life imprisonment. The offences include treason, spying, any terrorism offence defined under the Criminal Code and a variety of offences applicable to members of the military. In the case of terrorism offences, the conviction may be by a foreign court for an offence committed outside Canada, if it would also constitute a terrorism offence under Canadian law.[5] The UK law authorises citizenship stripping of naturalised citizens (but not birthright citizens) even if it renders them stateless. The Canadian law prohibits the creation of statelessness but puts the onus on the individual to satisfy the Minister that statelessness would ensue from revocation. The UK declines to publicly disclose the exact number, identities or circumstances of those deprived of UK citizenship, but investigative journalists estimate that at least 53 Britons have lost citizenship since 2002, over half on national security grounds. In 2013, the Home Secretary deprived 20 UK nationals of citizenship, more than all other years since 2002 combined.[6]

Citizenship revocation raises an array of practical, legal and normative questions: Does it advance a valid objective? Does it comply with domestic, constitutional and/or transnational law? Is it normatively defensible? The answers turn, in part, on one's underlying conception of citizenship as legal status. Defenders of citizenship revocation liturgically intone that 'citizenship is a privilege, not a right'. The rhetoric of citizenship-as-privilege trades on a popular and laudable sentiment that is sometimes expressed as follows: 'I feel privileged to be a citizen of Canada, or the UK, or Italy, etc., and I consider it my duty to demonstrate my commitment through actively participating in civic life, or joining the armed forces, and standing up for my country as a good and loyal citizen should do.' But a privilege in law is something different: A privilege emanates from the patron (here a government minister) and can be rescinded from an undeserving beneficiary (here the citizen) at the former's discretion.

In two US Supreme Court cases in the 1950s, Chief Justice Warren rejected the classification of citizenship as privilege, proclaiming that 'citizenship is not a licence that expires on misbehaviour'. Instead, he invoked Hannah Arendt's

---

[5] The law also permits revocation of a citizen who 'served as a member of an armed force of a country or as a member of an organised armed group and that country or group was engaged in an armed conflict with Canada.' This is not a criminal offence, though it is almost identical to the existing offence of treason, except that it includes non-state armed groups, whereas the offence of treason only includes armed forces of a state.

[6] Ibid.

famous depiction of citizenship as 'no less than the right to have rights.'[7] Framing citizenship as a right vests citizenship in the rights-bearer. Depicting it as a meta-right dramatically increases the justificatory burden for any curtailment, because it places all rights in the balance.

Yet the force of Arendt's 'right to have rights' aphorism may seem attenuated, at least with respect to liberal democratic states of the twenty first century. After all, permanent residents enjoy almost all the same rights as citizens, and even foreigners without status can, in principle, claim a long menu of basic human rights under international law and many domestic legal orders. But this rejoinder overlooks one crucial fact. The exercise of virtually all rights depends on territorial presence within the state,[8] and only citizens have an unqualified right to enter and remain on state territory. So once stripped of the right to enter and remain in the state, enforcement means that one is effectively deprived of all the other rights that depend (*de jure* or *de facto*) on territorial presence. This fact has not been lost on the present UK government: With two exceptions, all her targets were abroad when the Home Secretary chose to exercise her discretion to strip them of citizenship. This meant they were absent and unable to respond when the notice of intention to deprive was delivered, and therefore barred from entry *qua* alien in order to appeal the decision.

Another strand of citizenship discourse describes citizenship as a contract in which the citizen pledges allegiance to the sovereign in exchange for the sovereign's protection. Acts of disloyalty amount to fundamental breach of contract, and so citizenship revocation simply actualises in law the citizen's voluntary severance of the relationship. This was, more or less, the logic of constructive expatriation under US law[9]. But neither the rhetoric of contract nor privilege can mask the flagrantly punitive rationale for the citizenship

---

[7] The unattributed quote comes from Arendt, H. (1951), *The Origins of Totalitarianism*. New York: Harcourt & Brace, at 294. It was picked up by US Supreme Court Justice Warren in Perez v. Brownell, 356 US 54 (1958) at 64 and again in Trop v. Dulles, 356 U.S. 86 (1958) at 102. See discussion in Weil, P. (2013), *The Sovereign Citizen*. Philadelphia: University of Pennsylvania Press.

[8] Expatriate voting is one exception. Many people suppose that diplomatic or consular assistance is also a right available outside the territory of the state, except that states tend to deny that they owe a legal duty to extend assistance to their citizens abroad. See, e.g. R (Abbasi) v Foreign Secretary [2002] EWCA Civ 1598.

[9] The US model of expatriation implicitly relied on this metaphor to characterise a series of acts, from desertion, to voting in a foreign election, as acts signifying an intention to renounce citizenship.

revocation regimes currently in play in the UK and Canada: baldly stated, some citizens are very bad citizens, and therefore do not deserve to be citizens. The move from 'bad citizen' to 'not citizen' is explicit in the Canadian law, where conviction for a criminal offence is a condition precedent to revocation and eventual deportation. Citizenship revocation in the UK arguably turns on prevention of future risk rather than punishment for past wrong, but statements by UK politicians like 'We think that deprivation is a way of expressing extreme displeasure at the way in which someone has behaved', reveal that the difference is more apparent than real.[10]

Banishment as criminal penalty has a long pedigree, and dates to a time before the rise of penal systems that enabled states to segregate, punish, rehabilitate and reintegrate wrongdoers within the state. In other words, modern states have criminal justice systems and an infrastructure that obviates the utility of banishment. These systems can, and are, deployed in response to the range of conduct encompassed under the rubric of terrorism. Banishment is both superfluous and anachronistic.

One might counter that offences threatening national security are qualitatively distinct from other offences. For these putative 'crimes against citizenship', incarceration is insufficient and withdrawal of citizenship is uniquely appropriate as supplement or substitute. It bears noting, however, that none of the Canadian offences precipitating loss of citizenship on grounds of national security – including treason – apply exclusively to citizens. Moreover, the idea that 'national security' misconduct is an affront to the state and so warrants a distinctive punishment fails to take proper account of the fact that *all* crime is regarded as an affront to the state's maintenance of public order (the 'King's Peace' in common law systems) and its monopoly on the legitimate use of violence. It is this public dimension of criminal law that differentiates it from private law, and confers on the state the authority to investigate, prosecute and punish wrongdoers, in addition to and apart from any private remedy that an individual victim might seek in tort, contract or property.

---

[10] See See United Kingdom, Parliamentary Debates, HC Standing Committee E, 30 April 2002, col 54 (Angela Eagle), quoted in Thwaites, R. (2014), 'The Security of Citizenship?: Finnis in the Context of the United Kingdom's Citizenship Stripping Provisions', in F. Jenkins, M. Nolan & K. Rubenstein (eds.), *Allegiance and Identity in a Globalised World*, 243–266. Cambridge, UK: Cambridge University Press, at note 94.

The purported symmetry between 'crimes against citizenship' and denationalisation echoes the defence of the sovereign's other technique for permanent elimination of wrongdoers, namely the death penalty. Banishment fits the crime of disloyalty the way capital punishment fits the crime of murder. When tethered to expulsion, citizenship revocation effects a kind of 'political death'. A citizen stripped of nationality and banished from the territory is, for all intents and purposes, dead to the state. Once outside the territory, the state has neither legal claim nor legal duty in respect of the former citizen, and is relieved of any obligation to object if another state tortures, renders or kills one of its nationals.[11] Indeed, denationalisation is not only a political analogue to death, it may also be a prelude to it.[12] At least two former UK citizens were executed by US drone strikes after the Home Secretary deprived them of citizenship, and another was rendered to the United States for trial on terrorism charges.

As with the death penalty, denationalisation extinguishes the prospect of rehabilitation or reintegration. The paradigmatic subject of citizenship revocation – the terrorist – is excluded from the ambit of human dignity that underwrites contemporary penal philosophy and affirms capacity for autonomy, rational self-reflection and reform. He is, in that sense, not fully human and thus incapable of rehabilitation. Banishment operates as pure and permanent retribution. There is no re-entry into the political community, no life after political death. Even creative and sophisticated attempts to classify and isolate those crimes that merit denationalisation from those that do not still founder on the instability of the distinction and the legitimacy of pure retribution.[13]

---

[11] Since the United States' lethal drone strike on US citizen Anwar al Awlaki (and his son), the United States' position is that it may lawfully execute its own citizens without trial when they are abroad. This, of course, obviates the necessity to strip citizenship prior to execution. See 'US cited controversial law in decision to kill American citizen by drone', *The Guardian*, 23 June 2014, available at https://www.theguardian.com/world/2014/jun/23/us-justification-drone-killing-american-citizen-awlaki. See also Spiro, P. (2014), 'Expatriating Terrorists', *Fordham Law Review* 82 (5): 2169–2187.

[12] This was the case with the Nazi extermination of German Jewry, as Hannah Arendt recounted. First, the Nazi government stripped Jews of German nationality and then, when no country would take them in, proceeded to murder them.

[13] For a recent example, see Lavi, S. (2011), 'Citizenship Revocation as Punishment: On the Modern Duties of Citizens and Their Criminal Breach', *The University of Toronto Law Journal* 61 (4): 783–810, at 806.

One might object that that this parallel neglects the statelessness constraint. To the extent that a prerequisite of denationalisation is actual or potential possession of another citizenship, the individual has another political life to live somewhere else. This is also an answer to the complaint that stripping citizenship from dual nationals but not mono-nationals violates the principle of equality of citizenship.[14] The dual national is not similarly situated to the mono-national precisely because the former has another citizenship and the latter does not, so differential treatment does not constitute invidious discrimination. (Of course, the counter-intuitive consequence of this reasoning is that dual citizenship becomes a liability. Multiple citizenship becomes less than the sum of its parts: the mono-citizen is secure from revocation, while the dual or multiple citizen is not).

The cogency of this argument depends on how one characterises the impact of citizenship revocation. From an external, statist perspective, the function of nationality is to catalogue the world's population and to file each person under at least one state. Nationality provides states with a return address they can stick on non-citizens for purposes of deportation, and is one reason why statelessness is an inconvenient anomaly for states. And just as all sovereign states are formally equal under international law, so too are all citizenships. Within this framework, citizenship becomes fungible. Statelessness is the problem, and nationality the solution. So, it may not actually matter what nationality a person possesses – Canadian or Somali, Brazilian or North Korean – as long as he or she possesses at least one. All nationalities are equal for purposes of averting statelessness.[15] This formal equality of nationality may partly explain international law's diffidence, or at least ambiguity, on whether citizenship deprivation that does not induce statelessness may nevertheless be arbitrary and contrary to international law.[16] In any event, as long as an individual retains a nationality somewhere, denationalisation poses no human rights problem.

From an internal, individual perspective, however, citizenship is not fungible.[17] The revocation of citizenship severs a unique relationship between

---

[14] It does not, of course, answer the charge of discrimination against naturalised mono-citizens under UK law. They are exposed to the risk of statelessness whereas birthright citizens are not.
[15] One could even imagine how a creative government wedded to this view might venture that protecting mono-citizens from statelessness is really an affirmative action initiative under s. 15(2) of the Charter.
[16] See Spiro, P. (2011), 'A New International Law of Citizenship', *Am J. Int'l Law* 105 (4): 694-746, at 711–12.
[17] Thwaites makes a similar argument, supra note 9, at 263.

the individual and a specific state. It is unique in two respects: First, the formal equality of nationality suppresses the substantive inequality of citizenship. The bundle of social, political, economic, cultural and legal opportunities and entitlements to which citizenship provides access varies radically between countries. Canadian or Brazilian citizenship is dramatically and indisputably heftier than that of present-day North Korea or Somalia.

Secondly, the subjective experience of that legal bond, what the International Court of Justice in *Nottebohm v. Guatemala* calls 'the social fact of attachment'[18] is as infinitely diverse as the people who make up the citizenry. It may range from the 'nominal citizen' whose social attachment is highly attenuated, to the individual whose existence is, and has always been, wholly and exclusively embedded in the country of residence. Citizenships are not substantively equal in comparison to one another and the nature of the individual citizen-state relationship is not invariant. But my point is not to propose a metric capable of measuring the quantitative, qualitative, experiential, emotional, personal, familial, cultural, social, financial, linguistic and political impacts of exile on any individual, in order that some state official could determine precisely when citizenship revocation inflicts an appropriate versus excessive degree of punishment. Citizenship as legal status obviates both the need and the legitimacy of an on-going or comparative evaluation by state authorities of how much or how well a citizen performs as a citizen.[19] The very act of subjecting a subsisting citizenship to this kind of normative scrutiny subverts the security that distinguishes legal citizenship from other statuses that define the relationship between state and individual.

The history of banishment generates only cautionary tales about the inevitably arbitrary and prejudicial abuse of a discretionary power to identify the 'bad' citizen for purposes of relegating him or her to the non-status of non-citizen. The violence of rupturing the link between citizens and state is not negated by possession of citizenship status in another polity, if one conceives of the relationship (whatever its intensity, depth, etc.) between a state and a citizen as singular and unique. On this view, citizenship revoca-

---

[18] Nottebohm (Liechtenstein v. Guatemala), ICJ 4 (1955) at 23.
[19] This does not preclude an argument that the depth and duration of a resident non-citizen's relationship to a state could and should generate an entitlement to remain and to be put on a path to citizenship. See, e.g. Carens, J. (2013), *The Ethics of Immigration*. Oxford: OUP.

tion inflicts an intrinsically grave harm that is separate from (though exacerbated by) the harm of statelessness.[20]

I leave to one side an account of the myriad procedural and substantive deficiencies of the UK and Canadian denationalisation regimes that make them ripe for legal challenge. Nor do I dwell here on the dubious practical value of denationalisation in preventing terrorism or protecting national security. Suffice to say that if the aim of citizenship revocation is deterrence, there is no evidence that stripping citizenship will deter a potential terrorist any more or better than the prospect of a criminal conviction and lengthy imprisonment or, for that matter, the risk of blowing oneself up, getting killed or executed, or being detained indefinitely, rendered, or tortured. To the extent that exile supposedly makes a country more secure by removing dangerous people, the justification knows no limits: it is not obvious why Canadians or Britons would not also be made safer by exiling all citizens who commit violent offences. From the other side, expelling convicted or alleged terrorists is an oddly parochial response that transfers rather than reduces risk. Depending on the destination country, deportation may actually make it easier for the individual to engage in activities that pose a threat to global security.[21]

And, finally, the sheer absurdity of banishment as a response to the terrorist *qua* global outlaw is best illustrated by speculating on what would happen if all states behaved like the UK and Canada: Imagine a dual UK-Canada citizen who is convicted of a terrorism offence in the UK. Since terrorism is a global menace, Canada can treat a terrorism conviction in the UK as proof of being a bad Canadian citizen. Both Canada and the UK can lawfully denationalise him. But both states are also somewhat constrained in law not to create statelessness, and both want and need to find another state to admit the expelled person. And the only country that has a legal obligation to do is a state of nationality. So, now it becomes a race between Canada and the UK to see which country can strip citizenship first. To the loser goes the citizen.

Modern exile, as imagined under UK and Canadian law, is erected upon unsustainable and incoherent propositions about the nature of legal citizenship. If citizenship is irrevocable only where withdrawal causes statelessness, then citizenship is a right for mono-citizens but a privilege for dual or

---

[20] For a similar argument, see Rayner Thwaites, supra note 9.
[21] Macklin, A. (2001), 'Borderline Security', in R. Daniels et al. (eds.), *The Security of Freedom: Essays on Canada's Anti-Terrorism Bill*, 383-405. Toronto: U of T Press; 'Still Stuck at the Border', in C. Forcese & F. Crépeau (eds.), *Terrorism, Law and Democracy: 10 Years After 9/11*, 261–306. Montreal: Canadian Institute for the Administration of Justice.

multiple citizens. Legal citizenship can be contingent on normative criteria for one state if and only if it is not similarly contingent for another state. State A can deprive a national of citizenship and banish him because he is a bad citizen. But State A can do so lawfully if and only if State B is compelled to admit the individual simply because he is a citizen of State B, irrespective of whether he is a good or bad citizen of State B. One state's authority to deem the bad citizen a non-citizen presupposes another state lacking that same authority.

To contend that punitive denationalisation in the twenty-first century is an illegitimate and futile exercise of sovereign power does not refute or deny that social solidarity, belonging and allegiance have a place in conceptions of citizenship and deserve to be promoted. It is rather that these goals will not and cannot be advanced by citizenship revocation. Nor will citizenship revocation make any state, or the global community, more secure. Citizenship revocation only enhances the discretionary and arbitrary power of the executive, at the expense of all citizens, and of citizenship itself. Banishment deserves to be banished again. Permanently.

32

Expatriation of Terrorists and Counter Terrorism

Peter J. Spiro

I agree with the bottom line of Audrey Macklin's excellent kick-off for the Forum. New expatriation measures adopted by the United Kingdom and Canada are ill-advised and possibly unlawful. The UK and Canada moves make for a kind of trendlet, and other states (even human rights-pure Norway) are considering similar measures as the 'foreign fighter' phenomenon captures global attention. Denationalisation of terror suspects clearly merits the attention of scholars and activists; after decades of disuse, states are now stepping back into the practice of forced expatriation. Macklin sets the scene with a primer on recent developments and a powerful critique of the UK and Canadian measures.

But I would get to the destination along another path. I see denationalisation as anachronistic and toothless in the face of diminished conceptions of citizenship as an institution and changed locations of allegiance. The expatriation measures are empty gestures, a kind of counter-terror bravado to make up for the deficiency of more important material responses. Government officials must be seen to be doing something, and so they may (for appearances sake) throw expatriation into the counter-terror toolbox. But expatriation won't advance the counter-terror agenda in any real way. Given the lack of policy advantage, I expect that the human rights critique will suffice to suppress the broad use of denationalisation in this context.

In theory, expatriation could help shore up the boundaries of membership and national solidarity. Terrorist expatriation might be consistent with the historical practice of terminating nationality upon formal transfer of allegiance. This was once the near-universal practice; original nationality was lost automatically upon naturalisation in another state. Military and government service in another country would also typically result in expatriation, even when the other state was a friendly one. This practice helped police the boundaries of community. One could be a member of one or another polity, but not both. States that continue to prohibit dual citizenship still operate on this principle. A Japanese citizen who naturalises as an American, for example, automatically forfeits her Japanese nationality.

One might situate security-related expatriation in this tradition. To the extent that fighting for the Islamic State represents a shift of loyalty incompatible with loyalty to the United Kingdom, expatriation merely reflects social conditions on the ground. Membership in the United Kingdom would be exclusive of membership in forces associated with the Islamic State. Expatriation clarifies the 'us' and 'them' in a way that clarifies social solidarities and the special obligations that come with co-nationality. (Ayelet Shachar makes a similar argument with respect to 'hollow' citizens acquiring citizenship on the attenuated basis of descent.)

But this logic doesn't map out onto denationalisation in the current security context. There is no citizenship in the Islamic State (ISIL not being a state, the label notwithstanding). One cannot naturalise or be born into ISIL; there is no formal evidence of loyalty or membership. Expatriation doesn't work without the symmetry. To the extent that only dual nationals are subject to security-related expatriation, the criterion no longer makes any sense: the other citizenship is random, unrelated to the motivation for expatriation. (As Macklin points out, it could lead to a strange dynamic in which states allied against groups such as ISIL could race to expatriate foreign fighters in an effort to offshore putative threats.) The condition then arbitrarily discriminates against individuals on the basis of their dual-citizen status.

That takes care of the only normatively tenable rationale for the expatriation measures. The punitive basis is more easily dispatched. Punitive uses of expatriation have long been condemned. As early as 1958, the U.S. Supreme Court was able to observe that '[t]he civilized nations of the world are in virtual unanimity that statelessness is not to be imposed as punishment for crime.' The Canadian measure marks a return to the practice of exile. As Macklin argues, non-application to cases in which statelessness would result does not save it from this rap. A person may well feel a deep social attachment to one country while holding alternative nationalities (which themselves may be nominal). The denationalisation of a Canadian citizen long-resident in Canada will feel like banishment even as he holds another nationality, especially to the extent the latter is attenuated.

Finally, the protective rationale for terrorist expatriation makes little sense as a practical matter. The 'foreign fighter' problem is largely framed as a problem of return. Citizens radicalised by their experience in Iraq and Syria with brutal ISIL forces will return to their home countries in the West to undertake terror attacks. It's a potent narrative of weaponised citizens. Without citizenship, these individuals would have no right of re-entry, thus defusing their utility as ISIL operatives.

Or so our politicians would have it. In practice, denationalisation adds little counter-terror value. You can't take away someone's citizenship for being associated with ISIL before you know that he's associated with ISIL. But once the security apparatus is aware of the connection, it will have other, standard counter-terror tools to protect against the threat. There will be the possibility of criminal prosecution in many states on material support charges, with incarceration on conviction. (Canada's punitive scheme can hardly sustain even the pretence of a protective rationale.) Short of prosecution, watch lists and well-practiced surveillance techniques should prevent returning foreign fighters from undertaking terror attacks. Passport revocation and travel bans will help prevent citizens from becoming foreign fighters in the first place.

So terrorist expatriation advances counter-terror efforts not at all. It supplies yet another example of security-related theatre, a feel-good move that will be popular with some voters. (The features are shared with some Western responses to the vastly exaggerated Ebola threat, where politicians must be seen to respond dramatically even if dramatic moves make no sense in policy terms.) Terrorist expatriation is unlikely to have staying power against a powerful human rights critique. The UK and Canadian measures may well fall to legal challenges, domestic or international. Even if they are sustained in court, they are unlikely to be put to broad use. Few other states will follow suit (it is interesting that terrorist expatriation has almost no political traction in the United States, its aggressive counter-terror posturing notwithstanding). The failure will evidence an emerging norm against involuntary expatriation. If states can't make expatriation stick here, they won't be able to make it stick anywhere.

33

Attacking the Nation and the Question of Citizenship

Peter H. Schuck

Audrey Macklin's call for the banishment of banishment is eloquent and persuasive on many points. She is surely right that particular denationalisation regimes may suffer from a variety of fatal defects. The standards for revocation may be too vague to constrain official discretion or to provide adequate notice to the citizen concerning what conduct will risk revocation. Most important, the grounds for revocation must be limited to only the most extreme, unmitigated attacks on the nation's security, attacks that are consistent only with a desire to bring the nation to ruin. This conduct must be scrupulously-defined and highly specific conduct; mere malignant thoughts will not suffice. Revocation cannot be permitted to lead to statelessness and thus a loss of the 'meta-right' (as Macklin puts it) to have rights, especially the right to the territorial presence that in turn confers a broad panoply of liberal rights. The procedures for revocation must be robust in all respects, including of course the right to be actually or virtually present rather than having to contest the government's action ex post and from exile. The government's burden and standard of proof must be exceedingly demanding, perhaps even the proof beyond a reasonable doubt required for criminal convictions.

But even these extraordinarily demanding and rare preconditions are irrelevant to Macklin; she is utterly categorical in her rejection of the very notion of denationalisation. She would preclude denationalisation even if these (and other) strict conditions were met; indeed, no protections for the individual citizen – or for the threatened nation – would suffice. Here is where we disagree. I see no reason in logic or justice why a state should be powerless to protect itself and its people from imminent, existential threats (suitably defined) from an individual who has launched a dangerous attack (suitably defined and rigorously proved) on itself and its people, whose interestsm both international law and domestic politics obligates it to promote. And I see no reason in logic or justice why that state cannot defend itself and its people against such an attack by, among other things, severing the attacker's connection to a state with which he is manifestly at war, thereby making it much more difficult for him to succeed in that war. Should the individual's interest in maintaining that connection, which (by my definition, embedded in the preconditions listed above) can only be tactical and cynical, utterly and categorically outweigh the nation's interest in protecting those for whom it bears a sacred trust? This question, I submit, answers itself – and the answer is grounded not merely in a utilitarian balancing but in a deontological principle: the nation's fundamental duty to protect its people.

I also have some reservations about a few of Macklin's other, less fundamental arguments. First, she claims that denationalisation weakens citizenship by eliminating its security and thus rendering it a form of mere legal residence. I don't understand her logic. Am I less secure in my citizenship if I know that the state may execute me or imprison me for life if I murder a fellow citizen? I suppose that I am less secure, but that insecurity is warranted and I can easily avoid it. Moreover, there is a sense in which denationalising one who has demonstrably satisfied the exceedingly demanding conditions for revocation that I have specified does, contrary to Macklin's claim, strengthen citizenship by reaffirming the conditions on which it is based.

Second, she categorically condemns revocation in part because it categorically denies the individual the opportunity to rehabilitate himself. We should and ordinarily do protect a wrongdoer's opportunity to rehabilitate himself, but there are many situations in which we don't. An employer who catches an employee embezzling from the company may fire him without giving him an opportunity to rehabilitate himself there; if he wishes to rehabilitate himself, he will have to do so elsewhere, on his own time. When we sentence a murderer to life imprisonment without parole, we are denying him the right to regain his freedom through rehabilitation.

Third, it is true that denationalising a dual citizen would still leave him with a state while denationalising a mono citizen would not. But so long as we do not allow revocations that would render one stateless, this particular inequality between categories of citizens is hardly one that should trouble us – any more than we should be troubled that a dual citizen has an additional passport and can vote in an additional polity.

Finally, Macklin states that there is no evidence that denationalisation will deter a would-be terrorist if other, more conventional counter-terrorism measures fail to do so. I agree, but so what? Deterrence may be an important reason to punish wrongdoers but it is by no means the only reason to do so.

If we are justified in punishing them, that justification is not nullified by a claim that the punishment will not deter others. And if more conventional measures are indeed effective in eliminating threats, they should of course be our first and perhaps final resort. In such situations, denationalisation may well be a superfluous, unnecessary remedy. But this is a question of policy and prudence, not of moral principle.

Macklin is certainly right to worry about the possible abuses of denationalisation. The history of political banishment is hardly reassuring on this point. But a liberal constitutional regime can control such abuses by scrupulously controlling the state's exercise of this power through a variety of familiar institutions and practices. These include a careful definition and exacting limitation of the grounds for revocation; demanding procedural and evidentiary requirements before such a power can be exercised; a right to legal counsel; and an independent judiciary accustomed to challenging state power in the name of protecting individual rights. We have entrusted our precious liberties to the faithful working through of these institutions and practices. Some of these liberties are even more precious than our right to retain our citizenship when we have knowingly acted in horrendous ways that make it justifiable, under the safeguards I have described, for the state to declare that status forfeited.

34

Repudiation of Citizenship by Terrorists

Christian Joppke

The recent trend to strip international terrorists of their citizenship raises general questions about the changing nature of terror and of citizenship. Let us start with 'terror'. In the era of Marxist-inspired violence against the state (or rather 'capitalism', of which the state was suspected to be merely a servant), terror was a purely domestic affair, committed by the flower children of the elite, particularly its most educated and morally minded. No one would have fathomed stripping an Ulrike Meinhof or Andreas Baader, leaders of the 1970s' German Red Army Faction (RAF), of their German citizenship. The current 'return of banishment' is a response to an altogether different type of terror, one that transcends borders and is committed by people who explicitly posit themselves outside the political community of the nation-state—allegiance to the community of believers (ummah) cancels out the secular community of citizens, it is even deliberately mobilised against the latter. Only notice the cynical ritual of the Islamic State's henchmen to have a fellow-national do the mediatised head-chopping. By the same token, RAF limited its murderous acts to high-ranking representatives of the 'system' (of which ordinary citizens were seen as merely victims who thus stood to be recruited as fellow-fighters). Al Qaeda and its Islamic State sequel seek death for ordinary citizens, whose humanity is denied through being demoted to 'unbelievers'. Paul Kahn took the ubiquitous threat of terror to be today's ultimate moment of citizenship, the 'moment of conscription'.[1]

Indeed, Islamic terror is meant to be 'war', while RAF aspired to 'revolution' – two very different things, with obvious implications for citizenship in the former but not the latter. That terror against citizens should lead to reconsidering the citizen status of its culprits, who proved the ties to their state of citizenship to be at best 'tactical and cynical', as Peter Schuck writes in his contribution, seems logical. One is therefore astounded about the measured response by Western states, which have mostly respected the international norm of avoiding statelessness (only lately, in response to the unspeakable

---

[1] Kahn, P. (2011), *Political Theology*. Ithaca, N.Y.: Cornell University Press, p. 138.

atrocities committed by the fighters of the Islamic State, have there been cracks in this commitment, most notably in Britain). But academics cry out that 'banishment weakens citizenship', as Audrey Macklin does. They draw an idyllic and reality-resistant picture of 'singular and unique' ties between terrorists and the citizenship they despise; 'intrinsically grave harm' is said to be inflicted here, separate even from 'the harm of statelessness'. Evidently, more sympathy is invested on the culprits than on their victims.

Make no mistake. One should hold no illusion about populist, spin-doctored politicians, from Britain to America, Norway to Italy, who hide their chronic incapacity to lead in our contemporary 'audience democracies' behind the sable-rattling 'security' and 'War on Terror' rhetoric that the people wish to hear.[2] Macklin has a point when she finds that under the guise of 'security' only 'the discretionary and arbitrary power of the executive' is increased. Particularly the recent experience in Britain under Tory Home Minister Theresa May, with a rather capricious practice of citizenship stripping for the loosely defined reason of being 'conducive to the public good', with sometimes lethal and conspiratorially concocted consequences for the targeted individuals, lends itself to this interpretation. And Peter Spiro is on target that conducting the fight against terrorism on the citizenship front is 'empty gestures' and not likely to have much effect – though his proposal of 'passport revocation and travel bans' in lieu of denationalisation reads eerily off the mark after the recent tragedy of a would-be jihadist, who had been grounded by the Canadian government exactly in these terms, turning his rage about the passport denial against an innocent guardsman in Ottawa.

The practical question of effectiveness is secondary to the principled question whether citizenship for proven (naturally not just suspected or potential) terrorists who conduct war (in the literal sense) against Western states and their citizens should be unassailable. At heart, the issue is one of 'loyalty and allegiance', as the Canadian Immigration Minister, Chris Alexander, defended the 2014 Strengthening Canadian Citizenship Act in parliament. This act, representative of similar bills currently being considered in a number of European states, Australia, and the United States, allows the stripping of citizenship in the cases of treason, spying, taking up arms against the Canadian Forces, and terrorism, even if the latter is committed outside Canada and sentenced by foreign courts, should the action in question constitute a terrorism offence also under Canadian law. The expanded geographic scope for terrorism, which stirred controversy, was

---

[2] Manin, B. (1997), *The Principles of Representative Government*. New York: Cambridge University Press, Chapter 6.

clearly dictated by heightened security concerns. But it also recognises the global nature of the new terror and its affront to the secular state and citizenship at large, wherever it may occur; one might read it as a comity of nations response to a global challenge. In any case, it is not just bizarre but self-destructive to measure the 'strength' of citizenship in terrorists' unencumbered possibility to make tactical use of it in their war against the godless state and its unbelieving median citizen.

For calibrating banishment, next to taking into account the changing nature of terror, one also needs to recognise the changing nature of citizenship in a globalising world. Whoever has reflected for a second on the colossal injustice inflicted on the vast majority of mankind by being born into the 'wrong' kind of state that cannot guarantee its 'citizens' physical safety and the elementary means of survival[3], must be irritated to see citizenship depicted as something that an individual should never be able to lose, however randomly it had been assigned to her in the first place, and however much a particular individual has done to undermine or even destroy this very citizenship (and the state that guarantees it). Audrey Macklin sees the danger of banishment in 'making legal citizenship contingent on performance'. 'Performance' strikes me as a rather vague and anodyne term for the behaviour in question. It is one thing to make citizenship acquisition contingent on virtuous behaviour, which could never be exacted on born citizens (as Britain entertained for a while in its 'probationary' or 'earned' citizenship scheme that was never implemented); it is quite another to make a declared war against the secular state and its citizens a ground for renunciation. As much as one should eschew virtuous citizenship from a liberal perspective, one should welcome, even require the withdrawing of citizenship from someone to whom it is at best a tactical weapon.

It may warm the heart to elevate citizenship to a 'right to have rights', enunciated by US Supreme Court Chief Justice Earl Warren in a different time and context (voting in foreign elections[4] and desertion during World II[5], in both cases without any third-party harm inflicted and at best a vague and constructed violation of allegiance). The gospel of citizenship stripping as 'cruel punishment', pronounced in Trop v. Dulles (1958), needs reconsideration in the age of global terror. And the accompanying formula of citizenship as a 'right to have rights' obscures that persons without states

---

[3] See Shachar, A. (2009), *The Birthright Lottery: Citizenship and Global Inequality*. Cambridge, Mass.: Harvard University Press.
[4] Perez v. Brownell, 356 U.S. 54 (1958).
[5] Trop v. Dulles, 356 U.S. 86 (1958).

or citizenship are no longer the 'scum of the earth' they may have been in the late 1940s, when Hannah Arendt wrote the Origins of Totalitarianism. But most importantly, the formula 'rights to have rights' dodges the fact that, indeed, citizenship in a globalising world is increasingly 'privilege' and 'contract'. It is a privilege if one considers the mentioned exclusion from a lucrative OECD-state citizenship of most of mankind (that has to make do with less than US$ 2 per day). And it is a contract by definition for the ever growing number of immigrants who are not born with it but seek it out for their own benefit. In the post-feudal world, most states allow the possibility to renounce one's citizenship—this was the point of departure of 'democratic' America from 'monarchical' Britain. But then it is not outlandish (or illiberal) to concede the converse capacity to states to rid themselves even of born citizens who have despised or patently abused their citizenship through their actions (and why stop at the threshold of statelessness?).

Macklin claims that banishment is 'both superfluous and anachronistic' because states now have 'criminal justice systems' at their disposal to 'rehabilitate and reintegrate wrongdoers within the state'. This claim is misleading and paternalistic. International terrorists are not criminals but warriors—they don't want to be 'reintegrated'. The liberal state should acknowledge their claim, eye to eye, by taking away from them what they have factually renounced and even wish to destroy. Canadian minister Chris Alexander is right: 'They (terrorists) will have, in effect, withdrawn their allegiance to Canada by their very actions.' Peter Spiro lawyerly ups the ante by arguing that there could not be a 'shift of loyalty' on the part of Islamic terrorists because 'there is no citizenship in the Islamic State'. Does he want to wait until they have acquired a seat in the United Nations?

35

Citizenship: Us vs Them

Vesco Paskalev

The very passion and fury pouring from Christian Joppke's contribution should prompt both the lawyer and the political philosopher that he is wrong. I too am outraged by what ISIS fighters are doing, but it is well known that the function of constitutional rights, and of the constitutions themselves, is precisely to assure that the legislator is not driven by the passion of the day. One decade after 9/11 we know that the actions taken both by the President and the Congress of the US, based on the rationale that it is a new world that we have woken up into, were not all reasonable, to put it mildly. So may be today's rush to strip terrorist suspects of their citizenship. When watching the daily news on TV, one is easily tempted to think that we are living in extraordinarily dangerous times, which warrant a return to what the US Supreme Court considered to be 'cruel punishment' half a century ago. Yet as a matter of statistics, and despite our contrary impressions, violence of all kinds in the world is actually declining.[1] On the other hand, the capacity of law enforcement agencies for surveillance and control, especially in the OECD countries, has increased dramatically, so the return to practices which have long been abandoned is difficult to justify. This is not to say that that citizenship is a sacred cow and any return to abandoned practices is excluded by some historic laws of human progress. Nothing can be further from the truth. But it does follow that the proponents of banishment must provide a more subtle justification than we have seen so far.

Joppke has a point when distinguishing the old school revolutionaries from the contemporary jihadists, who conceive of themselves as members of the global ummah, and not of any state. (Do we know that for sure? ISIS aims to create an Islamic state after all). He also has a point that waging war against a country is a good reason to strip the warrior of the citizenship of that country. I can accept even stretching this argument to apply to all those who take up arms against any allies of that country, or even to those who

---

[1] Pinker, S. (2011), *The Better Angels of our Nature.* New York: Viking.

have taken arms against the international system of states. This would bring me already quite close to the position of the 'deprivationists'.

What I find difficult to accept is the unquestioned assumption that this gesture would serve any of the goals Joppke, and the politicians favouring banishment, may have. If the jihadists were as cosmopolitan as he takes them to be, deprivation would not have any meaning, neither for the actual fighters, nor for any like-minded followers. It might be the case that taking their passport will have the practical effect of preventing them from travelling to Syria or back, but as a person who is genuinely outraged by their deeds, I would rather see them locked up in prison rather than left at large in a legal limbo (in the Middle East out of all places!). For Joppke the practical side is only of secondary concern, but I am afraid his theoretical argument is self-defeating.

Now, if we accept that the jihadists just do not care if they are deprived of their western citizenships, let us consider whether this would still matter for anyone else. On the one hand, there are the 'normal' citizens of the same country who may wish to see the extremists publicly excommunicated. This is a legitimate concern. However, it is in no way different from the desire of many law-abiding citizens to see murderers and rapists sent to the electric chair. So the usual objections to the latter punishments apply here too. More importantly, while there is some commensurability between a murder and a death sentence, the very gravity of the offences of the jihadists make citizenship deprivation superfluous. Ironically, not the cruelty of citizenship deprivation, but its softness make it appear quite inappropriate for the case of terrorists. If we take into account also the practical difficulties arising in the prosecution of a foreigner, on balance it might be better to keep him as a citizen. On the other hand, the possibility or impossibility of revocation defines and redefines the meaning of the concept of citizenship itself – of our citizenship, not of theirs. That is why many academics, whose professional duty is to care for precisely such nuance, are so uneasy about the recent trend. I would be glad if this concern remains confined to the ivory towers of the academia, but I suspect that the conditionality of citizenship is more than a theoretical concern for those citizens who are not white, Anglo-Saxon and Christian and have only recently arrived from the wrong side of the OECD border.

One may argue, as Peter Schuck does, for deprivation administered under narrowly circumscribed conditions. Indeed, due process can alleviate some of the anxieties the conditionality of citizenship would create, but he does not provide much of a justification for this conditionality in the first place. He also relies on the intuitive, yet questionable assumption that citizenship deprivation serves to protect the state and its people. But all grounds for deprivation he suggests already constitute a serious crime, and if the perpetrator must be convicted to be denationalised as he suggests, then again, what difference would it make if those imprisoned for a very long time remain citizens or not? If deprivation were administered properly – for grave crimes and with due process, it becomes redundant.

Beyond these conceptual concerns, and paying due consideration to the all too present terrorist threats, I want the Islamic State bombed out of existence, and I want all jihadists punished for what they do. But as a citizen I also want my tax money spent on police to put the bad apples in jail, not on border patrols to keep them out.

36

Acquiring and Losing Citizenship

Bronwen Manby

The heading for this discussion makes a person focused on sub-Saharan Africa scratch her head somewhat. Which 'new' denationalisation policies are we talking about? In Africa, we have continued to see the same old denationalisation policies that have been in place since the 1960s. The context of national security has changed in some countries, especially the threat of 21st century terrorism methods in places such as Kenya or Nigeria, but the methods used by the governments in response have not changed.

The legal provisions

If we start from a survey of the laws, most African countries allow for deprivation of nationality acquired by naturalisation, some of them on quite vague and arbitrary grounds. The former British colonies borrow language from the British precedents and provide for deprivation on the grounds of 'disloyalty' or the 'public good'; while the francophone countries talk about behaviour 'incompatible with the status of a national' or 'prejudicial to the interests of the country'. However, more than half of Africa's 54 states forbid deprivation of nationality from a national from birth (of origin, in the

---

The original version of this chapter was revised. A correction to this chapter is available at.

This text was written in November 2014 and reflects events current at that time. Some important later developments are not reflected, including, most importantly, the readmission of Morocco to the African Union in January 2017 and the decision of the African Court on Human and Peoples' Rights in the *Anudo* case against Tanzania issued in March 2018.

civil law terminology), whether or not the person would become stateless.[1] And although a large number of the remaining countries have a provision framed along the lines provided in the 1961 Convention on the Reduction of Statelessness for a person who works for a foreign state in defiance of an express prohibition to lose their nationality,[2] only a small handful provide for deprivation of a birthright citizen in case of a crime against the state – Egypt, Eritrea and Mali.[3]

None of the sub-Saharan countries come close to the extremes of Egypt, where citizenship can be deprived from anyone (whether a citizen from birth or by naturalisation) if, among other things, 'at any time he has been qualified as Zionist'.[4]

On the positive side, the South African and Ethiopian constitutions provide blanket prohibitions on deprivation of nationality, whether from birth or naturalised (though South Africa then goes on to violate this prohibition in its legislation).[5] Several constitutions and laws create serious due process hurdles for governments seeking to revoke citizenship. In Kenya for example, the 2010 constitution requires a naturalised citizen (citizenship by birth cannot be revoked) to have been actually convicted of a serious crime, including treason;[6] less specifically, Burundi, Malawi, and Rwanda have

---

[1] Botswana, Burkina Faso, Burundi, Chad, Comoros, Ethiopia, Gabon, Gambia, Ghana, Kenya, Lesotho, Libya, Mauritius, Namibia, Nigeria, Rwanda, Seychelles, Somalia, South Africa, Swaziland, Tanzania, Uganda, Zambia and Zimbabwe. In the case of Botswana, Ethiopia, Libya, Tanzania and Zambia, dual nationality is not permitted, and voluntary acquisition of another nationality results in automatic loss. Lists from Manby, B. (2010), *Citizenship Laws in Africa: A Comparative Study*. Open Society Foundations, 2nd edition; updated information for a forthcoming 3rd edition. On the number of states in Africa: Morocco is not a member of the African Union, while the Sahrawi Arab Democratic Republic is: if both are counted, there are 55 states.

[2] Angola, Cameroon, CAR, Congo Republic, Côte d'Ivoire, Djibouti, Egypt, Equatorial Guinea, Eritrea, Guinea, Guinea Bissau, Liberia, Madagascar, Morocco, Mozambique, Sao Tomé & Príncipe, South Sudan, Sudan, Togo and Tunisia.

[3] Egypt Law No. 26 of 1975 Concerning Egyptian Nationality, Article 16(7); Eritrea Nationality Proclamation 1992 Article 8; Mali Nationality Code 1962, Article 43 (amended 1995).

[4] Law No. 26 of 1975 Concerning Egyptian Nationality, Article 16(7), translation from UNHCR website, http://www.refworld.org/docid/3ae6b4e218.html. Libya had similar rules until they were changed in 2010.

[5] South Africa Constitution 1996, Article 20; Ethiopia Constitution 1993, Article 33.

[6] Kenya Constitution, 2010, Section 17.

constitutional provisions forbidding arbitrary deprivation of nationality.[7] Meanwhile, Gambia, Ghana, Liberia and Rwanda all provide that deprivation can only be done by a court, on the government's application;[8] and a majority, though not all, others provide for judicial review of administrative decisions to deprive.[9] A few countries provide for protection against statelessness in deprivation cases: just Lesotho, Mauritius, and Zimbabwe (since 2013) provide in principle for protection from statelessness in all cases where nationality is revoked by act of the government; and Namibia, Rwanda, Senegal and South Africa provide partial protection, allowing statelessness to result in some circumstances.[10]

On the negative side, Botswana, Lesotho, Malawi, Mauritius, Seychelles, Tanzania, Zambia and Zimbabwe — notably, all with a British legal inheritance — explicitly state in their legislation that the decision of the minister on any matter under the nationality law cannot be reviewed in court.[11] These are all countries which do not allow for deprivation of birthright citizenship (though some provide for loss in case of acquisition of another nationality); but it's questionable what the protection against statelessness in deprivation

---

[7] Burundi Constitution 2005, Article 34; Malawi Constitution 1994 (as amended to 1998), Article 47 ; Rwanda Constitution 2003, Article 7.

[8] Gambia Constitution 1996, article 13; Ghana Constitution 1992 Article 9, Citizenship Act 2000, Article 18; Liberia Aliens and Nationality Law 1973, Articles 21.53; Rwanda Nationality Law No.30 of 2008, Article 20.

[9] Most of the civil law countries provide quite detailed procedures for nationality litigation through the courts; the Commonwealth countries tend to have weaker protections, and do not have the same tradition of providing procedures in the substantive law itself, but South Africa for example, provides for all decisions of the minister to be reviewable by the courts, as do Gambia and Kenya.

[10] Lesotho Constitution 1993, as amended to 2001, Article 42 (however, this provision is not respected in the Citizenship Order 1971 Article 23); Mauritius Citizenship Act 1968, as amended to 1995, Article 11(3)(b); Namibia Constitution 1990, as amended to 2010, Article 9(4); Rwanda Nationality Law 2003, Article 19; Senegal Nationality Code 1961 as amended 2013, Article 21; South African Citizenship Act 1996, as amended 2013, Article 8; Zimbabwe Constitution 2013, Article 39(3) (but this is not respected in the Citizenship Act, 1984, as amended to 2003, Article 11(3), which provides in principle prohibition of rendering a person stateless, but allows the minister to override if it is in the 'public good' to do so).

[11] Botswana Citizenship Act 1998, Article 22; Lesotho Citizenship Order 1971, Article 26; Malawi Citizenship Act 1966, Article 29; Mauritius Citizenship Act 1968 Article 17; Seychelles Citizenship Act 1994, Article 14; Tanzania Citizenship Act 1995 23; Zambia Citizenship Act Article 9; Zimbabwe Citizenship Act 1984 Article 16.

cases provided by Mauritius means, if the decision of the minister cannot be challenged. In Swaziland, where a certificate of nationality 'shall' be issued by the minister to a person who is qualified to be a citizen, it is also provided that the minister 'may revoke' a certificate and no grounds are specified.[12] Namibia allows deprivation of nationality on the grounds that a person was already deprived in another country, increasing the likelihood of rendering them stateless.[13]

In 2013, the Seychelles inserted a new article to its citizenship law expanding the grounds for deprivation of citizenship if the minister 'is satisfied' that the person has been involved in terrorism, piracy, drug offences, treason, and other offences, or has acted with disloyalty.[14] In 2010, the South African Citizenship Act was amended to provide for automatic loss of citizenship by a naturalised citizen 'if he or she engages, under the flag of another country, in a war that the Republic does not support', leaving lawyers wondering how you would know whether or not the Republic 'supported' a particular war (and would it matter which side the person was on?).[15]

The practice

But this review of deprivation provisions has a slightly unreal feel. These procedures are hardly used, so far as one can tell. Only South Africa publishes any statistics – or at least it used to do so – revealing that at least 17 people have been deprived of citizenship since 2001-02 (despite the constitutional ban on deprivation), though no details are given. Countries such as Kenya and Nigeria, both facing well-publicised and serious security threats from the Al-Qaeda-affiliated Al-Shabaab and Boko Haram are not known to have deprived any individual of citizenship through the formal procedures of the law on deprivation.[16]

---

[12] Swaziland Citizenship and Immigration Act 1992, Article 20.
[13] Namibia Citizenship Act 1990, Article 9(3)(e).
[14] Section 11A of the Citizenship Act, No. 18 of 1994, inserted by Act 11 of 2013.
[15] South African Citizenship Act 1996, as amended 2013, Article 6(3). This amendment came into force on 1 January 2013. The 1996 Constitution provides in Article 20 that 'No citizen may be deprived of citizenship.' It is possible that the phrasing of the revised Article 6(3) is designed to avoid this prohibition by providing for automatic loss. See further *Submission on the South African Citizenship Amendment Bill, B 17 – 2010*, Citizenship Rights in Africa Initiative, 6 August 2010.
[16] Email correspondence, November 2014, with Chidi Odinkalu of the Nigeria National Human Rights Commission and Adam Hussein Adam of the Open Society Initiative for East Africa, both following these issues closely.

The legal provisions on deprivation of citizenship are, in fact, more or less irrelevant in countries where (a) as described above, citizens from birth cannot be deprived of citizenship under law except in the rather rare circumstance of working for another state despite a formal request not to do so; (b) naturalisation is very difficult to obtain; and (c) the government has easily accessible other means of achieving the same result in relation to (people who believed they were) birthright citizens, obviating any need to amend the law on withdrawal of nationality.

As regards (b), statistics on naturalisation are hard to come by, but it seems that only a handful of people a year may be naturalised in most countries – even in Nigeria, with more than 150 million people, only around a hundred people acquire nationality by naturalisation or marriage annually – and those who are naturalised are mostly non-Africans operating in the formal economy, with all the panoply of lawyers and documents to support their claim.[17] So few people are involved, and the procedures for obtaining naturalisation are so highly discretionary, that it seems unlikely that anyone who has the slightest possibility of becoming a threat to the security of the state could pass that barrier – and therefore be at risk of subsequent deprivation. It's not impossible of course; but very unlikely. South Africa has had much more accessible naturalisation procedures, rendering it perhaps more vulnerable in this regard; but the numbers have dropped dramatically in recent years, without explanation.

Therefore, (c) comes into play. The methods traditionally used in Africa to 'denationalise' a person are simply to deny that he or she ever had nationality to start off with; to argue that the nationality documentation previously held was issued in error, or to fail to issue or renew a document providing proof of nationality (not even requiring an allegation of fraud). The key amendments to nationality laws in Africa have not been to increase government powers to deprive, but to restrict access to nationality based on birth and residence and to exploit any ambiguity in the rules applied on succession of states at independence.[18] These are the methods used against some high profile individuals: Kenneth Kaunda of Zambia and Alassane Ouattara of Côte d'Ivoire most famously; but also John Modise of Botswana, who found himself no longer considered a national by birth when he set up a political party in order to run for president. These cases reached the African Commission on Human and Peoples' Rights, but there are many others litigated only at national level involving politicians, journalists or activists.

---

[17] Manby, B. (2015), *Nationality, Migration and Statelessness in West Africa*. Dakar: UNHCR and IOM.

[18] Manby, B. (2014), 'Trends in citizenship law and politics in Africa since the colonial era', in E. F. Isin & P. Nyers (eds.), *Routledge Handbook of Global Citizenship Studies*, 172–185. Oxon; New York: Routledge.

UNHCR's clear guidance is that a retrospective finding that a person was not a national and was issued nationality documents in error is just as subject to rules on arbitrariness as any procedure under formal provisions on deprivation.[19] However, under national law, why bother with deprivation proceedings if you can manage matters so much more easily by other methods? And this applies especially when whole categories of people are seen as problematic, or potentially so.

It is, in fact, not the individual difficult cases that raise the greatest concerns in the African context, but the tendency to attribute collective responsibility to whole groups of citizens when a country is faced with a (real or perceived) security threat – or simply an organised opposition with support from a particular ethnic group. Faced with the challenges of 'nation-building' in states created by colonial fiat, the question of who belongs is not necessarily an obvious one to answer. African states have a history of mass expulsions based on ethnic grounds – there is even a style of bag known in Nigeria as a 'Ghana Must Go' bag, dating to one such episode in the 1980s when (actual or alleged) Ghanaians had to pack up and leave – and it remains the case that the usual approach is to assert that someone is a non-national, and then expel them.[20] The prevalence of such practices led to the inclusion of a specific provision banning mass expulsions, not found among similar treaties, in the African Charter on Human and Peoples' Rights.[21] Even where those who have been expelled fail to find recognition in their alleged country of origin, they may be unable to reclaim their status in the former country of residence: among those persons of Eritrean origin who were expelled by Ethiopia to Eritrea during the 1998 war between the two countries, a number subsequently became refugees from the highly repressive Eritrean regime. Even in their case, when some applied for reacquisition of Ethiopian nationality, they were reportedly told that they were security risks, so could not get papers.[22]

In Kenya, discriminatory measures in relation to documentation and identity have been sharply stepped up against Kenyan Somalis and coastal Muslims, tarred with the brush of the Westgate Mall siege and other out-

---

[19] Expert Meeting - Interpreting the 1961 Statelessness Convention and Avoiding Statelessness resulting from Loss and Deprivation of Nationality ('Tunis Conclusions'), UNHCR, March 2014, especially paragraph 9.
[20] See Manby, B. (2009), *Struggles for Citizenship in Africa*. London: Zed Books, Chapter 4.
[21] Article 12(5) of the African Charter.
[22] 'Ethiopians in Limbo: from statelessness to being a refugee in one's own country', *ECADF Ethiopian News and Views*, 14 February 2014, available at https://ecadforum.com/2014/02/14/ethiopians-in-limbo-from-statelessness-to-being-a-refugee-in-ones-own-country/

rages. In addition to a general round up and detention of suspected youth, the issuance of national ID cards has been suspended in the three counties that are located in the former North Eastern Province bordering Somalia (Garissa, Wajir and Mandera Counties, created by the 2010 Constitution), meaning that those without IDs cannot travel out of that zone, and effectively lose the reality of citizenship rights – without the need for the government to undertake any bothersome legal proceedings.[23] In Nigeria, the peculiar features of the country's federal system have led to the possibility of 'denationalisation' from a particular part of the country, even though such measures haven't been taken at national level. In the context of the threat from Boko Haram, governors of states in the south-east of the country in 2014 stepped up long-standing discrimination based on the idea of 'indigeneity' to adopt controversial measures to register and possibly deport 'non-indigenes', leading to an emergency meeting of the National Council of State in July 2014 to condemn these practices (but no action beyond establishing a committee to make recommendations).[24] Ghana's consul-general in Nigeria indeed recently blamed the Boko Haram insurgency on 'stateless people' excluded from the benefits of citizenship, and urged efforts to strengthen documentation across the sub-region.[25]

There are the beginnings of recognition that stronger guarantees around the right to a nationality may be part of the solution to some of the security challenges in the continent. The African Commission on Human and Peoples' Rights is working with the AU Commission in Addis Ababa to draft a protocol to the African Charter on the right to a nationality.[26] The African Committee of Experts on the Rights and Welfare of the Child recently adopted a General Comment on the rights of children to a name, birth registration and a nationality.[27] In parallel, there is a major push to improve docu-

---

[23] Email communication, Adam Hussein Adam, OSIEA, November 2014.
[24] 'Council of State moves to stop citizens' registration, deportation', *The Citizen*, 1 August 2014, available at https://thecitizenng.com/council-of-state-moves-to-%E2%80%8Estop-citizens-registration-deportation/. On the history of discrimination in relation to nationality in Kenya, see Manby, B. (2009), above n. 20, Chapter 6; on Nigeria and 'indigeneity', see Chapter 5.
[25] 'Envoy Blames Insecurity in Nigeria, Others on Stateless People', *Premium Times*, 29 April 2014, available at https://www.premiumtimesng.com/news/159587-envoy-blames-insecurity-nigeria-others-stateless-people.html
[26] See ACHPR Resolution 234 on the Right to Nationality, 53rd Ordinary Session, 9-23 April 2013, Banjul, The Gambia; Resolution 277 on the drafting of a Protocol to the African Charter on Human and Peoples' Rights on the Right to Nationality in Africa, 55th Ordinary Session, 28 April to 12 May 2014, Luanda, Angola.
[27] Available at the Committee of Experts website: http://acerwc.org/the-committees-work/general-comments/

mentation through the initiation or strengthening of requirements to hold a national identity card, for civil registration in general, and for the use of biometric data in these documents. But this push on information technology carries significant risks that governments will seek only to police the boundaries of their systems, excluding anyone of 'doubtful' nationality, while failing to reform legal provisions and administrative practices that restrict access to nationality for those who constitute no security threat at all. To date, the international agencies responsible on these issues — especially UNHCR, UNICEF and IOM — are also failing to join up the dots with a coherent approach on nationality and documentation in their interventions with national governments. Given the very real security threats they face, it remains an open question whether governments such as Nigeria's and Kenya's will commit to more secure rights to citizenship, rather than only more secure documentation.

37

The Politics of Revoking the Citizenship of Terrorists

Kay Hailbronner

Let's be clear: We are not in a dispute about the use of denationalisation policies to get rid of unwanted citizens who do not comply with a code of conduct how to behave as a 'good' or 'loyal' citizen. Nor are we talking about deprivation or revocation of citizenship on account of race, political opinion, religion, descent etc. There are clear rules of public international law prohibiting discriminatory citizenship policies and none of the policies discussed here call these into question. What we are discussing is the different and by no means absolutely novel issue of revoking the citizenship of persons who have given up or are irrefutably considered as having renounced that basic attachment which distinguishes citizenship from a residence permit. A recent report of de Groot and Vink for the European Commission[1] lists voluntary military service and non-military public service in nine, and eight EU countries respectively as a ground for revocation of citizenship, subject of course to some restrictions (prevention of statelessness) and exceptions.

In around half of the 28 countries included in the study, seriously prejudicial behaviour is considered as a ground for revocation of citizenship. The European Convention on Nationality of 6 November 1997 provides for revocation of citizenship for conduct seriously prejudicial to the vital interests of the State party (Art.7 para 1 lit.d). Very similar provisions on revocation are laid down in Art. 8 para 3 of the Convention on the Reduction of Statelessness of 1961.

What is new is the inclusion of a specific type of seriously prejudicial behaviour which is considered as endangering the safety of the population of a state and its security into this catalogue. The actors are not totalitarian or authoritarian regimes but democratic states with well-established

---

[1] de Groot, G.-R. & M. P. Vink (2015), *A Comparative Analysis of Regulations on Involuntary Loss of Nationality in the European Union*. Brussels: CEPS, available at https://www.ceps.eu/publications/comparative-analysis-regulations-involuntary-loss-nationality-european-union

institutions to protect human rights and to ensure the rule of law. Not that the democratic character of the states in question would dispense us from closely watching the transfer and exercise of powers to the executive branch, particularly in such a rights-sensitive area as denationalisation policies. Safeguards against arbitrary actions and abuse of power, conditions and procedures must be predominant on the watch list, as Peter Schuck rightly emphasizes. But why should revocation of citizenship of terrorists result inevitably in arbitrary and abusive exercise of power, as Audrey Macklin assumes?

What makes international terrorism so distinctive is not only its criminal and administrative relevance, but also its relevance for discontinuance of that special relationship established by citizenship. In order to answer this question it is not sufficient to conjure up emphatically the uniqueness of the ties between a citizen and a state. It is true that citizenship establishes a special relationship based upon security and stability. Security and stability on the side of the individual citizen require that denationalisation remains a rare exception. Citizenship implies rights, whether it is designated as a privilege, as a right to have rights or as a contract. For that reason deprivation of citizenship requires an overriding public interest and is subject to proportionality.

Ordinary crimes, even of a serious nature, have not been considered as sufficient under Art. 7 of the European Convention to destroy the bond of citizenship. Yet, fundamental and persistent alienation from the nation as a political community has – in spite of divergent interpretations and applications – frequently been considered as a justification for revocation of citizenship. Democratic states in the defence of their constitutional order and protection of the safety of their population and the security of the state are not restricted to a regime of criminal and administrative sanctions if their own nationals turn against them.

Legal comparison shows that there is no uniformity. States, according to their particular political conditions, and history that is sometimes reflected in constitutional provisions, have largely prohibited involuntary revocation of citizenship. Germany is one example, though it provides for loss of citizenship for voluntary service in foreign military services or in case of voluntary acquisition of a foreign citizenship. Other states, like Britain, have applied the concept to high treason, espionage, etc. International treaties, like the European Convention on Nationality of 1997 or the Convention on the Reduction of Statelessness provide further barriers. States may not provide for the loss of nationality if the person concerned would become stateless (except in case of fraud). One could discuss what this means if a state's national joins a group or organisation, such as the 'Islamic State', which is dominating a state-like territory and exercises state-like authority.

Discussion of the international and constitutional law prerequisites of revocation of citizenship is not the concern of Audrey Macklin. She argues primarily with illegitimacy. As a lawyer I have some difficulty with this term. If it is not illegal, what are the criteria for illegitimacy or immorality? Her personal idea of how democratic states should behave? That of course may be an acceptable political reasoning, provided I learn more about its ideological premises which I may share or not. I do understand Peter Spiro's objection about the revocation of citizenship as a 'security theatre' although I feel not confident on the basis of the facts to judge whether it is true that revocation of citizenship for international terrorists is impractical and irrelevant. The arguments of illegitimacy, in my view are hardly convincing. Assuming that revocation of citizenship is a (prohibited) form of punishment simply ignores the legal nature of revocation of citizenship. It is not destined to sanction acts of international terrorism, in addition to a potential criminal or administrative sanction. By untying the bond of citizenship, the former citizen can no longer rely upon his/her citizenship for unlimited entry and residence and free international travel. The further argument that there is no chance of rehabilitation is based on the same misunderstanding of revocation of citizenship as a special form of punishment. Citizenship of such persons is revoked because they have given up their attachment to a community by attacking the very fundament of that community, not by merely violating its internal rules of public order. To talk in this context of an inalienable right of rehabilitation, distorts the purpose of citizenship revocation.

The hard questions arise with the formulation of a precise and judicially reviewable provision authorising the executive to revoke citizenship. International terrorism as such is a term open to divergent interpretations. We do, however, have quite some experience, based upon the jurisprudence of national and international courts and Security Council Resolutions, in defining international terrorism. In order to be effective, a provision must include such actions as joining extremist organisations for training in order to use such training for participation in terrorist activities, as well as a membership in an organisation destined to fight against the state whose citizenship the person concerned possesses.

A further question is whether the introduction of a new provision on revocation of citizenship serves a useful purpose. Utility cannot be denied by reference to criminal law. It goes without saying that acts of international terrorism should be punished and that administrative action should, where possible, be taken to limit the use of passports for international travel for the purpose of preparing or assisting international terrorism – the technical and cynical use of citizenship rights, as Peter Schuck has phrased it. Criminal and administrative sanctions are always attached to specific activities. They do not cover the aspect of using citizenship in a general and in principle unforeseeable manner for acts destined to endanger the security of the state of which the perpetrators are citizens.

The cosmopolitan nature of this type of terrorism, as Christian Joppke has aptly described it, is misunderstood by Vesco Paskalev when he argues that the jihadists do not care about their citizenship. They might indeed not care about their attachment to the state whose citizenship they posses but they do care about the possibilities that a Canadian, US, British or German passport conveys with visa-free international travel, free entry and residence in their 'home' country and diplomatic protection if something does not go quite as smoothly as expected.

Revocation of citizenship means a substantial interference with individual rights. It can only be justified if tightly defined material conditions in accordance with the constitutional law of each country and its international commitments are fulfilled. Risk assessment and proof of an affiliation, assistance or membership in an international terrorist organisation will be essential elements in this procedure. Whether there is a practical value in revocation of citizenship for citizens engaged in international terrorism in addition to criminal and administrative sanctions is within the framework of law a matter of political expediency which may well lead to different results in different countries.

Where do the Terrorists Belong

Rainer Bauböck

Peter Schuck, Christian Joppke and Kay Hailbronner have provided strong arguments why liberal democracies should have the power to strip terrorist suspects of their citizenship. As good lawyers, Schuck and Hailbronner add that such power must be exercised with restraint and hedged in by the rule of law.

Everybody in this debate agrees that terrorists ought to be punished. Most would also agree that liberal states need exceptional powers in order to prevent terrorism and that this justifies some constraints on freedom of speech and association, for example by making incitement to terrorist violence or joining a terrorist organisation punishable crimes.

Terrorists commit particularly evil crimes. Yet denationalisation does not look like punishment for these crimes. First, it is normally based on executive order rather than court judgment. Second, it does not meet the standard purposes for criminal punishment. It cannot be justified as retribution, since it is not proportionate to the monstrosity of the crime. It does not promote rehabilitation, since the effect is to remove the criminal from the jurisdiction. And it is not effective in deterring or preventing terrorist crimes, since – as Vesco Paskalev has argued – global jihadists hardly care about losing citizenship status in a Western democracy that they detest.

Hailbronner points out that terrorists care about losing their right to travel, but restricting their freedom to move can also be achieved by other means, e.g. by invalidating their passports without denationalising them. Banishing jihadists to exactly those states where they want to go anyway to commit their atrocities can hardly count as an effective strategy against global terrorism. As a political scientist I suspect that governments have other motives apart from policy effectiveness when they seek denationalisation powers. They do not only want to do something against terrorism, they also want to be seen by voters as doing something. Stripping terrorist suspects of their citizenship is a strongly visible policy and for that reason possibly also a strongly symbolic one, as suggested by Peter Spiro.

This is not yet a conclusive refutation, since on some views it is exactly the symbolic nature of the sanction that justifies the denationalisation of terrorists. This argument starts from the assertion that liberal democracies are value-based political communities. Their basic values include freedom of conscience and religious practice, of speech and association and democratic self-government. Since these states are liberal, they cannot force their citizens to share their basic values. These are instead enshrined in their constitutions and their political institutions are designed to protect these values. Terrorists do not merely reject liberal values, they act to destroy the very institutions that protect these values. So why should liberal states not take away citizenship from those who attack the very foundations of liberal citizenship? Wouldn't this serve to defend these states' core values?

The answer is that the norms guiding the acquisition and loss of citizenship status have little to do with either the promotion or the defence of liberal values. In all states, including liberal ones, citizenship is acquired automatically at birth and normally retained over a whole life. Native citizens are never asked to show their commitment to liberal values as a condition for retaining their citizenship, nor are they stripped of their status when they commit crimes. Serious criminals are locked up in prison and thereby stripped of many citizenship rights, most importantly that of free movement. In some countries they also lose – and in my view much more questionably – voting rights. But they do not lose their citizenship status. Citizenship in our world has an extremely sticky quality. It does not have an expiry date, it can be passed on to subsequent generations and it can be carried abroad and increasingly also exercised from outside the state territory.

Yet many liberal states have introduced citizenship tests or naturalisation oaths in which immigrants are asked to affirm their commitment to the polity and its constitution.[1] Doesn't this show that acquisition of citizenship status and therefore also its loss may depend on a commitment to liberal values? No, it doesn't. Leaving aside the tricky question whether such commitments can be tested by filling in a questionnaire or taking an oath, naturalisation integrates newcomers into a political community that is based on birthright membership and equal citizenship. No matter how they have been selected and how they have acquired their citizenship, all citizens have equal

---

[1] See: Bauböck, R. & Joppke, C. (eds.) (2010), 'How Liberal are Citizenship Tests?', *Robert Schuman Centre for Advanced Studies-EUDO Citizenship Observatory Working Paper N. 2010/41*. Florence: European University Institute, available at: http://cadmus.eui.eu/handle/1814/13956.

membership status and those who have got it through naturalisation can retain it in the same way as if they had got it by birth.

This statement needs two minor qualifications. First, if citizenship has been acquired unlawfully, for example through concealing a criminal record, then it may be withdrawn. This reasoning cannot be applied to citizens who assert their commitment to a liberal constitution in a citizenship test or loyalty oath that they subsequently violate. Because liberal states cannot force ordinary citizens to support their core values, they also cannot claim that citizenship status has been acquired unlawfully if a naturalisation applicant was not sincere when swearing loyalty or was sincere and subsequently changed his views.

Second, the norm of equal treatment of native and naturalised citizens is not accepted by all liberal states – as we all know, the American President must be a native citizen. It is, however, enshrined in Art. 5 of the 1997 European Convention on Nationality and it is not difficult to see why unequal treatment of citizens based on their circumstances of birth is discriminatory and undermines the core value of equality. Faced with terrorism that is now no longer just imported but also home-grown, Western governments may anyhow be reluctant to limit the application of their denationalisation powers to naturalised immigrants.

There are two closely connected reasons why citizenship status is sticky and why it should not be taken away even for acts that attack the foundations of the polity. The first reason has to do with the function of nationality in the international state system. Citizenship is a mechanism for assigning responsibility for individuals to states. In its 1955 Nottebohm judgment the International Court of Justice asserted that citizenship should be based on a genuine connection in order to prevent states from abusively bestowing their citizenship on individuals residing abroad who want to escape a legal duty towards their host country. The same genuine link argument has been invoked by the European Parliament and Commission against Malta in January 2014 as an objection against the sale of EU citizenship to wealthy foreigners without a residence requirement.[2] If states can abuse their powers to confer citizenship by naturalising foreigners who lack a genuine

---

[2] See the press release of EU Justice Commissioner Vivian Reding 'Citizenship must not be for sale' (15 January 2014), available at http://europa.eu/rapid/press-release_SPEECH-14-18_fr.htm, the 'European Parliament resolution of 16 January 2014 on EU Citizenship for Sale', available at http://www.europarl.europa.eu/sides/getDoc.do?pubRef=-//EP//TEXT+TA+P7-TA-2014-0038+0+DOC+XML+V0//EN and Part I of this volume.

connection, they can also do so by denationalising their citizens in order to shift responsibility for them to another state. This is exactly what happens when Western countries deprive terrorist suspects of their citizenship. As Audrey Macklin has already explained, the effects can be particularly perverse for dual citizens. Since deprivation does not make them stateless, each of the two states involved has an incentive to act first so that the other state becomes responsible.

International law can thus not provide a full answer to our question. We must also consider what depriving terrorist suspects does to the citizenship bond as an internal relation between an individual and a state. Joppke points out that Germany did not expatriate the left wing terrorists of the Red Army Faction. They wanted to transform the German state whereas the global jihadists de facto renounce their membership by affiliating themselves with an Islamic pseudo-state. But the RAF was certainly as effective in shaking the foundations of a liberal Rechtsstaat by triggering illiberal responses as was Al Qaeda when it fell the twin towers in New York – and much more so than IS, which primarily wants to scare Western powers out of Iraq and Syria. In any case, the question here is not whether Ulrike Meinhof and Andreas Baader had a moral claim to German citizenship that jihadist terrorist suspects do not have. The question is whether Western democracies can shed responsibility for their home-grown citizen terrorists and shoulder it upon other states. This is what the new denationalisation policies are about.

Imagine for a moment that after 1945 Germany or Austria had posthumously denationalised Adolf Hitler. Would this symbolic act have strengthened their post-war liberal orders by demonstrating their abhorrence of Hitler's destruction of their liberal constitutions and his genocidal elimination of Jews and Roma from the political community? The answer is clearly no, because Hitler's denationalisation would have entailed a denial of responsibility for his crimes and their consequences and would thus have achieved the very opposite of the intended defence of liberal values. Moreover, if either Germany or Austria had taken such a decision, it would have signalled that they merely wanted to pass on the buck to the other state. Recognising that Hitler was 'our bad guy' was therefore crucial for building a liberal democratic consensus in both countries and good relations with other states that were the victims of Nazi aggression.

Why should this be different today with the jihadist terrorists? Joppke's answer involves an attempt to distinguish domestic from global terrorists. This may be often difficult, since Hitler turned out to be a global terrorist too. But the crucial point is that citizenship is by its very nature a domestic relation between an individual and a state. By cutting the bond, states deny their responsibility, including that towards the rest of the world upon whom they inflict the terrorist threat.

If denationalisation were a necessary and effective tool to prevent terrorism, it might be justifiable on such utilitarian grounds. But as a symbolic defence of the liberal values that terrorists attack it is entirely unconvincing.

39

Citizenship Rights and Human Rights

Daniel Kanstroom

This is an exceptionally rich and challenging discussion in which I am honoured to participate, though space limitations will inspire brevity. Audrey Macklin's essay reaches two major conclusions with which I heartily agree:

1. Citizenship-stripping weakens the concept of citizenship;
2. It is of highly-questionable efficacy and legitimacy as punishment;[1]

Despite my deep agreement with Macklin about the dangers of denationalisation trends in the UK, Canada, and elsewhere, I am not convinced that she has chosen the best way to counter them. In brief, I fear that Macklin may have missed some of the forest for the trees.

My view of the forest is this: Denationalisation should be situated against a broader backdrop in which pervasive rights deprivations against noncitizens – and even such extraterritorial rights deprivations against citizens as drone strikes – are central components. Macklin points us in this direction when she distinguishes the aspirational safe harbour of citizenship from a functional methodology:

> But my point is not to propose a metric capable of measuring the quantitative, qualitative, experiential, emotional, personal, familial, cultural, social, financial, linguistic and political impacts of exile on any individual, in order that some state official could determine precisely when citizenship revocation inflicts an appropriate versus excessive degree of punishment.

I fully support Macklin's desire to enhance 'the security that distinguishes legal citizenship.' I worry, though, about what certain approaches to such security might mean for 'other statuses that define the relationship between state and individual.' The challenge is to protect citizenship rights without relegating those 'other statuses' unduly tenuous and marginal.

---

[1] Though I agree with Kay Hailbronner that legitimacy is an elusive concept in need of further definition. I believe that one can do this relatively easily in this context.

Put simply, I suggest that the best way to do this is less (formally) citizenship–centred and more (functionally) rights-centred. By 'rights-centred,' I mean, essentially, a critical examination of state practices (including the government's intentions and justifications, and the practices' mechanisms, and effects) measured against the norms of a fully-developed human rights protection system.[2] More specifically, the important legal and policy questions raised by Macklin may be best answered by viewing denationalisation along a continuum of state practices that use citizenship status and territorial formalism to achieve policy goals with weakened (and in some cases no) rule of law encumbrances. This is one of the great human rights legal challenges of our times. It must be engaged fully – in all of its manifestations – in order to be properly understood and effectively engaged.

Macklin rightly notes that, '...citizenship revocation is best understood as a technique for extending the functionality of immigration law in counter-terrorism.' Moreover, '[s]ince 2001, states have turned to deportation to resolve threats to national security by displacing the embodied threat to the country of nationality.' However, the deep significance of these insights may be lost by too formalistic and narrow an examination of the particular practice of denationalisation. A basic reason for this is the powerful attraction – symbolic and practical – of citizenship as a safe harbour. That, in and of itself, is unobjectionable. But it risks denigration of the rights claims of noncitizens. Let me emphasize that I do not think that Macklin intends this at all. Still, her method may take us there.

Here is an example. Macklin writes, 'Banishment fits the crime of disloyalty the way capital punishment fits the crime of murder.' This works for me passably well as analogy (though, of course, the 'crime' of disloyalty is a much more complex proposition than murder). But the analogy prompts a question: How does banishment (of citizens) differ from what I have termed 'post-entry social control deportation,' which in the U.S. has resulted in lifetime exclusion of many thousands of long-term legal residents from their families and communities due to minor criminal offenses?[3] Does their lack of citizenship status render the death penalty analogy less apt? In another passage, Macklin correctly worries about 'arbitrary and prejudicial abuse of a discretionary power.' What do we make of the fact that such abuses are

---

[2] See e.g., A and others v Secretary of State for the Home Department [2004] UKHL 56, available at http://www.bailii.org/uk/cases/UKHL/2004/56.html

[3] See e.g., Kanstroom, D. (2007), *Deportation Nation: Outsiders in American History*. Cambridge: Harvard University Press; Kanstroom, D. (2012), *Aftermath: Deportation Law and New American Diaspora*. New York: Oxford University Press.

rare against citizens and troublingly common against noncitizens? Macklin is thus right, but perhaps insufficiently expansive when she asserts that the *particular* practice of denationalisation '*is* exile.' Is denationalisation categorically different from expulsion and removal of long-term legal residents because, as Macklin argues, it 'extinguishes a singular right of citizenship, namely the right to enter and to remain'? This seems formalistic and perhaps a bit circular. A fuller exploration might consider the actual effects of deportation and denationalisation on people of various statuses, various levels of assimilation, and various fears of harm. This would help explain *why* the 'right' to enter and remain is so crucial to protect against disproportionate or arbitrary state action against all people.

My main concern is about the potential implications of Macklin's methodology. The formalistic reification of citizenship may justify the relegation of noncitizens to a nether world of inferior balancing tests.[4] This is especially the case if that reification is connected to an implicitly exclusive set of rights claims to enter and remain. Noncitizens have such rights, too, at least under certain circumstances. Insufficient attention to such rights – though they are concededly still works–in-progress – is especially dangerous where the rights claims at issue include the right to life, to proportional punishment, to family unity, against arbitrary detention, and to procedural fairness.

Let us also consider the etiology and evolution of denationalisation. Harsh expulsion and exclusion practices against noncitizens can provide a conceptual matrix that facilitates similar practices against citizens. As Thomas Jefferson – writing to oppose the Federalists' Alien Friends Act, Alien Enemies Act, and Sedition Act – warned in 1798: 'The friendless alien has indeed been selected as the safest subject of a first experiment, but the citizen will soon follow...'[5] The best response to this concern, however, is *not* a regime of exclusive protections only for citizens. Rather, we should strengthen reasonable (procedural and substantive) human rights protections for all people, regardless of status or location. I expect that Macklin would not strongly disagree with this. Still, insufficient attention to such experiments against noncitizens have had metastatic tendencies in the past.

---

[4] I suppose that the opposite might also be true in certain circumstances. Rights gains won by citizens could form models that protect long term residents, albeit in depreciated form. But this pathway works best if citizenship is viewed on a continuum.

[5] The Kentucky Resolution, Documents of American History 181 (Henry Steele Commager ed., 6th ed. 1958).

Denationalisation should not be viewed as an anomalous practice that requires a unique normative critique grounded on a strong, formalistic conception of citizenship as the (supposed) Arendtian 'right to have rights.' Rather, it should be viewed as the *apotheosis* of an evolving array of exclusion and removal practices, as well as the episodic search by governments for what some termed Guantánamo Bay: 'a legal black hole.'[6] A more capacious analysis would thus not only critique the British, 'conducive to the public good' standard as relegating citizens to the status of permanent residents. It would equally question the standard's legitimacy and propriety for the latter group.[7] (Indeed, its attempted application to citizens might be ironically salutary, as political opposition will be more readily mobilised if it is practiced widely.)

Easy denationalisation deserves normative and practical critique, to be sure. As Rainer Bauböck properly highlights, citizenship is (and should be) 'sticky' and thus denationalisation must be justified as punishment. This practice is ill advised, problematic, and especially difficult to justify in liberal democracies for the reasons he highlights. However, critique should be primarily grounded in a broader set of human rights norms that apply *whenever* a state seeks to use its power disproportionately or arbitrarily against *anyone anywhere*. This is especially important for those who are strongly assimilated, who would be rendered juridically or functionally stateless or who would face severe harm, persecution, or torture.

In a similar vein, I would not recapitulate the rather formalistic and ultimately sterile debate between a 'right' and a 'privilege,' nor rely too readily on Justice Earl Warren's implicit references to Hannah Arendt. When Warren asserted that citizenship is 'the right to have rights,' he was tactically using this phrase to justify a particular position in a dissent in a 1958 case.[8] The case involved a U.S. citizen (by birth) who had lived most of his life in Texas

---

[6] *See Hamdan v. Rumsfeld*, 548 U.S. 557 (2006) (concluding: 'We have assumed ... that Hamdan is a dangerous individual whose beliefs, if acted upon, would cause great harm and even death to innocent civilians, and who would act upon those beliefs if given the opportunity. ... But in undertaking to try Hamdan and subject him to criminal punishment, the Executive is bound to comply with the Rule of Law that prevails in this jurisdiction.') See also, Steyn, J. (2004), 'Guantanamo Bay: The Legal Black Hole', *The International and Comparative Law Quarterly* 53 (1): 1–15.

[7] By which I mean conformity to the best understanding of the 'rule of law' in all its aspects, including procedural and substantive protections of basic rights.

[8] *Perez v. Brownell*, 356 U.S. 44 (1958).

and had voted there in 1946.[9] The court narrowly upheld the denationalisation (also called 'expatriation'). Justice Warren wrote a somewhat rambling dissent built around the (unattributed) reference to Arendt.[10] He concluded with two apparently contradictory propositions. The first was seemingly absolute, if a bit puzzling: 'The Government is without power to take citizenship away from a native-born or lawfully naturalized American.'[11] The second conclusion focused on the intention of the citizen: 'The citizen may elect to renounce his citizenship, and under some circumstances he may be found to have abandoned his status by voluntarily performing acts that compromise his undivided allegiance to his country.' Thus, even Justice Warren accepted that certain conduct could justify expatriation, so long as the conduct was voluntary.[12] But this fits poorly with the absolutist reading of the 'right to have rights.' Who would voluntarily relinquish the right to have all rights?

Later U.S. cases elaborated on the criterion of voluntariness, ultimately elevating it to the dominant principle.[13] However, as Justice Harlan once noted, the historical evidence limiting government power to voluntary

---

[9] The 1940 law at issue had been passed largely in response (ironically for our purposes) to voting by American citizens in a 1935 plebiscite relating to Hitler's annexation of the Saar region. As one member of congress put it. The legislation would 'relieve this country of the responsibility of those who reside in foreign lands and only claim citizenship when it serves their purposes.' Id. at 55 (in opinion of Justice Frankfurter).

[10] (joined by Justices Douglas and Black)

[11] Puzzling because the latter practice (denaturalisation) was well accepted in a wide variety of situations, such as where naturalisation had been illegally procured. The term, 'lawfully,' thus meant that one could not be denaturalised absent a finding that the naturalisation (viewed retrospectively, had been in some way unlawful).

[12] Cf. *Trop v. Dulles*, 356 U.S. 86 (1958) (in which Justice Warren, writing for a plurality, found denationalisation of a military deserter to be invalid for similar reasons, and also invalid as cruel and unusual punishment, because it resulted in 'the total destruction of an individual's status in organized society.')

[13] See e.g., *Aforyim v. Rusk*, 387 U.S. 253 (1967) ('First we reject the idea… that…Congress has any general power, express or implied, to take away an American citizen's citizenship without his assent.'); Vance v. Terrazas, 444 U.S. 252 (1980) ('[T]rier of fact must in the end conclude that the citizen not only voluntarily committed the expatriating act prescribed in the statute, but also intended to relinquish his citizenship.' Proof may be by a 'preponderance of the evidence' standard.) See also, Pub.L.99–653 (1986) (adopting this approach).

expatriation was questionable, to say the least.[14] Harlan highlighted a more functional, less formalistic defence of citizenship: 'Once obtained, citizenship is of course protected from arbitrary withdrawal by the constraints placed around Congress' powers by the Constitution....' This model seems to dovetail with Peter Schuck's proposal in this debate.[15] It has the powerful virtue of situating denationalisation within the rubric of well-accepted protections of the rule of law.

Finally, one should also note something obvious but worth highlighting: Hannah Arendt's position was *not* that citizenship *should be* the 'right to have rights.' Rather, as she expressly put it: 'The Rights of Man, supposedly inalienable, proved to be unenforceable...whenever people appeared who were no longer citizens of any sovereign state.'[16] Her concerns were practical: Such people lacked any real protection. When she explored the subject substantively her argument was much more nuanced: '...recent attempts to frame a new bill of human rights, which seem to have demonstrated that no one seems able to define with any assurance what these general human rights, as distinguished from the rights of citizen, really are.'[17] But Arendt published *The Origins of Totalitarianism* in 1951. It hardly needs to be said that – despite its evident challenges and deficiencies – the corpus of human

---

[14] Senator Howard, who had sponsored the Citizenship Clause of the Fourteenth Amendment, had conceded that citizenship could be 'forfeited' due to 'the commission of some crime.'

[15] It should also be noted that US law has long provide for such denationalisation for a wide variety of actions, including: 'committing any act of treason against, or attempting by force to overthrow, or bearing arms against, the United States, violating or conspiring to violate any of the provisions of section 2383 of title 18, United States Code, or willfully performing any act in violation of section 2385 of title 18, United States Code, or violating section 2384 of said title by engaging in a conspiracy to overthrow, put down, or to destroy by force the Government of the United States, or to levy war against them, if and when he is convicted thereof by a court martial or by a court of competent jurisdiction.' Immigration and Nationality Act Sec. 349. [8 U.S.C. 1481].

The operative standard, as noted, is the following:

'A person who is a national of the United States whether by birth or naturalisation, shall lose his nationality by voluntarily performing any of the following acts with the intention of relinquishing United States nationality- ...' Kay Hailbronner correctly highlights the prevalence of such standards elsewhere though I am less optimistic than he about the ability of states to define terrorism with sufficient precision to justify denationalisation.

[16] Arendt, H. (1966), *The Origins of Totalitarianism*. New York: Harcourt, Brace & World, Inc., 293.

[17] Indeed, Arendt herself defined the 'right to have rights' not as formal citizenship status as such, but as the right 'to live in a framework where one is judged by one's actions and opinions...' She distinguished this from the related 'right to belong to some kind of organized community.' (Ibid: 296–7)

rights protections is today more specific, more robust, and more widely enforced than was the case during the times she considered.

Arendt also poignantly described the 'calamity of the rightless' as 'that they no longer belong to any community whatsoever.' The main reason this was a calamity was that 'no law exists for them.'[18] The best way to avoid such calamities is not only to strengthen citizenship protections. That may well have the perverse consequences of, on the one hand, rendering citizenship ever harder to achieve, and on the other, relegating noncitizens to an increasingly rightless realm. We must do the harder, more basic work of defining and instantiating meaningful human rights protections for all people, regardless of status, or location. Focusing too specifically on the problem of deprivation of citizenship must not blind us 'to the numerous small and not so small evils with which the road to hell is paved.'[19]

---

[18] Ibid: 295.
[19] Arendt, H. (1994), *Essays in Understanding, 1930-1954: Formation, Exile, and Totalitarianism*. New York: Schocken Books, 271.

40

An American Perspective on Denationalization and Citizenship

Linda Bosniak

Unlike the several liberal states Macklin cites which have already, or will soon, deploy citizenship revocation as an anti-terrorism mechanism, the United States is unlikely to implement similar policies. The U.S. Constitution has been interpreted to prohibit unilateral citizenship-stripping as a tool of governance. Instead, denationalisation via expatriation in the U.S. requires the individual to specifically consent to relinquish the status, and such consent cannot be inferred from acts alone – even from acts which some (including some commentators in this symposium) would like to characterise as intrinsically antithetical to citizenship identity. The vigorous safeguarding of individual citizenship in US law is borne of the nation's history of race-based slavery and its aftermath. Today, courts quite stringently interpret the Fourteenth Amendment's guarantee of citizenship status for 'all persons born or naturalised in the U.S.' I realise the matter of slavery will seem remote from the concerns of contemporary transnational debates over citizenship-stripping in Europe and Canada (although it might be worth wondering, another day, if 'slavery' could ever serve – along with 'political death' – as a fruitful analytic metaphor here. Think, for example, of the recent mass denationalisation of Dominican-born Haitians in the Dominican Republic[1]). Nevertheless, we know that national citizenship law and policy look inward as well as outward. In the U.S., the legacy of slavery forms a part of a deep conversational grammar about citizenship in a way that will almost certainly stay the hand of congressional advocates of the 'Enemy Expatriation Act' and similar proposed measures.

That the US is not about to join Britain and Canada and other states in a politics of forcible expatriation, however, by no means implies that the US does not wish to 'permanently eliminate' suspected or confirmed terrorists, nor that it is unable to do so. Indeed, we have recently seen deployment by

---

[1] 'Stateless in the Dominican Republic: Residents stripped of citizenship', *Aljazeera America*, 4 May 2014, available at http://america.aljazeera.com/articles/2014/5/4/stateless-in-thedominicanrepublicresidentsstrippedofcitizenship.html

the U.S. of what Macklin calls 'the sovereign's other technique for permanent elimination' of such persons: namely: state-inflicted death. The 2013 assassination of U.S. citizen Anwar al-Awlaki in Yemen was a widely noted recent example of this policy (with the apparently accidental assassination Anwar's 16-year-old U.S. citizen son, Abdulrahman, a notorious follow-up.) For some commentators, state acts of this kind may appear more 'proportional' to the claimed offenses than expatriation is. Personally, I would not endorse any policy of assassination, much less when visited upon its target without application of due process. But my comments don't concern the policy's defensibility. Instead, I raise the al-Awlaki case to frame a few brief observations about the relationship between citizenship-stripping, targeted assassination and territoriality in the United States and beyond.

First, as Macklin points out, states strip citizenship not merely in order to territorially banish the affected going forward but sometimes perhaps, as a 'prelude to assassination,' whether by themselves or others. In particular, Macklin cites the cases of Britons who were denationalised and subsequently killed by US drone strike in Somalia.[2] Denationalisation here can be understood to have strategically relieved Britain of the imperative of protecting its own nationals from harm, including assassination, by another state party. In this scenario, denationalisation is not merely a form of political death; as Macklin argues, it may facilitate bodily death as well.

Nevertheless, we have also seen that since United States law makes it 'easier to kill than expatriate,' in Peter Spiro's succinct phrasing,[3] the U.S. government does not await denationalisation to assassinate its own citizens. We could, indeed, view assassination of al Awlaki senior as the nation's only route to denationalise him, with assassination serving as the actual mechanism for stripping his citizenship.

On the other hand, al Awlaki's assassination precipitated a fascinating debate in the United States about territoriality and citizenship which perhaps bears on our transnational conversation here. In the wake of the killing, a segment of the US political class erupted in concerted anxiety about whether

---

[2] See 'British terror suspects quietly stripped of citizenship... then killed by drones,' *The Independent*, 28 February 2013, available at http://www.independent.co.uk/news/uk/crime/british-terror-suspects-quietly-stripped-of-citizenship-then-killed-by-drones-8513858.html and 'Britain Increasingly Invokes Power to Disown Its Citizens', *The New York Times*, 9 April 2014, available at http://www.nytimes.com/2014/04/10/world/europe/britains-power-to-disown-its-citizens-raises-questions.html?_r=3

[3] Spiro, P. (2014), 'Expatriating Terrorists', *Fordham Law Review* 82 (5): 2169–2187, at 2177.

the government actually claimed authority not only to assassinate US citizens abroad but to do the same 'on US soil.' Senator Rand Paul led a filibuster against the confirmation of proposed CIA Director John Brennan, promising to 'speak as long as it takes until the alarm is sounded from coast to coast that our Constitution is important, that your rights to trial by jury are precious, [and] that no American should be killed by a drone on American soil without first being charged with a crime, [and] found...guilty by a court.' Much media fan-flaming followed, and eventually, Attorney General Eric Holder conceded that targeting any U.S. citizen for assassination within national territory – in the absence of imminent threat – is unacceptable. [4]

What was striking in this episode was the normative distinction taken up in popular discourse between in-country and out-of-country citizen assassination. The implied claim was that death of a citizen by its own government was somehow uniquely intolerable when accomplished *inside* national territorial bounds. For that moment, at least, the American political imaginary seemed to coalesce more around fear of tyrannical government than of the foreign terrorist within.

Of course, if government were in fact bound by this normative logic – i.e., that territorially present citizens are uniquely out of bounds for targeted killing – then the target would need to be denationalised and/or territorially expelled first and only executed thereafter. Yet since the US state is constrained in denationalising citizens, and since, like all states, it is precluded from expelling citizens, it would seem to have to await such person's travel outside the country in order to strike. This seems odd, yet it notably parallels the form denationalisation practices take in many countries – where, according to Macklin, governments tend to strip citizenship from those citizens who are already located abroad. In both settings, we see not only that territorially-present citizens are regarded as possessing more fundamental protections against government power than those territorially absent, but that governments make opportunistic use of citizen absence to act against them. Among other things, this amounts to a kind of penalty on citizen mobility, and seems to rest on an arbitrary locational distinction. This, at least, is what the US Supreme Court itself concluded in 1957 in a related context when it wrote that a citizen's constitutional rights may not 'be stripped away just because he happens to be in another land.'[5]

---

[4] For more extensive discussion and citations, see Bosniak, L. (2013), 'Soil and Citizenship', *Fordham L. Rev.* 82 (5): 2069–2075.

[5] Reid v. Covert, 354 U.S. 1 (1957).

Of course, territoriality's relationship with citizenship sometimes reaches back well beyond any possible denationalisation and assassination to the moment of the citizen's birth. For some, the Awlaki affair itself evoked long-standing debates about assignment of citizenship based on territorial presence at birth, with Awlaki an exemplar of the 'nominal citizen' whose extraterritoriality for most of his post-natal life rendered his social attachment to the nation 'highly attenuated' (to use Macklin's phrase). Yet in this setting as well, the United States will remain robustly-citizenship protective. The country's inclusive birthright citizenship rules are another stanchion of its post-slavery, post-Civil War, constitutionalism. Consequently, and much as some 'anti-birthers' wish it were otherwise, citizenship cannot be easily eliminated on the front end here, except by way more stringent immigration and border control policies to prevent, ex ante, potential parents' territorial presence. Broadly drawn and often selectively-applied grounds of inadmissibility and deportability based on 'terrorist activity' arguably go some of the distance in accomplishing that end.[6]

In short, citizenship status, especially for those in national territory, still remains more secure in the U.S. than it is in some other national settings. Our government works to counter the alleged 'bad guys' (Bauböck's shorthand) by different means.

---

[6] E.g., Legomsky, S. H. (2005), 'The Ethnic and Religious Profiling of Noncitizens: National Security and International Human Rights', *Boston College Third World Law Journal* 25 (1): 161-196.

41

Weakening of Citizenship by States

Matthew J. Gibney

I find a great deal to agree with in Audrey Macklin's trenchant and wide-ranging argument against denationalisation power's recent revival in Western countries. Yet I also understand where her critics are, somewhat abrasively, coming from. It is of course possible to imagine carefully fashioned cases where denationalisation seems a morally appropriate response as long as a range of guarantees are met (for example, when an individual represents a clear threat to the state, where there are no doubts about his guilt or intentions, and where he could be stripped of citizenship without being made stateless.) However, while this realisation might help us identify the terms on which the denationalisation of a particular individual is permissible, it tells us little about the broader consequences of piercing the norm of unconditional citizenship for punitive reasons.[1] I think that once we are realistic about the political dangers of conceding to the state powers to withdraw citizenship, we're brought back to a position compatible with Audrey Macklin's ban on denationalisation.

Before explaining why I think an absolute bar might be justified let make a couple of comments on the previous discussion. The first of these is on what one might call the statelessness constraint. All of the critics of Audrey Macklin's position start (with the possible exception of Christian Joppke) by accepting that individuals, even those who commit terrorist acts, should not be made stateless. This constraint against statelessness is not simply a matter of international or domestic law; it is also a normative constraint that stems from basic liberal commitments. The problem with statelessness is that it leaves individuals subject to state power without citizenship's basic protections against that power, including security of residence, political rights, and potentially a host of other entitlements. If we accept this normative rationale for guarding against statelessness, as I think we should, we will also want to

---

[1] My focus in this short piece is exclusively on the punitive withdrawal of citizenship. There are, of course, other reasons why states have sought to 'pierce' citizenship, for example, to address fraudulent acquisition of citizenship or to prevent dual nationality.

ensure that those denationalised are not made de facto stateless, that is, forced to rely on a state that is unable and unwilling to protect them or otherwise to deliver the fundamental rights citizenship (or nationality) is supposed to guarantee.[2]

Yet taking this additional constraint seriously is going to be very consequential. The secondary citizenships of the individuals Western states most want to strip of citizenship tend to be those of countries with dubious human rights records and histories of civil war and conflict (Somalia, Iraq, Eritrea, Sudan, to name a few).[3] If de facto statelessness is a bar, most of the prime targets are going to be out of denationalisation's reach. Of course, de facto statelessness does not establish a case for an absolute rejection of the state's power to denationalise. But it does show why the power's scope may be very narrow indeed, at least for liberals.

Second, I find myself attracted to the position of Rainer Bauböck that one reason denationalisation is unacceptable is because it involves states 'passing the buck' of their own responsibilities on to other states, a point that adds a different dimension to Audrey Macklin's claim that citizenship is, in important respects, not fungible. This view that banishment is unfair to other states is a very old one. None other than Voltaire argued against the practice of banishment on the grounds that it involves throwing into our neighbour's field the stones that incommode us in our own.

Powerful as it is, however, the consideration that there's something wrong with denationalising 'home grown' terrorists, wouldn't mean that denationalisation was always inappropriate. States might still claim the moral right to denationalise individuals who had held citizenship only for a short period of time or had spent most of their lives living in the other

---

[2] Cf. Barry, C. & L. Ferracioli (2013), 'Withdrawing Citizenship', paper delivered at the Australian National University, Canberra, 16 July 2013. I accept that specifying exactly what is included in the concept of 'de facto statelessness' is not necessarily clear, as is the relationship between de facto statelessness and simple human rights abuses. A good starting point for further consideration of this issue is Sawyer, C. & B. K. Blitz (eds.) (2011), *Statelessness in the European Union: displaced, undocumented, unwanted*. Cambridge: Cambridge University Press.

[3] Note, for example, the second nationalities of the denationalised individuals that the Bureau of Investigative Journalism has been able to track, available at https://www.thebureauinvestigates.com/stories/2014-12-10/what-do-we-know-about-citizenship-stripping.

country in which they held citizenship. Germany certainly should not have posthumously denationalised Hitler. But Hitler was the leader of the German state and celebrated in this role by a significant proportion of the German people during the 1930s and 1940s. Putting aside the question of what should be done posthumously, some citizens have a much more tenuous, even a merely nominal, relationship to the state. Not all are even grown at home.

These considerations help to clarify some of the constraints necessary for a liberal denationalisation power. Even from the short discussion here, we can identify plenty of others. Peter Schuck suggests that an individual's threat to the state needs to be 'rigorously proven' and Kay Hailbronner argues that citizenship deprivation must be 'subject to proportionality'. It's clear that satisfying all of these different requirements will make the construction of denationalisation law consistent with liberal principles a Herculean task. However, where I part company with the denationalisers is not so much over whether it's possible to identify a liberal starting point for the practice.[4] Rather, my concern is over the illiberal direction denationalisation seems likely to take once it returns to the political repertoire. Here my position has been greatly influenced by the recent experience of the UK.[5]

When denationalisation was first revived after over thirty years of desuetude by the Blair government in 2002, the power was tightly constrained: the definition incorporated was taken from the European Convention on Nationality, only dual nationals were targeted, and an automatic judicial appeal was to follow any decision by the Home Secretary. The government promised to use the power rarely. This modest beginning for denationalisation did not last. After the London bombings in July 2005, a new act passed by the Blair government in 2006 lowered the standard required for denationalisation. While previously the Home Secretary had to be satisfied that an individual had engaged in actions that threatened the 'vital interests of the UK' state, now he or she had only to be satisfied that taking away someone's citizenship was 'conducive to the public good'. The standard for continuing

---

[4] I discuss the normative complexities of denationalisation in Gibney, M. J. (2013), 'Should citizenship be conditional? The ethics of denationalization', *The Journal of Politics* 75 (3): 646–658.

[5] I give a fuller account of the history of UK denaturalisation power in Gibney, M. J. (2013), '"A Very Transcendental Power": Denaturalisation and the Liberalisation of Citizenship in the United Kingdom', *Political Studies* 61 (3): 637–655.

to hold British citizenship had now become the same as the one used to judge whether a non-citizen should be deported. Even after this radical change, it was possible to convince oneself that the government would use the power sparingly. Only a handful of people lost their citizenship under the Labour government's watch.

But with the coming of the Conservative/Liberal Democrat coalition government things have gone seriously awry. In the Cameron government's first year of office in 2010-11, no fewer than six people were stripped of their citizenship. This was more people than the Blair and Brown governments had denaturalised in the previous nine years (in the immediate aftermath of the terrorist events of September 11, 2001 and July 7, 2005). The enthusiastic use of deprivation power has continued apace in the years since, though almost always in secret. By May 2014, it was evident that Cameron's government had some 23 people stripped of citizenship on 'not conducive' grounds in the last three years. Almost all of these individuals were stripped of citizenship while outside the UK, undermining real access to appeal procedures. In January 2014 the government presented a bill to parliament requesting the power to strip citizenship from naturalised citizens even if they would be made stateless. The amendment passed, albeit, in a modified form. Under current law in the UK a naturalised citizen can be made stateless if the Home Secretary deems there are reasonable grounds for believing they have access to another citizenship.

Now it might be said – and Christian Joppke would probably be the one to say it – that the UK is an outlier. The unravelling of constraints on denationalisation evident in Britain is unlikely to be repeated elsewhere because other Western countries are less insouciant about protecting rights. But note that the circumstances that have geed along transformation in UK law are generally applicable: terrorist events (the 2005 Tube bombing) and a change of government (the coming of the Conservatives to power). Moreover, I'm not confident that other countries are as legally protected against creep of denationalisation power as they might seem. Australia has fewer rights based protections even than the UK; Canada has some alarming inclusions in its recent denationalisation legislation, including the state's ability to rely on a conviction for terrorist offences in another country; and, as I write, a large number of prominent US politicians (buoyed by public opinion polls) have effectively endorsed torture as a practice for dealing with terrorists past and future.

I thus find myself agreeing with Audrey Macklin's embrace of unconditional citizenship, albeit because I fear where we will end up if we try to pierce even a small – liberal size – hole into citizenship to punish terrorists.

Liberalism is not simply a set of principles, it's also a political stance – one that encourages a healthy scepticism of state attempts to encroach upon established rights and protections. In these fraught times, it is wise to adopt the stance as well as to protect the principles.

42

Citizenship Revocation

Reuven (Ruvi) Ziegler

Macklin's kick-off focused 'exclusively on denationalisation for allegedly disloyal conduct by a citizen, while a citizen'. Most contributions to this debate weighed the predicament of the former citizen against state interests. In my contribution, I offer a typology of cases in which revocation could be sought according to some of the contributors. I contend that disowning of citizens by their states is incoherent, tenuous, or disingenuous.

The first type of case involves acts which, according to Hailbronner, undermine the constitutional order by seriously threatening public safety and state security. Hailbronner contends that individuals performing such acts 'have given up their attachment to a community by attacking the very fundament of that community, not by merely violating its internal rules of public order'. However, this line-drawing exercise seems to be quite difficult: every crime may cause insecurity, threaten public order, and prevent democratic societies from functioning properly; citizens (and decision-makers, including those entrusted with citizenship revocation) will diverge, based on their ideological biases, as to whether particular crimes cross Hailbronner's threshold. For instance, did the perpetrators of the Brighton hotel bombing on 12 October 1984 cross the threshold in light of the potential ramifications of Thatcher's assassination for the stability of the United Kingdom? If so, would a person financing such an attack qualify, too?

Nevertheless, perhaps a 'core' case can be identified, such as a criminal conviction for treason. One of the constituent elements of such acts is often that they are committed by citizens qua citizens. For instance, Lord Haw-Haw (William Joyce) could be convicted of espionage for Germany in the Second World War because he possessed British nationality; he unsuccessfully argued that he did not owe loyalty to the Crown.[1] If the basis for Joyce's conviction was that his crimes against the state were committed as a British national, then disowning Joyce ex post facto seems incoherent: the state

---

[1] 'Lord Haw-Haw – The Nazi broadcaster who threatened Britain', *Lord Haw-Haw Collection, BBC Archive*, available at http://www.bbc.co.uk/archive/hawhaw/

must reject the claim that treasonous acts amount to renunciation of citizenship, because that would disable the state from prosecuting the perpetrator for treason (for an analogous argument concerning the legitimacy of disenfranchisement of convicted adult citizens, see my article[2]).

The second type of case involves crimes (including crimes defined as 'terrorism' under international treaties or domestic law) committed by a citizen of state A against individuals or institutions in state B. The fact that the person who has committed such crimes holds the citizenship of state A seems incidental. Consider the attack on the Jewish museum of Belgium in Brussels on 24 May 2014, which is likely to have been carried out by a French national affiliated with ISIL[3]. ISIL has been designated as a terrorist organisation by the EU, of which France is a member, as well as by the UN. Were France to revoke the citizenship of this member of an internationally designated terrorist organisation, it would be severing legal relations with a citizen even though the citizen's actions were not directed specifically towards the French state, its institutions, or its population. This seems rather tenuous.

Joppke argued that 'international terrorists are not criminals but warriors'. But the state exercises its sovereign powers vis-à-vis 'international terrorists' qua citizens. The fact that such persons commit acts that are of an international character does not make it more plausible for their state of nationality to legally disown them as a result. Hailbronner argues that '[w]hat makes international terrorism so distinctive is ... also its relevance for discontinuance of that special relationship established by citizenship.' I am not quite sure why engagement in international terrorism (such as the ISIL-sponsored attack on the Jewish museum) necessarily or even plausibly indicate that a citizenship bond has been severed by the terrorist. This seems to conflate the fact that their state of nationality perceives (and rightly so) the terrorist's act as heinous with a direct effect on that state.

The third type of case concerns acts which are committed by a citizen in the name of the Ancien Régime. Following political transformation, the state wishes to disassociate itself from such past acts by dissociating itself

---

[2] Ziegler, R. (2011), 'Legal Outlier, Again? U.S. Felon Suffrage: Comparative and International Human Rights Perspectives', *Boston University International Law Journal* 29 (2); *Oxford Student Legal Studies Paper No. 01/2011*. Available at SSRN: https://ssrn.com/abstract=1689665

[3] 'French suspect in Brussels Jewish museum attack spent year in Syria', *The Guardian*, 1 June 2014, available at https://www.theguardian.com/world/2014/jun/01/french-suspect-brussels-jewish-museum-attack-syria

from the perpetrators. As Bauböck rightly notes, Hitler's posthumous denationalisation by either Germany or Austria would have been considered 'a denial of responsibility for his crimes and their consequences'. In addition to the revocation's outward-looking dimension (towards the international community), it has an inward-looking dimension too. When Augusto Pinochet stood trial in in 2004, he was charged with crimes committed by him as head of the military junta which ruled Chile after the 1973 coup. He died in 2006 before the conclusion of his trial. Let's imagine that Pinochet had another (nominal) citizenship, and that his conviction would have resulted in his denationalisation. This would have seemed, rightly, as an attempt to undermine the fact that these acts were committed in the name of the Chilean state.

Paskalev asserted that, ironically, the 'softness of citizenship revocation makes it appear quite inappropriate for the case of terrorists'. However, even if (some) terrorists may be blasé about losing their citizenship, we ought to be concerned about states' eagerness to wash their hands of them.

43

Micro-Banishments of our Times

Saskia Sassen

I arrive late to this discussion, to these excellent pieces that cover much ground... not much left to cover. For the sake of debate and commentary, rather than scholarly analysis, let me throw into the discussion what is no more than a little wrench.

Denationalisation is an ambiguous concept. This discussion has given it one sharp meaning: being stripped of one's nationality and thrown out of one's country. In my own work I have used it to capture more ambiguous meanings, thereby giving it the status of a variable that can be applied to a range of domains, not only citizenship.[1]

Thus, I see denationalisation at work when, beginning in the 1980s, global firms pushed for and got most national governments to institute deregulations and privatisations so as to maximise their access into any national economy.[2] It meant that states had to denationalise key elements of the legal framing (i.e. protections) they had long offered their own firms, markets, investors. One might say that in doing so, these states instituted a partial 'banishment' of their own national firms from a legal framing that granted these national firms exclusive privileges/rights. This is a form of banishment that does not entail a physical departure from a country's territory. It only entails a loss of particular exclusive rights and protections. We can conceive of it as a kind of micro-banishment.

Similarly, I would argue that such internal micro-banishments are also present in the decisions of many national states, beginning in the 1980s and onwards, to eliminate a few rights here and there that their citizens may long have had. Examples for the U.S. are, among several others, Clinton's 1996 Illegal Immigration Reform and Immigrant Responsibility Act which took away the rights of citizens to bring legal action against the INS in lower

---

[1] See chapters 4, 5, and 6 in Sassen, S. (2008), *Territory, Authority, Rights: From Medieval to Global Assemblages*, 2nd ed. Princeton: Princeton University Press.

[2] Sassen, S (2017), 'Predatory Formations Dressed in Wall Street Suits and Algorithmic Math', *Science, Technology & Society* 22 (1): 1–15.

courts; or when credit card companies obtained the right to pursue payment even if a household had declared bankruptcy – a right so abusive it eventually got cancelled. We might argue that in these cases, citizens experienced a partial banishment from specific rights (even as some new rights were also attained, notably gay marriage). The better language to describe these losses may be what Audrey Macklin refers to elsewhere as civil death.[3]

Current examples for the gains of rights for global firms and the loss of protections for national firms and workers can be found in some of the clauses of both the Transpacific and the Transatlantic Trade Partnerships.

Long before we get to the dramatic figure of the terrorist, where the debate about banishment turns clearly pro or contra, I see a range of micro-banishments that take place deep inside national territory. If I wanted to give this image an extreme character, I would say that in today's interaction prone world (see, for instance, the earlier behind closed-doors negotiations between Iran and the U.S., or, for a period, between the U.S. and the Taliban) there is no more terra nullius for banishment.

If I were to use the term 'banishment,' I would want to use its conceptual power to get at the multiple little banishments that happen inside our countries and that often entail a move into systemic invisibility – the loss of rights as an event that produces its own partial, or specialised, erasure. I refer to these micro-banishments as expulsions, a term I intend as radically different from the more common term 'exclusion,' which refers to a condition internal to a system, such as discrimination.[4] I conceive of such expulsions as a systemic capability, clearly a use of the term capability that diverges from the common use which marks it as a positive. Thus micro-banishments can be seen as a profoundly negative systemic capability that is far more widespread than our current categories of analysis allow us to see.[5]

To conclude I would like to return to Audrey Macklin's argument.

I agree with Audrey Macklin's proposition that citizens should not be banished even when they engage in terrorist attacks on their own country. I share

---

[3] Macklin, A. (2014), 'Citizenship Revocation, the Privilege to Have Rights and the Production of the Alien', *Queen's Law Journal* 40 (1): 1–54, at 8.
[4] Sassen, S. (2014), *Expulsions: Brutality and Complexity in the Global Economy*. Cambridge, Mass: Harvard University Press.
[5] This also raises the possibility of an obverse condition: that the tissue constructed via the recurrence of micro-banishments inside a nation-state could, with time, become the tissue for a claim to transnational citizenship. Could it be that as citizens experience the limits of national citizenship, transversal notions of membership become more plausible? I am thinking here of substantive conditions for transnational citizenship, not just ideational ones.

her concern with the importance of protecting a robust form of citizenship. But I do so partly also from a transversal and dystopian perspective that may have little to do with the rationale put forth by Macklin. Let me clarify. It is not only terrorists that are destructive and attack the innocent; it is also predatory actors of all sorts – corporate firms that exploit workers worldwide, financial speculators, abusive prison systems. Further I agree with Macklin that a country should develop the needed internal instruments to deal with terrorists rather than banish them. But again, I would take this beyond terrorists who are citizens, and include the types of predatory actors I refer to above.

Beyond all of this, I am above all concerned with the larger history in the making that I refer to earlier in this short text. This larger history is shaping an epochal condition that takes me away from prioritising banishment as loss of citizenship and of the right to live in one's country as discussed in this Forum.

Briefly put, I would argue that the conceptual locus of the category banishment in today's world is not banishment in the historical sense of the term, but a new kind of banishment. It is one predicated on the formation of geographies of privilege and disadvantage that cut across the divides of our modernity – East-West, North-South. The formation of such geographies includes a partial disassembling of the modern national territorial project, one aspiring (and dependent on) national unity, whether actual or idealised. This then also means that there is a weakening of the explanatory power of the nation-based encasements of membership (for citizens, for firms, for political systems) that have marked our modernity. The micro-banishments I refer to are part of emergent (and proliferating!) geographies of disadvantage (for citizens, firms, districts) internal to a country.

44

Citizenship Revocation and its Conflicts with EU Law
Jo Shaw

The purpose of this short intervention in the debate on *The Return of Banishment* initiated by Audrey Macklin, where the pros and cons of various forms of deprivation policies pursued by, or sought by, liberal states have been fully debated, is to add an element of EU law. Specifically, in the light of the judgments of the European Court of Justice in *Rottmann*[1] and *Ruiz Zambrano*[2], how – if at all – are Member States' laws and procedures on involuntary loss of citizenship affected by EU law, given that the primary competence to determine the rules on the acquisition and loss of citizenship remains with Member States? At the time of the hearing, well informed observers[3] who followed the UK Supreme Court hearing in the case of *B2 (Pham) v SSHD*[4] concerned with the UK's rather extensive deprivation powers and the issue of statelessness indicated that they thought it likely that the Supreme Court would make a reference to the Court of Justice. It seemed that the judges would ask the CJEU if it really meant what it said when it decided the case of *Rottmann*. *B2 (Pham)*, like the earlier cases of *G1* (discussed below) and as well as the case of [5], a former Iraqi citizen who has

---

[1] C-135/08, available at http://curia.europa.eu/juris/liste.jsf?num=C-135/08
[2] C-34/09, available at http://curia.europa.eu/juris/liste.jsf?language=en&num=C-34/09
[3] Cox, S. (2014), 'Rottmann Rules UK? Can British citizenship be taken away without regard to EU law?', *EU Law Analysis*, available at http://eulawanalysis.blogspot.com.es/2014/11/rottmann-rules-uk-can-british.html; Woodrow, P. (2014), 'Statelessness, deprivation of nationality, and EU Citizenship…what is B2 in the Supreme Court really all about?', *freemovement*, available at https://www.freemovement.org.uk/statelessness-deprivation-of-nationality-and-eu-citizenshipwhat-is-b2-in-the-supreme-court-really-all-about/. In the event, no reference was made [comment added in June 2018 to text prepared in 2014].
[4] *Pham (Appellant) v Secretary of State for the Home Department (Respondent)* [2015] UKSC 19, available at https://www.supremecourt.uk/cases/uksc-2013-0150.html
[5] *Secretary of State for the Home Department v Al-Jedda* [2013] UKSC 62 (9 October 2013), available at http://www.bailii.org/uk/cases/UKSC/2013/62.html

twice been stripped of his UK citizenship as well as spending time in military detention in Iraq[6], all concern naturalised citizens who are suspected of some form of terrorist involvement, but against none of whom criminal proceedings have been brought in the UK.

We are likely, therefore, to be in a phase of further legal development – initially in iteration between the UK courts and the Court of Justice, but with implications for all of the Member States as quite a number of states have started to look closely at using expatriation measures in order to combat radicalisation and terrorist threats, even if many judge this approach to be ill-advised and inappropriate.

I will explain briefly what the issues are. The *Rottmann* case was the subject of an earlier Forum Debate[7] on the EUDO Citizenship website. *Rottmann* was a case of loss of citizenship conferred by naturalisation, after it came to light that the naturalisation had been obtained by fraud. In this case, Rottmann, an Austrian citizen, had failed to reveal that he had been the subject of unconcluded criminal proceedings in Austria when seeking naturalisation in Germany. Rottmann raised issues of EU law in his appeal against the deprivation decision before the German administrative courts, which led to a reference to the Court of Justice. He pointed out that having obtained German citizenship he lost Austrian citizenship, by operation of law. Thus, if he were deprived of German citizenship he would be stateless, and – furthermore – he would have lost his EU citizenship. One issue that had been raised – and which caught the attention of Advocate General Maduro in his Opinion – was whether this was a 'wholly internal situation' – i.e. a German court reviewing a decision of a German public authority regarding a German citizen. In that sense, it could be said, EU citizenship was not engaged at all. In response, the Court repeated its standard formulation when dealing with matters which fall outside the competence of the EU and its legislature. It reminded us that EU cannot adopt measures with regard to national citizenship, but none the less while national competence remains intact, it must be exercised 'with due regard' to the requirements of EU law in situations covered by EU law. Specifically, in this case, said the Court:

---

[6] 'Al-Jedda, "statelessness" and the meaning of words', *Freemovement*, 25 October 2013, available at https://www.freemovement.org.uk/al-jedda-statelessness-and-the-meaning-of-words/

[7] Shaw, J. (2011), 'Has the European Court of Justice Challenged Member State Sovereignty in Nationality Law?', *Robert Schuman Centre for Advanced Studies, EUDO Citizenship Observatory Working Paper No.* 2011/62, Florence: European University Institute, available at http://cadmus.eui.eu/handle/1814/19654

It is clear that the situation of a citizen of the Union who, like the applicant in the main proceedings, is faced with a decision withdrawing his naturalisation, adopted by the authorities of one Member State, and placing him, after he has lost the nationality of another Member State that he originally possessed, in a position capable of causing him to lose the status conferred by Article 17 EC [i.e. Union citizenship] and the rights attaching thereto falls, by reason of its nature and its consequences, within the ambit of European Union law (para. 42 of the judgment).

The Court went on to recognise that states may have legitimate reasons to withdraw citizenship, but it is worth noting that the Court of Justice does not, in this paragraph, focus on statelessness, but rather on the loss of the rights specific to EU law. In other words, this can be seen as an EU-specific reason for requiring the testing of any decision to withdraw citizenship against – as the Court went on to hold – a standard of proportionality. Factors to be borne in mind in assessing the proportionality of the withdrawal decision included the gravity of the original offence or deception, lapse of time, the impact on the subject of the decision and their family, the possibility of recovering the original citizenship lost at the time of naturalisation, and the availability of other less severe measures than withdrawal.

While some have suggested that the essence of *Rottmann* lay in the way that the claimant is strung across between the national citizenship laws of two EU Member States, one at least of which claims exclusivity and thus operates an automatic rule of withdrawal in the event that a citizen acquires the citizenship of another state, the point about loss of the benefits of EU citizenship as a freestanding principle of EU law without regard to prior movement from one Member State to another was given a further boost in the case of *Ruiz Zambrano*. In that case, the EU citizens threatened with losing their rights of citizenship were the children of the claimant, who were born in Belgium and who had acquired Belgian, and thus EU, citizenship at birth. Meanwhile, through a combination of circumstances their Colombian citizen father had not regularised his situation in Belgium (or had perhaps been prevented from doing so by a series of delays perpetrated by the Belgian authorities in relation to his case). Because the refusal of a residence permit for Ruiz Zambrano and his wife would, in effect, have meant that the EU citizen children would have been obliged to leave, with their parents, the territory of the EU and thus would not have been able to avail themselves of their rights as EU citizens (notably the right of free movement which they had not yet exercised, but which they might exercise in the future), the Court concluded that a Member State could not refuse to grant either a residence permit or indeed a work permit. The test that the Court articulated was whether the measure taken in relation to a third country national upon whom the EU citizen children were dependent was whether it would make them unable to exercise 'the substance of their rights' as citizens of the EU.

Neither *Rottmann* nor – in particular – *Ruiz Zambrano* have been met with unalloyed enthusiasm at the national level. It goes beyond the scope of this short comment to discuss how and why Member States and indeed their courts might react to challenging judgments of the Court of Justice that appear to extend the scope of EU law and, in particular, the scope of EU citizenship.[8] That said, there is no evidence to suggest that, thus far, *Rottmann* has had a significant or disruptive effect on national citizenship laws.[9]

The UK is one of the few states where *Rottmann* has thus far been discussed in national cases, but – until the case of *B2 (Pham)* which is before the Supreme Court – the limit of consideration had been a rather dismissive swipe at the Court of Justice taken by Lord Justice Laws in the Court of Appeal in the case of *G1 v SSHD*[10]. Laws LJ sceptically asked '[u]pon what principled basis, therefore, should the grant or withdrawal of State citizenship be qualified by an obligation to "have due regard" to the law of the European Union?' (para. 38), given that the grant and withdrawal of citizenship remains a matter of Member State competence.

The Supreme Court refused to give leave to appeal to the applicant in *G1*, but perhaps it was only a matter of time, given the salience of deprivation of citizenship in the UK at the present time, before it had to grasp the nettle of considering not only the meaning of statelessness in the context of the then applicable UK law (this having moved on somewhat since that time, as Gibney's contribution to the Forum highlights) but also the possible applicability of EU law as a restraint upon executive freedom, and as a standard

---

[8] Blauberger, M. (2012), 'With Luxembourg in mind ... the remaking of national policies in the face of ECJ jurisprudence', *Journal of European Public Policy* 19 (1): 109–126; Blauberger, M. (2014), 'National Responses to European Court Jurisprudence', *West European Politics* 37 (3): 457–474; Schmidt, S. (2014), 'Judicial Europeanisation: The Case of *Zambrano* in Ireland', *West European Politics* 37 (4): 769–785.

[9] See Shuibhne, N. N. & J. Shaw (2014), 'General Report General Report: Union Citizenship: Development, Impact and Challenges', in U. Neergaard, C. Jacqueson & N. Holst-Christensen (eds.), *Union Citizenship: Development, Impact and Challenges*. The XXVI FIDE Congress in Copenhagen, Congress Publications Vol. 2, Copenhagen: DJØF Publishing. at p. 154–155.

[10] *G1 v Secretary of State* [2012] EWCA Civ 867. Available at http://www.bailii.org/ew/cases/EWCA/Civ/2012/867.html

which UK courts, in exercising their review function, would need to uphold. Hence the appellant in *B2* has been given leave to appeal, with perhaps a reference to the Court of Justice still to come.

As the discussion by Simon Cox[11], a lawyer working with the Open Society Institute which intervened in this case[12], has made clear, it seems quite likely that if the applicability of EU law as a frame of reference against which UK deprivation legislation needs to be judged is duly established by the Court of Justice and accepted by the Supreme Court, then the proportionality standards which need to be applied by UK courts exercising their review function may differ from those otherwise applicable within UK public law. The key issue seems likely to surround the putative autonomy of EU citizenship: is there a freestanding EU law related concern with citizenship stripping, namely the loss of EU citizenship rights, which goes beyond the issue of statelessness? *Rottmann* seemed to suggest there was, but this is the issue on which the Supreme Court may probe the CJEU further. It should be noted that there may also be higher standards of disclosure of otherwise secret evidence, following the judgment of the Court of Justice in the *ZZ* case[13], if the applicability of EU law is accepted.

Finally, it should be pointed out that the OSI interest in the case is not directly with the *Rottmann* point, but concerns the definition of statelessness, which, they argue also has an EU element and should have a common EU level definition to which Member States are obliged to adhere. This call stems from the fear that in its earlier judgment in *B2 (Pham)* the Court of Appeal[14] created significant difficulties when it resolved that B2 was not to be judged as *de jure* stateless, once deprived of UK citizenship, because although the Vietnamese government indicated they did not recognise him as a citizen, it was clear that this was unlawful under Vietnamese law.

The UK courts, said the Court of Appeal, were bound by the rule of law. Therefore, they could not recognise an unlawful act of the Vietnamese government. This seems to be peculiarly Kafka-esque reasoning and the OSI, given its investment in the campaign against statelessness on-going under

---

[11] Cited above n. 3.
[12] Case No. UKSC 2013/0150, available at http://www.opensocietyfoundations.org/sites/default/files/b2-v-home-secretary-case-intervener-20 141105_0.pdf
[13] C-300/11, available at http://curia.europa.eu/juris/liste.jsf?num=C-300/11
[14] *B2 v Secretary of State for the Home Department* [2013] EWCA Civ 616 (24 May 2013), available at http://www.bailii.org/ew/cases/EWCA/Civ/2013/616.html

the leadership of the UNHCR, would be concerned if this reasoning were to take hold in the UK, which is bound to have further cases coming before the courts, given the remarkable rate[15] at which the state is now expatriating its citizens on grounds that this is conducive to the public good.

---

[15] 'Government release number of deprived of British citizenship since 2013', *The Bureau of Investigative Journalism*, 19 December 2014, available at https://www.thebureauinvestigates.com/stories/2014-12-19/government-release-number-deprived-of-british-citizenship-since-2013

45

A Glance at the Alien within

Audrey Macklin

Shortly after the last contributor posted a comment on this Forum, reports of the Charlie Hebdo attacks erupted in the media. The assailants were two French brothers (Cherif and Siad Kouachi) who claimed affiliation to Al Qaeda in Yemen. Hours later, an associate (Amiday Coulibaly) killed a police officer, then rampaged through a kosher Hyper Cacher supermarket and murdered four hostages. All three men were slain two days later in confrontations with French police and security. That same day, the notorious 'Finsbury Mosque cleric', British national Abu Hamza, was sentenced to life in prison by a US court for terrorism related crimes. Most recently, the French Conseil Constitutionnel upheld a law permitting denaturalisation of dual-national French citizens convicted of terrorist offences.[1] One cannot but wonder whether the Charlie Hebdo and Hyper Cacher attacks cast a long shadow over the Conseil Constitutionnel's deliberations, even though all three men were French by birth and therefore outside the purview of the denaturalisation law.

The horrific deeds of the French perpetrators struck at the heart of liberal democratic values: freedom of expression and religious tolerance. States understandably seek new and better tools to prevent future atrocities; the impulse toward retribution at such moments seems hard to resist. Do these attacks make the case for citizenship revocation? I remain sceptical that citizenship revocation advances the objective of protecting liberal democracies, or that pursuit of unalloyed retribution is an objective worthy of liberal democracies.

Defenders of citizenship stripping offer a mix of instrumental and non-instrumental justifications, but Kay Hailbronner, Christian Joppke and Peter Schuck lean toward the latter more than the former. Despite its rejection by

---

[1] The law permits denaturalisation of dual nationals who commit terrorism offences within fifteen years of naturalisation ('Moroccan-born man jailed on terror charges to lose French nationality', *The Guardian*, 23 January 2015, available at http://www.theguardian.com/world/2015/jan/23/moroccan-born-man-jailed-terror-lose-french-nationality-sahnouni)

the US Supreme Court over fifty years ago, both Hailbronner and Joppke revert to the legal fiction of constructive renunciation and insist that certain conduct communicates an irrefutable intention of terrorists to renounce their own citizenship. Schuck revises the fiction by acknowledging that perpetrators may not actually wish to renounce citizenship, but then discounts an intention to maintain citizenship for 'tactical and cynical' purposes. But however attractive the fiction of constructive renunciation, it does not become truer with repetition, or with the passage of time, or by writing new characters into the narrative. Citizenship revocation for misconduct while a citizen is not chosen by the citizen; it is inflicted by the state.

Joppke explains that Germany would have been wrong to regard members of the RAF as menacing enough to warrant denationalisation, and I suspect he would also condemn the United States denaturalisation of Communist citizens in the twentieth century as hysterical overreaction. But he remains confident that one can transcend historic patterns of panic-induced political myopia and he thus arrives at the conclusion that Islamic terrorists are uniquely suitable for citizenship revocation. Peter Schuck contends that citizenship revocation, when employed judiciously against terrorists, strengthens the value of citizenship itself. Kay Hailbronner adds that my arguments do not address the illegality of citizenship revocation under international or constitutional law, but rather proceed from unarticulated notions of legitimacy and morality. Space does not permit a proper reply to the last criticism. Readers are invited to read my published article on citizenship revocation in the Queen's Law Journal, which addresses citizenship revocation for misconduct under international and constitutional law.[2]

Consider citizenship revocation in relation to the goal of bringing perpetrators to justice. As I mentioned in my kick-off text, fear of citizenship revocation is unlikely to deter those bent on martyrdom, and the deaths of the Kaouchi brothers and Coulibaly seem to demonstrate that. As for Abu Hamza, it is worth noting that the UK did attempt to strip him of citizenship. It was thwarted because deprivation would have rendered the Egyptian-born cleric stateless. But the fact that Abu Hamza remained in the UK as a UK citizen made him available for extradition to face charges in the United States, where he was tried, convicted and sentenced to life imprisonment for terrorism offences after an open and fair trial. Had he been stripped of UK

---

[2] Macklin, A. (2014), 'Citizenship Revocation, the Privilege to Have Rights and the Production of the Alien', *Queen's Law Journal* 40 (1): 1–54.

citizenship and expelled to Egypt, he would never have faced justice in a US court, or anywhere for that matter.[3] I take the view that prosecution, trial and conviction are preferable responses to past acts. As for pre-empting incipient risks, various states have begun revoking passports of citizens allegedly bound for IS camps in Syria and Iraq. Restricting exit in this manner is only available in relation to citizens. Stripping citizenship permits states to shed their duty and responsibility toward nationals; it also deprives them of the authority to subject them to criminal prosecution and to thereby make a tangible contribution to bringing terrorists to justice under the rule of law.

Schuck, along with Hailbronner and Joppke, concede that existing practices of citizenship revocation breach basic norms of fairness. They regard these flaws as contingent defects that are severable from the abstract question of whether citizenship revocation for misconduct can be justified. I find the attempt to segregate theory from practice unconvincing in this context, and Matthew Gibney's intervention highlights the way in which attempts by the judiciary to hold the state to requirements of legality simply breed more tactics of state evasion. A chronic failure of a state practice to comply with fundamental norms of legality across time and space invites the inference that there is something about what the state is endeavouring to do that ineluctably and incorrigibly perverts the process of how it does it.[4] A fair process leading to banishment, like a fair process culminating in the death penalty, can only ever operate as a mirage that legitimates on-going practices that will – inevitably and necessarily – fail to meet basic norms associated with the rule of law.

This leaves a defence of citizenship revocation that does not depend on practicality or utility, but instead rests on the insistence that revocation is just and fitting punishment of those who abuse the privilege of citizenship. I argue that when citizenship becomes revocable for misconduct, citizenship

---

[3] Egypt does not extradite its nationals, and the Egyptian criminal justice system does not inspire confidence in its capacity to administer justice.

[4] This point draws on the insight of legal theorist Lon Fuller. He admitted that his principles of legality were formal in the sense that they did not stipulate any substantive moral content to law. But he also maintained that legal systems that were intent enacting morally repugnant laws would be hard pressed to reconcile achievement of those objectives with compliance with principles of legality. I extend Fuller's intuition to suggest that a chronic pattern of non-compliance with principles of legality in relation to a particular law supports an intuition that the law is normatively defective in substance.

as legal status is demoted from right to privilege. This is a specifically legal argument about the juridical fragility of a privilege compared to a right. Joppke's comment that citizenship in western states is a privilege because citizenship delivers so little to citizens of most non-western states is a non-sequitur. I may feel privileged to be a Canadian citizen and to benefit from the rights, entitlements and security of Canadian citizenship, but that does not make citizenship as such a privilege. And it would be peculiar indeed if only liberal democratic states that guarantee robust citizenship were entitled to revoke citizenship *qua* privilege, while poor and dysfunctional states that deliver only a meagre citizenship, were not so entitled. Schuck maintains that citizenship revocation, properly wielded, does not weaken citizenship, but can actually 'strengthen citizenship by reaffirming the conditions on which it is based.' I am not sure exactly what this means but his subsequent invocation of capital punishment does alert one to the rhetorical symmetry of his claim with similar assertions by death-penalty advocates: If one is convinced that the value of life is strengthened when the state executes a murderer, perhaps one will also be persuaded that citizenship is strengthened when the state denationalises a terrorist. The corollary also applies: If one is not attracted by the first proposition, perhaps one should resist being seduced by the second.

Jo Shaw's insightful intervention about the implications of denationalisation for EU citizenship brings to the discussion the important issue of proportionality, a matter Hailbronner also addresses briefly. Stepping back from the specificities of EU citizenship, a proportionality inquiry into citizenship deprivation directs us to the question of whether the state can achieve its objectives through less rights-infringing means than the impugned law. If one takes seriously the injunction against statelessness, the answer must surely be yes. However one frames the goals and purposes of citizenship deprivation, it remains true that states can and do deploy other means to address, contain and denounce threats to national security from mono-nationals.[5] They must do so because denationalisation is not a legal option,

---

[5] States can and do use the criminal law to prosecute people for terrorist related offences committed at home and abroad. Expanded police powers of investigation and surveillance enable detection. Passport confiscation that prevents travel to conflict zones restrains a right of citizenship (exit), and some states prosecute citizens who participation in combat abroad when the return. Some states also restrict the right of citizens abroad to re-enter in the name of national security. I consider this less defensible as a matter of law, both in relation to the excluded citizen and other affected states but cannot develop that argument here.

yet no state will be heard to say that it is disabled from protecting the nation adequately because it cannot denationalise mono-citizens.

Schuck proclaims that a state is 'powerless to protect itself and its people from imminent, existential threats', if denied access to denationalisation as a weapon. Not only does this ignore the resources currently available to states, it dramatically overestimates what citizenship revocation would add to the arsenal. Unless a state could mount evidence showing that dual citizens pose a qualitatively different and graver threat to national security than mono-nationals, I doubt that citizenship revocation for some citizens (but not others) could survive a rigorous proportionality analysis. And by advancing revocation as a response to 'imminent, existential' threats, he defeats his own claim that the process of citizenship revocation can, in principle, abide by standards of procedural fairness. Fair processes take time, so whatever threat revocation purports to eliminate, it cannot be imminent. And is it really a good idea to dump an 'imminent, existential threat' on another state and its people anyway?

Rainer Bauböck correctly and helpfully reminds us that what is at issue is citizenship as legal status. Legal citizenship, as an institution that regulates membership within and between states, performs certain specific functions that have formal implications. Among liberal states, equality of status and security of that status are two defining features of legal citizenship. The former speaks to citizenship's internal dimension by ensuring that all citizens within a state are recognised and treated as equal to one another. The latter speaks to citizenship's external dimension. In functional terms, nationality not only protects individuals from what Michael Walzer calls the 'infinite precarity' of statelessness, it also serves an international system of sovereign states in ensuring that at least one mailing address is affixed to every individual for purposes of state responsibility and deportation.

Apart from Joppke, all contributors accept statelessness as a constraint on citizenship stripping. In the world as we know it, where all habitable space is already assigned to some state, the claim that a citizen, by virtue of his or her conduct, does not belong to *this* state must, therefore, entail the claim that the person does belong to *that* state.[6] This exposes two related problems for conduct-based revocation. The first is that the people whom

---

[6] One could, I suppose, imagine a world where states re-appropriate statelessness in order to resurrect the figure of the global legal outcast (hostis humani, or perhaps homo sacer). Stripped of law's protection, this global outlaw could be killed or punished with impunity. I will set this aside this possibility, and I am unsure if this is what Joppke has in mind.

Joppke depicts as appropriate targets of denationalisation are not merely enemies of a particular state or government. On his view, they 'explicitly posit themselves outside the political community of the nation-state'. In other words, they repudiate citizenship as such or, if one prefers, pose as 'citizens' of a non-state entity that every other state in the world rightly regards as deeply threatening and inimical to their security. One expects that they will be as 'tactical and cynical' in their connection to one citizenship as to another. The Canadian citizenship revocation law validates this model of the global terrorist by making conviction for a terrorist-related offence in another country grounds for revoking Canadian citizenship. If another state regards a Canadian citizen as a terrorist, that is reason enough for Canada to conclude that his citizenship connection to Canada is inauthentic and warrants severance.

Joppke's own characterization of the terrorist's relationship to citizenship makes his argument about denationalisation self-defeating. If terrorists disavow citizenship as such, and are indeed hostis humani generi (enemies of all humanity), the same facts that would allow Joppke to pronounce that the Kouachis (for example) did not really belong to France must also yield the conclusion that they did not belong to any other state either. As a practical matter, if one state declares that formal possession of legal status is normatively insufficient to attach the terrorist to that state, it can hardly press the claim that legal status is sufficient to attach him to another state.

Joppke mocks Peter Spiro for making the sensible observation that neither al Qaeda nor Islamic State are states, which means that they are not deportation destinations. Hailbronner abets Joppke by musing about whether IS' military control over patches of land in the midst of violent conflict could be ratcheted up into something approximating statehood. If this is meant to hint at a viable legal option for where to dispose of otherwise stateless citizens, one might as well explore the equally plausible (from a legal perspective) option of launching them into space to orbit the globe aboard some inter-galactic Flying Dutchmen.[7] Alternatively, perhaps we are meant to

---

[7] It seems more likely that the UK will simply continue the practice of depriving citizens of their UK citizenship while abroad, now accompanied with a statement that the Home Secretary believes that target can obtain citizenship elsewhere. Even if the person does not, in fact, have access to another citizenship, the individual's physical location outside the UK and inside another state (to which they may have no legal relationship) will impose insuperable hurdles on challenging the decision or compelling the UK to repatriate him.

shrug off as a convenient fact that powerful states can opportunistically denationalise their citizens while they are abroad in conflict zones. Even if they are rendered stateless, they become some other [failing] state's problem.

Bauböck's contribution directs one to another dimension of belonging, which reveals the second problem with Joppke's approach. Citizenship stripping's revival traces back to the anxiety about so-called 'home-grown' terrorists who, unlike the iconic foreign menace, actually possess citizenship by birth. Revoking citizenship enables the state to recast them as the alien within, in order to then cast them out. Denationalisation serves the narrative of terrorism as always and essentially foreign to the body politic by literally transforming the citizen-terrorist into the foreign outcast. But the very term 'home-grown' refutes the premise. The Kaouchi brothers were French citizens. They were orphaned as children and raised as wards of the French state. It is difficult to see them other than as products of French society. The ideology that seized them originated elsewhere, but their receptivity to it also directs one's attention inward. Indeed, any viable anti-terrorism strategy must attend carefully and critically to the local conditions that produce a descent into disaffection, hatred and violence – whether of the Islamist, neo-Nazi or any other variety. The French assailants may have been alienated from France, but there is no state to which they belonged more.[8]

Ultimately, arguments about citizenship revocation turn on underlying conceptions of what citizenship is for, and expectations about what citizenship as legal status can achieve. Citizenship signifies membership, but beyond that general descriptor, citizenship inhabits multiple registers across many disciplines which are not reducible to or fully commensurate with one another. Citizenship as legal status is powerful because it carries the force of law, but also limited in what it can achieve for precisely the same reason. It is enabled and constrained because it is *citizenship* law and because it is citizenship *law*.

---

[8] One might object that the sample set is too limited: After all, there are dual citizens (especially those who naturalised as adults) who might reasonably be understood as more connected to their country of origin. A short answer is that even if true, it would be a clear conflict of interest to let one state of citizenship make that determination. A fuller answer, which lies beyond the scope of this intervention, would explain why this type of calculus is inimical to the security that distinguishes citizenship from other statuses.

States can and do use law to promote and endorse commitment, patriotism and active citizenship. They do it through public education, programmes for social inclusion, support and assistance, sponsorship of the arts and recreation, and other policies that build solidarity and encourage 'good citizenship'. These various spheres of public activity are enabled through legal frameworks, and so law plays an important role here. Citizenship law's chief constructive contribution lies in imposing (reasonable) requirements for naturalisation, such as residence and language acquisition, that genuinely facilitate integration and commitment to the national community.

The state must also be concerned about 'bad citizenship' and it falls to the criminal justice and national security regimes to address the most egregious conduct that endangers or harms the national community. To conclude that contemporary citizenship law is ill-suited to advancing punitive goals does not deny that some people are very bad citizens, or that law plays a crucial role in addressing that fact. It simply opposes the recruitment of citizenship law to punish bad citizens by demoting them to non-citizens.[9] A man who attacks his mother may be a terrible son who deserves to be prosecuted for his crime, but it is not the job of family law to disclaim him as the son of his mother. Citizenship law is not criminal law. Nor is it national security law. Nor should it be rigged to operate as a trap door that shunts citizens to immigration law.

Accounting for citizenship status' specific legal character also guides us toward what law can (and cannot) achieve. A number of plausible accounts of citizenship's normative foundation circulate in political theory. They typically involve some idea of commitment or allegiance, whether to the state, the constitution, or democratic self-government. I do not here express a preference among them, but rather observe that they tend to focus on the internal relationship between state and citizen, and the grounds upon which the relationship may be properly said to have ruptured. They do not attend to the external dimension of legal citizenship, namely the role of nationality in stabilising the international filing system for humanity, and they do not

---

[9] The various legal strategies currently in use to detect, deter, prevent and respond to terrorism can and do fail, sometimes tragically and spectacularly. Is this because states have not arrogated to themselves sufficient coercive powers, or do inadequate human, technical and financial resources explain more about operational failure?

furnish a satisfactory normative explanation for why the 'bad citizen' should be assigned to another state.

Citizenship law cannot subject to legal regulation the myriad values, practices and aspirations ascribed to citizenship-as-belonging. This is unsurprising: Citizenship status enfranchises citizens above the age of majority, but there is no legal compulsion to vote (except in Australia, Belgium, Brazil and a few other states) and citizenship law does not purport to penalise those who never exercise their right or duty of active citizenship. Nor does citizenship law purport to regulate access to most types of civil and social citizenship (in Marshallian terms), and I suspect most commentators agree that that is a good thing.

Nevertheless, defenders of revocation insist that citizenship law can and should regulate 'loyalty and allegiance' of citizens. The criminal law can punish people for intentionally committing wrongful acts, including treason, murder, and all other forms of horrific violence that concern us here. Some assailants may openly express contempt for their country of citizenship, while others (like the Ottawa shooter Joppke cites) display a messy history of mental illness, drug addiction and petty criminality preceding recent conversion to Islam. The putative value added by citizenship revocation is precisely that it makes lack of allegiance and loyalty the central element in defining crimes against citizenship. But to paraphrase Aldous Huxley, loyalty and allegiance are like happiness. They are by-products of other activities. Fostering love of country is a valid aspiration of states and worth cultivating. But it cannot be manufactured by the carrot of a citizenship oath (as Joppke has elsewhere[10] acknowledged), nor will it be conjured by the stick of revocation. Law is not adept at producing sentiment on command.

Space constraints have led me to focus on those submissions that directly challenge my own position, and I have not responded to the cogent, provocative and creative insights offered by so many contributors. My own thinking has been deepened and challenged by them, for which I express gratitude and appreciation. I admit that I took as my remit citizenship revocation only in the literal, legal sense. I also acknowledge the criticism that

---

[10] Bauböck, R. & Joppke, C. (2010), 'How liberal are citizenship tests?', *Robert Schuman Centre for Advanced Studies, EUDO Citizenship Observatory Working Paper No. 2010/41*, Florence: European University Institute, available at http://cadmus.eui.eu/handle/1814/13956

confining my focus to citizenship revocation does not pay due regard to the compelling claim, for example, that deportation of non-citizens may also constitute banishment in some circumstances, with attendant human rights implications. I hope that nothing I have said here gives the appearance of foreclosing or prejudging broader or different conceptions of banishment. There is always more to be said, and much to be done.

Part IV: Communities in the Digital Age

Abstract

New digital technologies are rapidly changing the global economy and have connected billions of people in deterritoralised social networks. Will they also create new opportunities for global citizenship and alternatives to state-based political communities? In his kick-off essay, Liav Orgad takes an optimistic view. Blockchain technology permits giving every human being a unique legal persona and allows individuals to associate in 'cloud communities' that may take on several functions of territorial states. 14 commentators discuss this vision. Sceptics assume that states or business corporations have always found ways to capture and use new technologies for their purposes. They emphasise that the political functions of states, including their task to protect human rights, require territorial monopolies of legitimate coercion that cannot be provided by cloud communities. Others point out that individuals would sort themselves out into cloud communities that are internally homogenous which risks to deepen political cleavages within territorial societies. Finally, some authors are concerned that digital political communities will enhance global social inequalities through excluding from access those who are already worse off in the birthright lottery of territorial citizenship. Optimists see instead the great potential of blockchain technology to overcome exclusion and marginalisation based on statelessness or sheer lack of civil registries; they regard it as a tool for enhancing individual freedom, since people are self-sovereign in controlling their personal data; and they emphasise the possibilities for emancipatory movements to mobilise for global justice across territorial borders or to create their own internally democratic political utopias. In the boldest vision, the deficits of cloud communities as voluntary political associations with limited scope of power could be overcome in a global cryptodemocracy that lets all individuals participate on a one-person-one-vote basis in global political decisions.

Keywords

Global citizenship · Digital technology · Blockchain · Cloud community · Virtual democracy · Legal persona

46

Global Citizenship and the Rise of Cloud Communities

Liav Orgad

The idea of global citizenship

About 70 years ago, an American peace activist named Garry Davis created a registered concept of 'world citizenship.' A naïve enterprise at its infancy, this concept looks more realistic today for three reasons. The first reason is *global interconnectedness*. The internet has profoundly changed the notion of public space. About 50 per cent of the world population uses the internet and global internet use is consistently growing – from 16 per cent in 2005 to 48 per cent in 2017. 71 per cent of the world's youth population (15-24) uses the internet, 94 per cent in the developed world.[1] 2.3 billion people use smartphones, almost one-third of the global population. Facebook and WeChat in China have an estimated 3 billion users together. Internet technologies and cloud computing enable people to establish digital IDs, which could eventually become recognised as an international legal personality, be connected with one another, disentangled from physical borders, and act at a distance.

The second reason is *identity*. Ever since Aristotle, membership in a political community denotes an identity of some kind. Shared identity is a cornerstone of citizenship – it creates a sense of community and a commitment toward a common good.[2] While the idea of global citizenship goes back to ancient Greece – the Greek philosopher Diogenes is credited to be the first to define himself as 'a citizen of the world'[3] – it is only in recent

---

[1] International Telecommunications Union (2017), *ITU Facts and Figures*. Geneva: International Telecommunications Union, available at https://www.itu.int/en/ITU-D/Statistics/Documents/facts/ICTFactsFigures2017.pdf
[2] Joppke, C. (2010), *Citizenship and Immigration*. Cambridge: Polity Press.
[3] Nussbaum, C. M. (1994), 'Patriotism and cosmopolitanism', *The Boston Review*.

The research is supported by the European Research Council (ERC) Starting Grant (# 716350). I thank Ehud Shapiro and Primavera De Filippi for inspiring discussions on the concept of self-sovereign digital identity.

years that a transformation of consciousness from local to global identities has been identified. Recent polls reveal that people are increasingly identifying themselves as global, rather than national, citizens. For example, a 2016 BBC World Poll shows that 56 per cent of the respondents consider themselves, first and foremost, as 'global citizens,' rather than national citizens.[4] A 2016 World Economic Forum Survey indicates that the vast majority of young people identify themselves first as 'human' (40.8 per cent) and 'citizens of the world' (18.6 per cent), while national identity only comes third (13 per cent).[5] National identity remains central, but, particularly in emerging economies, a perception of global social identity is on the rise.[6] For the first time in history, a large percentage of the world's population places global identity above any national or local identities; there is a growing sense of a global community that transcends national borders.

The third reason is *responsibility*, a central component of a republican conception of citizenship. In a republican view, members of a political community share public responsibilities to promote a common good and confront common challenges. Today, more than ever, human beings face common global challenges and human activities have a cumulative effect on the global scale.[7] Although there are no global individual responsibilities, at least not in the legal sense, private individuals are increasingly showing global responsibility in different policy areas (food consumption, global warming, animal rights) by taking actions (e.g., buying organic food, recycling, becoming a vegetarian) based on free choice and without state coercion. Some of the global challenges have become urgent and cannot be adequately addressed on the national level. By showing global responsibility, even if limited and with a weak sense of agency, individuals are participating in activities whose scope and target audience go beyond

---

[4] GlobeScan (2016), *Global Citizenship a Growing Sentiment Among Citizens of Emerging Economies: Global Poll*. Available at https://www.globescan.com/news-and-analysis/press-releases/press-releases-2016/383-global-citizenship-a-growing-sentiment-among-citizens-of-emerging-economies-global-poll.html

[5] World Economic Forum (2017), *Global Shapers Annual Survey 2017*. Available at http://www.shaperssurvey2017.org/static/data/WEF_GSC_Annual_Survey_2017.pdf; World Economic Forum (2016) *Global Shapers Annual Survey 2016*. Available at http://www.shaperssurvey2017.org/static/data/GSC_AS16_Report.pdf

[6] Buchan, N., M. B. Brewer, G. Grimalda, R. K. Wilson, E. Fatas & M. Foddy (2011), 'Global social identity and global cooperation', *Psychological Science* 22 (6): 821-828.

[7] Dower, N. (2003), 'Does Global Citizenship Require Modern Technology?' *Ideas Valores* 52 (123): 25-42.

national boundaries. The changing public opinion thus goes hand in hand with changes in individual actions motivated by a sense of global political responsibilities.

Status: international legal persona

Under the current structure of international law, individuals exist as legal persons only through a status conferred to them by a state. Individuals are citizens or residents of some state; an international legal status of a 'human being' is non-existent.[8] True, international law speaks in universal terms of international *human* rights law, even *natural* rights, but it makes them largely dependent on citizenship and territorial sovereignty, as if a person only legally exists through a state – a feudalist approach.[9] This state of affairs raises three issues. First, *human rights*: an estimate of 1.1 billion people, 15 per cent of the world population, lacks an official identification.[10] Without a national identification, one cannot have access to basic services and participate in modern life; one lacks, as coined by Hannah Arendt, the 'right to have rights'. For refugees and displaced persons, having no national identity can lead to detention and deportation. But even people with a national ID may wish to have a universal ID that allows them to choose an identity free of state limitations (think of national restrictions on gender identity, sexual orientation, and names). The legal source for an international legal personality can be found in Article 6 of the Universal Declaration of Human Rights, according to which 'Everyone has the right to recognition everywhere as a person before the law' (also Article 16, ICCPR).[11]

The second issue is lack of *self-governance*. Existing citizenship regimes are based on Westphalian sovereignty under which citizens govern their life

---

[8] It has a few exceptions: individual criminal responsibility and some civil liabilities in international law.

[9] Benhabib, S. (2005), 'Borders, Boundaries, and Citizenship', *Political Science and Politics* 38 (4): 673-677.

[10] Desai, V., M. Witt, K. Chandra & J. Marskell (2017), 'Counting the uncounted: 1.1 billion people without IDs', *The World Bank*. Available at http://blogs.worldbank.org/ic4d/counting-uncounted-11-billion-people-without-ids

[11] United Nations (1948), *Universal Declaration of Human Rights*. Available at http://www.un.org/en/universal-declaration-human-rights/; Also: United Nations (1966), *International Covenant on Civil and Political Rights. Adopted by the General Assembly of the United Nations on 19 December 1966*, available at https://treaties.un.org/doc/publication/unts/volume%20999/volume-999-i-14668-english.pdf

indirectly – through the state.[12] This means that the status of citizenship perpetuates the monopoly of the state to control the exercise of individual rights. On the national level, the exercise of rights is connected with the status of citizenship (though less today than in the past);[13] on the transnational level, following the development of a standard travel document, the passport, the exercise of freedom of movement outside the state has become connected with citizenship (perhaps more so today than in the 18th and 19th centuries).[14] It also means that the participation of individuals in international law-making, even in decisions that directly affect them, is only realised through state representatives and depends a great deal on who is included in the boundaries of the demos. Minorities that have minimal political influence or no citizenship rights remain unheard in international decision-making, and so are people who are ineligible to vote in national elections due to electoral law restrictions and citizens in authoritarian regimes.[15] The actual influence of individuals in the creation of international law is infinitesimally small.

The third issue is *unequal representation*. Since the 17th century, the Westphalian concept of sovereignty has been based upon two fundamental ideas that have marched together – nation-states and territories – accompanied by a third idea, equality: the notion that sovereign states are equal.[16] The Peace of Westphalia ended the medieval hierarchical system of power among rulers – though not among humans – and replaced it with a system of territorial sovereignty and sovereign equality of states (this idea is recognised today in Article 2(1) to the UN Charter).[17] Unlike sovereign states, individuals do not have an equal voice in international affairs. International law is organised on a 'one-state, one-vote' basis – a system that creates disparities in individual voting power. Citizens of San Marino (33,000 people)

---

[12] Peters, A. (2016), *Beyond human rights: the legal status of the individual in international law*. New York: Cambridge University Press (Huston J. tran.).

[13] Spiro, P. (2008), *Beyond Citizenship: American Identity After Globalization*. New York: Oxford University Press.

[14] Dehm, S. (2018), 'The Passport', in Hohmann J. & D. Joyce (eds.), *The Objects of International Law*. Oxford: Oxford University Press (forthcoming).

[15] Shaw, J. (2017), 'Citizenship and the Franchise', in Shachar A., R. Bauböck, I. Bloemraad & M. Vink (eds.), *The Oxford Handbook of Citizenship*, 290-313. Oxford: Oxford University Press.

[16] Walker, N. (2017), 'The Place of Territory in Citizenship' in A. Shachar, R. Bauböck, I. Bloemraad & M. Vink (eds.), *The Oxford Handbook of Citizenship*, 553-575. Oxford: Oxford University Press.

[17] United Nations (1945), *Charter of the United Nations*. Available at http://www.un.org/en/sections/un-charter/chapter-i/index.html

have the same voting power in the UN as citizens of India (1.2 billion). The disparity in individual voting power in governance of global issues (e.g., global warming and the environment) undermines the equal value of citizenship under international law.

Digital identity: blockchain technology

The UN Sustainable Development Goals recognise the importance of legal identity for all. Article 16.9 aims to 'provide legal identity for all, including birth registration' by 2030. Through the ID4D program, the World Bank assists in the promotion of the UN goal by financially assisting states to provide recognised IDs.[18]

The internet already offers the infrastructure for the realisation of digital IDs, yet new technologies, e.g. blockchain, are likely to bring further improvements necessary to turn the idea into reality. The internet is a system of interconnected computer networks, which allows for exchange and transfer of data. All present major internet applications are structured in a client-server application, where the participants access it via an app or a web browser (client) and the company providing the application runs the computations and data on their own computers (server). This structure gives these companies (and governments) total control over the service they provide and all the data produced by its users. Blockchain technology offers the first internet applications that works differently; it is designed as a peer-to-peer system that is not controlled by a central entity and in which data exchange is not stored in a single physical location. On the blockchain, shared data are hosted by all the computers in the network simultaneously and are publicly accessible to all. Blockchain technology is a game changer; it can provide people with *self-sovereign identity* – they are the ones who create and register their identity and they are the only ones who control what to do with it and with whom to share what. In such a decentralised system, one's identity is not owned by a central server (Facebook, LinkedIn, a state ministry), but by the person herself; she can decide which data to share and for what purpose. Hence, blockchain technologies can help achieving the UN goal of granting an ID to everyone, not just to those who can obtain it from a state, in a decentralised way that is not necessarily controlled by the UN or by states.

---

[18] Above n.11.

Several organisations are currently working on the creation of the technological infrastructure required for a trustworthy global digital ID.[19] The achievement of this goal involves some challenges: who will register people for a global ID? What will be the relation between a global ID and a national ID – will the global ID rely on national registries or be independent? When will a global ID be created – at birth, or at later age when the person can exercise control? Which details will be included – only a birth certificate, or also physical characteristics and biometric data? Will there be a standard form? Will the possession of a global ID be a right, or also a duty? How to create digital IDs for people in places where the required technology does not exist or in authoritarian regimes that restrict their subjects' access to information technology? How to create an ID that is immune to identity theft and fake identities? These are important questions, but the very idea of a global digital identity for everyone, giving all people a legal status as a 'human being,' is no longer a far-fetched possibility.

A global ID is not a status of citizenship – nor does it create, in and of itself, an international legal status, although it is a prerequisite for it. Yet, in my view, this is not supposed to be its main purpose. An international legal persona should not be seen as a replacement of national citizenships but rather as a status and identity *complementary* to national citizenships (it is thus not identical to cosmopolitan visions of global citizenship)[20]. It is a legal concept that will provide everyone with a global unique ID of a 'human being.' This status will be the *default* lifelong identity and membership for *every* person, which cannot be waived or withdrawn, and on top of it individuals will have other forms of membership, such as national citizenship.[21]

---

[19] E.g., ID2020; uPort; Accenture Unique Identity Service Platform; BITNATION; Democracy Earth Foundation, Jolocom, Evernym, Decentralized Identity Foundation.

[20] See discussions in: Shachar, A. (2009), *The Birthright Lottery: Citizenship and Global Inequality*. Cambridge: Harvard University Press, 45-48.

[21] My focus is on a formal legal institution – status – and the political deliberation that can follow it. Other issues that may be associated with an international legal status – e.g., rights (think of global basic income), duties (think of global tax system), or identity (think of global core curriculum) – require a different discussion.

Political participation: 'Cloud Communities'

Imagine that every person has a trustworthy unique international legal persona; what are we going to do with it? The range of applications is enormous. The question is not only which functions are technologically possible, but which ones are normatively desirable, i.e., which values should be achieved by using technology?

In international law, a 'state' possesses four qualities: a permanent population, a defined territory, government, and a capacity to enter into relations with other states (Article 1, Montevideo Convention, 1933)[22]. International law does not recognise the concept of a 'virtual state,' yet existing virtual communities, such as Bitnation (https://bitnation.co/) – a decentralised borderless virtual nation that functions as a government service platform – challenge the definition of a 'state,' and raise the question of why some of the institutional functions of the state, for which it was first established, cannot be effectively served also by a virtual political community?[23] Can we interpret a 'defined territory' to include cyberspace, or instead talk of 'state-like' non-territorial polities?

The concept of an international legal persona will enable individuals to establish 'Cloud Communities' of different kinds. Conceptually, cloud communities have traditional characteristics of political communities, but not necessarily a physical territory. The communal bond can be global in nature – such as a shared concern about climate change, ageing, veganism and animal rights (i.e., a universal community, open to everyone) – or ascriptive, such as a Jewish / *Bahá'í* faith / Diasporic Cloud Nations, a form of 'transnational nationalism' (i.e., a selective community, open only to certain members). It can be thematic or geographic – region, country, state, city, village – based on a shared interest or territorial identity, even if not corresponding to existing borders or legally recognised communities. Membership is based on consent; a person can be a member of several communities or none. The goal varies, but my focus is *political* communities. Cloud communities are not social networks, but political communities whose aim is political decision-making and in which individuals take part in a process of governance and the creation of law. The legal source for it can be Article

---

[22] *Convention signed at Montevideo December 26, 1933.* Available at http://avalon.law.yale.edu/20th_century/intam03.asp
[23] Tarkowski Tempelhof, S., E. Teissonniere, J. Fennell Tempelhof & D. Edwards (2017), *Bitnation, Pangea Jurisdiction and Pangea Arbitration Token (PAT): The Internet of Sovereignty.* Planet Earth: Bitnation.

25(1) of the International Covenant on Civil and Political Rights (ICCPR), according to which 'every citizen shall have the right and the opportunity ... to take part in the conduct of public affairs, directly or through freely chosen representatives.' Such a community may function in four areas: law (constitution, membership acquisition, registry), governance (political institutions, diplomacy, international agreements, taxes), welfare services (education, healthcare, social security), and economy (trade, corporate activities, fees). It can provide an ID registry, a dispute resolution system, collaborative decision-making, a virtual bank, and a voting system. In a sense, religions are a form of 'cloud communities': virtual and borderless, but not voluntary and decentralised.

Procedurally, cloud communities can be established in two ways. A top-down community can be set up by an international organisation, such as UN organs, as an advisory body to an existing UN organ (WHO, FAO, UNESCO), or in policy areas of global importance (the 17 UN Sustainable Development Goals is a good start). A bottom-up community can be set up by any number of international legal personas on a topic of common interest; as time passes by and the community reaches a certain numerical threshold, it can apply for a 'Consultative Status' at the UN (Article 71, UN Charter[24]). As in other mechanisms of advisory decision-making (e.g., advisory referendum), the outcome may become politically, even if not legally, binding.

Cloud communities are not a replacement for the state, but they offer global citizens sharing a common goal, interest, or identity new ways of interacting and collaborating with each other; they are 'state-like' entities.

The future of citizenship: dynamic and multilayered?

In today's world, one is a participating member in multiple political communities, each of which has different functions and comes with a different set of rights and duties. Citizenship is multilayered.[25] It is, for example, national and supranational, as demonstrated by European Union citizenship

---

[24] Available at http://www.un.org/en/sections/un-charter/un-charter-full-text/
[25] Bauböck, R. (2017), 'Political Membership and Democratic Boundaries', in Shachar, A., R. Bauböck, I. Bloemraad & M. Vink (eds.), 60-82. *The Oxford Handbook of Citizenship*. Oxford: Oxford University Press.

or – quite differently – an African Union passport.[26] It can be territorial and digital, as demonstrated by e-Estonia (https://e-estonia.com/), the first digital residency program in the world. In the blockchain-based digital society of e-Estonia, everyone can acquire e-residency in Estonia in order to access its digital governmental services; e-residents can establish a business in Estonia, register a company, participate in an e-school, open a bank account, and have an Estonian digital ID (e-residents are not entitled to physical residency in Estonia unless they fulfil the regular visa requirements – thus, they are e-residents without physical residency rights.) In July 2017, there were more e-residents than newborns in Estonia[27] and the country is planning is to reach 10 million e-residents by 2025, which will make its virtual population almost ten times larger than its territorial population (1.3 million in 2017).

Existing attempts to create 'cloud communities' – such as Bitnation and e-Estonia – already offer non-territorial forms of political membership, remodel the way people think about sovereignty, and challenge the definition of the state as we know it – as a legal entity that must have a physical territory and a centralised governance.[28] Citizenship, *à la* Bitnation and e-Estonia, resembles a business model where states are service providers and 'citizens' are billed for the service – from education to healthcare to infrastructure. In this model, there is no lifetime membership but fixed membership contracts, which can be renewed or become permanent.

If we had to design a new international legal system, given today's political and technological conditions, would it be like the current system? The world is ready, more than ever before, for realising of one of the most morally-desirable notions in human history – global citizenship

---

[26] The implementation of the African Union Passport, which is set to 2020, will facilitate the notion of an international legal persona as it would provide a legal identification to million Africans who currently lack a registered ID.

[27] Fraga, D. (2017), 'The Birth of a Digital Nation in Estonia', *Next Nature Network*, August 30, available at https://www.nextnature.net/2017/08/estonia-more-e-residents-than-babies/

[28] Certainly, e-Estonia and Bitnation represent opposite functions of cloud communities. While e-Estonia uses new technologies to expand the global reach of a nation-state, Bitnation seeks to disrupt the current system by offering an anarchic post-nation state world of voluntary virtual communities. I thank Rainer Bauböck for this point.

(*Weltbürgerschaft*) without a world state, as envisioned by Immanuel Kant in 1795. Such a vision is an addition to, and an improvement of the existing citizenship regimes that evolved in a completely different era. Are we ready to embrace the global citizenship that new technologies offer to us?

47

Cloud Communities: Progressive Potential and Possible Problems

Rainer Bauböck

We are in the midst of a digital revolution that could transform societies worldwide as profoundly as the agrarian revolution of the Neolithic age and the industrial revolution of the 19th century did. No doubt, new technologies will also deeply affect the structure and boundaries of political communities and the meaning of citizenship. Liav Orgad tells a hopeful story about the benefits of blockchain technology. It can serve to create an international legal identity for every human being and new forms of non-territorial political community in which citizenship is based entirely on consent. I share Orgad's sense of excitement about the speed and depth of change that we are witnessing. But I am less optimistic about the future of citizenship.

The progressive potential: providing global legal status and enabling global civil society

Orgad's first suggestion is that digital technologies will make it possible to provide every human being with an international legal persona, a '*default* lifelong identity and membership for *every* person, which cannot be waived or withdrawn' (original emphases). This would indeed be a major achievement. In less developed countries and autocratic regimes, millions of births are not registered. Unregistered persons are de facto stateless and cannot claim services or rights from governments that do not recognise them as nationals.[1]

Yet blockchain, the technology that he sees as most promising for this task, is not a tool to improve governments' administrative capacities. It is a decentralised ledger that is not under the control of any government or corporation. Individuals control themselves what their registered identity is (e.g. their chosen gender) and who gets access to their linked data (such as

---

[1] For Africa see Manby, B. (2016), *Citizenship Law in Africa. A Comparative Study*. New York: Open Society Foundations, 3rd edition, available at https://www.opensocietyfoundations.org/sites/default/files/citizenship-law-africa-third-edition-20160129.pdf

health or education records). This is why Orgad sees in blockchain technology a potential 'to provide people with *self-sovereign identity*' (original emphasis).

There is an obvious tension between these two goals: providing every human being with an unalterable and unique identity, on the one hand, and providing them with sovereign control over their identity related data, on the other hand. Births and deaths must be registered by someone else than the individuals concerned. Presumably adult individuals, too, are constrained in their choices because they must not opt out by deleting their international legal identity or subvert the global registry by assuming that of another person. More importantly, governments will not be out of business. Even if the act of registration is certified in a decentralised ledger, governments must recognise it in order for individuals to enjoy legal statuses and rights that only states can grant.

Orgad seems to be aware of this tension when he writes that a global ID is not a status of world citizenship and that it would supplement rather than replace national citizenships assigned by governments. But he also wants to put it to uses that would undermine the international system of sovereign states as we know it. When Orgad suggests that all individuals could be represented equally in making international law, he must have some form of global federal democracy in mind, e.g. a 'peoples' assembly' enjoying co-legislative powers with a body in which each state has one vote, as in the UN General Assembly.[2]

His main vision is, however, the emergence of alternative forms of political community at the sub-global level: cloud communities or virtual nations that individuals can join based on shared concerns or ascriptive identities that transcend the territorial boundaries of states. Orgad envisages two ways how these communities can come about: bottom up or top down. People concerned about global social justice could form cloud communities promoting this goal, whereas others may want to join a global ethnic or religious diaspora. The UN could initiate cloud communities that support its development or climate change goals, but also states or regions could set them up to empower their diasporas.

---

[2] Proposals for a UN reform along these lines have been made since the 1990s. See Archibugi, D. (1993), 'The Reform of the UN and Cosmopolitan Democracy: A Critical Review', *Journal of Peace Research* 30 (3): 301-315.

To me, these applications of cloud communities look like an expansion of civil society, of international organisations, or of traditional territorial polities into cyberspace, rather than like genuinely new forms of political community. If this is what they are, then cloud communities could provide great opportunities. They could mobilise individuals across the world for goals of global justice or climate protection. And they would provide new spaces for civil society in states that suppress individual liberty and oppress ethnic or religious minorities. I imagine that states and global corporations, even if they cannot control the underlying blockchain registries, will find ways to instrumentalise or hijack cloud communities for their own purposes, as they already do with the internet and social media. Autocrats have done so with new communication technologies ever since the invention of the printing press. Yet this is not my main worry. It would be wrong as well as futile to reject new technologies that enhance individual freedom because they can also be used to constrain it.

The threat to democracy: should we be ruled by voluntary associations?

My main worry is that cloud communities may provide new global spaces for citizenship as civic participation while undermining its foundation as equal membership in territorial polities. This tension emerges from contrasting mechanisms for determining membership in civil society and in political communities. Civil society is the realm of voluntary association in between the involuntary associations of families, firms and states.[3] In contrast with a global ID, which would register another form of involuntary membership, that of belonging to the human species, cloud communities must be voluntary associations. Individuals sort themselves into such communities by applying for membership or opting out while communities enjoy collectively powers to determine the conditions for admission. A vibrant sphere of voluntary associations is an essential element of democratic citizenship. And in an increasingly interconnected world it is indeed highly desirable to expand civil society so that individuals can act as global citizens in voluntary associations that pursue global agendas.

But they can do so only because and insofar as they have a secure territorial citizenship that protects their fundamental rights and makes them

---

[3] See Bauböck, R. (1996), 'Social and Cultural Integration in Civil Society', in R. Bauböck, A. Heller & A. Zolberg (eds.), *The Challenge of Diversity. Integration and Pluralism in Societies of Immigration*, 67-132. Aldershot, UK: Avebury.

equal members of a political community that most of them have not chosen to belong to. The social contract metaphor that has informed liberal thinking about citizenship since Hobbes, Locke and Rousseau is misleading in this respect. Citizenship as a legal status of membership in a territorial polity has never been based on consent. Citizenship in today's states is generally acquired at birth – either through birth in the territory or descent from citizen parents. Immigrants may opt in through applying for naturalisation but – as the word itself signals – they join a birthright community. Emigrants may opt out through renouncing their nationality, but they can generally do so only if they have already resided abroad for some time and have acquired another citizenship. The non-voluntary nature and automatic acquisition of citizenship are even stronger at local and regional levels. Local citizenship is, or should be, generally based on residence rather than birth. By taking up residence in another municipality I become a local citizen and acquire rights to be represented in local government. In an increasing number of democracies this principle of *ius domicilii* is also extended to foreign nationals who are granted voting rights in local elections.[4] Finally, regional citizenship in federal states or supranational unions is automatically derived from nationality. I am a citizen of the province of Lower Austria and a citizen of the European Union because I am an Austrian national. Birthright, residence and derivation are three complementary ways how territorial polities determine who their citizens are.[5] None of them is based on voluntary association.

But why should we not see cloud communities building on blockchain technology as finally realising the social contract ideal by enabling us to shed the coercive straightjacket of nonvoluntary citizenship and transforming all political communities into voluntary associations? My response is that this would be fatal for democracy. Already Aristotle knew that, unlike families, democratic polities are association of diverse individual. These have only one thing in common: a shared destiny that links the freedom and well-being of each to the collective freedom and good of all. The territorial bases and automatic attribution mechanisms of citizenship create political community among individuals that differ profoundly in their interests, identities and ideas about the common good. Democracy is a set of institutions and procedures that provide solutions to collective action problems and

---

[4] Arrighi, J.-T. & R. Bauböck (2017), 'A multilevel puzzle. Migrants' voting rights in national and local elections', *European Journal of Political Research* 56 (3): 619–639.
[5] See Bauböck, R. (2017), *Democratic Inclusion. A Pluralistic Theory of Citizenship*. Manchester: Manchester University Press, 57-87.

legitimacy for coercive government exercised over a set of individuals who have been thrown together in a territory instead of having chosen each other in a voluntary association.

Voluntary associations in civil society and territorial democracies are thus based on categorically different membership principles. Cloud communities could strengthen democratic citizenship if they contribute to expanding civil society to global scale. They would, however, undermine democracy if they took over the provision of public goods and functions of coercive government from territorial polities. Imagine what kind of cloud communities would be formed if these enjoyed powers similar to today's states. Individuals would sort themselves out into like-minded sets just as they do in the echo chambers of today's social media networks. The rich would form non-territorial polities that provide them with the best medical, educational and private security services worldwide without being taxed to finance adequate services also for the local poor. The dreams of nationalists of matching ethnocultural with political boundaries would finally come true if the latter are no longer territorial since, unlike territory, voluntary association is not a scarce resource. The boundaries of political communities would be constantly reshaped in efforts to get rid of minorities or lower classes who have become redundant in a digitalised economy.

This is in my views a dystopian rather than a utopian scenario. I do not think it is likely to happen any time soon, because states are powerful beasts that have been skilful in adapting to technological revolutions and using them for their purposes. I also think that most individuals are attached to territorial democracy and citizenship and will fight back politically against what they regard as excesses of globalisation. Unfortunately, they do so today often through voting for populist parties and politicians that promote an illiberal transformation of democracy. The task for liberal democrats is to strengthen the integration of territorial democracies by bridging the cleavage between mobile and globally oriented populations, on the one side, and immobile ones that experience a shrinking of their opportunities and lifeworlds, on the other side.

But maybe this is a period of transition and the next generations of digital natives will be much more footloose than today's sedentary majorities? A combination of a steep rise in global mobility with digital technologies empowering non-territorial political communities may make preserving territorial democracy and citizenship a hopeless goal. Individuals' primary political allegiances would then no longer be to a community of citizens rooted in a particular territory but to their self-selected cloud community.

It may happen, but democracy would then separate individuals living next to each other instead of uniting them as equal citizens in spite of their differences. This is not going to be Aristophanes' happy cloud cuckoo land.

48

Blockchain Technology and Citizenship

Primavera De Filippi

In the last decades, modern democracies have been witnessing a low rate of political participation and civic engagement with existing governmental institutions. Low voter turnout, especially with younger generations, is raising significant concerns for many representative democracies, and trust in public institutions has dropped to a point that it has become difficult for people to engage in political activity.[1]

Civic participation is not dead, however, it is only shifting to a new space. With the advent of internet and digital technologies, citizens of the world are coalescing into increasingly globalized social movements,[2] paving the way for new forms of political engagement.[3] With the blockchain, these individuals could find new ways to spontaneously organize and coordinate themselves into transnational 'cloud communities', and – as Liav Orgad suggests (chapter "Cloud Communities: The Dawn of Global Citizenship?") – even acquire their own self-sovereign identity that subsists independently of any nation-state. Those, I believe, are some of the most compelling developments of blockchain technology, which I have been following closely over the past few years.

But what makes blockchain technology a powerful tool for promoting disintermediation and decentralized coordination – i.e. a *trustless technol-*

---

[1] According to Pew Research, in 2016, only 19 per cent of Americans said they trust their government, among the lowest levels in the past half-century. See http://www.people-press.org/2015/11/23/beyond-distrust-how-americans-view-their-government/. The same is true at the international level. A GCF survey found out that 85 per cent of the respondents in eight countries believe that the UN needs to be reformed to better deal with global risks and 71 per cent support the establishment of a new supranational organization. See https://api.globalchallenges.org/static/files/ComRes.pdf

[2] Cohen, R. & R. Shirin (eds.) (2004), *Global social movements*. London: A&C Black.

[3] Della Porta, D., & S. G. Tarrow (eds.) (2005), *Transnational protest and global activism*. Lanham (MD): Rowman & Littlefield.

ogy – also constitutes one of its greatest limitations, especially when it comes to political deliberation. While politics is about reaching a compromise between conflicting interests and values, blockchain technology operates via distributed consensus and an exit-based conflict resolution system. As underlined by Rainer Bauböck, relying on voluntary cloud communities as a means to govern society could significantly increase inequalities, leading to an overall loss of democratic representation and wealth redistribution.

In a sense, I agree with the diverging views of both Orgad and Bauböck. When brought to an extreme, blockchain technology could create – simultaneously – a utopian society characterized by greater individual freedom and autonomy, and a dystopian society driven by market-based incentives and self-dealing. But reality is neither black or white; it often has many different shades of grey. I see blockchain technology as neither the cure nor the curse of today's political institutions. Rather, I see it as a tool that could enable us to experiment with new governance structures and alternative political systems – in a world where there is very little room left for experimentation.

Multiple shades of activism

Digital activism is a not a recent phenomenon. Social movements increasingly leverage the power of digital technologies to coordinate themselves and communicate to a broader audience – as illustrated by the role played by social media during the Arab uprisings in 2011.[4] But the internet also enabled the emergence of new communities of kinship, with a variety of online platforms (e.g *Facebook, Twitter, Whatsapp*) gathering people around specific interests or values, regardless of their political views. Some of these communities operate as tight social groups, providing members with a newfound sense of belonging and a collective identity.[5] While they do not engage in what we usually regard as political activity, these online communities play a key role in shaping the way people organize and coordinate themselves, in ways that significantly differ from those of existing political institutions.[6] Apart from the legal regime these communities operate in, they are gov-

---

[4] Howard, P. N., A Duffy, D. Freelon, M. M. Hussain, W. Mari & M. Maziad (2011), 'Opening closed regimes: what was the role of social media during the Arab Spring?', *Project on Information Technology & Political Islam Working Paper 2011.1*, available at https://papers.ssrn.com/sol3/papers.cfm?abstract_id=2595096

[5] Wellman, B. & M. Gulia (1999), 'Virtual communities as communities: Net surfers don't ride alone', in M. A. Smith & P. Kollock (eds.), *Communities in cyberspace*, 167-194. London; New York: Routledge.

[6] Norris, P. (2002), 'The bridging and bonding role of online communities', *Politics* 7 (3): 3-13.

erned by their own systems of rules and social norms – which members voluntary abide by.

In her book, 'Social Movements and Their Technologies: Wiring Social Change', Stefania Milan illustrates the different approaches of social movements in materializing their ideas into the world.[7] *Insiders* adopt a cooperative attitude: they recognise existing institutions as a legitimate source of power and actively engage in their game, through advocacy and traditional decision-making procedures.[8] *Outsiders* adopt a more confrontational attitude: they reject the rules of these institutions and choose instead to exert pressure from the outside, through campaigns, protest or other form of political resistance.[9] Finally, what she refers to as *beyonders* are a wholly different bunch. *Beyonders* simply refuse to engage with existing institutions: they do not want to fight them nor do they want to change them, they simply regard them as a leftover from a past era – which they are trying to render obsolete by building new systems.[10] Thus, relatively to the other two groups, *beyonders* operate in a way that is more autonomous or independent; they do not play for or against the established political system, they just decide to ignore it or bypass it.

Is it fair to conclude that *beyonders* do not play a political role in society? Clearly not. By creating an alternative to existing institutions, they exert an indirect pressure forcing them to adjust themselves to maintain their position. Perhaps more so than *insiders* and *outsiders*, who operate within a given political framework, *beyonders* are deeply concerned with social change. Their political action is the result of a constructive reaction to the current state of affairs. They are responding to their own needs using new schemes and methodologies, leveraging the power of communities to create new institutions that will help them fulfil their missions – through what essentially amounts to a new form of political organisation.

---

[7] Milan, S. (2013), *Social movements and their technologies: Wiring social change*. London: Springer, 118-136.
[8] Moe, T. M. (2005), 'Power and political institutions', *Perspectives on Politics* 3 (2): 215-233.
[9] Maloney, W. A., G. Jordan & A. M. McLaughlin (1994), 'Interest groups and public policy: the insider/outsider model revisited', *Journal of Public Policy* 14 (1): 17-38.
[10] Hintz, A. & S. Milan (2011), 'User rights for the Internet age: Communications policy according to "Netizens"', in R. Mansell & M. Raboy (eds.), *The handbook of global media and communication policy*, 230-241. Chichester, West Sussex; Malden, MA: Wiley-Blackwell.

Beyond the blockchain

Today, in the shadow corners of the internet, a new group of *beyonders* is emerging, looking at blockchain technology as a means to replace many of our traditional institutions. While most of the attention was put, initially, on Bitcoin disrupting banks and other financial operators,[11] as people understood the full potential of blockchain technology, they saw it a means to implement new governance structures that could potentially replace some of our existing systems of governance.[12]

At the extreme end of this spectrum are those who envision the creation of new blockchain-based virtual nations, with a view to ultimately replace the nation-state. This is the case, for instance, of *Bitnation*: an initiative aimed at creating a new sovereign jurisdiction that operates only and exclusively in cyberspace, independently of any geographical boundaries. Founded in 2014, *Bitnation* describes itself as a *decentralized borderless voluntary nation* that anyone can join or leave as they wish:[13] a transnational community of global citizens that spontaneously coordinate themselves, with no recourse to coercion.

To early internet pioneers, this might sound familiar. Already in 1996, in the 'Declaration of the Independence of Cyberspace', John Perry Barlow described the digital world as an independent space that simply could not be regulated, because – he claimed – governments did not have the right nor the capacity to exert their sovereignty over it[14] (even though history has eventually taught us otherwise).

---

[11] De Filippi, P. (2014), 'Bitcoin: a regulatory nightmare to a libertarian dream', *Internet Policy Review* 3 (2): 43.

[12] Davidson, S., P. De Filippi & J. Potts (2016), 'Disrupting governance: The new institutional economics of distributed ledger technology', available at SSRN: https://ssrn.com/abstract=2811995

[13] According to the Bitnation website, Bitnation is a decentralized is fostering 'a peer-to-peer voluntary governance system, rather than the current "top-down", "one-size-fits-all" model, restrained by the current geographical apartheid, where your quality of life is defined by where you were arbitrarily born.' See https://bitnation.co/join-the-team/

[14] '*Governments of the Industrial World, you weary giants of flesh and steel, I come from Cyberspace, the new home of Mind. On behalf of the future, I ask you of the past to leave us alone. You are not welcome among us. You have no sovereignty where we gather.*' Barlow, J. P. (1996), *Declaration of Independence of Cyberspace*. Available at http://homes.eff.org/~barlow/Declaration-Final.html

Barlow was essentially a *beyonder* – mocking the various governmental attempts at regulating the internet landscape, in ways that he considered to be ineffective in this new digital era. Similarly, *Bitnation* is mostly the result of a *beyonders'* approach to governance, trying to create a new sovereign nation that ignores the rules and procedures of existing nation-states, regarded as obsolete in this new digital world. Because it operates on a transnational and decentralized peer-to-peer network (the *Ethereum* blockchain), *Bitnation* is not under the control of any one government. Indeed, by relying on blockchain technology, *Bitnation* is creating a system that not only tries to escape from the hegemony of nation-states – because it has no single point of failure, or control – but also tries to compete with existing institutions and governmental systems – by providing self-sovereign identities, notarization services, property rights and company registration, dispute resolution systems, etc. which are usually associated with the functions of the public administration. The Ethereum blockchain is particularly useful in this context, because – as a public and transnational blockchain – it provides the necessary transparency, verifiability, incorruptibility and trust that one would expect from these governmental services.

'*Governance in the real world is so fucked. We have to start thinking about how to build it in the virtual world*' said Lawrence Lessig in an interview[15], after he resigned from the 2016 presidential campaign. While Lessig was referring to the creation of a massive multiplayer online game[16] inviting players to experiment with different forms of governances, it might be worth investigating whether initiatives such as Bitnation, and other attempts at creating blockchain-based virtual nations (such as *Cultu.re*) or even blockchain-based virtual worlds (such as *Decentraland*) could actually provide a new space of experimentation, allowing people to experiment with new political systems that operate outside of any defined territory. Indeed, these initiatives – which rely on decentralised blockchain-based systems – are not located in any given jurisdiction: they subsist in a transnational space, which has yet to be colonised by new governance structures and experimental political regimes.

---

[15] '"Governance in the Real World Is So Fucked:" Lawrence Lessig Is Working on an MMO', *Motherboard*, 8 June 2017, available at https://motherboard.vice.com/en_us/article/neweqm/lawrence-lessig-is-working-on-an-mmo-game-seed

[16] 'Think the government is doomed? See if you can build a better one in "Seed"', *Digital Trends*, 8 March 2017, available at https://www.digitaltrends.com/gaming/seed-mmo-interview-democracy-lawrence-lessig/

Blockchain-based virtual nations

Can these blockchain-based systems support the emergence of a new framework for *global citizenship* (as suggested by Liav Orgad, amongst others[17]) where people pledge allegiance not to an existing government or nation-state, but to a global community that transcends national boundaries?[18] Can they support a new understanding citizenship as *collective identity,* providing new opportunities for collective action and civic participation in a post-national world?[19] As with many things today, the answer is not a simple one. The concept of blockchain-based virtual nations is interesting because it is highly controversial. It is, in fact, supported by different groups, for very different purposes.

On the one hand, the concept of a virtual nation is appealing to many libertarians, who see it as an opportunity to reduce the room for governmental intervention, by creating new ad-hoc governmental structures aimed at creating a society governed by (unregulated) market forces, and nothing else. This is the vision brought forward most prominently by Peter Thiel, who envisions the creation of a new sovereign nation on an offshore artificial island[20], built 200 miles off the Californian coast. This vision is also shared by a number of crypto-libertarians,[21] such as the team behind *Bitnation*, who believe that – since we have lost trust in our governments – we shall now

---

[17] The notion of 'world citizen' has been endorsed by a variety of scholars, activists and social movements. See, in particular, Ulrich Beck's notion of 'cosmopolitanism' and discussions on the 'post-westphalian' international system. See Beck, U. (2003), 'Toward a new critical theory with a cosmopolitan intent', *Constellations* 10 (4): 453-468; Beck, U. & N. Sznaider (2006), 'Unpacking cosmopolitanism for the social sciences: a research agenda', *The British Journal of Sociology* 57 (1): 1-23.

[18] See also the work of Tölölyan, K. (1996), 'Rethinking diaspora(s): Stateless power in the transnational moment', *Diaspora: A Journal of Transnational Studies* 5 (1): 3-36; Grewal, I. (2005), *Transnational America: feminisms, diasporas, neoliberalisms*. Durham: Duke University Press; and Van Hear, N. (2005), *New diasporas: The mass exodus, dispersal and regrouping of migrant communities*. London: Routledge (on diasporas as transnational entities).

[19] Sassen, S. (2002), 'Towards post-national and denationalized citizenship', in E. F. Isin & B. S. Turner (eds.), *Handbook of citizenship studies*, 277-292. London: Sage.

[20] 'Libertarians Seek a Home on the High Seas', *The New Republic*, 29 May 2017, available at https://newrepublic.com/article/142381/libertarians-seek-home-high-seas

[21] May, T. C. (1994), *Crypto anarchy and virtual communities*. Available at http://aom.jku.at/archiv/cmc/text/may_n01.pdf

rely on blockchain technology to create *trustless systems* (*i.e.* systems where trust is no longer needed) with a view to support and facilitate a series of atomic peer-to-peer interactions in a seemingly stateless environment.[22]

On the other hand, there are people who see virtual nations as an opportunity to overcome the lack of trust in governmental institutions, through the creation of new trusted communities with a global scope. These communities can experiment with new institutional structures that operate independently from, or as a complement to existing institutions. They can support the emergence of grassroots initiatives intended to fill the gaps generated by the progressive shrinking of the welfare state – *i.e.* the provision of public services and shared infrastructure, the pursuit of the common good, and the protection of individual and collective rights.[23] Blockchain technologies could provide new mechanisms of social or political coordination, allowing for transnational communities and activist groups (such as human rights defenders, internet freedoms advocates and climate change campaigners) to gather around a newfound sense of identity and organise themselves as a collective.

The idea is not to replace nation-states with new or competing forms of sovereignty, but rather to provide new means for global communities to mobilise and experiment with new ways of engaging in civic life. If political participation no longer finds its place in the context of traditional governmental structures, perhaps these virtual communities – or *cloud communities*, as Orgad calls them – might be able to bring civics back to life. Indeed, if citizenship refers not only to a legal status, but also to an individual's political activity and collective identity,[24] we might soon witness the emergence of new global citizens, who regard these new virtual nations as *polities* and self-identify as their members.

This is the vision supported by initiatives like *Democracy Earth* and *Aragon*, two blockchain-based platforms providing tools for small and large organisations to operate in a globalised post nation-state world, through their own governance rules and dispute resolution systems. Without trying

---

[22] Atzori, M. (2015), 'Blockchain technology and decentralized governance: Is the state still necessary?', available at SSRN: https://ssrn.com/abstract=2709713 or.

[23] Feigenbaum, H., J. Henig & C. Hamnett (1998), *Shrinking the state: The political underpinnings of privatization*. Cambridge: Cambridge University Press.

[24] Dalton, R. J. (2008), 'Citizenship norms and the expansion of political participation', *Political Studies* 56 (1): 76-98; Eisenstadt, S. N. & B. Giesen (1995), 'The construction of collective identity', *European Journal of Sociology* 36 (1): 72-102.

to replace the role of the state as a political institution, these initiatives are exploring whether (and how) some of the functions undertaken by governmental authorities – e.g. the issuance of identity cards, recordation of vital records and maintenance of public registries, etc. – could be transposed into a blockchain-based system.

People are ideally free to decide, on a case-by-case basis, whether they want to rely on traditional institutions and governmental frameworks, or whether they would rather adopt these new experimental systems, whose values they might feel more attuned with. As a general rule, citizens cannot easily revoke their allegiance to a particular nation-state, because – as highlighted by Rainer Bauböck – the *social contract* described by Hobbes and Rousseau is not a negotiable contractual agreement entered into by consent (*i.e.* citizenship as a legal status is generally something that one does not chose and that, once acquired, cannot be easily gotten ridden of). Yet, to the extent possible, they could choose to acquire additional citizenships, becoming members of multiple communities based on affinity and consent. Insofar as they provide valuable services to their citizens, these virtual communities (or *virtual nations*) may be competing with one another – and potentially with nation-states – so as to expand their user-base.

While this might sound speculative at best, we are already seeing glimmers of this new world. For several years, the republic of Estonia has been trying to create a 'digital nation for global citizens,'[25] as illustrated by its e-residency program, which provides a government-issued digital ID to all individuals requesting it. Inspired by the notion of *government as a platform*,[26] e-Estonia is trying to become the hub for every governmental service, providing all of its electronic residents with a secure identification system, notarisation services, and even the ability to run a company or open a bank account, without ever putting foot into Estonia. With over 28,000 e-residents from all over the world, today, the state of Estonia increasingly operates on a digital layer, enabling people to interact with its governmental platform independently of their country of citizenship or residency.[27]

---

[25] 'E-Residency is a new digital nation for global citizens, powered by the Republic of Estonia.' See https://e-resident.gov.ee/
[26] O'Reilly, T. (2011), 'Government as a Platform', *Innovations* 6 (1): 13-40.
[27] According to Taavi Kotka, Chief Innovation Officer of Estonia since 2013: '*Countries are like enterprises. They want to increase the wealth of their own people.*' Heller, N. (2017), 'Estonia, the Digital Republic', *The New Yorker*, 18 December, available at https://www.newyorker.com/magazine/2017/12/18/estonia-the-digital-republic

Competing sovereignties

Competition between nation-states, trying to collect new members by providing more efficient or reliable governments services, has already begun. If Estonia can collect e-residents on a global scale – in spite of its national boundaries – what would prevent virtual nations from doing the same, without a physical territory? Are we actually moving towards a world in which multiple nations are competing to attract more citizens, in the same way as companies are today competing to attract more customers?[28]

Of course, things get murky when we move from purely administrative tasks – like identity, property and company recordation – to more political tasks, involving policy and decision-making. If people could choose to become citizens only of the communities with whom they agree, they would essentially engage in a generalised version of nation-shopping, constantly trying to find the jurisdictions that seem the most advantageous for them. When brought to an extreme, this would ultimately mean the end of politics.

Politics is all about compromises, in order to accommodate different viewpoints without entering into a conflict. An *opt-in* or *exit-based* political system essentially eliminates the notion of politics, because it removes the need for compromise. People with different values or opinions would no longer need to argue and deliberate in order to reach consensus, because if they're in disagreement, they can simply leave.

As Bauböck recognises, there are significant challenges in letting people choose which nation they want to pledge allegiance to. The state as a sovereign entity – Hobbes' *Leviathan* – is not only responsible for preserving the public order, it is also in charge of promoting the general interests, producing common goods and creating a collective sense of redistribution and justice. All these functions could disappear as we move towards a more market-based approach to citizenship.

I am, however, more pessimistic than Bauböck when it comes to the way nation-states will adapt to these technological changes. Given the progressive disengagement of citizens in local politics, and the growing distrust in existing institutions – whose legitimacy is increasingly put into question – it might not be surprising to see a new wave of nationalism emerging all over the world, with nation-states drawing on nationalist and anti-immigration

---

[28] According to its website: '*Bitnation is creating a new world where thousands or millions of nations actually compete for customers by providing better services, instead of using force. It's a world where everyone can choose.*' See http://bitnation.co

narratives to reinforce their hegemony over the territory, essentially redefining on-going relationships between citizens and non-citizens.[29]

At the same time, due to the increasing trends towards globalisation, large internet corporations, like Google or Facebook, are progressively taking on some of the functions that were once specific to the nation-state: from the task of supporting the discourses in the public sphere to their role as identity providers.[30] With several billions of users on their platforms, these corporations are slowly turning into *de facto* corporate nations, with their own system of rules that they unilaterally define and impose on their 'citizens'. Traditional nation-states might, therefore, soon have to compete not only with virtual nations, but also with these new transnational corporate nations – similar to Neal Stephenson's *franchulates* as science-fiction fans will certainly point out.[31]

New opportunities for experimentation

It is in this convoluted (and daunting) context that I see the rise of blockchain-based virtual nations as a positive omen. Perhaps the reference to *virtual nations* is not the most accurate one, because the term has a strong political connotation and somewhat gives the impression that these communities are assuming the role of traditional nation-states. While some of these communities do intend to replace the figure of the nation-state (e.g. Bitnation), others are simply trying to experiment with new and allegedly *apolitical* governance systems,[32] which nevertheless play a crucial political function.

Because they rely on voluntary association, virtual communities might well remove the need for compromise within a single community, yet they do not eliminate the need for compromise between multiple communities. Hence, politics are not gone, they are simply moving into a different layer. By aggregating people with similar values and opinions, these virtual communities could in fact strengthen the voice of certain minorities – usually stifled by the majority's opinion – and create a more lively debate and political discourse at the outside (rather than on the inside) of these communities. As such, they could end up participating in conventional politics, along with other real-world interests groups.

---

[29] Mitchell, K. (1997), 'Transnational discourse: bringing geography back in', *Antipode* 29 (2): 101-114.
[30] Habermas, J. (1991), *The structural transformation of the public sphere: An inquiry into a category of bourgeois society.* Cambridge, MA: MIT press.
[31] Stephenson, N. (1992), *Snow crash.* New York: Bantam-Random.
[32] Atzori, M. (2015), 'Blockchain technology and decentralized governance: Is the state still necessary?', available at SSRN: https://ssrn.com/abstract=2709713 or.

To conclude, let me take the stance of a *beyonder* for a moment. As a member of *Creative Commons*,[33] I have always been fascinated by its solution. Instead of trying to reform copyright law from the inside or fight it from the outside, Creative Commons introduced an alternative legal regime for creative works that coexists with the existing regulatory framework (in fact, it is based on it) for authors to experiment with new business models that do not rely on the exclusivity and artificial scarcity of copyright law.

Today, with the advent of blockchain technologies, a new wave of innovation is underway in the realm of governance. This innovation is one that will benefit everyone: the *insiders*, i.e. governmental authorities like Estonia, relying on blockchain technology to increase the transparency and accountability of public administrations; the *outsiders*, like Peter Thiel, trying to create new self-sovereign nations with the intention to escape from the laws and control of existing nation-states; and, of course, the *beyonders*, like Bitnation et al., eager to use the technology to support the coordination of transnational communities of voluntary association that operate independently of traditional nation-states, but are capable of peacefully coexisting with them. It is the latter which I am the most excited about, and which I believe could contribute to developing new governance models that might help us build a real global democracy.

---

[33] Creative Commons is an organisation devoted to expanding the range of artistic, academic, and other content available for people to share and build upon. See http://creativecommons.org

49

Global Citizenship and National Borders

Francesca Strumia

Technological advances sometimes alter our experience of well-established notions. The night is as dark today as in the 18th century. However streetlights have pierced its veil. The distance between Turin and Rome is the same today as it was in the first century AD. Yet what was once at least a week-long journey has become with high speed trains a commute of a few hours. Similarly, distributed ledgers technology, by making it technically possible for every individual to create and maintain a globally recognised digital identity, has the potential to materially alter the experience and the meaning of citizenship.[1] Such technological advances, and their possible applications, make global political participation, moral commitment and rights claiming as envisioned by global citizenship theorists one touch closer to reality.[2] Liav Orgad and Rainer Bauböck emphasize from different perspectives that new technologies are not meant to supplant citizenship as we know it; they rather add to it. The notion of an international legal persona – explains Orgad – is a complement to national citizenship. And cloud political communities are – in Bauböck's view – an extension of existing political communities. Hence, global citizenship comes to flank long-established notions of citizenship.

I agree with them on the complementary nature of global citizenship in respect to traditional one. And in this contribution I focus on the latter rather than on the former. I propose to consider how the prospect of technology-enabled global citizenship alters the concept, legal structure and scope of citizenship as we know it. The possibility of novel virtual frontiers challenges further traditional citizenship as a state-based, non-voluntary and

---

[1] For an overview of the technology and its applications, see: UK Government Office for Science (2018), *Distributed Ledger Technology: beyond block chain.* Available at https://www.gov.uk/government/uploads/system/uploads/attachment_data/file/492972/gs-16-1-distributed-ledger-technology.pdf

[2] Archibugi, D. (2008), *The Global Commonwealth of Citizens: towards Cosmopolitan Democracy.* Princeton, N.J.; Woodstock: Princeton University Press; Falk, R. (1994), 'The Making of Global Citizenship', in B. van Steenbergen (ed.), *The Condition of Citizenship,* 127-140. London: Sage.

bounded membership. A web of relations beyond the bilateral one between state and individual comes within the purview of the concept; consensual citizenship acquires a new role; and citizenship becomes increasingly unbounded from national borders.

A network model of citizenship

Cloud communities can cause a conceptual shift as they strike at the heart of the role of states in shaping citizenship. As Bauböck observes, global citizenship cannot push the state out of business. States remain responsible for providing a range of fundamental services and benefits. Yet the advent of distributed ledgers technology potentially breaks the state's monopoly in attributing and authenticating citizens' identities.[3] This nuances in turn the state's role as the main counterpart of the citizen. Citizenship no longer focuses on a binary relation between lord and vassal, sovereign and subject, state and individual. While that relation loses part of its feudalist character, to echo Orgad, citizenship comes to express a relation between different classes of 'belongers' to a legal and political community: the birthright members, the voluntary joiners, the reluctant leavers, the engaged passers-by, to mention just a few. Blockchain and other technologies will mean that their interactions are no longer exclusively mediated by the state and its rules. They would rather articulate through a web of virtual relations enabled by encrypted and self-governed digital identities.

A network model of citizenship pushes us to rethink, and possibly reframe, the legal structure and scope of citizenship as we know it. First, consent potentially gains a heftier role than it has traditionally played in the domain of citizenship. Second, cross-border citizenship receives a new lease of life.

More room for consensual citizenship

Consensual citizenship is traditionally the exception rather than the rule. The vast majority of humans are attributed a citizenship through a birthright lottery.[4] A tiny minority exercises consent to change citizenship through

---

[3] For an explanation in this sense, see Dumbrava, C. (2017), 'Citizenship and Technology', in A. Shachar, R. Bauböck, I. Bloemraad & M. Vink, *Oxford Handbook of Citizenship*, 767-778. Oxford: Oxford University Press.

[4] Shachar, A. (2009), *The Birthright Lottery: Citizenship and Global Inequality*. Cambridge: Harvard University Press.

processes of naturalisation,[5] or renounces a citizenship automatically received. And consent is still only exercised within the narrow tracks designed by states for attribution and removal of citizenship. But otherwise citizenship is the legacy of blood relations or territorial connections one has never chosen.

With technology enabling participation of virtual citizens in cloud communities, the relative weight of consensual citizenship potentially changes. This is because participation in a cloud community could allow citizens to virtually vote with their feet.[6] It would enable everyone to decide to spend their digital identity in a community other than the territorial one to which one is assigned at birth. With the opening up of opportunities for virtual exit from the cage of territorial citizenship, the negotiating balance in the relation between state and individual changes. The question 'why am I a citizen of this nation state' no longer finds an obvious answer and individual citizens gain more clout against the states to which they automatically belong. On the one hand, this transformation may lead to rethink the opportunities for birthright members to confirm or withdraw their consent to membership.[7] On the other hand, it may result in states pushing their efforts to attract consenting passers-by into the ranks of their territorial citizenry, as they already do in part with investor citizenship programs.[8]

More room for consensual citizenship is not necessarily good news, as Bauböck observes. There are risks linked to consent. Bauböck sees the non-voluntary character of citizenship as a condition for preserving democracy: non-voluntary determination of citizenship is the only guarantee that political communities, whether territorial or virtual, preserve a healthy level of diversity. A further risk is that consensual cloud communities are resorted to

---

[5] For instance, in the US out of a population of ca 300,000,000, only 19.8 million are naturalised citizens. See Pew Research Center, *Recent Trends in Naturalization 1995-2015*, June 29 2017, available at http://www.pewhispanic.org/2017/06/29/recent-trends-in-naturalization-1995-2015/ (consulted 19th January 2018).

[6] For an argument about voting with one's feet in federal states, see Tiebout, C. (1956), 'A Pure Theory of Local Expenditures', *The Journal of Political Economy* 64 (5): 416-424.

[7] For the theory of voice and exit see Hirschman, A. O. (1970), *Exit, Voice and Loyalty: Responses to Decline in Firms, Organizations and States*. Cambridge/London: Harvard University Press.

[8] See Shachar, A. & R. Bauböck (eds.) (2014), 'Should Citizenship be for Sale', *Robert Schuman Centre for Advanced Studies, EUDO Citizenship Observatory Working Paper 2011/62*, Florence: European University Institute, available at cadmus.eui.eu/bitstream/handle/1814/29318/RSCAS_2014_01.pdf

as a means to harden the link between citizenship and territory rather than to loosen it. Cloud communities may easily become a tool for amplifying cultural traditions and national sentiments. They offer a platform for joining virtually different territorial pockets of supporters of closure and exclusion. From this perspective cloud communities risk to widen the gap between the mobile and globally oriented citizens on the one hand, and the immobile ones on the other hand, as Bauböck points out.[9] Should this cleavage come to inform the competition among virtual nations that Primavera de Filippi envisions, global society could end up split between the virtual communities of those engaged across borders and the ones of those living in splendid isolation.

But technology-enabled global citizenship does not only nudge states gently towards consensual citizenship. It also enhances qualitatively the prospects of cross-border citizenship. Enhanced cross-border citizenship may hold the key to the bridge across the above referred gap between the mobiles and immobiles.

A citizen's stake beyond national borders

It goes without saying that digital identities and their applications multiply the opportunities for long-distance citizenship. They can help states to engage their diasporas through virtual communities. Or enable expats to receive benefits and services issued by their state of origin in a state of residence. In this sense, technology supports and complements the legal infrastructure underpinning cross-border movement and transnational citizenship.[10]

Beyond this, cloud communities of digitally identified participants have the potential to alter the very nature of cross-border citizenship. They open up opportunities for extending the reach of citizenship beyond the national territory even without cross-border movement. Cloud communities indeed offer to individuals the option to raise their voice, or claim benefits and ser-

---

[9] For an insightful analysis of the new gap between supporters and opponents of 'drawbridges up', see 'The New Political Divide', *The Economist*, 30 July 2016, available at https://www.economist.com/news/leaders/21702750-farewell-left-versus-right-contest-matters-now-open-against-closed-new (consulted 19 January 2018)
[10] Infrastructure that has one of its more sophisticated expressions in the citizenship of the European Union. See Strumia F. (2017), 'Supranational Citizenship', in A. Shachar, R. Bauböck, I. Bloemraad & M. Vink, *Oxford Handbook of Citizenship*, 669-693. Oxford: Oxford University Press.

vices, in territorial communities to which they do not physically belong. States can open their communities to new classes of e-citizens along the lines of Estonia's e-residence program.[11] And sedentary citizens could negotiate virtual membership in states to which they will never travel.

In this sense, digital identities and cloud communities may create the right to have, and exercise, a stake in legal and political communities beyond the borders of one's own nation.[12] On a practical level, they enable states to recognise forms of ad hoc political citizenship and temporary virtual admission to accommodate the stakes of non-citizens. Relevant non-citizens could be given voice in selected deliberations of the territorial political community, touching upon the interests of a larger cohort of virtual denizens. On a conceptual level, the right that technology enables, if adequately recognised and framed within the legal structure of national citizenship, could fundamentally alter the scope of traditional citizenship. It would no longer be just the right to have rights, and raise a voice, within a bounded national territory but the right to have rights and to participate wherever interests, careers, affective life, chance or just curiosity bring one's stakes.

In a similar scenario, the counterpart of the citizen would no longer be just one state (or two in the case of dual nationals), but potentially the plurality of states within whose territorial boundaries a person's virtual interests unfold in the course of a lifetime. 'Why should states even bother to open their virtual borders to such virtual denizens?', one could wonder. In part, because a state's citizens would reciprocally benefit from the same opportunity in other states. Hence a state would accommodate virtual denizens to protect the interests of its own citizens. Further, states may have an economic, or even political interest, in activating the stakes of some external e-citizens. Relevant citizens may contribute capital or economic initiative. Or they may support governmental policy choices.

Global citizenship for the stay-at-homes

The citizen's right to have a stake beyond national borders potentially bridges the cleavage between the globally mobile and the immobile. It belongs to, and appeals to the interests of, both classes of citizens. It can be exercised physically by the former group, and virtually by the latter through

---

[11] See Republic of Estonia e-residency program, available at https://e-resident.gov.ee/
[12] For the concept of stakeholder citizenship see Bauböck, R. (2017), *Democratic Inclusion. Rainer Bauböck in Dialogue*. Manchester, UK: Manchester University Press.

the novel channels that technology opens up. It is this very right that holds the potential to respond to nationalist and protectionist stances variedly represented in the contemporary political spectrum of several western countries. To the extent that these stances are driven by fear and insecurity, the concrete conferral of a right to have a stake beyond one's borders can teach the 21st century citizens an important lesson: that protection and security do not come from populist retrenchment into closure and exclusion. They rather come from the broadening of the umbrella under which citizenship claims can find accommodation.

As the night has become less dark and millenary cities have grown closer, also national citizenship can change to track not only the territorial boundaries of nation states but also the virtual ones of human stakes and interests. Never mind the gap between the mobiles and the immobiles. New technology brings about the gift of global citizenship for the stay-at-homes.

50

Removing Law and Politics

Robert Post

I have read with great interest the stimulating contributions of Liav Orgad, Rainer Bauböck, Primavera De Filippi, and Francesca Strumia. It is important to ask how a universal internet will affect the nature of citizenship, the status of which has heretofore been dominated by territorially-defined nation states.

I confess, however, that I know nothing about blockchain technology. So I accept Orgad's assertion that blockchain technology 'can provide people with *self-sovereign identity* – they are the ones who create and register their identity and they are the only ones who control what to do with it and with whom to share what.' I accept that nation states can off-load this identification function to some technological mechanism.

But Orgad seems to believe that this mechanism creates the possibility of 'realizing one of the most morally-desirable notions in human history – global citizenship without a world state.' This is because the mechanism potentially shatters a Westphalian system in which legal personality is conferred by nation states.

Orgad writes that 'the concept of an international legal persona will enable individuals to establish "Cloud Communities" of different kinds. Conceptually, cloud communities have traditional characteristics of political communities, but not necessarily a physical territory. The communal bond can be global in nature – such as a shared concern about climate change, ageing, veganism and animal rights (i.e., a universal community, open to everyone) – or ascriptive, such as a Jewish / Bahá'í faith / Diasporic Cloud Nations, a form of "transnational nationalism" (i.e., a selective community, open only to certain members). It can be thematic or geographic – region, country, state, city, village – based on a shared interest or territorial identity, even if not or legally recognised communities. Membership is based on consent; a person can be a member of several communities or none.'

So described, cloud communities are, as Rainer Bauböck properly observes, 'an expansion of civil society.' It is a far jump from expanding international civil society to creating global citizenship. A global citizen must be a member of a global *political* community. Orgad acknowledges this point. He states that his 'focus is *political* communities. Cloud communities are not social networks, but political communities whose aim is political decision-making and in which individuals take part in a process of governance and the creation of law.'

It is at precisely this point that I lose track of the argument. Orgad is correct to observe that the defining characteristic of political communities is the production of 'governance and the creation of law.' What I do not understand is how cloud communities produce governance and law.

By imposing sanctions of expulsion, any given cloud community can govern itself; it can create its own law. But this is true for every group within civil society. Every church has its rules and its criteria for excommunication. The point about a political community, however, is that it imposes law upon those who, as Bauböck observes, are not voluntarily members. Political communities govern all those within their jurisdiction. That is precisely the difference between political communities and a private organization. It is why law ultimately must have recourse to force, even to violence (as Max Weber observes).

A world in which every community is voluntary is a world in which every norm is also voluntary. It is therefore a world without law. Because politics is the social form by which we create law, it is also a world without politics.

If I commit murder, the necessity of my punishment is not bounded by my consent. Cloud communities, which are defined by consent, are thus irrelevant. The question is who we will entrust with the fearsome power of involuntary punishment, which is not a purely textual, purely mediated consequence. To the extent that punishment operates on the body of the guilty, it cannot be within the purview of cloud communities.

De Filippi shrewdly observes that the attraction of blockchain technologies is to create '*trustless systems* (i.e. system where trust is no longer needed).' The hope that technology will remove the human element is an old one. We all long to leave behind the flesh and live only in the spirit. But this is merely a fantasy. There is always corruption, and for that reason we can never escape the need for politics, police, and law.

Suppose someone infiltrates the blockchain and manipulates it for nefarious ends. To whom will we entrust the power of ensuring the integrity of the chain? And don't think that it can never happen. It always happens. All technology is ultimately wielded by human hands that can become dirty. Who will have the power (to use an old-fashioned word) to cleanse the chain and restore the system? And how will that power be legitimised? How will we come to trust that power?

Politics is what we use in the face of such problems, when we must confront each other as distinct human beings and reach accommodation about essential matters in which we differ. Another way of seeing this point is this: If cloud communities create, as Strumia writes, 'citizens' who can 'virtually vote with their feet,' who will protect global citizens as they travel between cloud communities?

At their best, cloud communities can inspire all the virtues that de Tocqueville saw in civil associations. They can train us in the benefits of participation and sociality. But in the contributions of Strumia and Orgad, I sense also another value, that of free, autonomous, marketplace consumers. Orgad writes that e-Estonia 'resembles a business model where states are service providers and "citizens" are billed for the service.' Strumia imagines e-states that provide services to expats or 'virtual denizens.'

Strumia and Orgad emphasise real and important developments. But it is a mistake to confuse these possibilities with the creation of political communities. Strumia and Orgad are instead describing ordinary marketplace consumer transactions. If states can sell services more cheaply than a private entity, and if they can sell these services internationally, that may be all to the good.

But what does this have to do with law and governance? To answer this query, we need to ask questions like: Who can (involuntarily) tax virtual denizens? Who can determine the commercial law that will govern the market transactions that a state conducts with virtual denizens? and so forth. Every market transaction presupposes a legal environment that is outside the transaction itself. Setting the requirements of that environment is a political task.

It is quite true that traditional states can offload services that now we associate with governmentality. Perhaps states can offload the determination of identity status to a blockchain. As the EU has taught us, it is a mistake to confuse government sovereignty with the particular shape in which it is presently exercised. But insofar as we wish to deploy *government* sovereignty – insofar as we wish to exercise state functions backed by the force of law – it is a fearsome and unstable thing to do so without a corresponding political community, as the EU has also taught us.

If the very definition of cloud communities is that they are voluntary and exist only at the whim and interest of members, I do not see how blockchain cloud communities promise the creation of global citizenship. They seem instead to signal the emergence of global civil society or at most a global market in government services. And, to the extent that cloud communities are involuntary, I must ask how their members are conscripted and governed. I must also ask how blockchains or any other technological device can offer hope that governance will be more just or more democratic than what presently exists in traditional territorially-bounded nation states.

51

Relationship between Violence, Cloud Community and Human Rights

Michael Blake

The creation of novel forms of information technology will put pressure on traditional forms of state sovereignty. The future, then, will be unlike the past. That much – to me, at least – seems beyond question. The more interesting subject, though, is whether we will be able to predict – from where and when we now are, with the technologies and histories we now inhabit – what that future will look like. Liav Orgad, in his lead essay, offers us a compelling – and profoundly optimistic – vision of one possible future. In that future, our current world of sovereignty, in which human rights are nested in territorially limited sovereign states, is supplemented by a pluralistic and polycentric network of voluntary communities, mediated by information technology based upon self-sovereign forms of digital identity. The notion of global citizenship, in that world, might move from useful metaphor to lived reality; we could, at last, inhabit a world of our own choosing – a world in which, as Francesca Strumia adds, we might join new worlds while never leaving home.

It is my lot, in these debates, to provide reasons to worry. I want to highlight and describe problems that stand in the way of moving from where we are now to where Orgad thinks we might soon be. I want to present these worries, not as permanent obstacles to the forms of life Orgad describes, but as problems we would have to solve before that world could be made real. The worries I describe stem from features of the state system that I think are poorly replicated in the world of cloud community and voluntary association; territorial states right now provide us with goods that cannot be provided by even the best systems of informational technology. To denigrate the importance of territorial states, in favour of these voluntaristic forms of association, might make things worse, rather than better.

I follow the lead of Rainer Bauböck, who notes the ways in which diversity of thought might be placed at risk in voluntary association, and Robert Post, who argues that the power of the state to punish cannot be replicated by a virtual and voluntary community. My own challenge is broader: the protection of human rights, I believe, can only be accomplished by means of violence and force, in both policing and in punishment – and this violence is in our world reserved (as a matter of right, if not reality) for use by states. Orgad's polycentric vision, in other words, must either acknowledge the continued relevance of the state system, and provide space for the preservation and maintenance of that system – or it must provide us with the resources to move beyond that system, by showing how violence might be rightly used by dispersed forms of intentional community. What I think cannot be done – or, at any rate, cannot be done easily – is to insist that informational technology has fundamentally transformed political reality, in the world in which we live. It might do so, of course; but I do not think it has done so yet – and there is a great deal of work to do, for philosophers and politicians alike, before that transformed world is open to us.

To see this, we might begin by looking at the notion of a failed state. What does such a state look like? A failed state, in the first instance, involves the absence of a political community sufficient to provide the means of survival; food, shelter, water, and so on.[1] But the state rarely actually provides these goods itself; we do not expect the government to actually deliver us food and water, unless circumstances (or that government) have become very dire. What the state provides, instead, is coercion – coercion directed, in the first instance, at those people who would steal our food or water; at people who would break contracts with us as regards our labour; and so on. A state fails when it fails to provide the coercive means needed to preserve these liberties – or, on a broader vision of failure, when it sometimes provides the means of survival, and sometimes refrains from doing so.[2]

This is, to be sure, a minimal account of what a state must do; but it is already instructive. We should note, to begin with, that the use of coercion by the state is not here an optional part of its toolkit; coercion – which is to say, violence – is required of any state that is doing the job of the state. The second thing to note is that a great deal of political philosophy amounts to understanding what particular forms of violence might be justified specifically to the people gathered together within the coercive grasp of the state.[3] Most of us, after all, regard the state as having a duty to do more than avoid failure; it has to be *just* in how it deploys these coercive powers that make it distinct. The state must, therefore, do justice to those people over whom it claims the power of rightful coercion. The final thing to note is that the state

---

[1] Rotberg, R. I. (ed.) (2003), *When States Fail: Causes and Consequences*. Princeton: Princeton University Press.
[2] Easterly, W. R. (2002), *The Elusive Quest for Growth*. Cambridge: MIT Press.
[3] Rawls, J. (1989), *Political Liberalism*. New York: Columbia University Press.

is supposed to be capable of offering, in any particular dispute about what justice demands, something very much like finality. Once the state has decided some matter of controversy, it is entitled to insist that its determination shall be non-optional for the political community over which it rules.[4]

Why, though, is any of this relevant to our discussion of blockchain and cloud community? It is relevant, I think, because of how our most important rights are linked to the state's use of violence. Our human rights are conceptually linked to violence; Hannah Arendt's often-cited 'right to have rights' demands the existence of an agency that will deploy force against those who would presume to deny or trespass on those rights.[5] Our civil rights, too, are conceptually linked with violence; the reason I have the right to vote in the United States and not France, goes the argument, is that the law of the United States – and not France – gets to order me around, and to coerce me if I resist. This sort of coercion, though, is unavailable to even the most robust and well-developed forms of virtual association. We have, I think, very little sense of what it would be for them to have such coercive rights; and we have some good reason to worry that a world in which they had such rights might be a bad one indeed.

We can use these thoughts to develop some more specific worries about the examples used by Orgad in his essay. Take the notion of political participation in a virtual political community. Orgad suggests that such communities would form valuable spaces for political negotiation. I agree – so long as we are aware that such communities are *political* in only a secondary and derivative sense. The political community of the United States must engage in discourse whose aim is to determine what sorts of things the law of the United States shall do. This sort of political community is, I think, political in a *primary* sense; if the discourse were to stop, the justice of coercive law in the United States would necessarily cease. Other forms of political association, though, are political communities only in a *secondary* sense. If they were to cease their discussions, the world of discourse would likely be impoverished; but the justice of United States legal determinations, for example, would not be automatically placed into doubt. I think we might usefully call the United States' citizenry, and Amnesty International, political associations; certainly, they both seem associative, and they both seem political. But the two are distinct in how they relate to violence. The United States uses violence. Amnesty International offers *criticism about how that violence is used*. The latter sort of political community, in short, could not

---

[4] Hart, H. L. A. (1961), *The Concept of Law*. Oxford: Clarendon Press.
[5] Arendt, H. (1994 [1951]), *The Origins of Totalitarianism*. New York: Harcourt.

even in principle replace the former. It might make the political deliberations in the former more robust, and more likely to do justice. (Certainly, a world without Amnesty International would likely have worse states in it than our own world.) But the virtual political community cannot do the job of the state's political community. The fact that we can use the phrasing of *political community* in both contexts should not obscure the vast differences between the two sorts of human association.

I would suggest that something similar might be felt about blockchain cryptography, which produces self-sovereign forms of identification. These forms of identification are *sovereign,* in that they are initiated with and controllable by the individual; but the individual has no greater *sovereignty,* in the sense used in international law, after her digital ID than before it. What the digital ID would provide, after all, is information. Information, we say, is power; but so too is, well, power, in the ordinary sense in which states use military might to preserve their sovereignty. What is required for rights to be protected, following on our discussion above, is a set of powerful agents willing to deploy violence against those who would do violence against us. The digital ID might be used to frustrate some forms of malignant state action – and, of course, allow others. What it cannot do is provide the violence that is conceptually linked with our human rights. If one is not possessed of a state willing and able to use violence on one's behalf prior to the digital ID, one is not provided with one once that ID is created.

I suspect similar things might be said of the Estonian experiment. People have long been able to engage in contracts with foreign companies, and foreign states, for particular ends; we engage in international trade, we accept particular patterns of dispute resolution, we agree to the terms limiting our rights as foreign visitors, and so on. It is not clear what, in particular, changes with the creation of a computer system capable of centralising and administering our dealings with a foreign state. I am open to being convinced otherwise, but my initial reaction is that registering as an e-Estonian no more makes me Estonian than changing planes at Heathrow makes me British. The Estonian state has obligations to its own citizens that it does not – or, at least, does not yet – have to me. So long as the e-Estonian system leaves that fact fundamentally unchanged, it is not clear to me that the virtual association it creates is even a pale shadow of a genuine political community.

All this, I should repeat, is intended not to defeat Orgad's vision, but to outline what I take to be significant worries about how we might make that vision real. Orgad does not want these voluntary forms of transnational institution to take the place of states, but insists upon their validity and power as 'state-like entities.' It is this latter point with which I take issue. If these institutions are to become genuinely state-like, they must have some part in doing what it is that states do; and we must understand how they could do that sort of thing, and how we could move from where we are to where we might be. If, in contrast, these institutions are merely places for debate and for the creation of solidarity, then we have had them for a very long time indeed; Amnesty International has been helped by the digital revolution, but had a life prior to that revolution. It is not clear what these tools provide us with except for scale and ease. Either way, I suggest, we have some work to do. Orgad is, I believe, well-positioned to help with this work; as I noted at the beginning, his vision is profoundly hopeful, while my own is not, and I genuinely hope I can be proven wrong.

52

Citizenship and the Internet

Peter J. Spiro

Liav Orgad offers a characteristically insightful and provocative speculation on how novel technologies will facilitate global citizenship. Global interconnectedness is transforming individual identity composites to include transnational elements, and the migration of identity is, as Orgad argues, establishing more pervasive understandings of global responsibility. Along these three dimensions of interconnectedness, identity, and responsibility, we are assimilating an understanding of global citizenship. A recent worldwide poll[1] found that a majority of respondents consider themselves more global citizens than citizens of their own countries.

Orgad is also to be congratulated for identifying the citizenship-related possibilities of blockchain technologies, which might further enable that sense of global identity. Blockchain could deliver a formal identity detached from national citizenship and sovereign control. Indeed, a blockchain identity could plausibly displace the passport as the standard form of identification in the same way that Bitcoin might plausibly displace national currencies. So long as it were insulated from the surveillance capacities of states and powerful non-state actors, a blockchain ID might enhance individual autonomies on a global landscape.

I am less taken by the concept of cloud communities as such. The internet facilitates the making of transnational and non-state communities, but for the most part these are communities that exist on the ground. Eliminating friction in long-distance global communication, the web enables connectedness among individuals who might otherwise maintain only thin or even non-existent ties. This is the case with almost all real-space identities that are not based on territorial location. The Web collapses location, allowing territorially dispersed communities to establish dense networks.

True, some communities exist only or primarily on the web. The community of video gamers, for example, is mostly an online identity, constituting

---

[1] 'Identity 2016: "Global citizenship" rising, poll suggests', *BBC News*, 28 April 2016, available at http://www.bbc.com/news/world-36139904

(perhaps) a genuine cloud community. But even as our online selves become more prominent in our everyday lives, they are now and will be for the foreseeable future only a slice of our identity composites. (Remember Second Life?) There is also the interesting phenomenon of e-residence as innovated by Estonia. But that 'residence' doesn't represent community, even in its virtual sense; really, the label is misplaced. No sense of solidarity is likely to flow from e-citizenship in that form any more than individuals with bank accounts in the Cayman Islands compose a community on that basis. It's a market convenience and little more.

The false dichotomies of political community

Of course, one way in which the web facilitates communities is as a vehicle for community self-governance and in turn, global self-governance. Almost all communities are political. In this respect, I would part ways with the dichotomization of political, state-based communities and civil society that appears in other contributions to this Forum (Rainer Bauböck's and Robert Post's in particular). At the very least, it is a continuum rather than a binary. The web will as a general matter enhance transparency. The web allows voices to be heard. No organisation, community, identity group, or movement can be governed in an insulated, top-down fashion.

So the web (more so than cloud communities as such) is already enhancing self-governance. It will not solve the problem of unequal representation. As Orgad notes, the international system continues formally to work from the principle of sovereign, not individual, equality, so that the citizen of San Marino has much greater clout than the citizen of China, both countries having one vote in international institutions but San Marino having many fewer citizens deciding how that vote will be cast. It's an extreme departure from the one person, one vote benchmark of democratic governance. But sovereign equality masks vast power disparities that in many pairings will more than compensate for inequality at the level of the individual. The citizen of China may be one of almost one and a half billion, the citizen of San Marino, one of thirty thousand, but China's global heft surely gives its citizens a more powerful voice (however measured) than those of its pipsqueak counterpart.

The web does help level the playing field against state power generally. In that sense the web may mitigate political inequality. Global governance is not the sole preserve of state representatives, as Orgad appears to have it; non-state communities are exercising increasing powers, formal or not, at the international level. The web supplies an important channel of global influence that does not institutionally favour state-based communities (it may even disadvantage them, insofar as bureaucracy inhibits technological adaptation). That translates into greater global self-governance capacities, and a redistribution of power away from states. The citizen of San Marino who is an environmentalist, who has an LGBTQ identification, or for that matter is a Catholic has alternate vehicles of representation at the global level, and those vehicles are empowered by the revolution in global communications.

But inequalities will persist, even if they are redistributed. I agree with Bauböck that Orgad's implication of a world federalism based on blockchain equality present an improbable prospect. In this respect, the technology does not answer standing objections to one-person, one-vote at the global level. Cloud communities, such as they exist, will themselves operate on the basis of internal formal equality in limited contexts only.

Corroded Leviathan

The corrosion of state power, meanwhile, will accelerate. Francesca Strumia articulates a new question, 'why am I a citizen of this nation-state?' That question has new salience, most dramatically with the rise of investor and other forms of instrumental citizenship. But it also begs the question, 'why should I care that I am a citizen of this (or that) nation-state?' It is no doubt true that possessing a premium passport expands life opportunities.[2] But within the universe of developed states, the question is not so obviously answered. There are inevitable spatial elements to our physical existence that are best governed through territorially delimited community, but those necessities need not be addressed at the level of the state. Many are better addressed at the subnational level, with respect to which 'voting with your feet' is practicable as a preference-sorting mechanism into 'like-minded sets', in Bauböck's formulation.

This gives the lie to the other misplaced critique of cloud communities, that they are voluntary and monolithic where states are involuntary and diverse. Here again, a descriptive spectrum is more appropriate than an artificial binary. It is true of course that most individuals are born into the states of which they will remain members (at the same time that a growing number change nationality after birth). But many are effectively born into non-state communities as well. Religion supplies an obvious example. In some contexts, the exit costs – perhaps a better metric than voluntariness – of leaving

---

[2] The Henley & Partners – Kochenov Quality of Nationality Index, available at https://www.henleyglobal.com/quality-of-nationality/

a religious community[3] are higher than leaving a state-based one. Communities based on race, ethnicity, and sexual orientation are more or less involuntary. They can also be remarkably diverse, sometimes more so than state-based communities. The Catholic Church represents a more diverse constituency than does Austria, for example, and its internal dynamics surely implicate politics in any but the most formalistic definition of the term.

I understand the liberal nationalist tendency to lament the corrosion of state-based communities. There was a time (the latter half of the twentieth century) when the state impressively if imperfectly delivered on redistributionist solidarities. But wishing a return to that era is starting to look somewhat sentimental. States are powerful beasts, as Bauböck observes. They will linger in the way of other once-dominant legacy institutions (think the Holy Roman Empire). But they are clearly in crisis, and it seems unlikely that we will be able to re-right the ship to its formerly commendable course.

In the meantime, we should be setting our sights on making the new world a better one than it might otherwise be. They are many dystopian possibilities (some of them almost apocalyptic) if the state collapses and other locations of power replace it. Wishing the resurrection of the state will do us no good to the extent that the state can't withstand material developments on the ground. A necessary first step will be to map the new institutional landscape, of which cloud communities will clearly be a part.

---

[3] 'Off the path of Orthodoxy', *The New Yorker*, 31 July 2015, available at https://www.newyorker.com/news/news-desk/off-the-path-of-orthodoxy

53

Algorithms, Cloud Communities and Citizenship

Costica Dumbrava

In his thought-provoking kick-off contribution, Liav Orgad enthusiastically embraces the idea of a global digital citizenship that could remedy some of the deficiencies of the present system of territorial national citizenships and, potentially, transform the meaning of democratic citizenship. Technologies such as blockchain could allow people to create virtual communities based on shared interests and sustained by instantaneous consent, beyond the reach of nosy governments and regardless of national borders. By widening access to rights, expanding political voice and creating more secure and diverse identities, digital citizenship could address current challenges related to the imperfect attribution of status and rights (statelessness, disenfranchisement), widespread political apathy among citizens and artificial divisions created by national borders. To paraphrase the text of a famous cartoon: 'on the internet nobody knows you are a foreigner'.

Other contributors to this Forum have pointed out several important tensions and dangers lurking in Orgad's proposal. Rainer Bauböck worries that replacing political communities, which are based largely on ascribed but equal citizenship, with freely chosen cloud communities would be 'fatal for democracy'. Purely consensual political communities cannot work because political associations need coercive systems capable to enforce laws. As 'exit-based conflict resolution systems' (Primavera De Filippi), virtual communities are too volatile to ensure stable membership and commitment to rules. They are also ill equipped to do the policing and punishing required by political organisation (Robert Post, Michael Blake). Orgad's cloud communities could be seen instead as akin to civil society organisations. As novel forms of coagulating solidarity, interests and identities, they can be instrumental for checking, challenging or complementing governments, but they have neither the means, nor the legitimacy to replace democratic citizenship.

I agree that technologies may offer surprising opportunities for improving and reimagining our social and political life (Francesca Strumia, Peter Spiro). Information and communication technologies already offer to some people better access to legal status (digital IDs), allowing them to participate more effectively in political deliberations and decision making (e-forums, e-voting), to mobilise against authoritarian regimes (twitter revolutions) and to transcend borders in order to engage with communities of origin (diaspora politics).[1] Using powerful computers, myriads of sensors and sophisticated algorithms, 'smart cities' can identify and address public issues and concerns, such as traffic congestions and security threats. However, I worry that we too often take technologies for granted and fail to discern between technological opportunity and mythology.

My contribution to this debate is to raise two general points about the risks involved by linking citizenship to technology, namely making citizenship vulnerable to biases and failures that typically affect technology and increasing citizenship's dependence on technology.

Technologies are not neutral. They are embedded in and tend to reinforce certain values, norms and expectations to the detriment of others. For example, predictive algorithms used by police are more likely to identify black persons as suspects of crime[2] and facial recognition software seems to recognise better white male faces.[3] When they are not biased by design, smart technologies may quickly pick up biases from their surroundings. In 2016, Microsoft created Tay, a chatbot that used machine learning to emulate a teenage user on Twitter. However, after a few hours of 'learning' on the social media platform Tay began posting Hitler-praising and other racist

---

[1] Dumbrava, C. (2017), 'Citizenship and Technology', in Shachar, A., R. Bauböck, I. Bloemraad & M. Vink (eds.), *Oxford Handbook of Citizenship*, 767–788. Oxford: Oxford University Press.

[2] 'Big data may be reinforcing racial bias in the criminal justice system', *The Washington Post*, 10 February 2017, available at https://www.washingtonpost.com/opinions/big-data-may-be-reinforcing-racial-bias-in-the-criminal-justice-system/2017/02/10/d63de518-ee3a-11e6-9973-c5efb7ccfb0d_story.html?utm_term=.5513fe110740

[3] 'Facial recognition software is biased towards white men, researcher finds', *The Verge*, 11 February 2018, available at https://www.theverge.com/2018/2/11/17001218/facial-recognition-software-accuracy-technology-mit-white-men-black-women-error

and sexist remarks[4], which forced Microsoft to shut it down with an apology. Bitcoin, the most well-known blockchain technology, can also be regarded as deeply political, a product of particular 'right-wing, liberation, anti-government politics.'[5] Such ideological bias makes blockchain unsuitable for becoming the repository of democratic citizenship. If the platform itself is biased towards a particular conception of the good, how can we expect it to serve as an arena and mediator between different conceptions of the good?

Technologies often fall short of expectations and are usually hijacked, if not initiated, by authoritarian governments and powerful groups. For example, India's population biometric database, Aadhaar, which is intended to provide more than a billion people with digital identities and access to public services, has been criticised for its rigidity and security problems, which affect particularly the poor.[6] The Chinese government is currently toying with a Social Credit System[7] designed to measure citizens' trustworthiness that would further mould their behaviour to align it with the government's priorities and ideology. Blockchain gurus and their followers claim that this technology is highly secure. However, this has not prevented a hacker to steal about 60 million USD - worth Ether (another major cryptocurrency) in the so-called DAO attack.[8] Indicative of the ideological underpinning of the blockchain movement, and deeply troubling from many perspectives of social justice, is that some members of the cryptocurrency community sug-

---

[4] 'Microsoft's disastrous Tay experiment shows the hidden dangers of AI', *QUARTZ*, 2 April 2016, available at https://qz.com/646825/microsofts-ai-millennial-chatbot-became-a-racist-jerk-after-less-than-a-day-on-twitter/https:/qz.com/653084/microsofts-disastrous-tay-experiment-shows-the-hidden-dangers-of-ai/

[5] Golumbia, D. (2015), 'Bitcoin as Politics: Distributed Right-Wing Extremism', in G. Lovink, N. Tkacz & P. de Vries (eds.), *MoneyLab reader: An intervention in digital economy*, 118–31. Amsterdam: Institute of Network Cultures.

[6] 'In Rajasthan, there is "unrest at the ration shop" because of error-ridden Aadhaar', *Scroll.in*, 14 April 2018, available at http://scroll.in/article/805909/in-rajasthan-there-is-unrest-at-the-ration-shop-because-of-error-ridden-aadhaar

[7] 'Big data meets Big Brother as China moves to rate its citizens', *Wired*, 21 October 2017, available at http://www.wired.co.uk/article/chinese-government-social-credit-score-privacy-invasion

[8] Reijers, W., F. O'Brolcháin & P. Haynes (2016), 'Governance in Blockchain Technologies & Social Contract Theories', *Ledger* 1 (1): 134–151.

gested that the attacker should keep the money as s/he did not break the rules but simply exploited a flaw in the system.

As other products of digital technologies, the blockchain exists in online clouds that depend on critical physical infrastructures. Online clouds are no less fragile than on-the-sky clouds. Online systems are emanations of a bunch of machines connected to various grids that require an awful lot of things, such as electricity, computers, data centres, internet servers, etc. Since this enabling infrastructure is vulnerable to hacking and shutdown, so is democratic citizenship if embedded in digital technologies. If digital identities could be compromised (as in the Indian case) and cryptocurrency stolen there is little assurance that digital citizenship solutions, such as universal IDs, e-voting systems and blockchain-based cloud communities, would not succumb to the same illness.

My second point is about the risk of making citizenship (too) dependent on technology. As we regularly worry about our children's addiction to tablets, online gaming and other technologies that could affect their social development, we should also worry about our society's dependence on technologies that might affect its capacity for self-government. It is not only about a technologically mediated withdrawal of citizens from the physical public space, á la Putnam,[9] but also about the dangers of making democratic citizenship dependent on specific technological systems and artefacts.

Exercising citizenship has always involved some forms of technology, from voting pebbles in Ancient Greece to ballot boxes and electoral districting algorithms[10] in modern representative democracies. However, the high levels of sophistication and, ultimately, opaqueness of technologies such as blockchain must be a real concern should we decide to entrust these technologies with the role of embodying democratic self-government. We are asked to take for granted the promises of new digital technologies and are kindly invited to take our places in shiny new cloud communities. However, we rarely understand how these technologies work, who designs and oversees them and whether we would be able to dispense of them if we find them wanting.

---

[9] Putnam, R. D. (2000), *Bowling Alone: The Collapse and Revival of American Community*. New York: Simon & Schuster.
[10] 'Of the Algorithms, by the Algorithms, for the Algorithms', *Slate*, 13 January 2009, available at http://www.slate.com/articles/news_and_politics/politics/2009/01/of_the_algorithms_by_the_algorithms_for_the_algorithms.html

Some religions tell you that the true God is in the clouds; tech enthusiasts tell you that the true community is in the cloud. I recommend examining the sky carefully before you start packing.

54

Dividing Territory and State

Yussef Al Tamimi

The contributions on cloud communities and citizenship in this blog raise both hopes and fears. The reality of an idea initially as outlandish as citizens of a digital cloud is materialising as we ponder and debate its practices. Political theory and the law must attempt to keep up with these rapidly changing circumstances. This comment raises some questions regarding three assumptions in this debate:

1. Cloud states[1] have no **territory**
2. Cloud states cannot exert **violence**
3. Cloud state membership is based on **choice**

To illustrate and perhaps formulate a response to these assumptions, it might benefit this futuristic debate to consult experiences from the past. As suggested by the other contributors, the current transformation of the state as a consequence of the 'digital revolution' is profound. Nothing less than a separation of the state from its traditional connectedness to territory is suggested. The historic event that comes close to matching such a seismic shift in the structure of the state was the American and French Revolutions, which set in motion the institutional untying of state and church. A historical parallel is quickly drawn: if these revolutions led to the *separation of Church and State* that resulted in secular states, will the digital revolution lead to the *separation of Territory and State* that results in cloud states?

---

[1] I use the term 'cloud state' rather than 'cloud community', as the latter unnecessarily obscures the fact that, at least in this debate, the question is whether clouds can fulfill certain political functions traditionally belonging to the state, such as conferring citizenship. Assuming that these political functions can indeed be performed by clouds, this leaves no reason to call a cloud anything else than a 'state', except to dissociate the cloud from the negative connotations of the state and calling it by the more cozy term community. However, in my opinion, one should not appropriate the political function of the traditional state and simultaneously obscure the responsibility – which states sometimes fail to exercise – that is inherent to that function.

Assumption 1: Cloud states have no territory

Robert Post, focusing on legislation in his blog post, argues: 'A world in which every community is voluntary is a world in which every norm is also voluntary. It is therefore a world without law. Because politics is the social form by which we create law, it is also a world without politics.'

For Post, a cloud state, which does not impose legislation, is not a state at all. One can imagine that arguments sounding very similar were once raised by opponents of the separation of Church and State: 'a secular, neutral state, which does not impose public morals, is not a state at all.' I raise this parallel not to disagree with Post. Rather, it is to show that after centuries of debate on secularism we have come to understand that 'neutrality' of the state is an impossibility; a state always makes choices that impact a state's public sphere. That is to say that the opponents of the separation of Church and State were wrong in the first place because the starting premise of their critique, that the secular state would be neutral, was incorrect.

The starting premise of the cloud state is that it is nonterritorial. Now that we have come to know that 'neutrality' does not really exist, the question arises if we have to conclude that 'nonterritorial clouds' do not really exist either. In other words, *is the cloud itself not territory?* I do not mean this in the strict physical sense that clouds have servers that are located in territorial states, which itself is a valid point; yet the development of serverless cloud computing in the future might undermine such an argument. To think of the cloud as somehow territory-less and border-less is incongruous if one appreciates that territory itself is not a natural phenomenon but a man-made construct the meaning of which is dynamic and can come to encompass non-physical spaces.

Assumption 2: Cloud states cannot exert violence

Focusing on violence in his comment, Michael Blake states: 'My own challenge is broader: the protection of human rights, I believe, can only be accomplished by means of violence and force, in both policing and in punishment – and this violence is in our world reserved (as a matter of right, if not reality) for use by states.'

Blake argues that cloud states cannot protect human rights. A comparison with anti-separationists in the French Revolution is again not far away: they would claim that 'secular states cannot protect God's law'. To make his argument, Blake relies heavily on state force. But why could cloud states not impose their own forms of digital violence? Perhaps an obvious damage they could inflict is to one's reputation. An example of this is the social credit system proposed by the Chinese government, which is a national reputation system that assigns social credit to citizens. The flipside of such reputation systems that aim to promote 'good citizenship' behaviour is the potential social devaluation of 'bad' citizens, which can go as far as seriously harming their wellbeing and possibilities in life. A punishment in terms of such social devaluation imposed by the cloud state is conceivably more painful and restricting to the individual than traditional methods of punishment, such as fines or jail.

As with territory, one could counter this claim by saying that what matters for statehood is physical, rather than non-physical, violence. In that case, the actual core of the matter is the physicality of the traditional state's territory and violence compared to the non-physicality of the cloud state's territory and violence. That raises a question that is yet to be addressed by proponents of cloud states: What is desirable about the non-physicality of territory and violence that makes cloud states and their citizenship superior to traditional states and their citizenship?

Assumption 3: Cloud state membership is based on choice

Focusing on the idea of consent-based cloud communities, Rainer Bauböck writes: 'My response is that this would be fatal for democracy. Already Aristotle knew that, unlike families, democratic polities are associations of diverse individuals. The territorial bases and automatic attribution mechanisms of citizenship create political community among individuals that differ profoundly in their interests, identities and ideas about the common good.'

In short, for Bauböck choice cannot be constitutive for political membership (citizenship). Hence, the chosen membership of cloud states is not citizenship. This is a difficult topic, and the parallel with the earlier (French) revolution escapes me. The reason for this is that in the secular revolution separating Church and State the 'onus' of choice fell on the Church and not the State: It was religion and the freedom to choose individually one's religion that was guaranteed by the secular state. By contrast, in the digital revolution separating Territory and State the opening up of choice is focused on the newfound states among which individuals can choose. In fact, one might even be limited in exiting from a territory (think refugees, political activists) yet have the freedom to select from a range of cloud states one wants to join.

Yet, the notions of choice and voluntariness applied in this context leave many questions unanswered. It is still unclear in what way we understand membership in a cloud state to be a 'choice'. The Chinese social credit system mentioned earlier may become mandatory as of 2020. Such a turn towards explicitly mandatory membership will probably not always happen, but what idea of choice do we have in mind when saying that cloud membership is a 'choice'? Is it rational choice theory, which has long been refuted in psychology? The conditions that move people to decide on their cyber membership, as well as their non-rational motivations, have to be taken into account for a more realistic conception of choice.

The question of chosen membership is closely related to issues concerning identity. The idea that individuals are able to 'create' their own identities, which is implicit in Liav Orgad's contribution, is mistaken. Iris Marion Young makes a helpful distinction between associations and social groups to tease out the distinct role of identity when membership is based on choice. Young argues that that the contract model of society applies to associations but not to social groups: 'Individuals constitute associations; they come together *as already formed persons* and set them up, establishing rules, positions, and offices.' (my emphasis).[2] In contrast, social groups, in which our identities are implicated, involve a much more complex process: 'Group affinity (...) has the character of (...) "thrownness": one finds oneself as a member of a group, whose existence and relations one experiences as always already having been.' This does not mean that one cannot change one's group affinity, for example by changing one's gender identity as transpersons do. For Young, these cases illustrate thrownness precisely because such changes are 'experienced as a transformation in one's identity.' This phenomenological approach to social groups shows that a deeper affinity is involved in the process of membership and that social groups, which implicate our identity, cannot be explained solely by 'choice'. Young and Bauböck therefore agree that citizenship and choice are irreconcilable, though they do so from different standpoints: for Bauböck the presence of choice in communities leads to a democratic deficit, for Young it leads to a social defi-

---

[2] Young, I. M. (1989), 'Polity and Group Difference: A Critique of the Ideal of Universal Citizenship', *Ethics* 99: 250–274, at 260.

cit, a lack of social affinity or belonging. To respond to this complex debate relating to membership, the nature of cloud membership requires further clarification as to its position on citizenship, identity and choice.

55

Citizenship and Governance: A Futuristic Perspective

Jelena Džankić

I have always been fascinated by the human capacity to imagine future worlds and describe what humanity would look like in the years or decades ahead. In the second half of the nineteenth century, Jules Verne wrote about electricity, submarines and flying balloons. A few decades later, Thea von Harbou and Fritz Lang gave birth to the world of *Metropolis,* which in many ways is a metaphor of contemporary societies. In the 1970s and 1980s, Isaac Asimov wrote about psychohistory, a discipline that combines statistics, psychology and history to predict how the behaviour of large groups would shape future events. Just as most of the things described by Verne, von Harbou and Lang, or Asimov seemed technologically and politically distant or unimaginable at their times, so do meaningful digital communities seem to be today.

Liav Orgad sees tremendous potential in digital technologies for reconstructing the traditional notion of citizenship by shifting status, identity and the exercise of rights away from the state and closer to the individual. He believes that blockchain could enhance the current structure of international governance by strengthening human rights through the attribution of digital identities and by offering new models for political participation through cloud communities, which in turn would decrease the inequality engrained in, for instance, the principles of voting in the United Nations. In other words, with further development of blockchain technologies, states would no longer be the sole determinants of an individual's legal status, or have the monopoly over the exercise of individual rights, or be the core community for identity ascription. In this sense, I am in agreement with Orgad, Primavera De Filippi and Francesca Strumia that we cannot but acknowledge that rapidly developing technologies are likely to 'outsource' many of the state's functions to cyberspace. Even so, as has been pointed out by other contributors (Rainer Bauböck, Robert Post, Michael Blake and Peter Spiro), blockchain technologies and cloud communities raise a number of concerns about governability and the exercise of self-sovereignty.

They want citizenship? Let them have digital identities instead!

In his kick-off contribution Orgad highlights that 1.1 billion people, or a sixth of the global population lack an official identification. Such people, including many refugees, displaced persons, nomadic pastoralists or socially marginalised minorities like the Roma are consequently excluded from participating in or accessing services of modern states. According to Orgad, blockchain technologies already provide the infrastructure for attributing such people global digital IDs, which would grant them recognition as 'human beings'. Blockchain-based digital IDs would enable individuals to create and register their own identity. This identity would be validated through multiple decentralised network nodes. It would also be permanent and immutable.

I agree with the general need to recognise every human being before the law. However, the attribution of a global digital ID scarcely resolves this problem for two reasons. The first one is recognition. Our legal status is attributed by states recognising us as legal persons. The international system of mutual recognition among states allows us to be considered a legal persona elsewhere precisely because the status that we have has been confirmed by a state. Hence, any global digital ID would still need to be recognised by states or an international organisation in order to have external validity. Initiatives, such as ID2020[1] speak about the need to tackle the problem of the lack of 'officially recognised identity' through digital technology but offer scarcely any practical pointers as to how these identities would be recognised and by whom. Furthermore, if such digital identification were to create a 'status and identity *complementary* to national citizenships', I am wondering what kind of status and rights it would yield for those whose predicament Orgad seeks to resolve. If a digital ID has no external recognition, it has little value for a person with no other proof of identity. They will still lack the status that a digital identity could complement but cannot substitute for. Isn't the offer of digital identity for them a bit like Marie Antoinette's cake for the hungry crowds in revolutionary Paris?

---

[1] *ID2020 Alliance at a Glance*, available at https://static1.squarespace.com/static/578015396a4963f7d4413498/t/5a5f92bcc8302548e722dff3/1519157409748/ID2020+Alliance+Doc+-+Jan+2018.pdf

Governance by blockchain: digital hierarchies or direct democracy?

Orgad's second claim looks prima facie stronger. Recent experiments with blockchain-based virtual communities, such as Bitnation, indicate that blockchain technology has the potential to substitute or complement some elements of state governance. In theory, in a blockchain-based cloud community, members agree on a set of laws regulating their interaction, and these laws are then amended by consensus.

Pazaitis, De Filippi and Kostakis give the example of Backfeed (http://backfeed.cc/) protocol as a conceptual model 'for a new form of governance with an incentivisation system implemented on the blockchain.'[2] This system would be materialised through an organisational structure of decentralised cooperation based on peer-to-peer evaluation and a reputation system as grounds for allocating communal influence. This kind of cooperation would presume that a number of members come together to establish a digital community and reach a consensus on what values underpin that community. Members of the community own certain initial amounts of 'reputation' tokens and they are incentivised to participate in communal decisions through a system that provides reputational gains to those who are best aligned with communal values. Those contributing voluntarily to 'values' receive a reward if 50 per cent of the tokens representing the community's reputation have been invested in the evaluation of the voluntary contribution. The reward takes the form of reputation tokens, which are shared between the contributor and those who reached the consensus on the evaluation. Whenever a person evaluates a new contribution, they also give away some of their existing reputation to it.

Let's translate this into a thought experiment. Imagine there is a Backfeed-based community called Scientia, in which the core value were 'knowledge'. Scientia has been created by five members (A, B, C, D, and E), each of whom originally had 10 reputation tokens (i.e., the community has a total of 50 tokens). Member A comes up with a proposal to create an encyclopaedia of cloud communities and the proposal is put to communal vote. Votes can range from 1 to 5 (1 lowest contribution, 5 highest contribution). The proposal will go through if at least 25 reputation tokens have been invested in the evaluation.

---

[2] Pazaitis, A., P. De Filippi & V. Kostakis (2017), 'Blockchain and value systems in the sharing economy: The illustrative case of Backfeed', *Technological Forecasting and Social Change* 125: 105–115, at 111.

Now, imagine a scenario where A invests 8 out of her initial 10 reputation tokens with a vote of 5; B invests 5 tokens with a vote of 5; C invests 3 tokens with a vote of 3; D invests 5 tokens with a vote of 4; E invests 7 tokens with a vote of 5. A total of 28 tokens have been invested, with three contributors voting 5, and hence the proposal is accepted. C and D will lose the 8 tokens they invested, and these will be distributed between A (4 tokens), B (3 tokens), and E (1 token) in line with their initial reputation investment. The new count of reputation tokens would be 14 for A, 13 for B, 7 for C, 5 for D, and 11 for E. In evaluating the subsequent proposal, A, B and E would have greater voting power, as they would hold three quarters of the community's reputation tokens.

In my view, there are three problems with this kind of decision-making. First, the 'overall evaluation of a specific contribution is based on the reputation score'.[3] This implies the use of a system of weighted voting, whereby individuals with higher reputation (i.e., with more tokens) have a greater say in communal decision-making. Paradoxically this would make the principles of deciding in such digital communities closer to those in ancient Rome, feudal Prussia, or French colonies where votes were weighted on grounds of 'wealth' than to contemporary democracies based on the equality of votes. In other words, this kind of system would perpetuate inequality of membership in a similar way as the Chinese social credit system described by Costica Dumbrava does. Second, even though the general idea of Backfeed-based governance is to incentivise participation through rewards, those with high rewards from previous rounds of evaluations may be less inclined to participate in new evaluations as that may result in their loss of reputation. Equally, 'losers' in the communal vote (such as the examples of C and D above) may face obstacles in putting forward or voting for any proposal due to limited resources at their disposal. Third, such a system could create incentives to bet with the winners rather than to invest into the values that one truly believes are in line with communal ones. This is antithetical to democracy and turns into a market where people pursue reputational gains instead of deliberating on what values they share. That is, a system in which reputation is gained and lost by 'betting' on the levels of contribution to communal value has the potential to create a stratified society in which decisions are made by a small number of those willing to speculate on communal value.

An alternative to this would be to think how direct democracy could work in cloud communities. Presumably, protocols could be developed

---

[3] Above n. 1 at 110.

that – unlike Backfeed – base decision-making on equal voting power for each digital identity and that offer a platform for deliberation rather than only for voting. Such communities would be similar to voluntary associations of individuals that adopt statutes providing for internally democratic governance: *all* members (independently of their duration of membership and place of residence) and members *only* can participate in decisions taken by the 'demos' of the association.

Now, let's go back to the example of Scientia. Imagine that this time, Scientia were a voluntary decentralised blockchain-based community that operates on the basis of equal votes of its members A, B, C, D, and E. The community votes on A's proposal for the encyclopaedia of cloud communities and the proposal passes due to positive votes of A, B, and E. Unlike in the previous example, since there are no reputational gains or losses, C and D will have the same voting power in the next ballot. Hence such a model would not disincentivise those who opposed the initiative. However, it would then not provide incentives for contributing in the future, as Backfeed is supposed to do. As Pazaitis, De Filippi and Kostakis rightly point out, this would lead to 'to the gradual dissipation of the community members, who could no longer reflect themselves into the value system of the new entity.'[4]

So there is a dilemma of blockchain governance in cloud communities: will they be based on incentives that create hierarchies or on direct democracy with scarce mechanisms for motivating participation?

Citizenship as a business model?

In his kick-off contribution Orgad notes that the future of citizenship is dynamic and multi-layered. Yet so is the present, and so has been its past. The key question is whether we are ready to embrace a new approach to citizenship, based on 'smart contracts' operating in cyberspace and regulating needs of individuals, just as a business model would do. For Spiro the recent trend towards a global market for passports exemplifies such an approach to citizenship: individuals with multiple passports have more choice where to settle, pay taxes, send their children to school, etc. Hence, in some respects, citizenship (albeit for a small number of people who can benefit from investor citizenship programmes) is already merely an access point to a market of goods and services that different providers (in this case states) offer.

As new technologies develop, digital markets will allow individuals to choose the services previously provided by the state from private companies.

---

[4] Ibid.

Indeed, some functions of the state have already been outsourced to companies operating in the digital world (e.g., online education instead of public schooling, car-sharing schemes instead of public transport, etc.). Perhaps the utopian vision of the 'sharing economy' is that public goods would be produced through horizontal and voluntary cooperation among consumers. Yet examples such as online degrees, Airbnb, Uber, and the likes prove the contrary. They follow the logic of the market and reveal the huge potential for corporate power based on network effects and 'cartelisation' of services.[5] In considering the effects of citizenship as a business model, we also need to think about possible implications for some other core functions of the state, including adjudication and the provision of security.

And even if, in the spirit of the introductory paragraph, digital technologies bring along numerous benefits we have to recognise that their *á la carte* approach is hardly conducive to the creation of a community of shared values among members. That is, it is hardly conducive to citizenship.

---

[5] Atzori, M. (2015), 'Blockchain technology and decentralized governance: Is the state still necessary?', available at SSRN: abstract=2709713.

56

Global Citizenship and Access to Digital Devices

Lea Ypi

There is no doubt that we live in an age of global communication. But who is able to communicate and how is access to the means that enable that communication (computers, mobile phones, internet lines) distributed?

Consider again the facts of global interconnectedness with which Liav Orgad begins his piece. But consider them from a different perspective, not that of the wealthy Western academic who blogs about cloud communities. If half of the world population spends time online, it means that the other half does not. While 94 per cent of the youth population in the developed world has access to the internet, 70 per cent of youngsters in least developed countries do not. While almost one-third of the global population uses smartphones, the other two-thirds (the vast majority) does not. If global internet use in 2017 was at 48 per cent, 52 per cent of the world's population was left out. In the least developed countries only 15 per cent of households have access to the internet from their homes and 85 per cent rely on schools, offices, libraries or other public connections to access the web. The proportion of men using the internet is higher than the proportion of women, and the proportion of private internet access in developed countries is twice as high as in developing ones.[1]

All this suggests that the narrative of global interconnectedness on which the ideal of global citizenship rests is only half true and true only for half of the world. There is of course the claim that even for the half of the world that is connected, the technology might not work very well. There are the dangers of digital identities being stolen and of data centres, internet servers, and the rest of the infrastructure being vulnerable to hacking, as Dumbrava emphasises in his contribution. But my problem is even more basic. One of the most attractive features of global citizenship based on blockchain technologies

---

[1] International Telecommunications Union (2017), *ITU Facts and Figures*. Available at https://www.itu.int/en/ITU-D/Statistics/Documents/facts/ICTFactsFigures2017.pdf

seems to be that it does not entail the right to exclude. But either proponents of that ideal start with the world as it is, or they do not. If they take the world as it is, they endorse an even more pernicious form of exclusion, the exclusion of those who have no access to the internet from the community of those that do, and they proceed to reify the separation between the two. If they start with the world as it ought to be, they owe us an argument on how we can get from here to there. How can we make sure that the half of the world that has no access to the internet can do so? How are we going to take care of the costs of IT provision? What will put an end to the inequalities that make it the case that for some people (like me) mobile phones are an extension of themselves and for some others only an aspiration? Who controls the production of the tools that lead to differentiated access of the means of connection?

It will be clear from my lines above that I approach the question of global citizenship presented in Orgad's piece from a radical egalitarian perspective, concerned with inequalities of access to the material means of production, and the related power positions of those who control such access. In the contemporary world this means raising very basic questions, such as who owns Apple and Microsoft, and how we can make sure that everyone has a mobile phone that works as well in central London as it does in the remote areas of Albania (where it typically does not). Apple and Microsoft are the modern equivalents of cotton and spin factories. We have the same reasons to worry about who controls their ownership and who has access to the technologies that they enable as much now as we did in the past. But if we ignore the problem of asymmetrical access and proceed as if the internet was already within everybody's reach, we run the risk of entrenching one of the most problematic divides of our time.

Given the perspective I have offered, I hesitate to show enthusiasm for Orgad's proposal for reasons very different from those of Robert Post, Michael Blake or even Rainer Bauböck. My argument is not that cloud communities based on voluntary membership do not offer the benefits of a collective coercive system of rewards and punishments like the one offered by modern states. I do not think that states are necessarily either more just or more democratic than cloud communities, or that they 'provide us with goods that cannot be provided by even the best systems of informational technology' as Michael Blake suggests. If you are a representative of the half of the world that has nothing to do with the internet you are of course failed by IT providers, but you are also failed by your state. Indeed, you are failed by those providers precisely *because* you are failed by your state. It is because the state is captured by powerful groups who merely exploit you and who are uninterested in guaranteeing you access to those basic goods that the state is supposed to guarantee (at least according to the liberal myth) that you are excluded within the state as much as outside.

When we assess the benefits and limitations of state citizenship versus a voluntary model of global citizenship, we have to make sure that we compare like with like. We have to make sure we don't compare an ideal of the state with the reality of failing blockchain technologies, for example. We need to compare the reality of the state with the reality of cloud communities or the ideal of the state with the ideal of cloud communities. Speaking about ideals, like Orgad, I am attracted to a system of voluntary membership where citizenship does not come coupled with the right to exclude, and like De Filippi I can see the advantages of '*trustless systems* (i.e. system where trust is no longer needed).' Indeed, both of those things are compatible with the kind of utopian society Marx thought would come after capitalism had been superseded and when the need for a state (understood as a collective coercive system of punishment) would have withered away. But speaking about reality, capitalism is alive and kicking: capitalist relations control the state and they will control cloud communities. Without remedying the asymmetries of access to the means of connection, and the exclusions they generate, the ideal of global citizenship will be as illusory as the ideal of a state that is effective in distributing social goods. But while in the case of the state, we have at least a history of political mobilisation and, if lucky, democratic learning processes and institutions on which to rely when seeking change (as Bauböck also points out in his piece), nothing of that sort is available in the cloud. So we should probably hold on to state citizenship for the conflictual period of transition and leave cloud communities to the future utopian society that may become accessible once interconnectedness is truly global. If it ever does.

57

Neo-Feudalism, Escapism and Technology

Dimitry Kochenov

This contribution agrees with Rainer Bauböck's reaction to Liav Orgad's opening statement. I am, too, 'less optimistic about the future of citizenship'. My reasons are different though. There are different ways to go about technological leaps: to turn technological breakthroughs into the tools of improving the long-established reality, or to revolutionize society based on technological advancements. Nikolai Fëdorov, to give an ambitious example, aimed at conquering death and resurrecting all those previously living.[1] Liav Orgad's text proposes technology-inspired change. I suggest, respectfully, that by not going far enough, what is proposed by Orgad could turn out to be dangerous and unwelcome for a large share of the world population outside of the richest countries. Echoing Lea Ypi's contribution, I suggest that it will do more harm than good. The reason for this is that it puts technology to the service of the mythology of citizenship, instead of interrogating citizenship's essence and functions and questioning its darker corners.

The core of the problem, to my mind, is the concept of citizenship as such, not the documentation of identity, which the blockchain proposal addresses. Virtual nations, as long as they replicate existing national structures that randomly ascribe strict identities and reinforce deep global inequalities, will make the world worse off, especially among its poorest half. Even if they miraculously end up playing a significant role, the citizenship framing of the issues Orgad aims to address seems to be unhelpful and problematic, especially in the context of his rhetoric aspiring to reach out to 'global' citizenship, whatever this could mean.

Citizenship is a racist and sexist status of randomised violent segregation of the world population into relatively closed groups of varying objective value from the point of view of individual rights.[2] Some come with far-reaching rights – others with liabilities. Both are significant both in real life

---

[1] Fëdorov, N. F. (1906), *Filosofija obshchego dela*. Moscow: Vernyj.
[2] Kochenov, D. (2019), *Citizenship: An Alchemist's Promise*. Michigan: MIT Press (forthcoming).

and in the cloud. If someone is assigned a humiliating set of liabilities in real life, say, a Central African Republic citizenship, instead of a noble and democratic status boosting one's rights, say the citizenship of France, cloud communities will not change that, unless the distinction between being assigned to CAR as opposed to France is thereby undermined, and based on Orgad's suggestion it won't be. The 'real life' problem thus derives from real life inequalities between citizenships as bundles of rights and liabilities. It is not only that citizenships by definition exclude. It is the difference between different citizenships that matters. As long as these two premises persist in shaping our day-to-day reality, a 'global' cloud community is a meaningless proposition for those who hold inferior citizenships, reinforcing the gaps between CAR citizens and the French.

Citizenship's core function throughout history, alongside sexism and a deep exclusion of women, has been to establish and police global race- and wealth-based hierarchies of opportunities and rights, while providing an impenetrable and punishing noble façade of equality and self-determination. In this, citizenship has been very effective: it took US women almost hundred years to get the right to vote and the Dutch ones waited until 1986 to have a citizenship status independent of that of their husbands. Compared with women, all the colonial subjects fared significantly worse. While African Americans obviously have not been enjoying the same rights as 'Caucasian' US citizens throughout the history of US citizenship, the same is true for the European and Asian empires as well. Emmanuelle Saada explains how arbitrary and uniquely based on skin-colour the ascription of Frenchness in the colonies of the Republic was.[3] What decolonisation brought, however, was a racial segregation of the world under the banner of equal citizenship *among* equal states. All the former colonial subjects are now confined to the places around the world reserved uniquely for the losers of Ayelet Shachar's infamous birthright lottery.[4] The only difference compared with seventy years ago is that there is no more French judge in the former colony, whom you can beg for a drastic status upgrade for your child, capitalising on her unexpected blue eyes – racism is outlawed, remember?

The world has thus both changed and remained the same. It changed, because since the Second World War the Western world has come to accept women as the bearers of citizenship status independent of their sexual

---

[3] Saada, E. (2012), *Empire's Children: Race, Filiation, and Citizenship in the French Colonies*. Chicago: Chicago University Press.
[4] Shachar, A. (2009), *The Birthright Lottery: Citizenship and Global Inequality*. Harvard: Harvard University Press.

partners and even grants them political rights. Racial minorities within 'first world' states are also respected – both on paper and often in practice too. The façade of citizenship as a status of equals seems to have met – for the first time since its proclamation by Aristotle – its promise. Yet the world has also remained hugely unequal. Branko Milanovic teaches us that, although global income inequalities have recently declined when measured by country averages, country of residence is more important than class today.[5] Even the 'occupy Wall Street' guys belong in fact to the world's elites, they are only not able to realise the depth of misery of others. Indeed, those locked into the poorest former colonies do not inhabit the same narrative as Europeans and Americans. The main purpose of citizenship has been upgraded: from a neo-feudal mechanism of sexist and racist governance, it is turning into one of the core instruments of preservation and justification of global inequality, hiding its functionality behind the old façade of political self-determination, which had been effective to brush away women and minorities before.

Citizenships are thus about preserving inequality worldwide. As long as segregating remains citizenships' main function, cloud communities are powerless in their mission: identities are irrelevant as long as all the life chances or the lack thereof depend on a random legal status of ascription to authority distributed at birth. Worse still, humiliation and randomness are routinely sanctified: while upholding and perpetuating inequality, citizenship supplies a powerful and ultimately pointless narrative justifying random privilege through the glorification of expediency in territorial governance.

The lack of any rights worldwide coming with some citizenships as opposed to a huge bundle of rights coming with others can be measured. By comparing GDP, HDI, travel freedom and settlement and work rights abroad it is easy to see why being born French – with a status welcoming you to the job market of 41 countries and all the other perks included – is infinitely better than being a Ukrainian or, God forbid, an Afghani. The Quality of Nationality Index, which I designed together with Chris Kälin shows this in the most graphic way (http://www.nationalityindex.com). For ordinary people this is not all theory: the boats crossing the Mediterranean are full and they cross the sea in one direction only. My point is, they will be going the same way no matter what cloud communities are introduced, since the

---

[5] Milanovic, B. (2012), 'Global Income Inequality by the Numbers: In History and Now', *Policy Research Working Paper No. 6259*, The World Bank, available at http://documents.worldbank.org/curated/en/959251468176687085/Global-income-inequality-by-the-numbers-in-history-and-now-an-overview

violence of global segregation that citizenship inflicts cannot be affected by the technology proclaiming an abstract 'global citizenship' to be a value and reaffirming it in the cloud.

Before discussing the potential benefits of a set of quasi-citizenships in the cloud it is crucial to be fully aware of the drastic differences between citizenships in 'real life' and fully internalise their ability to punish besides simply segregating at random. *Pace* Arendt's 'right to have tights' citizenship is a status associated with rights in a handful of countries only. In many others, it is a severe and undeserved liability and sometimes a mortal one. What blockchain offers to a Frenchmen will thus be radically different from what it offers to a Congolese (pick your Congo!). When refugees arrive in Europe or America, they often destroy, sometimes even eat, their passports. Have you tried to consider why? It is because many citizenships are so terribly poisonous and dangerous that you might be infinitely better off as a stateless person. This is because with a Central African Republic passport your child born in Brussels will be a Central African, not a Belgian, because you will need to wait for naturalisation longer and, ultimately, because CAR will have to accept you back once you are out of the Belgian asylum system. To be identifiable is always as bad a liability as the citizenship or the place of birth you will be identified with. It can ruin lives. This is where cloud communities come in as an impermissibly rosy dream. The proposal ignores the complexity of the world and fails to fully come to terms with its own dangers in the context of the current functions of citizenship behind the self-justificatory sacred façade put up uniquely for those who somehow happen to belong to the right country in order to let them sleep tight at night.

Citizenship's inescapable evil does not stem from the fact that it is a randomly assigned benefit, but from the reality that it is about branding as deficient those who are randomly proclaimed not to belong while treating such exclusion as self-explanatory and just. This justice is ethically void, however, as long as we believe that it is humanity that counts morally and that obliges us to respect others' desire to live a worthy life, as Joseph Carens has demonstrated.[6] Should this indeed be our starting point, any serious work to perfect the current citizenship paradigm – either on the ground or in the cloud – is nothing else but work that opposes ethical imperatives we all share. The untenability of citizenship's ethical narrative, no matter which way of telling it one chooses, is the elephant in the room, which ultimately explains the on-going demise of the citizenship of the 'good old times': a random supremacist status for armed white boys who belong and believe in

---

[6] Carens, J. (2013), *The Ethics of Immigration*. Oxford: Oxford University Press.

the greatness of their land, whatever it might be, often at the expense of all their neighbours.

How do the cloud communities proposed by Orgad fit Joppke's story of the 'inevitable lightening of citizenship'?[7] In the former imperial centres such luxury as new online associations emerging through the individual sovereign governance of identity with the help of blockchain as Orgad describes it is only welcome – our world is open and ripe with opportunities – in the cloud and on the ground. About the rest of the world I am somewhat sceptical: as Robert Post has already suggested in his contribution, life in the place where you are is something that is of crucial importance, more than your cloud identity, whatever that would come to mean. And as Michael Blake points out, violence in the physical world is equally crucial. Work and education of your choosing, residence abroad, freedom of belief and expression, an ability to be with your loved ones, to go places – this is what a Saudi citizenship, now grotesquely granted to a robot, will no doubt deny you, especially if you are a woman. Using technology for escapism is something that falls far short, it seems to me, of its potential. A cloud community will not even save you from beheading in Saudi Arabia for confessing atheism online, for instance, or, if you happen to be a Chinese national, spending three years in jail for calling Mr Xi a 'steam bun' in a private chat conversation in your cloud.

Once escapism has been discarded, it becomes necessary to consider what cloud communities could be good for. And in doing so it is our imperative not to replicate the repugnant nature of citizenship as a justificatory label for random privilege and for explaining away global inequality. Here Estonia shows the way, as Poleshchuk has demonstrated.[8]

It is not the cloud identity, – I am gay in the cloud since otherwise the government will kill me – it is the functional added value of the virtual statuses and 'residences' that should come to the fore. What I am saying is that clubs, no matter whether offline or in the cloud, have nothing to do with citizenships, since citizenships are involuntary and do not foster common interests or values. Consequently, calling any cloud identities 'citizenship' is a misconception. One needs to move on from citizenship when technology allows. What is possible today – and this is a great beginning Estonia

---

[7] Joppke, C. (2010), *Citizenship and Immigration*. London: Polity.
[8] Poleshchuk, V. (2016). '"Making Estonia Bigger": What E-Residency in E-Estonia Can Do for You, What It Can Do for Estonia', *Investment Migration Working Papers*. Available at https://investmentmigration.org/download/making-estonia-bigger-e-residency-e-estonia-can-can-estonia/

started – is to use online residences as compensation mechanisms for the deficiencies of the statuses of citizenship, which the vast majority of the world's population got by birth. You are born in Afghanistan? Fine, with an Estonian residency online you can at least open a proper bank account and have access to basic state services – notaries, company registers etc. This is a primary use of new digital technologies.

A second purpose – and this one should be based on a broad agreement between states – is to use attested individual identities to judge people by those, rather than their passports. Crucially, these cannot go hand in hand. The core added value would be to replace one with the other. We are a long way from here and the connection between the cloud and 'real life' is crucial here, but what one can envisage is a world where babies in Afghanistan or Pakistan are born without at least some of the drastic harmful effects of the original sin of nationality and that peoples' worth at international borders is assessed via some factors other than the particular state that has been claiming the possession of them from birth. This should be the future of technological thinking to bring true liberation from the neo-feudal essence of a poisonous status, which is ethically vacuous, its political expediency notwithstanding. A technological revolution should not become a servant of the *status quo*, erecting yet higher walls between the haves and have-nots.

58

Digital Technologies, Materiality and Cloud Communities

Stefania Milan

As a digital sociologist, I have always found 'classical' political scientists and lawyers a tad too reluctant to embrace the idea that digital technology *is* a game changer in so many respects. In the debate spurred by Liav Orgad's provocative thoughts on blockchain-enabled cloud communities, I am particularly fascinated by the tension between techno-utopianism on the one hand (above all, Orgad and Primavera De Filippi), and socio-legal realism on the other (e.g., Rainer Bauböck, Michael Blake, Lea Ypi, Jelena Dzankic, Dimitry Kochenov). I find myself somewhere in the middle. In what follows, I take a sociological perspective to explain why there is something profoundly interesting in the notion of cloud communities, why however little of it is really new, and why the obstacles ahead are bigger than we might like to think. The point of departure for my considerations is a number of experiences in the realm of transnational social movements and governance: what we can learn from existing experiments that might help us contextualize and rethink cloud communities?

Three problems with Orgad's argument

To start with, while I sympathise with Orgad's provocative claims, I cannot but notice that what he deems new in cloud communities – namely the global dimension of political membership and its networked nature – is indeed rather old. Since the 1990s, transnational social movements for global justice have offered non-territorial forms of political membership – not unlike those described as cloud communities. Similar to cloud communities, these movements were the manifestation of political communities based on consent, gathered around shared interests and only minimally rooted in physical territories corresponding to nation states.[1] In the fall of 2011 I observed with earnest interest the emergence of yet another global wave of contention: the

---

[1] Tarrow, S. (2005), *The New Transnational Activism*. New York: Cambridge University Press.

so-called Occupy mobilisation. As a sociologist of the web, I set off in search for a good metaphor to capture the evolution of organised collective action in the age of social media, and the obvious candidate was... the cloud. In a series of articles[2] and book chapters,[3] I developed my theory of 'cloud protesting', intended to capture how the algorithmic environment of social media alters the dynamics of organized collective action. In light of my empirical work, I agree with Bauböck, who acknowledges that cloud communities might have something to do with the 'expansion of civil society, of international organizations, or of traditional territorial polities into cyberspace.' He also points out how, sadly, people can express their political views – and, I would add, engage in disruptive actions, as happens at some fringes of the movement for global justice – only because 'a secure territorial citizenship' protects their exercise of fundamental rights, such as freedom of expression and association. Hence the questions a sociologist might ask: do we really need the blockchain to enable the emergence of cloud communities? If, as I argue, the existence of 'international legal personas' is not a pre-requisite for the establishment of cloud communities, what would the creation of 'international legal personas' add to the picture?[4]

Secondly, while I understand why a blockchain-enabled citizenship system would make life easier for the many who do not have access to a regular passport, I am wary of its 'institutionalisation', on account of the probable discrepancies between the ideas (and the mechanisms) associated with a Westphalian state and those of politically active activists and radical technologists alike. On the one hand, citizens interested in 'advanced' forms of

---

[2] Milan, S. (2015), 'From social movements to cloud protesting: the evolution of collective identity', *Information, Communication & Society* 18 (8): 887–900; Milan, S. (2015), 'When algorithms shape collective action: Social media and the dynamics of cloud protesting', *Social Media + Society* 1 (2): 1–10.

[3] Milan, S. (2015), 'Mobilizing in Times of Social Media. From a Politics of Identity to a Politics of Visibility', in L. Dencik & O. Leistert (eds.), *Critical Perspectives on Social Media and Protest: Between Control and Emancipation*, 53–71. New York: Rowman & Littlefield. Available at SSRN: https://ssrn.com/abstract=2880402; Milan, S. (2013), 'WikiLeaks, Anonymous, and the exercise of individuality: protesting in the cloud', in B. Brevini, A. Hintz & P. McCurdy (eds.), *Beyond WikiLeaks: Implications for the Future of Communications, Journalism and Society*, 191–208. London: Palgrave Macmillan.

[4] I am aware that there is a fundamental drawback in social movements when compared to cloud communities: unlike the latter, the former are not rights providers. However, these are the questions one could ask taking a sociological perspective.

political participation (e.g., governance and the making of law) might not necessarily be inclined to form a state-like entity. For example, many accounts of the so-called 'movement for global justice'[5] show how 'official' membership and affiliation is often not required, not expected and especially not considered desirable. Activism today is characterised by a dislike and distrust of the state, and a tendency to privilege flexible, multiple identities.[6] On the other hand, the 'radical technologists' behind the blockchain project are animated by values – an *imaginaire*[7] – deeply distinct from that of the state.[8] While the blockchain technology is enabled by a complex constellation of diverse actors, it is legitimate to ask whether it is possible to bend a technology built with an 'underlying philosophy of distributed consensus, open source, transparency and community' with the goal to 'be highly disruptive'[9] ... to serve similar purposes as those of states?

Thirdly, Orgad's argument falls short of a clear description of what the 'cloud' stands for in his notion of cloud communities. When thinking about 'clouds', as a metaphor and a technical term, we cannot but think of cloud computing, a 'key force in the changing international political economy'[10] of our times, which entails a process of centralisation of software and hardware allowing users to reduce costs by sharing resources. The cloud

---

[5] Della Porta, D. & S. Tarrow (eds.) (2005), *Transnational Protest and Global Activism*. Lanham, MD: Rowman & Littlefield; Juris, J. S. (2012), 'Reflections on #Occupy Everywhere: Social Media, Public Space, and Emerging Logics of Aggregation', *American Ethnologist* 39 (2): 259–279; McDonald, K. (2006), *Global Movements: Action and Culture*. Malden, MA and Oxford: Blackwell.

[6] Bennett, L. W. & A. Segerberg (2013), *The Logic of Connective Action Digital Media and the Personalization of Contentious Politics*. Cambridge, UK: Cambridge University Press; Milan, S. (2013), 'WikiLeaks, Anonymous, and the exercise of individuality: Protesting in the cloud', in B. Brevini, A. Hintz & P. McCurdy (eds.), *Beyond WikiLeaks: Implications for the Future of Communications, Journalism and Society*, 191–208. Basingstoke, UK: Palgrave Macmillan.

[7] Flichy, P. (2007), *The Internet imaginaire*. Cambridge, Mass.: MIT Press.

[8] Reijers, W. & M. Coeckelbergh (2018), 'The Blockchain as a Narrative Technology: Investigating the Social Ontology and Normative Configurations of Cryptocurrencies', *Philosophy & Technology* 31 (1): 103–130.

[9] Walport, M. (2015), *Distributed Ledger Technology: Beyond blockchain*. London: UK Government Office for Science. London: UK Government Office for Science, available at https://assets.publishing.service.gov.uk/government/uploads/system/uploads/attachment_data/file/492972/gs-16-1-distributed-ledger-technology.pdf

[10] Mosco, V. (2014), *To the Cloud: Big Data in a Turbulent World*. New York: Paradigm Publishers, 1.

metaphor, I argued elsewhere,[11] is an apt one as it exposes a fundamental ambivalence of contemporary processes of 'socio-legal decentralisation.' While claiming distance from the values and dynamics of the neoliberal state, a project of building blockchain-enabled communities still relies on commercially-owned infrastructure to function.

Precisely to reflect on this ambiguity, my most recent text on cloud protesting interrogates the materiality of the cloud.[12] We have long lived in the illusion that the internet was a space *free of geography*. Yet, as IR scholar Ron Deibert argued, 'physical geography is an essential component of cyberspace: *Where* technology is located is as important as *what* it is' (original italics).[13] The Snowden revelations, to name just one, have brought to the forefront the role of the national state in – openly or covertly – setting the rules of user interactions online. What's more, we no longer can blame the state alone, but the 'surveillant assemblage' of state *and* corporations.[14] To me, the big absent in this debate is the private sector and corporate capital. De Filippi briefly mentioned how the 'new communities of kinship' are anchored in 'a variety of online platforms'. However, what Orgav's and partially also Bauböck's contributions underscore is the extent to which intermediation by private actors stands in the way of creating a real alternative to the state – or at least the fulfilment of certain dreams of autonomy, best represented today by the fascination for blockchain technology. Bauböck rightly notes that 'state and corporations… will find ways to instrumentalise or hijack cloud communities for their own purposes.' But there is more to that: the infrastructure we use to enable our interpersonal exchanges and, why not, the blockchain, are *owned and controlled by private interests subjected to national laws*. They are not merely neutral pipes, as Dumbrava reminds us.

---

[11] Milan, S. (2015), 'When Algorithms Shape Collective Action: Social Media and the Dynamics of Cloud Protesting', *Social Media + Society* 1 (1): 1–10.

[12] Stefania, M. (2018), 'The Materiality of Clouds. Beyond a Platform-Specific Critique of Contemporary Activism'. In M. Mortensen, C. Neumayer & T. Poell (eds.), *Social Media Materialities and Protest: Critical Reflections.* London: Routledge.

[13] Deibert, R (2015), 'The Geopolitics of Cyberspace After Snowden', *Current History* 114 (768): 9–15, at 10.

[14] Murakami Wood, D. (2013) 'What Is Global Surveillance?: Towards a Relational Political Economy of the Global Surveillant Assemblage', *Geoforum* 49: 317–326.

Self-governance in practice: A cautionary tale

To be sure, many experiments allow 'individuals the option to raise their voice ... in territorial communities to which they do not physically belong,' as beautifully put by Francesca Strumia. Internet governance is a case in point. Since the early days of the internet, cyberlibertarian ideals, enshrined for instance in the 'Declaration of Independence of Cyberspace'[15] by late JP Barlow, have attributed little to no role to governments – both in deciding the rules for the 'new' space as well as the citizenship of its users (read: the right to participate in the space and in the decision-making about the rules governing it). In those early flamboyant narratives, cyberspace was to be a space where users – but really engineers above all – would translate into practice their wildest dreams in matter of self-governance, self-determination and, to some extent, fairness. While cyberlibertarian views have been appropriated by both conservative (anti-state) and progressive forces alike, some of their founding principles have spilled over to real governance mechanisms – above all the governance of standards and protocols by the Internet Engineering Task Force (IETF), and the management of the Domain Name System (DNS) by the Internet Corporation for Assigned Names and Numbers (ICANN).[16] Here I focus on the latter, where I have been active for about four years (2014–2017).

ICANN is organized in constituencies of stakeholders, including contracted parties (the 'middlemen', that is to say registries and registrars that on a regional base allocate and manage on behalf of ICANN the names and numbers, and whose relationship with ICANN is regulated by contract), non-contracted parties (corporations doing business on the DNS, e.g. content or infrastructure providers) and non-commercial internet users (read: us). ICANN's proceedings are fully recorded and accessible from its website (https://www.icann.org/); its public meetings, thrice a year and rotating around the globe, are open to everyone who wants to walk in. Governments are represented in a sort of United Nations-style entity called the Government Advisory Committee. While corporate interests are well-represented by an array of professional lobbyists, the Non-Commercial Stakeholder Group

---

[15] Barlow, J. P. (1996), *Declaration of Independence of Cyberspace*. Available at http://homes.eff.org/~barlow/Declaration-Final.html
[16] The system of unique identifiers of the DNS comprises the so-called 'names' standing in for domain names (e.g., www.eui.eu), and 'numbers', or Internet Protocol (IP) addresses (e.g., the 'machine version' of the domain name that a router for example can understand). The DNS can be seen as a sort of 'phone book' of the internet.

(NCSG), which stands in for civil society,[17] is a mix and match of advocates of various extraction, expertise and nationality: internet governance academics, nongovernmental organisations promoting freedom of expression, and independent individuals who take an interest in the functioning of the logical layer of the internet.

The 2016 transition of the stewardship over the DNS from the US Congress to the 'global multistakeholder community' has achieved a dream unique in its kind, straight out of the cyberlibertarian vision of the early days: the technical oversight of the internet[18] is in the hands of the people who make and use it, and the (advisory) role of the state is marginal. Accountability now rests solely within the community behind ICANN, which envisioned (and is still implementing) a complex system of checks and balances to allow the various stakeholder voices to be fairly represented. No other critical infrastructure is regulated by its own users. To build on Orgad's reasoning, the community around ICANN is a cloud community, which operates by voluntary association and consensus,[19] and is entitled to produce 'governance and the creation of law'.[20]

But the system is far from perfect. Let's look at how the so-called civil society is represented, focusing on one such entity, the NCSG. Firstly, given that everyone can participate, the variety of views represented is enormous, and often hinders the ability of the constituency to be effective in policy

---

[17] Technically, of the DNS, which is only a portion of what we call 'the internet', although the most widely used one.

[18] Civil society representation in ICANN is more complex than what is described here. The NCSG is composed of two (litigious) constituencies, namely the Non-Commercial User Constituency (NCUC) and the Non-Profit Operational Concerns (NPOC). In addition, 'nonorganizedd' internet users can elect their representatives in the At-Large Advisory Committee (ALAC), organized on a regional basis. The NCSG, however, is the only one who directly contributes to policy-making.

[19] ICANN is both a nonprofit corporation registered under Californian law, and a community of volunteers who set the rules for the management of the logical layer of the internet by consensus. See also the ICANN Bylaws, available at https://www.icann.org/resources/pages/governance/bylaws-en (last updated in August 2017).

[20] This should at least in part address Post's doubts about the ability of a political community to govern those outside of its jurisdiction. One might argue that internet users are, perhaps unwillingly or simply unconsciously, within the 'jurisdiction' of ICANN. I do believe, however, that the case of ICANN is an interesting one for its being in between the two 'definitions' of political communities.

negotiations. Yet, the size of the group is relatively small: at the time of writing, the Non-Commercial User Constituency (the bigger one among the two that form the NCSG) comprises '538 members from 161 countries, including 118 noncommercial organizations and 420 individuals'[21], making it the largest constituency within ICANN: this is nothing when compared to the global internet population it serves, confirming, as Dzankic argues, that 'direct democracy is not necessarily conducive to broad participation in decision-making'. Secondly, ICANN policy-making is highly technical and specialised; the learning curve is dramatically steep. Thirdly, to be effective, the amount of time a civil society representative should spend on ICANN is largely incompatible with regular daily jobs; civil society cannot compete with corporate lobbyists. Fourthly, with ICANN meetings rotating across the globe, one needs to be on the road for at least a month per year, with considerable personal and financial costs.[22] In sum, while participation is in principle open to everyone, *informed participation* has much higher access barriers, which have to do with expertise, time, and financial resources.[23]

As a result, we observe a number of dangerous distortions of political representation. For example, when only the highly motivated participate, the views and 'imaginaries' represented are often at the opposite ends of the spectrum.[24] Only the most involved really partake in decision-making, in a mechanism which is well known in sociology: the 'tyranny of structurelessness',[25] which is typical of participatory, consensus-based organising. The extreme personalisation of politics that we observe within civil society at ICANN – a small group of long-term advocates with high personal stakes – yields also another similar mechanism, known as 'the tyranny of emotions',[26] by which the most invested, independently of the suitability of their curricula vitae, end up assuming informal leadership

---

[21] 'Our membership', available at https://www.ncuc.org/about/membership/
[22] ICANN allocates consistent but not sufficient resources to support civil society participation in its policymaking. These include travel bursaries and accommodation costs and fellowship programs for induction of newcomers.
[23] See for example: Milan, S. & A. Hintz (2013), 'Networked Collective Action and the Institutionalized Policy Debate: Bringing Cyberactivism to the Policy Arena?', *Internet & Policy* 5 (1): 7–26.
[24] Milan, S. (2014), 'The Fair of Competing Narratives: Civil Society(ies) after NETmundial', *IPO Blog*, 10 September. Available at http://globalnetpolicy.org/the-fair-of-competing-narratives-civil-societyies-after-netmundial/
[25] Freeman, J. (1972), *The Tyranny of Structurelessness*. Available at http://www.jofreeman.com/joreen/ tyranny.htm
[26] Polletta, F. (2002), *Freedom Is an Endless Meeting: Democracy in American Social Movements*. Chicago: University of Chicago Press.

roles – and, as the case of ICANN shows, even in presence of formal and carefully weighted governance structures. Decision-making is thus based on a sort of 'microconsensus' within small decision-making cliques.[27] To make things worse, ICANN is increasingly making exceptions to its own, community-established rules, largely under the pressure of corporations as well as law enforcement: for example, the corporation has recently been accused of bypassing consensus policy-making through voluntary agreements ad private contracting.[28]

Why not (yet?): On new divides and bad players

In conclusion, while I value the possibilities the blockchain technology opens for experimentation as much as Primavera De Filippi, I do not believe it will really solve our problems in the short to middle-term. Rather, as it is always with technology because of its inherent political nature,[29] new conflicts will emerge – and they will concern both its technical features and its governance.

Earlier contributors to this debate have raised important concerns which are worth listening to. Besides Bauböck's concerns over the perils for democracy represented by a consensus-based, self-governed model, endorsed also by Blake, I want to echo Lea Ypi's reminder of the enormous potential *for exclusion* embedded in technologies, as digital skills (but also income) are not equally distributed across the globe. For the time being, a citizenship model based on blockchain technology would be for the elites only, and would contribute to create new divides and to amplify existing ones. The first fundamental step towards the cloud communities envisioned by Orgad would thus see the state stepping in (once again) and being in

---

[27] Although a quantitative analysis of the stickiness of participation in relation to discursive change reveals a more nuanced picture (see, for example: Milan, S. & N. ten Oever (2017), 'Coding and encoding rights in internet infrastructure', *Internet Policy Review* 6 (1): 1–17). See: Gastil, J. (1993), *Democracy in Small Groups. Participation, Decision Making & Communication*. Philadelphia, PA and Gabriola Island, BC: New Society Publishers.

[28] 'ICANN Drifting Toward Online Content Regulation, Says Law Professor', *Circle ID*, 28 February 2017, available at http://www.circleid.com/posts/20170228_icann_drifting_toward_online_content_regulation_says_law_professor/

[29] Bijker, W. E., T. P. Hughes & T. Pinch (eds.) (2012), *The Social Construction of Technological Systems. New Direction in the Sociology and History of Technology*. Cambridge, MA and London, England: MIT Press.

charge of creating appropriate data and algorithmic literacy programmes whose scope is out of reach for corporations and the organised civil society alike.

There is more to that, however. The costs to our already fragile ecosystem of the blockchain technology are on the rise along with its popularity. These infrastructures are energy-intensive: talking about the cryptocurrency Bitcoin, tech magazine Motherboard estimated that each transaction consumes 215 Kilowatt-hour of electricity – the equivalent of the weekly consumption of an American household.[30] A world built on blockchain would have a vast environmental footprint.[31] Once again, the state might play a role in imposing adequate regulation mindful of the environmental costs of such programs.

But I do not intend to glorify the role of the state. On the contrary, I believe we should also watch out for any attempts by the state to curb innovation. The relatively brief history of digital technology, and even more that of the internet, is awash with examples of late but extremely damaging state interventions. As soon as a given technology performs roles or produces information that are of interest to the state (e.g., interpersonal communications), the state wants to jump in, and often does so in pretty clumsy ways. The recent surveillance scandals have abundantly shown how state powers firmly inhabit the internet[32] – and, as the Cambridge Analytica case[33] reminds us, so do corporate interests. Moreover, the two are, more often than not, dangerously aligned.

---

[30] 'One Bitcoin Transaction Now Uses as Much Energy as Your House in a Week', *Motherboard*, 1 November 2017, available at https://motherboard.vice.com/en_us/article/ywbbpm/bitcoin-mining-electricity-consumption-ethereum-energy-climate-change

[31] Also see: Mosco, V. (2014), *To the Cloud: Big Data in a Turbulent World*. New York: Paradigm Publishers.

[32] Deibert, R. J. (2009), 'The geopolitics of internet control: censorship, sovereignty, and cyberspace', in A. Chadwick & P. N. Howard (eds.), *The Routledge Handbook of Internet Politics*, 323–336. London: Routledge; Deibert, R. J., J. G. Palfrey, R., Rohozinski & J. Zittrain (eds.) (2010), *Access Controlled: The Shaping of Power, Rights, and Rule in Cyberspace*. Cambridge, MA: MIT Press; Lyon, D. (2015), *Surveillance After Snowden*. Cambridge and Malden, MA: Polity Press.

[33] 'Cambridge Analytica case highlights Facebook's data riches', *Financial Times*, 19 March 2018, available at https://www.ft.com/content/c1f326a4-2b24-11e8-9b4b-bc4b9f08f381

I do not intend, with my cautionary tales, to hinder any imaginative effort to explore the possibilities offered by blockchain to rethink how we understand and practice citizenship today. The case of Estonia shows that different models based on alternative infrastructure are possible, at least on the small scale and in presence of a committed state. As scholars we ought to explore those possibilities. Much work is needed, however, before we can proclaim the blockchain revolution.

59

Virtual Public Spaces and Blockchain Technology

Dora Kostakopoulou

While developments in information technology have always sparked lively debates about democratic participation and citizenship, the advent of blockchain technology promises to change the concept and nature of participatory citizenship by providing an inclusive, secure and transparent mechanism of data sharing among an unlimited number of members. Liav Orgad has written a powerful contribution about the promise of blockchain technology. I fully share his thoughts and his optimism. Blockchain participants are able to interact, share information, collaborate and have access to an incredible amount of information organised in blocks without the intervention of a centralised authority and without any reliance on a centralised platform. More importantly, everyone's copy of the distributed database will be kept updated and will be immutable; information can be added by any member of the global network, but cannot be deleted. Blockchain is thus a platform for worldwide information sharing, interaction and collaboration. As such, it has the potential to enhance political participation, trigger civic mobilisation and to provide the substratum for public action on a global scale.

Such a bottom up, participatory and size-neutral (the network could consist of billions of people) digital network does not merely offer a glimpse of what might be possible in terms of global citizenship but, as Liav Orgad has explained, casts doubts on any arguments about the impossibility of global citizenship. This is because blockchain simply removes three of the main obstacles for its realisation; namely, the impermeability of state borders, the size of the demos, and certain costs associated with political participation. Participants just need to have internet access in order to join a network comprising millions of citizens from diverse regions and remote locations of the globe who could be mobilised in influencing public policies and taking part in public actions.

In what follows, I will thus sidestep questions about the feasibility of global citizenship in order to examine how the new technological revolution will lead to innovations in political life and will create Hannah Arendt's public spaces of 'virtual' citizenship. By so doing, I take it for granted that blockchain is a 'game-changer' and that it *could* have significant transformative effects on societies, politics and citizenship. I use the verb 'could' because I do not wish to embrace determinism or to imply the existence of a causal relation between technology and political processes. Blockchain has the potential to transform the way we think about public spaces, citizenship and political participation, but this potential can only be realised if technology is put to uses which can enhance democratic political processes.

My critics might object here that we do not need technological advancements in order to procure new conceptions of public space. Analyses informed by the thinking of philosophers, such as Henri Lefebvre, and geographers, such as Doreen Massey and Edward Soja, have highlighted that spaces are not given but are constructed in different ways by politics and discursive practices. Readers might recall Peter Maier's anthology on the changing boundaries of the political in the late 1980s.[1] In it, Maier mapped the blurring of the distinction between the state and civil society, while a few years later, Gilles Deleuze commented on the shifting of borders and the proliferation of political spaces within contemporary societies of control.[2]

While all this is true, blockchain promises to realise those ideas in unprecedented ways. It also holds the promise of generating huge publics beyond (and across) geographical borders and territorially defined communities and thus of opening up new citizenship spaces. Rainer Bauböck and Peter Spiro have noted this in their contributions. Citizenship relies on the existence of public spaces of communication, of exchange of ideas, arguments and contested viewpoints and of joint decision-making. For a significant period of time, the agoras of the direct democratic experimentation in ancient Athens became remnants of a distant past that had no chance to be replicated in the present and future. Now, virtual agoras 'containing' millions of active and activist individuals can be built onto blockchain.[3] The mythical space of a distant past becomes connected with, and re-enacted within, the contemporary world of an embodied digital network that makes citizenship a network good.[4]

---

[1] Maier, C. C. (ed.) (1987), *The Changing Boundaries of the Political.* Cambridge: Cambridge University Press.
[2] Deleuze, G. (1992), 'Postscript on the Societies of Control', MIT Press October 59: 3–7. Available at http://www.jstor.org/stable/778828.
[3] Isin, E. & M. Saward (2013), *Enacting European Citizenship.* Cambridge: Cambridge University Press.
[4] Kostakopoulou, D. (2008), *The Future Governance of Citizenship.* Cambridge: Cambridge University Press, 107–110.

This is essentially the realisation of Hannah Arendt's conception of 'virtual' public spaces. Virtual 'agoras' built on blockchain will become shared common worlds of continuous flows of speech and action, that is, spaces where people would recognise one another as equals or at least equally entitled to express their views, to 'deal only with one's peers' and to decide on common actions at national, international and global levels.[5] As Arendt had eloquently noted, the (public) space of speech and action 'can find its proper location almost any time and anywhere'.[6] By transcending topological as well as institutional accounts of the 'public space', blockchain technology not only lends credence to Arendt's conception of public space, but it also promises to open up decentralised public spaces in which all participants can be contributors, deciders and holders of institutional memories. The participants' geographical location does not matter. In an unprecedented border-transcending move, new spaces of citizenship appear 'almost any time and anywhere' as Arendt had argued. What ties all the blockchain participants together in the virtual public space of citizenship is simply their ongoing concern and active engagement.[7] These are, in reality, the characteristics that sustain all communities, be they virtual or not: members are visibly concerned about the common state of affairs and want their claims, needs, and aspirations to be heard.

This development can bring about a complete reconceptualisation of the nature of international society; non-statist ways of defining it will gain prominence. Hedley Bull's envisaged transformation of international society from a society of states to a society of peoples will be progressively realised.[8] Cloud agoras will also prompt a rethinking of communitarian ways of defining communities and international society which see society and culture as interlocked. This is because they do not rely on some form of cultural homogeneity or conformity to a majority's ideas and narratives; the rely, instead, on the coming together of strangers[9] in order to share their concerns and information, express their interests, make demands on the political system and to articulate proposals for common action. All this is bound to give rise to interesting questions about ways of constructing political order and legitimacy in international relations and politics.

---

[5] Arendt, H. (1958), *The Human Condition*. Chicago: Chicago University Press.
[6] Above n. 5, at 198.
[7] Kostakopoulou, D. (1996), 'Towards a Theory of Constructive Citizenship in Europe', *Journal of Political Philosophy* 4 (4): 337–358.
[8] Bull, H. (1977), *The Anarchical Society*. London: Macmillan.
[9] Young, I. M. (1986), 'The Ideal of Community and the Politics of Difference', *Social Theory and Practice* 12 (1): 1–26, at 21–23.

While cloud agoras have the potential of dislocating citizenship from its statist reference point and stimulating citizen involvement by delivering the affirmative requirements for an active citizenry, namely, information sharing, the exchange of ideas and preferences, capability for action and the means of exerting influence and pressure, they will not be able to resolve the 'problem of equality of voice'. Claude Lefort, Nancy Fraser, Jürgen Habermas and others have commented on the inequalities that persist in democratic public spheres. Some voices will be louder and more influential than others and women will always struggle to find time to engage even virtually. Socio-economic disparities measured in terms of education, income and occupation will also allow certain participants to easily convert their possessed resources into political involvement. The cognitive and linguistic skills for political articulations and activity are not uniformly distributed. Nor do they exist independently of individuals' socio-economic setting and geographical location across the globe. Peter Spiro, Lea Yip and Stefania Milan correctly highlight this problem. Cloud agoras therefore will not be able to transcend the difficulties of ensuring full inclusion in the open public grid. They will certainly be more inclusionary that the existing publics, but they will still represent a stratified model of political community or public space(s). They will also have their own 'spinners', exploiters and manipulators of public opinion. I recall Jean Mansbridge's observations about the dark world of domination and manufactured invisibility of actors underpinning deliberative democracy.[10]

Although it is true that participatory parity cannot be easily achieved even in cloud agoras, it is equally true that the common world of citizenship beyond borders, states and nations could be more activist. And this is good news for democracy in general. It would be relatively easy for millions of blockchain members to mobilise on specific issues and to demand change in law and policy regionally, nationally and globally. It would also be more difficult for decision-making elites to ignore the voices of so many people and to pretend that they do not count or that their claims do not matter. Civic awakenings and political mobilisations in cloud agoras are also likely to exert influence on other public spaces that are more conventional and delineated across national and statist lines. For the boundaries of public spaces, virtual and non-virtual ones, will always be porous and issues will leak from one domain to another. The dawn of global citizenship will thus be a combination of the activation of an international or global society and of a more activist citizenship. Virtual global citizenship promises to be more virtual, in

---

[10] Mansbridge, J. (1995), 'Does Participation Make Better Citizens?', *The Good Society* 5 (2): 1–7.

the republican sense; citizens will continually question aspects of public life, make public disclosures of wrongdoing, take an active part in public affairs and engage in regular, assertive action.

That this is good news for citizenship, democracy and politics in general cannot be denied. The virtual public space of blockchain communities will make citizens think, engage and act more virtually. In other words, the virtual reality of cloud agoras will have an impact on institutions and the participants themselves; it will yield pressures for more open, transparent and accountable institutions and will result in more virtuous, that is, actively engaged, citizens. Whether cloud agoras will prove to be decisive public spaces and strong promoters of democratic processes that make wealth, power and privilege accountable or merely subaltern counter publics will depend on the intentions and actions of their participants. In other words, the answer to the question whether the virtual public space of global citizenship will have a decisive influence on global, regional and national public policy-making is not theoretical or scholarly; it will be a contextual one.

60

Exploring the Possibility of a Global Cryptodemocracy

Ehud Shapiro

The fascinating discussion kicked-off by Liav Orgad addresses the interplay between the clouds and earth: How do cloud citizens and cloud communities relate to their earthly counterparts?

Arguments by Orgad, Primavera De Filippi, Francesca Strumia, Peter Spiro and Dora Kostakopoulou espouse the potential benefits of global citizenship, ordained by the clouds, and cloud communities that such global citizens can form, inhabit and govern. Counterarguments by Rainer Bauböck, Robert Post, Michael Blake, Costica Dumbrava, Yussef Al Tamimi, Jelena Dzankic, Lea Ypi and Dimitry Kochenov suggest that what happens in the cloud stays in the cloud, and may not be helpful or relevant to, or at least cannot substitute for, earthly dominions, due to fundamental differences between the two. I will try to counter these counterarguments.

A key introductory point made by Bauböck is that Orgad 'must have some form of global federal democracy in mind', yet that 'his main vision is, however, the emergence of alternative forms of political community at the sub-global level'. It is this main vision of Orgad that much of the weighty and thoughtful criticism is directed at.

To address it, I recall a strategy from mathematics: When faced with a difficult problem, namely a difficult theorem to prove, turn it into an even bigger problem: Define a more general and broader theorem, prove it, and then the original theorem easily follows as a corollary. This seemingly-paradoxical strategy works sometimes since a higher vantage point may offer a clearer view of the crux of the matter. I try to apply this strategy here: I will not address criticisms directed at sub-global political cloud communities directly. Instead, I will paint a vision of a global democracy, enabled by the internet and the emerging technologies of blockchain and cryptocurrencies, explain how subsidiary communities based on shared territory or common interests, as envisioned by Orgad, can emerge and operate within it, and respond to criticism from this broader and more encompassing perspective.

From the outset, key criticisms that apply to subsidiary cloud communities do not apply to a global democracy, whether on or off the cloud (we note in parenthesis the respective critics): It has a clear territory (Bauböck, Post, Blake, Al Tamimi) – Planet Earth; it has diverse membership (Bauböck, Blake) – humanity at large; membership is involuntary (Bauböck, Post, Al Tamimi, Ypi) and by decree – just as earthly states conscript citizens by decree; it has room for political communities 'that differ profoundly in their interests, identities and ideas about the common good' (Bauböck, Al Tamimi); and, due to all the above, it is clearly political (Bauböck, Post, Blake, Al Tamimi). Key remaining criticisms not answered by generalising the vision to incorporate all of humanity are those related to the use of coercion in community governance (Bauböck, Post, Blake, Dumbrava, Al Tamimi), lack of inclusivity (Ypi and Kochenov), and the risks of new technology (Dumbrava), which I will answer now in turn.

For our envisioned global democracy to be worthy of its name, it must uphold democratic values[1], including *sovereignty*, *equality*, *freedom of assembly*, *the subsidiarity principle*, *transparency*, and the conservation of the natural and imprescriptible human rights: *liberty, property, safety and resistance against oppression*.[2]

A fundamental advantage of blockchain technology is that it is the only technology to date that can uphold *sovereignty*: The multitudes participating in the operation of the blockchain are its sovereign; no member, third party or outside entity has omnipotent 'super user' or 'administrator' capabilities over the system, and no-one can pull the plug on it: it will survive as long as there are interconnected participants who are able and willing to continue its operation.[3] Hence, the answer to Stefania Milan's question, 'do we really need the blockchain to enable the emergence of cloud communities?', is: Yes, if we want cloud communities to be sovereign and not subservient.

The situation is not as rosy with *equality*. Governance trepidations of the 'cloud communities' of the leading cryptocurrencies, Bitcoin and Ethereum, which consist of their developers, miners and owners, resulted in community

---

[1] Shapiro, E. (2017), 'Foundations of e-Democracy', *Computers and Society*. Available at https://arxiv.org/abs/1710.02873
[2] Ibid.
[3] I acknowledge Milan's point that such interconnectedness (but not the computers being connected!) would most-probably be commercially-owned, and that it is essential that such interconnectedness be neutral and unhindered, even if owned and controlled by private or government interests. Given that, global citizens can be the true sovereign of the global democratic blockchain outlined below.

breakups termed 'hard forks'. Hence, second- and third-generation cryptocurrencies attempt to address their self-governance from first principles.[4] However, they offer only plutocratic solutions,[5] espousing 'one coin – one vote' instead of the 'one person – one vote' principle necessary for *equality*. It may be ironic, given the thrust of our discussion, that the only approach available today to realise equality on the blockchain is to piggyback on identities issued by earthly governments. Besides defeating the purpose of freeing cloud communities from the grasp of their earthly counterparts, this approach cannot mix and match governments or identity-granting authorities, lest people with multiple government-issued identities have multiple votes in the cloud; and it excludes people, such as refugees, who may be hard pressed to present a government-issued identity.

Realising truthful, unique and persistent global digital identities for all, a precondition for making an egalitarian blockchain, is a major open challenge.[6] But, for the sake of the vision we wish to paint, please suspend disbelief and assume that: (i) a worthy method for granting global digital identities to all has been devised, allowing any individual to claim a global identity (which functions as the 'attested individual identities' Kochenov aspires for); call the rightful owners of such global identities *global citizens*; (ii) unhindered internet access has been globally recognised as a basic civil right and is provided, directly or via a proxy, to any individual wishing to become a global citizen. While disbelief regarding the first assumption could be discharged in a decade, the second one will take longer. However, stating the goal of universal access as a basic civil right, taking concrete steps to implement it effectively, and making interim amends to compensate for its temporary lack, are all essential for our vision to be legitimate (and to address the justified criticisms of exclusion by Ypi and Kochenov). With this in mind, let us explore the vision of bringing about a global democracy of global citizens.

---

[4] Bitshares (2018), *Technology*. Available at https://bitshares.org/technology/; Tezos (2018), *Governance*. Available at https://www.tezos.com/governance
[5] Buterin, V. (2018), 'Governance, Part 2: Plutocracy Is Still Bad', *Vitalik Buterin's Website*, 28 March, available at https://vitalik.ca/general/2018/03/28/plutocracy.html
[6] Disclosure: My team at Weizmann aims to address this global challenge. Note that it will not be solved just by achieving broader coverage of local government-issued IDs ('Identification for Development', available at http://www.worldbank.org/en/programs/id4d).

As much as disbelief is suspended, a method for granting global digital identities will never be perfect. Hence, the global democracy will have to grapple with fraud (fake, duplicate and stolen identities, Sybil attacks), extortion (the $5 wrench attack) and negligence (lost/forgotten password). Resolving such matters with due process would require a court. Such a court would need to rule according to a constitution. And the operation of the court (populated most likely by a combination of people and machines) will have to be financed. So we have hardly left the doorstep in our journey towards a global cloud democracy, and already discovered that in order to realise *equality* we need a global court, a global constitution, and a global currency.

That the global democracy needs a currency immediately suggests a cryptocurrency. But, how can we entrust the future of humanity to the hands of an environmentally-harmful[7], plutocratic regime? The answer is of fundamental importance: Current cryptocurrencies were architected on the premise that participants are anonymous and trustless, and resorted to the deliberately wasteful (Milan) proof-of-work protocol to cope with trustlessness. If indeed we have a mechanism for granting truthful and unique global digital identities that is reasonably resilient to attacks (e.g. at most one third of the global identities are compromised at any time)[8] then the global democracy can deploy an egalitarian and planet-friendly cryptocurrency with a democratic governance regime; let's call such a cryptocurrency a *democratic cryptocurrency*.

Let's take stock: We have a democratic cryptocurrency governed by sovereign global citizens that are subject to a global court that rules according to a global constitution and is financed by the democratic cryptocurrency. This may sound a bit circular, but that's exactly how earthly states finance their operation. For example, the democratic cryptoeconomy can be fuelled by a universal basic income to all global citizens.[9] Income, wealth and trans-

---

[7] Present-day cryptocurrencies are unsustainable, even environmentally-harmful, since the proof-of-work protocols that underlie, for example, Bitcoin and Ethereum are unfathomably energy-wasteful on purpose: The ongoing operation of Bitcoin alone consumes as of today more energy than does the entire state of Israel, with its more than 8 million inhabitants (Bitcoin Energy Consumption Index, available at https://digiconomist.net/bitcoin-energy-consumption)
[8] Algorand (2018), *Algorand Website*. https://www.algorand.com/
[9] Flynn, J. (2018), 'The Cryptoeconomics of Funding a Universal Basic Income', *Technophile Musings*, 21 March, available at https://jamespflynn.com/2018/03/21/the-cryptoeconomics-of-funding-a-universal-basic-income/

actions could be taxed, progressively if the global democracy decides so. Tax revenues would be disbursed to finance the operation of the global democracy, in particular the court and the underlying computational infrastructure ('mining'), as well as other purposes, according to a democratically-formed budget.[10] To prevent speculative manipulation of the exchange rate of the democratic cryptocurrency, a global central bank may be established, with authority to purchase and sell foreign (crypto)currency to hinder such manipulations; the bank can similarly set an interest rate. The constitution will have to be updated as the global democracy develops, and subsidiary legislation will have to be adopted. So, in just a few short paragraphs we have come to realise that the global citizens of a global cloud democracy that has its own cryptocurrency and cryptoeconomy will have to recreate almost all the functions of earthly states; let's call this resulting specific vision a *global cryptodemocracy*, to distinguish it from the more general and abstract idea of a global democracy. If successful, it would show that a technology built with an 'underlying philosophy of distributed consensus, open source, transparency and community' can be both 'highly disruptive' *and* 'serve similar purposes as those of states' (Milan); and it could achieve that without a reliance on the private sector and corporate capital that would necessitate paying undue attention to their interests and lobbying (Milan).

Additional key criticisms concern the ability of our global cryptodemocracy to protect human rights (Bauböck, Blake, Kochenov), collect taxes (Bauböck, Post) and in general enforce the rule of the law, given that physical coercion is possible on earth but not in the clouds (Bauböck, Post, Blake, Dumbrava, Al Tamimi). To redress crimes against global identities, we propose that global identities be realised as programmable software agents, aka 'smart contracts', programmed to obey certified court orders. Thus, coercion is achieved through design and programmability, without violence: If the court determines a global identity to be fake, then it can directly order it to terminate; if determined to be a duplicate, then it can be ordered to merge into another identity, and if stolen then to change its owner. Regarding Milan's observation that 'activism today is characterised by [...] a tendency to privilege flexible, multiple identities', we cannot hold the stick at both ends: aspire for egalitarian rule of law in a global democracy, and undermine it with flexible (and hence unaccountable) and multiple (and hence unfairly privileged) identities.

---

[10] Shapiro, E. & N. Talmon (2017), 'A Condorcet-Consistent Democratic Budgeting Algorithm', *Computer Science and Game Theory*, available at https://arxiv.org/abs/1709.05839

We propose to integrate the global citizen's global identity with her democratic cryptocurrency wallet into one entity, termed *global persona*. A global persona is the global citizen's proxy in the cloud: it is entrusted with the global citizen's identity information and crypto-assets, and it performs financial transactions and civic duties in the global cryptodemocracy on behalf of the global citizen it represents. Being unique and persistent makes a global persona accountable for the global citizen it represents. Hence, in addition to the court orders described above, a court may also issue fines against a global persona, payable immediately from her wallet, or deducted from her future (universal basic) income. As the global persona is programmed to obey court orders, no force is needed to collect such fines either. Income, wealth and transaction taxes can be similarly collected without the use of force, by programming global personas to obey the (democratically instituted) tax rules that are in effect. Of course, the court must be open to appeals on any decision and transaction.

A key remaining criticism relates to relying on and overseeing the technologies that will underlie our envisioned global cryptodemocracy (Post, Dumbrava). The criticism is valid, but is mostly equally valid of any technology on which humanity depends today, and there are many. Perhaps one key technological vulnerability is related to the democratic process itself, ensuring that elections and more generally voting on the blockchain at least stand up to earthly standards.[11] Regarding overseeing blockchain technology, blockchain governance is indeed an issue of active research and experimentation, with the recognition that a change of underlying technology of a blockchain is as akin to, and as grave as, a change of constitution in a democracy. The global cryptodemocracy would employ the constitutional approach to its core technology, allowing constitutional change by its sovereign global citizens via a democratic process. Such a process must dampen the immediacy of internet communication, lest mob dynamics may rule, by employing hysteresis measures such as special majority requirements.[12] Recovery mechanisms would also be established, and invoked, by democratic decision.

Let us now consider Orgad's vision of multiple cloud communities with a shared concern or ascriptive, thematic or geographic memberships 'whose

---

[11] European External Action Service (2018), *Compendium of International Standards for Elections*. Available at https://eeas.europa.eu/sites/eeas/files/compendium-en-n-pdf.pdf

[12] Shapiro, E. (2018), 'Foundations of e-Democracy', *Computers and Society*. Available at https://arxiv.org/abs/1710.02873

aim is political decision-making and in which individuals take part in a process of governance and the creation of law.'

First, we note that all these communities can be subsidiary communities of the global cryptodemocracy, potentially with multiple levels of hierarchy (e.g. subsidiary animal rights or Bahá'í communities, with their own subsidiary communities based on country of residence); that the ability to form them is a manifestation of *freedom of assembly* in the clouds; and that allowing them to conduct their affairs without outside intervention is in line with the *subsidiarity principle*.

Second, such communities, within the context of a functioning global cryptodemocracy, may have at least one clear political goal: To draft and promote, within the parent global cryptodemocracy, policy and legislation that pertain to the rights and goals of their (possibly minority) community members. Recall the second article of the 1789 Declaration of the Rights of Man and Citizen: 'The goal of any political association is the conservation of the natural and imprescriptible rights of man. These rights are *liberty, property, safety and resistance against oppression*'. To uphold these, the conduct of all subsidiary cloud communities must be *transparent* in order to ensure that no subsidiary community aims to harm the liberty, property or safety of other communities or global citizens.

Third, within these rich and multi-faceted cloud communities, a virtual punishment with a global scope against one's global persona, e.g. temporary suspension or even just a public reprimand, applied to all subsidiary cloud communities, would be severe indeed. Hence, the higher the value of the subsidiary cloud communities to peoples' lives, the mightier the coercive power of the global cryptodemocracy.

While we have implicitly assumed an egalitarian, democratic decision-making process at the core of global cryptodemocracy and in its subsidiary communities that will choose to adopt it, we have not specified this process. Such a mechanism faces many challenges, including 'tyranny of structurelessness', 'tyranny of emotions', decision-making by 'microconsensus' within small cliques (Milan) and many others. The question of how to best reach a democratic decision has been investigated sporadically for centuries (e.g. by Llull, Condorcet, Borda), and intensively for the last 70 years within Social Choice theory. Much theory was developed, much confusion was sowed, and confidence in democracy has eroded, mainly due to Arrow's impossibility theorem and its follow-on work. I will just hint that adding a taste for reality to social choice theory can undo much of this damage and restore trust in democratic decision making, on and off the cloud.[13]

I have aimed to show that a vision of a global cryptodemocracy, with a rich set of subsidiary cloud communities, is realisable and have tried to address many of the criticisms raised in this debate. But, even if a global cryptodemocracy is realisable, and successfully addresses criticism, is it desirable? My personal answer is positive for two reasons: First, I believe that, since the days of Kant and even before,[14] the proponents of a world government own the moral high ground, and the weakness of their position was practical: Until now, for a world government to materialise, local governments have to volunteer to cease some of their power; and giving up of power is not known to happen voluntarily. Fortunately, earthly democracies are sufficiently free so that the formation of a global cryptodemocracy does not require their consent. True, dictatorial regimes may prevent their citizens from participating, but this would, eventually, be at their own peril, as the interests of their people will not be represented as well. And true, the full power of a global cryptodemocracy will not be realised until proponents of global democracy become majorities in the majority of their respective earthly states. Yet, embryonic as it may be, the global cryptodemocracy vision presented here may very well be the only concrete proposal towards the ultimate realisation of a global democratic government based on currently available technologies.

And this relates to my second reason. I believe that for representative democracies to rebounce from their worldwide decline, they should undergo a major revision and adopt the practices of one of the oldest and most successful democracies in the world, namely the Swiss federal direct democracy. Given that those in power never give it up voluntarily, and that direct democracy disempowers representatives, such a major shift cannot happen without a major outside force in its favor. And new technology can offer such a force. In particular, political e-parties, formed as subsidiary cloud communities of the global cryptodemocracy, sharing the same technology and networking to share winning practices and methods, may be able to win earthly elections and change earthly democracies for the better. This in turn

---

[13] Shapiro, E. & N. Talmon (2018), 'Incorporating Reality into Social Choice', *Computers and Society*, available at https://arxiv.org/abs/1710.10117

[14] Global Challenges Foundation (2018), *Global governance models in history*. Stockholm: Global Challenges Foundation, available at https://api.globalchallenges.org/static/files/GG%20models%20in%20history%20EN.pdf

may result in such earthly democracies officially supporting[15] the global cryptodemocracy in its rise into a *bona fide* egalitarian democratic world government of all global citizens.

---

[15] For example, a state may create government-attested global personas for all its citizens, place them in the escrow of the state notary, and assign them to citizens upon their presentation of a government-issued ID. This would immediately turn all state citizens into global citizens. A state citizen who already owns a global persona will have to merge it with the received government-attested global persona, lest she would be guilty of owning duplicate global personas.

61

Citizenship: Future Perspectives

Liav Orgad

This has been an insightful discussion that touches upon some of the most fundamental concepts in political theory – communities, states, citizenship, and sovereignty. New technologies challenge the meaning and essence of these terms and blur the lines between physical and digital, local and global. The nature of the transformation is still a puzzle, but sooner rather than later the 'Fourth Industrial Revolution' will reach the institution of citizenship. The possible effects are promising but, as this GLOBALCIT debate shows, scary too.

My celebration of the potential of blockchain technologies to advance the idea of global citizenship lost in the GLOBALCIT digital agora, at least if we count 'votes.' There are four firm supporters (Primavera De Filippi, Francesca Strumia, Dora Kostakopoulou, Ehud Shapiro), five strong objectors (Robert Post, Michael Blake, Peter Spiro, Lea Ypi, Dimitry Kochenov), and five people who are somewhere in between, acknowledging the potential yet expressing concerns (Rainer Bauböck, Costica Dumbrava, Yussef Al Tamimi, Jelena Dzankic, Stefania Milan). The objections are wide – theoretical and practical, empirical and normative, methodological and conceptual. The idea of blockchain-based global citizenship, which can lead to the development of cloud communities that seek to take part in international decision making, is seen as 'techno-utopianism' (Milan), 'escapism' (Kochenov), and 'exclusion[ary]' (Ypi), a risk to 'territorial democracy' (Bauböck) that may bring a 'world without law' (Post) and 'legitimate coercion' that is so essential for the protection of human rights (Blake).

My kick-off had several premises. When discussing the need for an international legal persona for all human beings, I indicated three fundamental problems: human rights concerns (1.1 billion people do not have an official identification), lack of self-governance (individuals have no direct voice in international law-making), and unequal representation (the principle of 'one-state, one-vote' leads to disparities in individual voting power). I identified three developments – the rise of global interconnectedness, identity, and responsibility – that, taken together, can end up with the creation of an international legal persona and digital identity (as a form of 'global citizenship'), thereby mitigating some of these problems. I also indicated one possible outcome of global citizenship – the emergence of (top-down and bottom-up) decentralised 'cloud communities' in which global citizens, sharing a common bond, can be politically organised and collaborate with the purpose of influencing international decision making and, eventually, becoming part of it. The authors in this debate have not addressed the premises, yet challenged my observations (e.g., global interconnectedness) and my conclusion – the potential of global digital citizenship to do more good than harm. I cannot do justice to all the subtle replies, so let me first express my gratefulness to the participants – this has been enriching experience, although it has not changed my optimistic view – and briefly address below some issues that I see as central.

Cloud computing

A large percentage of humanity is already engaged with some forms of cloud computing on a daily basis. Whenever you use Google Drive, Apple iCloud, and Dropbox, you spend time 'in the cloud.' Whenever you use audio and video streaming, online storage, and mobile services, you are 'in the cloud.' Government services, research data, medical records, and consumer services are available 'in the cloud.' Social networks too are 'in the cloud.' I have never physically met most of the authors who contributed to this debate, but I meet them on a daily basis on Facebook. The reason why we call these digital structures 'cloud' is not due to the lack of territory – the hardware is located somewhere – but because territory is largely *irrelevant* for the user and the service.

Cloud computing does not create, in and of itself, a 'community' (Post, Spiro), let alone a political community (Blake). Facebook is a social network, not a political community. It is commercial and dictatorial – members have no common bond and cannot create law or engage in governance – and it does not guarantee a truthful unique identity. Yet, in recent years there have been attempts to create cloud-based 'communities' by using blockchain and other technologies. This started as private initiatives, such as Bitnation, but spread into government initiatives, as illustrated by Estonia's e-residency. True, e-Estonia is far from creating a 'community'; Estonia's e-residents do not interact with one another or cooperate for political purposes. They are a group of clients more than a sovereign. It is also true that the notion of DBVNs (Decentralized Borderless Voluntary Nations), where anyone can build a 'community' in a Pangea jurisdiction – an IKEA-style do-ityourself nation – is unrealistic and undesirable. Still, the idea of a political community in which territory is largely irrelevant for certain political functions is worth considering. Thus far, it has been regarded as radical because it was promoted by anarchists and like-minded people looking for disruptive technologies to replace the nation-state. But as technology becomes more developed, it is just a matter of time until the idea will crystallise.

Political community

Even if the idea crystallises, can we really call cloud networks a 'political community,' or would they be like a 'community of video gamers,' to use Spiro's analogy, or just an addition to global civil society (Bauböck, Post, Milan)? The essence of the community I envision is indeed political, having members who share a common bond (say, the protection of animal rights) and seek to become part of national (and mainly international) decision making. There are similarities between cloud communities and global civil society (Bauböck, Post, Milan) as they are both voluntary, political in nature, civil (in the sense of non-governmental), and usually non-profit. But there are some differences. The global civil society is not composed of sovereign political entities where decision making is based on a 'one person, one vote' principle; global civil society organisations are acting *on behalf of* a group, while decentralised cloud communities can form themselves democratic collectives acting on a global scale.

Do cloud communities merit being called 'political communities'? It depends on the nature of such a community and how it will be developed. At least three components should come together: 1) members should have a self-perception as belonging to a collective entity, a shared consciousness of forming a political community; 2) members should have political relations and act with a collective responsibility; 3) members should be capable of acting collectively with regard to some functions. Take immigrants, for example. If all international migrants – more than 250 million people in 2017 – joined a virtual community, it would be the world's fifth largest 'country' (after China, India, USA, and Indonesia). It could act as a self-governed collective at the international level, negotiating with states and UN agencies, collecting taxes, and promoting immigrant rights worldwide – all based not on representatives or NGOs, but on direct decision-making by its members.

Digital coercion

What about coercion – how can there be a political community without a recourse to force (Bauböck, Post, Blake, Dumbrava)? Normatively, the coercive force of law can be independent of the state or its territory; it requires authority. Such authority exists also in a blockchain-based community with one main difference – it is decentralised. If, for example, the 'migrant cloud community' decides collectively to stop migration to a certain country that does not respect migrants' rights or to buy products from certain retailers, and a migrant who is a member violates the rules, s/he can be sanctioned (through fines, suspension, limited access to rights/data, or termination of membership). As long as membership provides some benefits, particularly the ability to influence and shape decisions that affect the member's life, these sanctions are not minor or trivial.

Technologically, since membership is virtual, coercion is realised via software. As Shapiro notes, one's virtual identity (or 'global persona') is programmed to obey the community's decisions ('coercion is achieved through design and programmability, without violence'). In fact, state laws represent 'weak coercion'; there are papers that set rules (e.g., a prohibition of murder or crossing a red light) and one decides whether to follow the rules or violate them, in this case there are punishments and sanctions. Internet protocols are one step further. They are a form of 'strong coercion'; internet codes (e.g., restrictions and blockings) are stronger than papers because the law of the software is more difficult to violate – it is not in the discretion of an individual but requires knowledge and effort. A digital society represents a form of 'absolute coercion.' Transaction monitoring (e.g., voting, tax, or registry) is governed by blockchain rules that one cannot violate.

Socially, 'punishment' in a digital society is of a different type. A person cannot be sent to jail, but her reputation can be discredited. In the digital era, reputation capital is a valuable asset and a factor for providing services and products (think of Airbnb, Uber, eBay). In other words, online reputation has a real-world value. As Al Tamimi observes, 'A punishment in terms of such social devaluation imposed by the cloud state is conceivably more painful and restricting to the individual than traditional methods of punishment, such as fines or jail.'

Functional sovereignty

The territorial dimension of states has been seen central to citizenship (Bauböck, Post, Blake). Indeed, territory is considered the state's most characteristic feature; states are, by definition (Article 1, Montevideo Convention, 1933[1]), territorial units. Territory is considered necessary for assuming most of the normative functions of the state – for instance, as a source of security and identity,

---

[1] Available at http://avalon.law.yale.edu/20th_century/intam03.asp

and for managing natural resources. Against this background, the concept of a deterritorialised state – or cloud communities that would replace the state and fulfil all of its functions – is politically inconceivable. But this does not entail that none of the state's essential functions can be reconceptualised. Cloud communities are not a state-replacement, but an improvement – they seek to add a circle to the already dynamic and multi-layered rich dimensions of citizenship. They are not supposed to act in the physical world – and thus have no sovereignty on issues like murder (Post) – but to govern the transaction of values or data that exist in the digital world (voting, registries, certificates, etc.). However, as cloud communities become politically more important, what happens there will not remain confined to the cloud but influence real-world political decision-making.

The idea of 'concentric circles' of citizenship – to use Cicero metaphor – with each circle having a different normative function, is not foreign to the theory of sovereignty. There are three options: cloud communities can be seen as sub-sovereign entities, semi/quasi-sovereign entities, or functional sovereign entities. Let me focus on the third option – functional sovereignty. Under this approach, sovereignty is divided by functions, with each being governed by a different entity. Think of federal systems, a condominium of states, mandate/trusteeship, autonomy (e.g., Quebec or Puerto Rico), or municipalities (where certain functions are governed by local sovereignty). Divisible sovereignty can be exercised over territories – e.g. Andorra, which was a condominium before independence in 1993 and still had two heads of state (the French president and a Catalan bishop) – or peoples. Sovereignty can be divided between political entities, as in federations or in the European Union, or between political and nonpolitical entities – think of religion (in Israeli law, for example, religious law is sovereign in family issues). The idea of functional sovereignty, as coined by Willem Riphagen in 1975,[2] enables entity *A* to have sovereignty over social welfare, entity *B* to be the sovereign on financial issues, and entity *C* to enjoy sovereignty over security – all in the same territory. It also makes it possible for different political authorities to exercise functional sovereignty over different peoples in the same space. The switch is from a jurisdiction over territories to a jurisdiction over functions, peoples and services. As this is not a new concept, we can understand how it could be applied to blockchain-based cloud communities as well.

The normative functions of cloud communities remain an open question in the debate. My focus has been on global topics – global warming, the

---

[2] Riphagen, W. 1975. 'Some Reflections on Functional Sovereignty', *Netherlands Yearbook of International Law* 6: 121–165.

environment, and other issues of global sustainability – but it is for the states to decide which functions to delegate to self-sovereign communities. Ultimately, states would set the boundaries and decide the sensitive areas in which sovereignty cannot/should not be divided or shared.

Coda

We can construct theoretical models of digital citizenship but, as this debate has shown, there are plenty of uncertainties – political, technological, and psychological ones – before it can become actually operative. I agree with Milan that 'much work is needed . . . before we can proclaim the blockchain revolution.' In particular, I share the concern about global inequality generated by ideas of cloud communities due to lack of internet access (Dzankic, Ypi, Kochenov) – this gap, however, has tremendously (and rapidly) narrowed and in 104 states more than 80 per cent of the youth population (aged 15–24) are now online. The situation will further improve if a right to internet access is universally recognised. And I cannot but share Bauböck's worries about the tyranny of the majority in the cloud – addressing it is a matter of constitutional design of voting mechanisms (note, however, that there will be judicial review, decisions that require supermajority, and perhaps even veto rights in the digital world as well). Discussing these (and others) concerns will keep theorists and policy makers busy in the years to come. While the focus of this debate is on global citizenship and virtual communities, I see it as a broader invitation to reflect on the nexus between new technologies and the future of citizenship.

Permissions

All chapters in this book were first published by Springer; hereby published with permission under the Creative Commons Attribution License or equivalent. Every chapter published in this book has been scrutinized by our experts. Their significance has been extensively debated. The topics covered herein carry significant information for a comprehensive understanding. They may even be implemented as practical applications or may be referred to as a beginning point for further studies.

The contributors of this book come from diverse backgrounds, making this book a truly international effort. We would like to thank all the contributing authors for lending their expertise to make the book truly unique. They have played a crucial role in the development of this book. Without their invaluable contributions this book wouldn't have been possible. They have made vital efforts to compile up to date information on the varied aspects of this subject to make this book a valuable addition to the collection of many professionals and students.

This book was conceptualized with the vision of imparting up-to-date and integrated information in this field. To ensure the same, a matchless editorial board was set up. Every individual on the board went through rigorous rounds of assessment to prove their worth. After which they invested a large part of their time researching and compiling the most relevant data for our readers.

The editorial board has been involved in producing this book since its inception. They have spent rigorous hours researching and exploring the diverse topics which have resulted in the successful publishing of this book. They have passed on their knowledge of decades through this book. To expedite this challenging task, the publisher supported the team at every step. A small team of assistant editors was also appointed to further simplify the editing procedure and attain best results for the readers.

Apart from the editorial board, the designing team has also invested a significant amount of their time in understanding the subject and creating the most relevant covers. They scrutinized every image to scout for the most suitable representation of the subject and create an appropriate cover for the book.

The publishing team has been an ardent support to the editorial, designing and production team. Their endless efforts to recruit the best for this project, has resulted in the accomplishment of this book. They are a veteran in the field of academics and their pool of knowledge is as vast as their experience in printing. Their expertise and guidance has proved useful at every step. Their uncompromising quality standards have made this book an exceptional effort. Their encouragement from time to time has been an inspiration for everyone.

The publisher and the editorial board hope that this book will prove to be a valuable piece of knowledge for students, practitioners and scholars across the globe.

Index

A
Abolishment, 90, 96, 128, 137
Advisory Committee, 28, 302-303
Allegiance, 50, 150-151, 156-157, 163-166, 191, 222-223, 248, 250-251
Amendments, 1, 7, 29, 55, 98, 174

B
Birthright Citizenship, 34, 36, 75-79, 87, 92, 96-98, 102, 110, 118-119, 127-129, 133-135, 137, 140, 142-143, 172, 197
Blockchain Technology, 225, 231, 237-238, 240, 243-244, 246-247, 249, 252-253, 260, 275, 285, 288, 300-301, 305-306, 308, 310, 314, 318

C
Citizenship Acquisition, 1, 4-5, 21-22, 104, 116, 122, 165
Citizenship Act, 7, 29, 147, 164, 172-173
Citizenship Revocation, 145, 147-156, 180, 187-188, 194, 203, 205, 207, 209, 215-221, 223-224
Citizenship Transmission, 73, 85, 88, 90, 92-95, 109-110
Cloud Communities, 225, 227, 233-235, 237-241, 243-244, 249, 255-258, 260-263, 285-287, 289-291, 293-296, 298-301, 318-320, 322-324, 326-327
Cloud Computing, 227, 279, 300, 323
Commodity, 32-33, 35
Communal Decision, 286
Communal Vote, 285-286
Constituency, 272, 303-304
Constructive Renunciation, 216
Court of Justice, 4, 7, 47, 51, 53, 154, 184, 209-213
Criminal Conviction, 148, 155, 203

Cryptocurrency, 275-276, 306, 316-318

D
Democratic Community, 4, 33-34, 38, 55
Democratic Institutions, 39, 41, 72
Denationalisation, 145, 147-148, 152-153, 155-162, 164, 170, 176, 178-179, 182-192, 194-201, 203, 205-206, 216, 218-221
Digital Identities, 255, 257-258, 275-276, 283-284, 289, 315-316
Diplomatic Protection, 16, 32-33, 47, 112, 181

E
Egalitarian, 10, 23, 35-36, 290, 315-317, 319, 321
Empirical Evidence, 137-138
Existential Threat, 219

F
Federal Democracy, 238, 313
Freedom of Assembly, 314, 319

G
Genetic Descent, 116-117
Genetic Relationship, 67, 69
Global Citizens, 228, 234, 239, 246, 249-250, 262, 269, 313-319, 321, 323
Global Citizenship, 174, 225, 227-228, 232, 235-236, 243, 248, 254-255, 257-261, 263-264, 269, 289-291, 295, 308, 311-313, 322-323, 327
Global Cloud Democracy, 316-317
Global Cryptodemocracy, 225, 313, 317-321
Golden Residence Programmes, 4

Index

I
Immigration Policy, 15, 91
Inclusionary, 60, 74, 84, 311
Inherited Privilege, 33, 116
International Legal Personas, 234, 299
Investor Citizenship, 1, 5, 9, 15, 17, 20, 25, 30-31, 42, 44, 256, 287

J
Judicial Review, 172, 327

L
Legal Citizenship, 147, 154-156, 165, 187, 219, 222
Legal Instrument, 101-102
Legal Structure, 254-255, 258
Long-term Relations, 12, 39

M
Microconsensus, 305, 319
Migration Status, 71, 77
Modernisation, 93, 95

O
Ordre Public Exemption, 112, 123

P
Political Community, 4, 6-7, 9, 11, 14, 35-36, 64-65, 70-72, 77-78, 92, 95, 112, 117, 129-130, 227-228, 233, 237-240, 255, 258, 270, 280, 303, 311, 313, 323-324
Political Division, 96-97
Political Members, 72
Political Sphere, 38
Populist, 164, 241, 259
Pre-war Citizens, 138

R
Radical Technologists, 299-300
Reproductive Choices, 71, 76, 95, 101

S
Same-sex Marriage, 85
Scientia, 285, 287
Social Contract, 15, 70, 240, 250, 275
Social Credit System, 280-281, 286
Social Parenting, 93, 97
Sovereign Control, 238, 269
State-based Communities, 270, 272
Subsidiarity Principle, 314, 319
Surrogacy, 62, 66-69, 87-88, 112-114, 124

T
Technological Advances, 254
Territorial Boundaries, 238, 258-259
Terrorism Offences, 149, 215-216
Transparency, 8, 247, 253, 270, 300, 314, 317

U
Universal Basic Income, 316

V
Virtual Public Space, 310, 312
Voluntary Association, 239-241, 252-253, 264, 303

W
Warrant Protection, 117

Printed in the USA
CPSIA information can be obtained
at www.ICGtesting.com
LVHW010341230923
759035LV00005B/343